INSIGHT
GUIDES
CataLonia

Edited by Roger Williams
Managing Editor: Andrew Eames
Photography: Bill Wassman and others

A P A
PUBLICATIONS

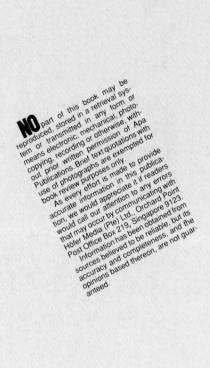
Catalonia

First Edition
Printed in Singapore by Höfer Press Pte. Ltd

ABOUT THIS BOOK

Catalonia has too often been overlooked by foreign writers who, upon reaching Spain, don't stop until the sun is searing their skin in the south. For some time this had been a source of disappointment to **Roger Williams**, the project editor of this Insight Guide. A London-based writer and editor, he has a home on the Costa Brava where he collects books about the region. Since the mid-1950s only two books have been published in English, both excellent, and Williams lost no time in signing their authors up as contributors. The first was *The Catalans*, a history by **Jan Read**, which won compliments from the Catalan president, Josep Tarradellas, when it came out in 1978. It was followed 10 years later by *The Essence of Catalonia* by **Lord Kilmarnock**, who writes his urbane travel books under the name of Alastair Boyd.

In his own book, Boyd casts himself as cicerone: "sly, cunning, knowledgeable, up to all tricks and full of ingenuity in furthering your interests." As our guide here, he explains the history of the 19th century, the glories of Romanesque architecture, the mysteries of Montserrat and the grandeur of the Cistercian monasteries further south.

Read, who has written the chapter on Catalonia's heyday as master of the seas, is a Scot and prolific author. He has written extensively on the history, food and wine of Spain, often with his Spanish wife, the cookery writer Maite Manjón. When on holiday in Catalonia, they frequently stay with the Torres family, friends of long standing, in Penedès.

The Torres family is one of the subjects of the Wine Dynasties chapter, written by **Desmond Begg**. A restless traveller, Begg spent a year in Granada, has visited all the wine regions of the peninsula and has written two books on the wines of Spain.

Marimar Torres runs the family wine business in California, but she is also author of *The Spanish Table* and an expert on local cuisine. In the chapter on country food, she recalls the delights of the family kitchen and other tasty treats of her childhood in Penedès. "La Boqueria market in the Rambla in Barcelona is one of my favourite spots to show visitors," she says. "It has unparalleled produce and provides an unforgettable memory of Catalonia."

Much of the good food in the region is either on four legs or flying through. **Oriol Alamany**, Catalonia's most exciting wildlife photographer, would rather it was shot with a camera. His contributions are added to those of the New York-based photographer **Bill Wassman**, an old Apa hand who spent many weeks touring the region.

While Insight Guides can claim, with this book, to have the most colourful, diverse and... well, *insightful* guide to the region, it also has to be admitted that at its outset it was not the only one in the production line—a fact uncovered as further specialist writers were sought. **Paul Gogarty**, a London-based travel writer who covers the province of Lleida, had been writing one. **Colm Tóibín**, a former editor of *Magill* magazine in Ireland, had been writing two: one fact, one fiction. He lived in Barcelona from 1975 to 1978 and frequently returns to visit. His contribution to this book is a chapter on artists and, the most difficult chapter of all, an analysis of the character of the people.

Although he speaks Catalan, Tóibín also had some assistance in writing his book from **Tony Strubell**, who was born in Oxford and whose mother is Catalan. Strubell, who now

Williams   *Boyd*   *Tóibín*

lives in the Basque country, is a teacher and translator, and he spends his summers working in the Aiguamolls wildlife sanctuary. From him comes the expertise on Pyrenean wildlife and the birds of the Ebre delta, as well as 20th-century history and the chapter on Jacint Verdaguer, the subject of a film script for which he was awarded a prize by the Catalan Generalitat.

Strubell is the grandson of Dr Josep Trueta, the author of *The Spirit of Catalonia*, written while in self-imposed exile in England after the civil war. Trueta married the daughter of Josep Ensesa, owner of the legendary Hostal de la Gavina, the subject of **Alex Scott**'s chapter on Tourism.

Scott is a journalist and he lives in Castelldefels with his Catalan wife Núria and their daughter Emma. He was ideally situated to write the chapter on tourism, and the guide to the province of Barcelona. (He has a complaint about Catalan restaurants: they serve the food too fast, he says, and then leave you waiting hours for the bill.) Another recruit from Barcelona's Press Centre was **Patrick Kelly**, a specialist on architecture and design (he couldn't be in a more inspirational place), who has written on the subject for this book.

Also in Barcelona is **George Semler Jr**, whose subjects are the Great Outdoors and Mushroom Mania. Semler, a former Barcelona ice-hockey coach, always seems to have his Jeep full of family and friends heading off on some caper or expedition. Another *barcelonese* is **Carolyn Montserrat** who is married to an Andorran, and her intimate knowledge of this little country makes her an invaluable guide.

An outsider is **Jan McGirk**, who has been living for a number of years in Madrid, though she once worked as a flamenco dancer in a bar in Tossa de Mar. She has written a book, *Exploring Rural Spain*, and she loves to go skiing in the Vall d'Aran, which is why she wrote the chapter about this beautiful valley.

Vicky Hayward has been going to Spain since the age of two in the 1950s. She remembers eating large quantities of *pa amb tomàquet* and riding on the little steam railway that ran down to Palafrugell. A writer with many enthusiasms, her contributions are the fashion and textile chapter, the guide to Tarragona and the Tarragona half of the Costa Daurada, and the piece on the chocolate wizard Antoni Escribà.

Ward Rutherford, author of numerous travel books, kicks off the history section with The First Catalans. He and his wife have a house just over the border in "north Catalonia", in France. He also tackled Barcelona city, and fared rather badly when his Spanish wife was mugged in the early evening walking down Carrer de Ferran. It could happen in any city, but be warned just the same.

Bringing the good news is **Kendall McDonald**, who has been diving on the Costa Brava since the 1950s, which he writes about here. Most of his three dozen books have been about diving, though anyone staying at the Aiguablava hotel in Fornells should look out for his very funny *Xiquet Letters*.

Pam Barrett wrote the chapter on Festivals and compiled the indispensable Travel Tips at the back of the book. A Spanish speaker, she lived for three years in Barcelona and now has a home on the Costa Brava where she and her husband, and daughter Joby, spend just as much time as they can.

The maps were drawn by **Berndtson & Berndtson**, proof-reading and indexing were handled by **Kate Owen**, and the text was guided through computers by **Jill Anderson**.

Hayward

Scott

Barrett

Strubell

CONTENTS

INTRODUCTION & HISTORY

23   **Introduction: Benvinguts**
—by Roger Williams

27   **The First Catalans**
—by Ward Rutherford

37   **The House of Barcelona**
—by Jan Read

40   *Masters of the Sea*
—by Jan Read

47   **Nineteenth-Century Renaissance**
—by Alastair Boyd

57   **The Twentieth Century**
—by Tony Strubell

FEATURES

67   **A People Apart**
—by Colm Tóibín

73   **Verdaguer: Father of Modern Catalan**
—by Tony Strubell

83   **Festivals, Music and Dance**
—by Pam Barrett

86   *The Sedate Sardana*
—by Roger Williams

93   **Glorious Romanesque**
—by Alastair Boyd

103   **Modernism to Modern**
—by Patrick Kelly

111   **Generations of Artistic Talent**
—Colm Tóibín

119   **The Wine Dynasties**
—by Desmond Begg

120 Which Wines to Try
—by Desmond Begg

126 The Country Kitchen
—by Marimar Torres

130 Mushroom Mania
—by George Semler Jr

137 Textiles Come Into Fashion
—by Vicky Hayward

145 Tourism on Spain's First "Costa"
—by Alex Scott

153 The Great Outdoors
—by George Semler Jr

PLACES

169 Introduction
—by Roger Williams

173 Lleida Province
—by Paul Gogarty

187 Vall d'Aran
—by Jan McGirk

193 Andorra
—by Carolyn Montserrat

201 Pyrenean Wildlife
—by Tony Strubell

211 Girona Province
—by Roger Williams

214 Fountains and Spas
—by Roger Williams

220 A Jewish Inheritance
—by Roger Williams

227 The Costa Brava
—by Roger Williams

232 When the Wind Blows
—*by Roger Williams*

241 Diving in the Medes Islands
—by Kendall McDonald

247 The Maresme
—by Roger Williams

253 Barcelona City
—by Ward Rutherford

260 Chocolate Maestro
—*by Vicky Hayward*

273 Barcelona Province
—by Alex Scott

274 The Holy Mountain
—*by Alastair Boyd*

278 Keepers of the Flocks
—*by Roger Williams*

283 Costa Daurada
—by Alex Scott

293 Birds of the Ebre Delta
—by Tony Strubell

300 The Cistercian Triangle
—by Alastair Boyd

303 Tarragona Province
—by Vicky Hayward

MAPS

170 Catalonia
177 The Catalan Pyrenees
218 Girona town
229 The Costa Brava
254 Barcelona city
304 Tarragona town

TRAVEL TIPS

GETTING THERE
314   By Air
314   By Road
314   By Rail
314   By Sea

TRAVEL ESSENTIALS
315   Visas & Passports
315   Customs
315   Health
315   What to Wear
316   What to Bring
316   Animal Quarantine

GETTING ACQUAINTED
316   Government & Economy
316   Geography & Population
317   Climate
318   Weights & Measures
318   Electricity
318   Time Zones
318   Language
319   Business Hours
319   Holidays
319   Festivals
319   Religious Services

COMMUNICATIONS
320   The Media
320   Postal Services
320   Telephones

EMERGENCIES
321   Security & Crime
321   Consulates

GETTING AROUND
322   Railways
322   The Metro
323   Driving
324   Buses
324   Hitchhiking
324   Boat Trips
324   Natural Parks
326   Wine Routes

WHERE TO STAY
326   Hotels
327   Camping
327   Farmhouse Holidays
327   Youth Hostels

FOOD DIGEST
328   What to Eat
328   Market Produce
329   Reading the Menu
330   Restaurants & Hotels

SPORTS
338   Sailing
339   Diving
340   Golf
341   Walking
341   Hunting & Fishing
341   Skiing
343   Miscellaneous Activities

CULTURE PLUS
343   Architecture
344   Museums
346   Music

NIGHTLIFE
347   Clubs & Discos
347   Casinos

SHOPPING
348   What to Buy
348   Where to Buy
349   Export Procedures
349   Complaints

SPECIAL INFORMATION
349   Children
350   Disabled

FURTHER READING
350

USEFUL ADDRESSES
351   Tourist Offices
352   Airlines
352   Motoring Organisations

Suddenly all the signs are written in neither French nor (Castilian) Spanish, but in abrupt, slightly familiar words from a language which belongs on its own. Beaches are not *plages* nor *playas*, but *platjas*, good day is *bon dia*, please is *si us plau*, and welcome is neither *bienvenu* nor *bienvenidos* but *benvinguts*.

Since the return of democracy in 1975, and with it some degree of autonomy, Catalonia has blossomed, as has Catalan. A whole generation is now growing up, taught in the language which has always been spoken in the home. With this blossoming has come a renewed, overt pride: a remembrance, for example, that Catalonia was one of the great seafaring nations, that it has been and often still is a leader in the arts and in industry, that its food and wine are unparalleled... in fact, just about everything concerning its people and their land is special.

Catalans do indeed have a lot to be pleased about, especially in their climate and diverse landscape, which has attracted visitors since Caesar retired his officers to seaside villas at L'Escala. Many Europeans today were first taken abroad, as children, to the Costa Brava and Costa Daurada. It was warm and beautiful and wonderfully cheap and wine seemed to pour free from the taps.

The low prices attracted cheap tourism and it wasn't long before hotels and package tours had besmirched the name of the *costa*. But Catalonia's coasts, among the first to feel mass foreign invasion, had also been long appreciated by Catalans from Barcelona as well as Spaniards from other parts of Spain and lessons were quickly learned. Today there are green belts and natural parks, both on land and in the sea. The visitor, too, has become more discerning. And so have the travel guides.

To help follow the signs, all the spellings in this book are in Catalan. The counts are called Joan or Jaume, not Juan or Jaime or even John or James, mountain ranges are *serres*, not *sierras* and, when it arrives in the region, the River Ebro becomes the Ebre.

Preceding pages: Hospital de Vielha valley, Pyrenees; olive groves, Cap de Creus; moonshine over Sitges; Barcelona city. <u>Left</u>, festive costume.

Fossils found at Banyoles, near Girona, have been dated to about 200,000 BC, but there is evidence that humans have lived in Catalonia for as much as half a million years. The first known Catalans were Neanderthals, characterised by heavy bone ridges over the eyes—a trait also found among the apes—and a thickness of skull limiting brain capacity. But between 25,000 and 30,000 years ago the true ancestors of modern humanity, the Palaeolithic hunters, began arriving on the peninsula, probably from the Near East, bringing new techniques and new skills in the manufacture of flint tools and weapons. That they were also gifted artists is shown by the famous cave-paintings, found particularly in Cantabria in north Spain. One example in Catalonia, at Ulldecona, just to the south of the Ebre delta, shows a typical hunting scene in a style similar to the cave-paintings of Algeria and Tunisia.

The first communities: The transition from Palaeolithic (Old Stone Age) to Neolithic (New Stone Age), from around 5000 BC, was marked in Catalonia by a gradual shift away from the precarious dependence on the environment to the shaping of the environment to human needs. Land was cleared for cultivation and there is evidence of animal husbandry; caves and lean-to shelters gave way to purpose-built stone dwellings huddled together as villages.

The Neolithic period also saw the rise of communal activities like flint-mining as well as the introduction of new ones such as spinning, knitting and ceramics, with potters producing bell-shaped utensils with geometric designs. At the same time, the discovery of artefacts made from foreign materials like ivory, turquoise, obsidian and amber indicates trade links.

With this were associated the religious practices typical of agricultural peoples, based on the Great Earth Mother. Worship of a feminine principle of fecundity may help to explain the forms of the massive, stone-slab built passage-graves, such as those at Baix

Empordà and Alt Urgell, which began to appear about 3000 BC. Their originators were probably colonists from the Near East who later moved up the Atlantic seaboard through France into Britain and Scandinavia, and many scholars have suggested that the passage-graves were intended to imitate the vagina and uterus.

The complexity of organisation and the enormous resources of labour involved in building these structures also sheds light on the nature of the society responsible for

them. Plainly intended as mausoleums for selected members of the community, they imply that it was one based on a wealthy ruling class, particularly when taken with the other evidence of communal activity.

The second millennium BC witnessed the dawning of the Bronze Age, bringing with it a demand for ore. Deposits of copper, which with tin is one of the constituents of bronze, as well as of gold and silver, existed in the Guadalquivír valley of southwestern Spain. It may well have been this that attracted a previously unknown seafaring people to settle on what may have been the site of modern Seville, the city the Bible refers to as

Preceding pages: Jaume I (the Conqueror) during the Mallorca campaign. Left, dolmen at Roses. Right, cave-painting from Ulldecona.

"Tarshish" and the Classical writers as "Tartessus".

As the Tartessians were a literate people, their arrival in the peninsula represents the line of demarcation between prehistoric and historic culture—the invention of writing. Though there is little evidence that they had a direct influence on regions as far east as Catalonia, their thriving metal trade, as well as their many other activities, can hardly have failed to bring them at least into trade relations.

In any event, Tartessian prosperity would inevitably cause others to cast an emulative gaze in the direction of Spain and, by their coming, influence the destiny of and contrib-

now Roses. (The Greek name for Empúries, *Emporion*, root of our own word "emporium", simply means a trading-post. Rhodes, the name of the Aegean island, means "roses".) These Greek settlers are usually credited with introducing the vine and the olive tree to Spain.

In 545 BC, when Izmir was overrun by the Persians, the flood of Greek fugitives which reached Empúries necessitated the building of a second town, called Neapolis (New Town) to distinguish it from the original one which came to be called Palaiapolis (Old Town).

Greek artefacts found at the two sites include coins, statuary, bronzes and coins. A

ute their genes to, the ethnic group the Greek geographers were to classify as Iberian, probably from the River Ebre (Greek: *Iberos*).

Trading posts: Among the first to follow the Tartessians were the Phoenicians, inhabitants of a group of city-states in what is now the Lebanon. Arriving from about the end of the second millennium BC, they founded a chain of trading-posts from Cádiz to Málaga.

In their wake came Greeks. Some, from the area round the Gulf of Izmir in Turkey, installed themselves at the present Empúries, then an offshore island; others, from the island of Rhodes, went to what is

great many are housed in the local museum, but in some cases the pieces on show are reproductions, the originals being in the Archaeological Museum in Barcelona.

More or less coincidentally with the second Greek influx, two other ingredients were being added to the ethnic mix. The first came from beyond the Pyrenees when waves of Celts began crossing from Gaul. Though in many areas they maintained their separateness, in others their assimilation gave rise to the racial sub-group known to history as the Celtiberians. However, the greatest significance of the Celts arose from the fact that they were an iron-using people and adoption of the new metal saw the waning of the bronze-based prosperity of Tartessus.

The second ingredient came from Carthage, a Phoenician colony in what is now Tunisia. The main Phoenician cities in the Lebanon were in the process of being swallowed up by the Assyrians, leaving Carthage sole mistress of its overseas possessions, including those in Spain. Carthaginians began arriving in large numbers in the 3rd century BC after a naval victory over the Greeks gave them undisputed control of the Mediterranean. The Greeks had always had friendly relations with the Tartessians and the new occupiers were quick to punish this partiality by sacking Tartessus.

The continuation of Hamilcar's aggressive policies by his son Hannibal led to the Second Punic War in 218 BC and it was from Spain that he made his famous descent on Italy with elephants, crossing the Pyrenees and scaling the Alps. The Romans responded with their first landings in Spain, under Scipio Africanus, at Empúries, the beginning of a campaign to expel the Carthaginians from Iberia. After their initial victory in 201 BC, much of Catalonia was absorbed into a swathe of littoral called Hither Spain.

For the next six centuries the Romans were masters and Iberia was to play an important role in their subsequent history,

Barca's town: At the same time they also gave Barcelona its first name, Barcino, in honour of their general and leader, Hamilcar Barca. He, for his part, had a personal ambition. His plans for an empire in Sicily had been thwarted by the Romans, and he now hoped to create one in Iberia. The natural effect of implementing this policy was to renew the conflict with Rome, the protector of the Greek coastal cities, in what came to be known as the First Punic War ("Punic" comes from the Poeni or Phoenicians).

<u>Left</u>, Cova d'en Daina Neolithic passage-grave.
<u>Above</u>, Empúries, Rome's first foot in Spain.

among other things as the birthplace of three Roman emperors, Trajan, Hadrian and Theodosius. Tarragona, under the name of Tarraco, became one of the imperial capitals and is still the site of impressive Roman remains. Towards the end of the 3rd century Barcelona, renamed Colonia Faventia Julia Augusta Pia Barcino, was encircled by its first city wall, evidence of growing status, though at that time it was overshadowed by the *dipolis* or twin-cities at Empúries.

Apart from its importance as a port, Empúries was also considered a health resort by the ancient world. Evidence of this is provided by the discovery there of a temple dedicated to Hygiea, goddess of health, and a 4th-century statue of Asclepius, the god of healing.

The region re-entered Roman history briefly during the leadership struggle between Julius Caesar and Pompey in the second half of the last century BC. In the April of 49 BC Caesar crossed into the peninsula with six legions to deal with the army of Spain which was loyal to Pompey, met it at Lleida and, in a 40-day campaign, so outmanoeuvred it that it was forced to surrender, leaving Hither Spain in his hands.

Roman veterans' colony: Caesar was not quite finished with it. Before leaving, he installed a colony of veterans on the heights

However, the period was also one in which Roman rule was faltering. Its benefits had been immeasurable. The cities had become, as Jan Read put it in *The Catalans*, "miniature Romes", connected by a system of roads such as the Via Augusta which crosses the Pyrenees at La Junquera to run through Girona, Barcelona, Tarragona and on to Valencia and Alicante. The Latin of the legionaries had laid the basis of the language which was to evolve into Catalan, a close relative of the *langue d'oc* of the troubadours, spoken throughout most of southern France. But, most of all, it had ensured a period of peace, security and prosperity. All three fled with the departing legions as the

above L'Escala, overlooking Empúries. This was no doubt because of its reputation as a health resort, but it must also have been because he wanted stalwarts of his own in the country.

The close of the period of Roman occupation saw the establishment of Christianity as the official religion of the empire. Catalonia is said to have been an early participant in the conversion, although a legend that St Paul preached at Empúries is probably apocryphal. In any event, a basilica was built at Palaiapolis, possibly on the site of a temple to Artemis of Ephesus, and the town became the seat of a bishop.

coastal areas became prey to Germanic raiders. Barcelona, Tarragona and Palaiapolis were all sacked, the last so thoroughly it never recovered.

Arian Visigoths: Over the ensuing 150 years what had been raids turned into full-scale invasions. The occupation of Spain by Germanic tribes was completed in the 5th century when Visigoths, already established in southern France, moved into Catalonia and, in the next decades, ousted the other invaders as they headed south.

These were by no means the bearded, horn-helmeted and spear-flourishing barbarians of popular stereotype. Since AD 411 they had been allies of Rome and this influence on them had extended to religion, though Visigoths were Arian Christians who doubted Christ's divinity. This was obviously antithetical to the orthodox Christians of Spain. Nonetheless the two were able to coexist. Nor did the Visigoths try to impose their own political system, with its elective monarchy and assemblies of free men. The indigenous population continued to be ruled by a system of laws derived from Rome which included a prohibition on mixed marriages between Christian Iberians and heretical Visigoths.

Such difficulties as this might have caused were resolved when the Visigothic king,

Reccared, converted to the Christianity of Rome, an event which marked the full assimilation of the two peoples and, at the same time, the abolition of Germanic in favour of Roman law.

The period directly after Reccared's conversion was a high water mark for Visigothic Spain, followed by one of decline. In AD 710, the king, Witzia, died and his son and heir, Akhila, governor of a region which included Catalonia, was passed over. Arab sources claim that his aggrieved family

Left, Roman sarcophagus in Sant Feliu, Girona.
Above, Arc de Berà on the road to Tarragona.

immediately sent envoys to North Africa to seek their help.

Saracen "liberators": If they did make such an appeal, it was answered with gratifying speed. The following year Saracens invaded the peninsula, and defeated Visigothic troops at Guadalete. The defeat was due, it was said, to the Witzia family's treachery. Whatever the truth, the Saracens were initially regarded as liberators in all of Akhila's former domains, thereby fuelling an enduring suspicion of the Catalans, especially among the Franks of neighbouring Gaul who were to become deeply embroiled in the subsequent struggle with Islam.

The Saracens soon demonstrated they had ambitions more extensive than the restoration of a Visigothic dynasty, for they immediately turned their attention to the total conquest of Spain. In AD 717, with the fall of Barcelona—promptly renamed Barjalunah—the Catalans realised it was occupation and not liberation that they had brought down on themselves.

Many of the Visigothic rulers fled to the mountains of the north where a group of Christian states came into being. In AD 722 this federation had its first success in the Battle of Covadonga in the western Pyrenees, which was followed by the repossession of Galicia. These events were hailed as the beginning of what came to be known as the *Reconquista*.

However, if defeated on one front, the Saracens had others to exploit. Crossing the eastern Pyrenees they continued their advance to occupy Septimania, the coastal strip of Gaul south of the Massif Central between the Rhône and the Pyrenees, and its capital, Narbonne.

To meet the growing threat, the powerful Pepin family, who were Christian Franks and rulers of Gaul in all but name, had been concentrating their forces. It was these which, 10 years after the Battle of Covadonga, were responsible for the real turning point. A Saracen army, sallying into Aquitaine, was surprised at Poitiers by that of the Frankish leader Charles Martel and routed. Though there were further engagements, it was not until 20 years later that Septimania was cleared of the invader.

Charlemagne's legacy: By AD 771 government of the increasingly powerful Frankish kingdom was firmly in the hands of Charles

Martel's grandson, to be known to the world as Charlemagne or Charles the Great (*Carolus Magnus*, hence "Carolingian" as the name of his dynasty).

His immediate preoccupation was with the pagan Saxons harrying his borders on the Lower Rhine, but their submission in AD 777 was attended by Saracen emissaries seeking his aid in an uprising against the Emir of Córdoba, the Moorish ruler of Spain. As anxious to secure his southwestern as his northern flanks, in 778 Charlemagne crossed the frontier, only to find the expected Saracen support not to be forthcoming. He still attempted to take Zaragoza but, repulsed, was forced to retreat through the passes at

Roncevalles northeast of Pamplona. His rearguard was ambushed and massacred in the battle commemorated in the *Chanson de Roland*.

Catalonia is named: Having invited retaliation by this ill-starred adventure, Charlemagne created a buffer-zone running the length of the Pyrenees. To administer it, he placed it under the charge of one of his sons, Louis, later to succeed him as Louis I (the Pious), and divided it into feudal counties. Those in the eastern Pyrenees, spilling over into what is now France, were Roussillon, Empúries, Girona, Besalú, Urgell, Osona and Barcelona. At the same time, his foray

had revived hopes of independence in these counties of the Spanish March (*Marca Hispanica*) which by Louis's reign had become known as Catalonia. Many Catalans slipped across the border to join Louis's forces, according to a contemporary Frankish chronicle, accepting Carolingian authority "freely and spontaneously", an act to have deeper consequences later.

The Christian armies, returning to the offensive, took Girona in AD 785, putting Barcelona at risk. Its Moorish governor, refused reinforcement, is said to have travelled to Aix-la-Chapelle, Charlemagne's capital, with an offer of surrender. After his experience with the Emir of Córdoba, Charlemagne was not minded to accept such an offer. However, in AD 801 the city was taken by the Franks, but 12 years later was sacked with such carnage that the piled heads of the slaughtered were said by an Arab commentator to have overtopped a lance struck into the ground. Notwithstanding such setbacks, the struggle against the Saracens continued, with ground gradually being repossessed.

It was now that the consequences of the Catalans' voluntary submission to Frankish authority became manifest. They had made it in the belief it would be the means of recovering independence and this seemed confirmed by Charlemagne's assertions that he intended to liberate the Christian lands from the infidel and restore them to their proper overlords. Instead, once having freed an area, he continued in occupation while permitting the restoration of local government. This was partly because of the ingrained distrust of the Catalans, who had retained a reputation for preferring infidel Moors to Christian Franks. Indeed, a second Saracen attack on Barcelona in AD 828 was said have been made with local support. However, the primary consideration was the Franks' determination to create a broad *cordon sanitaire* between themselves and the areas still in Saracen hands.

Under the aegis of this Spanish March, Catalonia became a dependency, soon to be free of the Moorish rulers who were to remain on much of the rest of the peninsula for a further 600 years.

Above, Spanish-born philosopher Seneca, a 14th-century manuscript from Sant Cugat del Vallès. **Right**, Roman statue, Barcelona.

& pfocauonem cordis ab ece[?]
et In rubra sine dubio eamũ
placabra cum eo. & deserens eum
lurena aie surgabra huc? apparet
dicece. Domus nia est. & eo
ehr abitauor. sicut ipse dicta.
Qui diligit me diligitur a patre
meo. et ego diligam eum. & manifestabo
 si me ipsum. et
ego appacia ad eum uemuenu. et
man sionam apur eum faciemur.
e apofet hanc cotepcionem. quid
boni accerif pro mat aia dicta.
Qui iniecera. dabo illi cala meũ
In ealam meam sicut & ego mei
et eo cum patre mo In trono
ipsus. Conferotam quam die[?]
puam cipam poterit eam promat[?].
Nam cum dicat In cale puarit
redire quomodo cum illo re
debia qui incet. cum ipse uni
geniuur In cale puarit poterau
te calaur. sicut ipse ula.
Celum et terram ego Impleo.
quid era ego In trono di redire
ni si qui trcet. et tari cum do
oc est beaur ud sis est tribuna
libur. aeas In concursa peceam
aia. Illur felicitae quid ece.
Qui habet aure audiat di audiat ea
quid spr dicat petitis.

EXPLICIT STORIE SEPTEM

ECLESIARUM NUMERA

THE HOUSE OF BARCELONA

The Catalan flag, with its four red bars on a yellow ground, is the subject of a picturesque legend. It is said that while fighting against the Moors with Charlemagne's grandson, Charles II, the Catalan leader, Guifré el Pilós (Wilfred the Hairy), was wounded. Charles dipped his fingers into the blood and, drawing them across Guifré's gilded shield, made a grant of arms on it.

Charles was doing no more than recognise the service of a loyal vassal, but by his death in AD 897 Guifré had taken the first steps towards separating the principality from the Carolingian empire. He had consolidated under his rule the counties of Cerdanya, Urgell, Barcelona, Girona, Osona and Conflent and founded a spiritual home in the monastery of Santa Maria in Ripoll, on the site of a church built by the first Catholic Visigothic king, Reccared. The House of Barcelona he thus founded was to guide the destinies of Catalonia for five centuries.

The final break with the Franks took place a century later when the power of the Moors was on the wane and after the death of al-Mansur, who had sacked and burnt Barcelona to the ground in July AD 985. Catalonia remained a small state struggling for its existence, but by a sudden reversal of roles it was now the Muslims who, in return for protection or, at least, freedom from attack, became tributaries of the Christians.

The money which began to flow into the coffers of the Counts of Barcelona paved the way for economic expansion. Ramon Berenguer I (1035–76) extended his territories to both the north and the south, but made his most significant contribution in the promulgation of the *usatges*, a written code defining the reciprocal rights and responsibilities of the sovereign and his subjects, which preceded *Magna Carta* by 150 years. For example, his subjects were charged with supporting him in the defence of the realm (*Princeps namque*); on the other hand *Strate et vie publice* established that the prince does not have outright dominion over roads, running water, pastures and woods, which were for the benefit of the community as a whole.

By the time of Ramon Berenguer III (1096–1131) the southern boundary of the principality had been pushed south to Tarragona by its capture from the Moors, and, by annexation or alliance, the Counts of Barcelona controlled half a dozen small counties in the north, including Roussillon and Foix beyond the Pyrenees. Ramon Berenguer III achieved still more when in 1113 he married

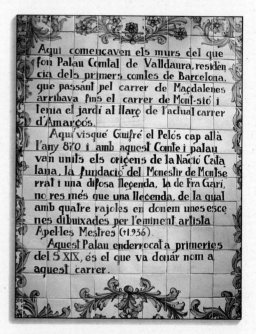

Dolça, the heiress to Provence, and united her territories with his own. As Frédéric Mistral describes, the Count Berenguer embarked from Barcelona with a fair wind swelling the white sails of his fleet, sailed up the Rhône, and gained the hand, the crown and the diamonds of the princess. Catalonia and Provence were to remain closely linked for almost a century and a half.

The ties of language, the bond of a shared Roman heritage and the poetry of the Provençal troubadours contributed to the cultural awakening of Catalonia; while a community of interests in trade and maritime communications led to an expansion of commerce and

Preceding pages: Mozarabic *Beatus* from Girona. **Left**, Ramon Berenguer III who took the hand and the land of the princess of Provence. **Above**, site of the Counts' Barcelona palace.

opened European horizons to a state which had previously been inward-looking and isolated.

Counts to kings: Ramon Berenguer IV (1131–62) bettered his father with an even more spectacular marital coup. Relations between Catalonia and its powerful neighbour, Castile, were not good and, when the imperialistic Alfonso VII of Castile attempted to enlarge his domains even further by marrying his son Sancho to the infant daughter of the king of Aragón, Catalonia's very existence was at stake. In fact, the future of the whole peninsula hung on obtaining the hand of two-year-old Petronilla.

In this bizarre contest, it was Ramon Ber-

who was to set Catalonia on the path of large-scale expansion in the Mediterranean, was fathered by the ill-fated Pere I when his mother, Maria of Montpellier, whom Pere had deserted, was smuggled into his bedchamber in place of his awaited mistress. Pere has also gone down in history for losing most of the Catalan territories beyond the Pyrenees to the French after embracing the cause of the Albigensian heretics in the Midi, who were opposed to the Roman Church partly because of the corruption of its priesthood. He was killed during a disastrous defeat by Simon de Montfort at the Battle of Muret in 1213.

Jaume was only six at the time, but by the

enguer who emerged the victor when in August 1137 King Ramiro pledged his daughter to him, together with his kingdom. Petronilla was to be known as Queen of Aragón, but Ramon Berenguer contented himself with the title "*Princeps Aragonum*", and only after his death were his successors titled "King of Aragón and Count of Barcelona". It was Catalan dynamism which later resulted in the acquisition of a Mediterranean empire, but since Aragón was a kingdom and Catalonia a principality, the combined realm was henceforth known as the "Crown of Aragón".

Jaume I (James the Conqueror, 1213–76),

age of nine he succeeded in escaping from the castle of Monzón, west of Lleida, where he had been kept prisoner by a regent, and at 13 was married to Eleanor of Castile. His great military successes included the capture of Mallorca from the Moors in 1229 and of Valencia in 1238.

Jaume was far-sighted in his policy for repopulating the conquered territories. Unlike successive Castilian monarchs of Andalucía, who rewarded the nobility from the north with vast estates, he was alive to the need for a fairer sharing out of the land, once remarking to Alfonso X of Castile that every hundred brave men who had been well endowed could be expected to rally to the Crown in its hour of need.

Thus in 1272 he wrote to his counsellors in Barcelona: "We have surveyed the Kingdom of Valencia and we have found that in the whole realm there are only thirty thousand Christians... Seek out, therefore, those men in your city who are of courage and have no heritage enabling them to live comfortably; and if there are two or three brothers, and one has an inheritance and the others not, we wish that those who are heirs should not be so in this kingdom which God has given us."

Tall and commanding in presence, Jaume el Conqueridor was a man of powerful passions and his infatuation for his second wife, of the country—the great *Llibre del Consolat de Mar*, a compendium of maritime law, was written in the vernacular during his reign—Jaume paved the way for writers such as Ramon Llull and the flowering of Catalan literature in the decades following his death. And he was undoubtedly loved by his subjects.

Maritime power: Jaume's death in 1276 marked the end of an era. Catalonia had reached the limits of expansion within the peninsula and he had already laid the foundations for its future and much more important role as the major maritime power in the Mediterranean. One such move was the marriage in 1260 of his first-born, the future

Violante of Hungary, unduly influenced him in political decisions, notably the disastrous provisions of his will dividing the kingdom between his sons. He has been condemned as an illiterate barbarian, yet his *Llibre dels Feits* was the first of the four great Catalan chronicles (the others were those of Ramon Muntaner, Bernat Desclot and Peter the Ceremonious) which, it has been said, can be compared with the leading historiographers of the time.

By making Catalan the official language

Left, baronial courtyard in Tarragona. **Above**, 11th-century Tapestry of the Creation, Girona.

Pere II (Peter the Great), to Constance, daughter of Manfred, king of Sicily, a step taken in accordance with the wishes of the Barcelona merchants and maritime community and aimed at extending island bases for Catalan shipping and commerce.

The marriage was consummated in the teeth of stubborn opposition by the Pope, who had plotted with his French compatriot Charles of Anjou to expropriate Manfred; and since his overthrow and death in 1262 Sicily had been occupied by the French. Pere II seized the opportunity to recover the island in the name of his wife when the rebellion known as the Sicilian Vespers broke out on

MASTERS OF THE SEA

Catalonia was already famous for its seamen when, in the late 14th century, Ramon Llull wrote his *Arte de Navegar*, in which he describes the use of charts and astrolabes for navigational purposes and makes the first mention of the magnetic needle. A century before Columbus, he had realised that the earth was spherical and that there must be land on the far side of the Atlantic, "a continent against which the water strikes when displaced, as happens on our side, which is, with respect to the other, the eastern one".

The first full-scale Catalan naval expedition was that of Jaume I (James the Conqueror) which sailed for Mallorca in September 1229 from the ports of Tarragona, Cambrils and Salou. "The whole sea," as the king wrote in his *Chronicle*, "seemed white with sails, so great was the fleet." Mallorca was taken from the Moors, but only after a fiercely contested landing and heavy losses.

Most famous of Catalan naval commanders during the 13th century was Roger de Llúria, whose father had been killed while fighting by the side of King Manfred of Sicily against the forces of Charles of Anjou. He had his revenge in 1283 when he was admiral of the fleet which defeated the Provençal navy off Malta. In hot pursuit, de Llúria jumped aboard the galley of the Provençal admiral, Guillén Corner, and slew him in single combat. The following year de Llúria drubbed a huge Provençal armada along the coast of Calabria, but his greatest triumph was the rout of another great French fleet in the Gulf of Roses in 1285. This ended the massive French invasion of Catalonia aimed at dispossessing Pere II of Aragón.

No less colourful was Roger de Flor, admiral of the fleet for King Frederick of Sicily during Charles of Anjou's last attempts to recapture the island. He was at the time, as the Greek chronicler George Pachymeres describes him, "a man in the prime of life, of terrible aspect, quick in gesture and impetuous in action", and the troops whom he commanded during the campaign were the formidable Catalan and Aragonese mercenaries known as the Almogàvers. It came as a relief to Frederick when Roger proposed that he ship his bellicose companions to Constantinople to fight for the Byzantine emperor, Andronicus II, in his struggle against the Ottoman Turks.

The Grand Company arrived in September 1303 and consisted of 1,500 cavalry, 4,000 foot-soldiers and 1,000 sailors, making a total of 8,000. They formed a savage and ruthless fighting machine and had soon routed the Turks in Anatolia, killing some 10,000 of the enemy.

However, it was not long before reports came back that the Almogàvers' barbarities were worse than any committed by the Turks; soon they became the scourge and terror of the whole region. Roger de Flor was murdered by the emperor's son Michael in 1305; but the Company soldiered on under new commanders, finally occupying the Duchy of Athens, which remained a dependency of the Kingdom of Sicily until 1387.

By the 14th century Catalonia was the largest mercantile country in the Mediterranean, with its fleet bringing back gold and slaves from North Africa, and spices from Syria and Egypt. That its merchant ships did not share in the lucrative trade with the New World during the 16th century was not, as is often stated, because of a Castilian monopoly, but because it was not then feasible to pass through the Strait of Gibraltar against current and winds without risking men and ships.

The 16th century also saw widespread piracy and depredation of the Levante coast at the hands of the Barbary corsairs. Barcelona was finally stirred to action; pine, birch and oak logs were torn down from the Pyrenees. Don Juan of Austria's flagship *El Real*, which has been rebuilt as the centrepiece for the city's Maritime Museum (pictured here), consumed 300 mature oak logs in hull timbers alone. The shipyards rang to activity and, when the grand fleet finally set sail in 1571, there was a large Catalan contingent under the admiral, Lluís de Requesens, and including captains from Palamós and Sant Feliu de Guíxols. Meeting the Turkish fleet off the Greek coast at Lepanto, the Christian fleet of Don Juan won a spectacular and decisive victory in the biggest battle the Mediterranean has ever seen.

Easter Monday 1282 as the people were leaving church in Palermo.

Coincidentally or not, Pere was engaged in operations along the North African coast with 140 ships and an army of 15,000 men and was prompt to respond when the Sicilians asked him to intervene. All attempts by the French to regain the island were beaten off, and, although Sicily and the Crown of Aragón were at first ruled by separate branches of the House of Barcelona, it became an advance base for Catalan mercantile enterprise along the North African coast and for the spice trade with the Near East.

The Pope meanwhile responded by excommunicating Pere; and Charles of Anjou, August 1285. Its stubborn defence nevertheless gained time for the invincible Roger de Llúria to fall upon and utterly destroy the French fleet in the Gulf of Roses. This ended the invasion; the French straggled back across the Pyrenees, leaving enormous booty in the hands of the victorious Catalans.

Pere el Gran's short reign had seen the emergence of Catalonia-Aragón as a major Mediterranean power, and he well merited Dante's description of him: "*D'ogni valor portò cinta la corda*" ("Today he wears courage like a belt").

Consolidation of the Catalan-Aragonese empire in the Mediterranean proceeded apace during the reign of Pere III (Peter the

who had been soundly drubbed by the great Catalan admiral Roger de Llúria, challenged Pere to personal combat in Bordeaux. On discovering that an ambush was being prepared for him and his retinue, Pere returned to Aragón to learn that the Pope had conferred his kingdom on Charles of Valois, son of Philip III of France, and that a huge French force of 100 ships, 16,000 knights and 100,000 infantry was advancing on him. It proved impossible to hold the passes of the Pyrenees and Girona fell to the invaders in

Above, Santa Maria, Castelló d'Empúries, built for a bishop's see which was never confirmed.

Ceremonious, 1336–87). The Balearics, a perpetual bone of contention because of the habit of the kings of the House of Barcelona to leave the islands to their younger sons, were reintegrated in the Crown of Aragón; Sardinia was pacified at some cost; and even the Duchy of Athens was under Catalan control. Sicily was ruled by a junior branch of the family and Pere reverted to the old ploy of the Counts of Barcelona by marrying his daughter to Frederick, king of Sicily. As insurance, when his wife died, he himself married Frederick's sister.

Pere was a man of boundless ambition, who, in the words of Oxford professor P. E.

Russell, "in the end found himself irretrievably imprisoned in diplomatic webs of his own weaving". Nowhere is this more apparent than in his war against Pedro the Cruel of Castile—in which the Black Prince fought on Pedro's side. The only eventual winner was Enrique of Trastamara, who murdered his brother Pedro to achieve his ambition of becoming King of Castile.

To all outward appearances the 14th century was a period of spectacular expansion for the Crown of Aragón. Catalan merchants rivalled those of Genoa and Venice in the traffic of spices from Alexandria and its sailors ranged from the Sea of Azov to England and Flanders. Nevertheless the outbreak of the Black Death in 1348 signalled a

Young), the last of his line, died suddenly in 1409 while on an expedition to Sardinia. The shock was traumatic. In the eyes of the Catalans, especially the all-important mercantile classes, the country's health and prosperity depended on the survival of the dynasty. Even today Catalan historians, among them the illustrious Ferran Soldevila, attribute the country's subsequent decline and "Castilianisation" to the events surrounding the succession at the time of Martí's death.

Martí el Jove's father, Martí l'Humà (Martin the Humane), survived his son by only a year and failed to make clear his wishes as to a successor. In the upshot the field was narrowed to two candidates, Jaume

break of the Black Death in 1348 signalled a period of economic depression and labour shortages throughout Western Europe which put the Crown of Aragón at a serious demographic disadvantage compared with its much larger neighbour, Castile. Pere's successors, the last two kings of the House of Barcelona, were faced with organised protests from the *pagesos de remença* (labourers tied to the land) and proved unable to reconcile the differences between the landed proprietors and the peasants any more than those between their feuding nobility.

End of the line: In these circumstances, the heir to the throne, Martí el Jove (Martin the

of Urgell, favoured by most Catalans, and Ferran of Antequera (the second son of Juan I of Castile and Eleanor, daughter of Pere el Ceremoniós), who was Regent of Castile and, even more important, had enlisted the support of the most influential man in the Crown of Aragón, the Anti-Pope Pere de Luna.

With conspicuous fairness, the Catalan Corts (the form of parliament first established in 1218 during the reign of Jaume el Conqueridor) proposed that *parlaments* be convoked from all three divisions of the kingdom—Catalonia, Aragón and Valencia—to decide between the claimants. In the event the delegates were dominated by de Luna's men and only one of the *compromissaris* voted for Jaume of Urgell.

For all the talk of the "denationalisation of Catalonia", Ferran was scrupulous in acknowledging the rights of the Corts and its standing committee, the Generalitat, as set out at the time:

"The affairs of the Principality are not to be judged by reference to those of other kingdoms and provinces, where the kings and lords are sovereign lords, with such power that they make and unmake laws and rule their vassals as they will; and where, after making laws, they themselves are not bound by them… In Catalonia, the supreme power and jurisdiction over the province belongs not to His Majesty alone, but to His Majesty and the three estates of the province [the nobility, the clergy and well-to-do citizenry], which together possess supreme and absolute power to make and unmake laws… These laws we have in Catalonia are laws contracted between the king and the land, and the prince can no more exempt himself from them than he can exempt himself from a contract…"

Ferran's son, Alfons V (The Magnanimous), was criticised for installing his Castilian followers in positions of authority, but he can hardly be accused of furthering the interests of Castile at the expense of the Crown of Aragón. His life was devoted to expansion in the Mediterranean, and above all to 20 years of bitter campaigning for the Kingdom of Naples, which he finally won in 1442—only to leave it to his bastard son, Ferran de Calabria, and for it to be separated from the Crown of Aragón.

In the meantime all of Catalonia's internal problems were aggravated by Alfons's constant demands for money to finance his foreign adventures. Matters went from bad to worse during the reign of his son, Joan II (1458–79). There was renewed conflict between the landed proprietors and the *pagesos de remença* who worked the land and on whom they depended for their income. The king in the main took the part of the *pagesos*. Most of the nobility, the clergy and bourgeoisie and the institutions representing

them, such as the Corts, Generalitat and municipality of Barcelona, were ranged on the other side.

Finally it all boiled over into civil war, with the king calling in Louis XI of France, who improved the occasion to seize the counties of Rousillon and Cerdanya, and the Corts appealing to Enrique IV of Castile. King Joan played his last card by marrying his 16-year-old son Ferran to Enrique IV's half-sister Isabel, and the whole messy business was patched up, but only at the expense of ensuring the future paramount role of Castile in ordering the affairs of the peninsula. (As the first of the Castilian kings to rule Catalonia, Ferran is given his Spanish

name, Fernando, as will all the monarchs from this point on.)

The writers of the Renaixença, the romantic and nationalistic literary movement of the 19th century, laid most of the ills of a depressed 16th-century Catalonia at the door of Fernando the Catholic. This is hardly borne out by the facts. Fernando's marriage to Isabel of Castile did not imply the amalgamation of the two countries; Isabel remained ruler of Castile and Fernando ruler of the Crown of Aragón. It was only after the accession of their Habsburg grandson, the Emperor Carlos V, that the kingship was combined in one person. Even then, the ruler

Left, Lleida Cathedral, disused since Felipe V exacted retribution on Catalonia in 1716. **Right**, the harvesters' revolt in Barcelona.

became not "King of Spain", but "King of the Spains".

Fernando proved to be a fair-minded and decisive ruler. The historic Sentencia Arbitral de Guadalupe of 1486 granted the *pagesos* personal liberty and the use of the land which they occupied, and an agreement with the Corts in 1481 stated that any royal measure considered in breach of the laws and usages of Catalonia should forthwith be declared null and void. It was a different story when it came to the Inquisition. This was forced on a country rootedly opposed to it and it promptly led to mass emigration. After the *remença* civil war production and commerce had declined by more than a quarter, inflation was rampant and the florin had slumped, while the population of Barcelona had declined to some 20,000—the lowest figure since the 11th century. "How can the city and country survive such a blow?" the councillors demanded of the king and his extension of the Inquisition to Catalonia. His reply was uncompromising; what he intended to do was *"al servei de Nostre Senyor Déu"* ("in the service of God").

Catalonia plumbed the depths of depression about 1487, but this was followed by an upswing. Fernando made his own contribution by encouraging agriculture, by his measures for combating the piracy rampant in the Mediterranean and, above all, by protecting basic industries such as the manufacture of cloth.

Fernando the Catholic, born in Navarra and fluent in Aragonese and Catalan, took a lively interest in the affairs of the principality. But the position changed radically during the period of his 17th-century Habsburg successors, when Spain became a world power, of which Catalonia, Valencia and Aragón were only a small unit. Even the gold and silver of America were now proving insufficient to finance Castile's imperialistic aims in Europe. Why, it was now argued in Madrid, should not practical form be given to the loose union? Why should the Crown of Aragón not play its part by repealing outdated laws forbidding the raising of troops and by contributing towards the expense of foreign campaigns?

Egged on by his chief minister, the formidable Count Duke of Olivares, Felipe IV paid several visits to Catalonia to persuade the Corts to collaborate—to no effect. Olivares rode roughshod over all objections; Catalan troops were raised and sent to France and an army of 9,000 men was billeted on the principality. By now the inhabitants were seething and rose up in revolt. In a bloody climax in June 1640, a mob of *segadors* (harvesters) broke into Barcelona and converged on the palace of the viceroy, the Count of Santa Coloma; he was murdered attempting to escape on a Genoese galley.

Ultimate banishment: The Catalans paid dearly for their decision to support the Archduke Charles of Austria during the War of the Spanish Succession. Felipe IV of Anjou, who had been crowned King of Spain with the support of Louis XIV of France, offered the Catalans generous concessions, but in 1705 a British fleet arrived off Barcelona and the Archduke made a triumphal entry.

The war followed a chequered course in Spain, but by 1713 the allies had lost interest and were less than scrupulous in implementing their solemn guarantees to the Catalans. As a result Barcelona closed ranks and prepared for a heroic defence which was to stir all Europe and last for 14 months. The city was unable to withstand Felipe's army of some 20,000 reinforced by French troops under the mercenary Duke of Berwick.

The price paid by the Catalans was high. In proclaiming the Decreto de Nueva Planta in January 1716, the Council of Castile declared: "It is necessary to abolish, efface and suspend in their entirety the privileges, usages and customs of the principality… and to impose the laws of Castile… to employ the Castilian language… so that books in Catalan must be forbidden, nor must it be spoken or written in schools and instruction in Christian doctrine must be in Castilian…"

Books were collected and destroyed, the universities of Barcelona, Girona and Lleida were closed and Lleida's cathedral, which Felipe's troops had made a barracks, would never be used as a place of worship again.

Such was the vitality of the region, however, that Catalonia was to rise above its trials. The last decades of the 18th century saw an explosion of economic activity and the population doubled to reach a million; while the patriotic movements of the 19th century revived all the Catalan's latent pride.

Typical Catalan wall tiles showing the crafts and industries of the town and countryside.

Any account of the 19th century in Catalonia has to answer these questions: why and how did this region become the first in Spain to develop a market mentality and an industrial proletariat? Why was Richard Ford, writing in the late 1830s, able to describe Barcelona as "the Manchester of Catalonia, which is the Lancashire of the peninsula"?

The Catalans were not rich in coal or iron ore like the Basques (whose industrialisation came a little later); their principal natural resource lay in their five rivers. These certainly provided hydraulic power but the region's economic success seems to lie less in water power than in will power. The germ probably lay far back in the past, when the Mediterranean conquests of the count-kings of the Catalan-Aragonese federation were enthusiastically supported by merchants in search of markets. This was a time when Castile was fully concentrated on the war with Islam, to the exclusion of any mercantile thoughts whatsoever.

Also, a kind of determination is associated with Catalans. An old saying runs: *"El Catalan de las piedras saca pan"* ("The Catalan will get bread from stones"). The Catalan historian J. Viçens Vives believed that industrialism "made headway because of the enormous sacrifices of individuals and because of an indomitable will to triumph".

During the previous century three additional factors had contributed to Catalonia's industrial revolution. The system of land tenure based on middle-sized family holdings called *masies* (sing. *masia*), transmitted through primogeniture, encouraged younger sons to move into the towns and set up small businesses, usually with family support. The rapid growth of the population provided markets and profits for farmers, who were thus able to purchase the products of the factories.

But, perhaps most importantly of all, that enlightened despot Carlos III opened up the American colonial trade (for two and a half

centuries the monopoly of Seville and Cádiz) to Catalonia. The need for commercial capital was thus able to be met by agricultural exports, notably wine and spirits to South America and cork to world markets. It was the profits from these ventures that provided the funds for investment in the textile industry, which was to dominate the Catalan economy in the next century.

War with France: The war of 1793–95 with the French revolutionaries and the Peninsular War (1808–14), always known in Spain

as "the War of Independence", were serious interruptions to the industrial process. Because of the shared border running through the Pyrenees, the French naturally occupied Catalonia at an early stage. Barcelona fell at the outset of the War of Independence, in February 1808, deceived by a ruse. But it soon became the haunt of *afrancesados*, those who believed that the French influence would be beneficial in modernising Spain.

There was, however, fierce resistance elsewhere. Roses on the Costa Brava held out for a while with the aid of a British squadron under Lord Cochrane. Tarragona, Manresa, Montserrat and Hostalric defied

Left, the Company of Santa Barbara were the heroines in the breaches during the historic defence of Girona in 1809, while Lord Cochrane, **above**, sailed to the aid of Roses.

the French for varying periods. Girona, having repulsed its first siege in 1808, put up a heroic resistance to its second siege in 1809, which lasted seven months and five days. English volunteers played a gallant part. The women of the city enrolled themselves in a militia devoted to Santa Barbara, the patroness of Spanish artillery, and fought in the breaches.

The governor, Mariano Alvarez, became delirious and, with his collapse, Girona fell. He was later said to have died in his cell in the prison of Figueres, where he is generally thought to have been murdered. This sturdy but unavailing defence has passed into Spanish legend.

If the Peninsular War was a distraction from the main thrust of Catalan development, so too—but more insidiously because it was an internal conflict—was the first Carlist War (1833–39). As from 1827 a Carlist party began to form around the person of Don Carlos, brother and heir presumptive of Fernando VII, then still childless. But the king's last wife, Maria Cristina of Naples, bore him a girl, Isabel. The Queen's faction at court persuaded Fernando to publish a "pragmatic sanction", naming his daughter as heiress to the throne under the regency of her mother, in defiance of Don Carlos's claim under the Salic law,

which had been imported into Spain by the first Spanish Bourbon, Felipe V.

When the king died in 1833, a civil war immediately followed. Maria Cristina was forced, rather against her natural instincts, into an alliance with the Liberals, and on the world scene the war came to be seen as one between the great principles of liberalism and reaction. According to the British historian Raymond Carr, Carlism was always presented by Liberals as the "revolt of monks and low people" against the spirit of the century.

The Carlist strongholds were confined to those regions where the preservation of medieval autonomous rights or *fueros* was most jealously guarded—the Basque provinces, Navarra, Aragón and, to a lesser extent, Catalonia, where the movement was confined to the foothills of the Pyrenees and soon degenerated into mere brigandage.

The Convention of Vergara in 1839, which recognised Isabel as Queen, brought the first Carlist War to an end. But there was to be a resurgence in 1846–49 under Don Carlos's son, the Count of Montemolin, which aroused some support in the Catalan countryside; and again after the Liberal *coup d'état* in 1868.

Despite its political and military defeats, Carlism showed a hardy capacity for nostalgic survival as an expression of an older Spain, disgusted with industrialism, liberalism and free thought. Latter-day Carlists, sporting red berets and known as *requetés*, joined General Franco's National Movement and were rewarded after his victory in 1939 with some concessions to their traditional rights.

King cotton: Despite Carlism, Catalan industrial growth continued apace. Catalans visited England and introduced modern manufacturing equipment on their return home: between 1830 and 1840 the production of cotton goods almost tripled and it doubled again in the following five years. The industry relied predominantly on horse and water power in the 1830s, but by 1845 there had been a dramatic shift to steam. The first railway line in Spain was completed from Barcelona to Mataró in 1848.

And it was not only industry that developed. The agricultural sector continued to flourish: Reus, near Tarragona, became a world centre of trade in almonds, hazelnuts and dried fruits, while the cork forests did well from the growing popularity of Champagne. All the same, cotton textiles, reinforced to some extent by wool, remained the staple of the Catalan economy almost to the end of the century, thanks in part to fierce demands for protective tariffs from manufacturers whenever threatened by recession.

La Renaixença: It is impossible to venture any further into the 19th century without addressing la Renaixença, Catalonia's home-grown "Renaissance". This was not a Risorgimento on the Italian model. It did not initially formulate any political goals. Its first stirrings in the 1830s were literary, coinciding with the growth of the Romantic

sance was entirely cultural and élitist. It also had a popular, progressive and republican side, linked with the emerging workers' associations. The popular tongue had survived through almost three centuries of repression and "decatalanisation" by central government; its literary luminaries could not have turned it into a potent instrument, later to be taken up and used by politicians, if it had not remained alive and well among the population at large. Business interests at first treated the Renaissance purely as a cultural phenomenon but later sought to exploit its political offspring, Catalanism.

The bourgeoisie: The leading contributors both to economic and to cultural life—the

movement in England. Its first text was *L'Oda a la Pàtria* by B.C. Aribau, published in 1833. The bourgeoisie began to rediscover the Catalan language. Literary and satirical magazines sprang to life. The Jocs Florals were revived in 1859 in imitation of the medieval contests of the troubadours. Jacint Verdaguer and Joan Maragall became popular romantic poets.

It should not be assumed from its emergence in poetic garb that the Catalan Renais-

two are strongly linked in Catalonia to this day—were members of a bourgeoisie very different in its outlook from the middle class of soldiers and bureaucrats in the rest of the country, whom they derided as parasites. They reserved especial scorn for the "artificial" economy of Madrid, whose trades were confined to such peripheral items as umbrella factories, silversmiths, printing works, guitar-string makers and even manufacturers of false teeth.

Yet not everything was blooming in the Catalan industrialists' garden. Expansion was constantly curtailed by the limited purchasing power of the Spanish agrarian

Left, Queen Isabel, favoured by the Liberals, against whom the Carlists, <u>above</u>, by the Olot School's Berga i Boix, sporadically fought.

masses. This turned Catalan employers into vociferous protectionists and led them into frequent conflict with Liberal governments in Madrid wedded to free trade. Also, as the century progressed, they faced mounting labour unrest.

With the boom in cotton textiles, a unique type of industrial organisation grew up in the shape of *colonies industrials*. These were situated along the rivers, where hydraulic power was available for the mills. Prominent among these were the Colònia Rosal at Gironella and the Colònia Güell at Santa Coloma de Cervelló, both on the upper Llobregat.

In essence the factory, the workers' housing estate, the church, the school and the owner's residence were all enclosed in a single compound like a barracks. There was an early morning bell to wake employees in time to allow for a little procreation before clocking in: the future workforce had to be assured. Educational provision was made with the genuine aim of alleviating the brutalisation of labour by the factory system. Magnates such as Count Eusebi Güell employed leading architects—Antoni Gaudí, for example—to build their colonies.

In this sense, the Catalan *haute bourgeoisie* may be seen as progressive reactionaries. But their combination of paternalism and intrusiveness, which has been described as semi-feudal, became increasingly obnoxious to the budding workers' movements.

Workers' rights: The cultural enlightenment of the Catalan employers was not accompanied by any enthusiasm for workers' rights. Confrontation with the progressive government of General Espartero (1840–43) led to the bombardment of Barcelona by government troops in 1842. While demanding state protection for their own interests, the employers resisted all attempts by Madrid to introduce measures to protect workers against abusive practices. Laws limiting the daily hours of female labour to 11 and prohibiting the employment of children under the age of 10 were not finally forced on Catalonia till 1907.

Taken in conjunction with the legal ban on workers' associations, not permanently lifted until 1881, the kindling for urban radicalism and revolt was well and truly laid. Despite the ban, workers' movements of a mutualist and co-operative nature continued

to gather strength, culminating in a general strike in 1855.

The bourgeoisie was even more shocked by the palace revolution of September 1868 by Generals Prim and Serrano and Admiral Topete, which sent Queen Isabel into exile, partly on account of her politics and partly of her scandalous private life. Her departure was followed, to their horror, by the introduction of universal suffrage, the right of association, and press and religious freedom.

The anarchists: The (bloodless) revolution of 1868 gave rise to a new outbreak of Carlism by the conservative peasantry of the north, including Catalonia. In the very same year anarchism was introduced into Spain by

Giuseppe Fanelli, a missionary of Bakunin's revolutionary Alliance of Social Democracy, which was shortly to be disowned by Marx. Fanelli's extraordinary achievement was, without a word of Spanish, to lay the foundations of Spanish Anarcho-Syndicalism which was to colour and disrupt the politics of the left for decades to come.

The new movement gathered support, through its union, the CNT, not only from the disillusioned urban proletariat of Catalonia but also from the landless rural labourers of Andalucía. Though later contaminated by its reputation for violence, anarchism built initially on a millenarian, idealistic streak which is attractive in Spaniards. Some writers have seen the anarchist ideal of independent sovereign municipalities as a doctrine ideally suited to the individualism of Spaniards, in contrast with the doctrinaire conformity of Marxism.

The Spanish socialist union, the UGT, was founded in Barcelona in 1888 in the hope that it would convert the industrial workers there, but its failure in Catalonia was so complete that it removed its headquarters to Madrid in 1899, leaving the field to the anarchists. Centralising socialism was simply not congenial to the Catalan spirit.

Catalanism: While the proletarian movements were increasingly seeking their inspi-

ration abroad, the conservative right was still demanding protectionism at home and the Progressive Federalists, led by Valentí Almirall, author of the seminal *Lo Catalanisme* (1886), were demanding regional autonomy. In 1885 the bourgeoisie presented a Memorial de Greuges (Memorandum of Grievances) to the restored Bourbon monarch Alfonso XII but without any concrete results. From this time on, they took up the banner of Catalanism no longer as a cultural and literary plaything but as an instrument to

Left, mosaic ceiling from Gaudí's Colònia Güell. **Above,** satirical cartoon of "bomb city".

advance their own interests against the central state.

The period from 1890 to 1910 was marked by a number of mainly right-wing Catalanist groupings and regroupings whose objective was to demand either protectionist legislation or regional autonomy, or both, from the central government. The Lliga de Catalunya of 1889 evolved into the Unió Catalanista two years later, which approved the Bases de Manresa, a home rule project which again did not prosper.

In 1895 rebellion broke out in Cuba and in 1898 the last straw came for the Catalan bourgeoisie when Cuba, the Philippines and Puerto Rico—all important trade outlets—were lost for good through, as they saw it, the incompetence and indolence of Madrid. These disasters led to the foundation of the first exclusively Catalan political party, the conservative-inspired Lliga Regionalista in 1901, with the objective of fighting the national elections on a regionalist ticket.

There was then a further attempt at an all-party Catalanist movement under the banner of Solidaritat Catalana. The leaders of these various permutations and combinations were men of high calibre: Cambò, the industrialist, and Prat de la Riba, author of *La Nacionalitat Catalana* (1906), both intelligent conservatives; Almirall, the inspiration behind Catalanism; and Lerroux, the republican. Ultimately their efforts came to little because the discrepancies between left and right could never be papered over for long and, more importantly, because Catalanism was not supported by the urban proletariat.

The working classes were supremely unimpressed by these various Catalanist manoeuvres. In 1893 Paulí Pallás attempted to kill General Martínez Campos (who had been instrumental in restoring Alfonso XII in 1874) and was executed. Two bombs were dropped by way of reprisal in the packed Liceu opera house, favoured haunt of the bourgeoisie, killing 20 and wounding many more. Bomb city was in business. The campaign of terrorism continued with the bombing of a Corpus Christi procession, which killed 10 bystanders, followed by the assassination of Cánovas del Castillo, the conservative statesman (who had been deeply influenced by Edmund Burke).

The most violent incident of all was the Setmana Trágica (tragic week) of 1909, when workers' organisations rose against the government's call-up of reserves to fight in Morocco in defence of Spanish mining interests which were threatened by Rif tribesmen. This was the classic instance, bloody in its outcome, of the Catalans' deep desire to have nothing to do with the incompetent militarism of Madrid: 116 people died and some 300 were injured before the uprising was suppressed. Executions followed, giving rise to an international outcry, as a result of which the government fell.

Modernism: However great the political turbulence, it would be wrong to leave the 19th century on a negative note. Though politics left many tensions unresolved, the

spirit of improvement and even of optimism was in the air throughout much of the period. Whatever the shortcomings of the bourgeoisie in industrial relations, they spectacularly maintained their devotion to culture, education, architecture and the arts.

This was seen especially in the movement called Modernism, which embraced all the art forms but is most accessible to the visitor through its buildings. Many of these were put up for the Universal Exhibition of 1888, in which Barcelona demonstrated to the world its financial muscle and industrial strength. Architecturally, Modernism was eclectic in its inspiration: it drew on Moor-

ish, Gothic and Renaissance motifs and abhorred cold neo-classicism; it preferred friendly brick to monumental stone; it loved variegated decoration, both inside and out, employing iron, ceramics, wood and all the crafts. It is sometimes thought of as a Spanish brand of Art Nouveau, but that fails to do justice either to its exceptional élan and vitality or to its idealistic revolt against industrial squalor.

Some of Modernism's main practitioners were polymaths, also active in civil and political life. The architect Lluís Domènech i Montaner (1850–1933) was president of the revived Jocs Florals, president of the Lliga de Catalunya and a signatory of the Bases de Manresa. He was twice elected to the national parliament in Madrid. He also wrote a general history of art with Josep Puig i Cadafalch (1867–1957).

Puig, likewise an architect, was the arch-eclecticist, a sort of Catalan Edwin Lutyens. He wrote the major work on Catalan Romanesque art. He, too, had a distinguished political career, culminating in the presidency of the Mancomunitat (the very limited type of regional government finally granted in 1913 to appease Catalanism and abolished by General Primo de Rivera after his *coup d'état* in 1923).

Though the polymaths expressed the spirit of their times, their more famous colleague Antoni Gaudí was a religious traditionalist who led a very private life. The town house he built in Barcelona for his patron, Count Eusebi Güell, was a reversion to the urban fortress-dwelling favoured by prominent and frequently feuding families in the Middle Ages. This brilliantly executed yet sinister building reflects the architect's view of the industrial magnate as feudal overlord.

But there can be no doubt about Gaudí's creative vitality, which well outstripped that of his eminent contemporaries, so it is fitting that his best-known work, the church of the Sagrada Família, should have become to Barcelona what the Eiffel Tower is to Paris and Big Ben to London. Its enormously ambitious scale and the fact that it is unfinished and likely to remain so, say much about the thrusting aspirations of the Catalans: never fully satisfied but never extinguished.

Left, Modernist decoration, Casa Lleó Morera, Barcelona. Right, sausage factory, Girona.

53

When looking back over this century's history, it is hard to know whether to think of Catalonia as an uppity region or a frustrated state. Whichever is nearer the truth, the two *coups d'état* which brought Spain a total of 45 years' dictatorship were to some extent sparked off by right-wing reaction to a small degree of home rule granted to Catalonia.

In 1914, the moderate campaign of the Catalan conservative party, La Lliga, had resulted in the recovery of some autonomy for Catalonia. It had been the first step on the road to home rule since the loss of independence in 1714. The establishment of the Mancomunitat (an administrative council for the four Catalan provinces) had enabled its president, Enric Prat de la Riba, to exercise powers and responsibilities in areas such as library administration, health and education. The Mancomunitat also adopted and promoted Noucentism, the rather austere, classical and somewhat élitist cultural movement which followed Modernism.

Despite some degree of social unrest, things seemed to go well for this small, prospering nation, until 1923 and the unexpected *pronunciamento* (*coup d'état*) of Barcelona's military governor, General Primo de Rivera (1870–1930). But his seven-year dictatorship of Spain had a boomerang effect, stirring up support for the republican and Catalan national causes it had tried to suppress. In the end Primo de Rivera was dismissed by King Alfonso XIII, who had initially given his blessing to the military regime. A year later city council elections were seen as a referendum on the monarchy, and the king abdicated.

"Granddad" Macià: The Catalans' 20th-century hero is undoubtedly Francesc Macià (1875–1933), more affectionately known as *L'Avi* (Granddad). His charisma may be matched only by Tito's in Yugoslavia or Churchill's in England during World War II. He began his career as an army officer in the Spanish engineer corps; but in November

1905, he resigned his post in Lleida as a result of the "*Cu-cut* affair", when officers broke up the satirical magazine's printing presses which had published an unflattering cartoon about the army. Macià soon became a nationalist leader.

It wasn't until 1926, however, that he became a household name. A small force he was secretly gathering in French Catalonia to fight Primo de Rivera's dictatorship was discovered. The subsequent trial held in Paris was to prove a triumph for him and the

Catalan cause. Macià's name hit the headlines in America and Europe and he was pictured in the "personality of the week" section of the *Illustrated London News*.

In 1927, after a token sentence served in Paris's La Santé prison, Macià went to rally the support of exiled Catalans in South America. On being refused a visa into Argentina by a government reluctant to fall out with Madrid, he risked life and limb crossing the River Plate to meet up with followers in Buenos Aires.

A few weeks before the 1931 elections Macià returned to Catalonia to a hero's welcome. Just after the election results were

Preceding pages: nationalist demonstration, Girona. **Left**, Macià proclaims the Catalan Republic, 1931. **Above**, the long, dark ride into exile in 1939 at the end of the civil war.

known, Macià, the new president, proclaimed the Catalan Republic in opposition to the "Bourbon monarchy we have overcome". Not surprisingly, the new Madrid government was unhappy with this declaration of sovereignty, and after three days of bitter negotiation, Macià was forced to accept a rather deflated solution: the re-establishment of the old 14th-century government of Catalonia, the Generalitat, and the drafting of a new Statute of Autonomy. Although the statute had massive support in a referendum later that year, it was subsequently watered down by the parliament in Madrid.

President Macià, who had come to politics late in life, was now an old man. He died on Christmas Day 1933. The period of Catalan history associated with Macià and his successor, Lluís Companys (1883–1940), was seen as progressive both inside and outside Catalonia. English observers visited the country to look at what had been termed the "educational miracle" of the Catalans; and the Macià Plan was drawn up by the architect Le Corbusier for the creation of a vast worker holiday city at Castelldefels. But the *coup d'état* headed by General Francisco Franco nipped the project in the bud, as it did the alternative Olympics that had been organised in opposition to Hitler's Berlin Games. They were to have started on 19 July 1936, just as the civil war began.

On 6 October 1934, in solidarity with the Asturian miners who had declared their region a socialist republic, President Companys had once again proclaimed the Catalan Republic. This time Madrid called out the army. In Rambla Santa Mònica there is a plaque commemorating the site where several trade unionists were killed when the building was shelled. Companys and other members of the Catalan government were sentenced to life imprisonment.

But in early 1936, following the election of the popular front in Madrid, Companys was released from prison to preside over the Catalan government once again. Shortly afterwards, Franco's Nationalist rebellion began. Companys remained in Barcelona until early 1939, when he fled to France; there he was captured by the Gestapo, handed over to the Spanish authorities and executed barefoot on Montjuïc hill. The wall against which he was shot is half a kilometre from the Olympic Stadium.

The civil war: The Nationalist rebellion was an insurrection by a substantial right-wing element in the army against the Republican government. It began on 16 July 1936, with the uprising of Spain's Africa Army in Morocco, led by General Franco, and was followed by rebellions in garrisons throughout Spain. At 4 a.m. on 19 July the army in the Bruc barracks near Pedralbes in Barcelona, declaring for Franco, marched down the Diagonal towards the centre of the city. But the Republican civil authorities and the anarchist unions had access to arms and after many hours of bitter fighting, the rebels' last stronghold in the telephone exchange in Plaça Catalunya fell. Their leader, General

Goded, who had hoped to take over Catalonia, was tried and executed.

In neighbouring Aragón, however, the army had taken control of the capital, Zaragoza. Columns were somewhat haphazardly recruited by the Anti-Fascist Brigades and sent off, ill-equipped, to regain the city. With more ideology than organisation, the venture failed, though the troops remained in sight of the city for 18 months.

In November 1936 the Republican government left Madrid for Valencia and the following October it retreated to Barcelona. In March 1938 the Nationalists began their Aragón offensive and the Ebre front became the bloodiest battleground of the war. The Catalan troops, reorganised on Stalinist lines, always lacked equipment and weapons. France and England were set on nonintervention and the few cannons sent from Russia seldom arrived with ammunition.

Lack of supplies had sapped morale, as had the shelling of the coast and the air raids by Mussolini's Italian air force units stationed in Mallorca. Once Franco decided to march on Catalonia with a sizeable force, resistance crumbled within a few months. By late 1938, Catalan forces withdrew in tatters to the frontier, surrendering the capital without firing a shot.

The defeat of the Republic by the fascist

forces meant not only that progress, democracy and human rights were wiped off the map of Spain generally but, in the case of Catalonia, the identity of a whole nation was put in jeopardy.

Many Catalans today feel the events of the civil war were too confusing to draw any clear-cut conclusions. Long years of proregime schooling and the benign nature of the political transition have undoubtedly contributed to this. For example, most are

Left, President Lluís Companys, who was executed barefoot on Montjuïc. **Above**, the victors' vision of the crucial Ebre battle.

unaware that, as it moved into Catalonia, Franco's army changed its name from "army of liberation" to "army of occupation", clearly betraying its new motives. Between the end of the war and 1964 Catalans were singled out by the regime to pay a special 1 percent "punishment tax". But these factors do not seem to have left deep scars.

Franco abolished the Statute of Autonomy as soon as his troops trod on Catalan soil. Just before occupying Lleida in 1938, the fascist planes bombed the city on a market day. It was the same story as Guernica, but no artist recorded it and the event has been pushed out of people's minds. When Franco's troops took the town, one of their first tasks was to remove volumes 150 and 151 from the civil registry where all the deaths caused by the raid had been recorded.

The post-war years: Once Catalonia had fallen, shopkeepers who still had anything to sell were given a few hours to take down any signs in Catalan. More than 200,000 Catalans went over the Pyrenees into exile. Many were concentrated in camps in French Catalonia. A further 200,000 were killed in the post-war repression, and in Barcelona the early morning executions at Camp de la Bota were commonplace for years. Catalan books were burnt in their thousands. The language was banned in schools and in public, and Catalans were told to speak in *Cristiano* (Spanish). Even the *sardana* dance was initially forbidden.

Despite their bitter experience of Anglo-French non-intervention in the war, exiled Catalans had pinned high hopes on the premise that, once Hitler and Mussolini had fallen, the Allies would rid Europe of its last fascist regime. This was the hope of the *Consell Nacional Català* operating in London. But the visit to Spain of General Eisenhower in 1959 confirmed Franco as an ally of NATO and the West.

The Franco regime was not entirely without support in Catalonia. The richer classes that had suffered persecution, expropriation and insecurity during the civil war years were often fervent Franco supporters, though few Catalans were appointed to government posts. Many upper-middle-class families adopted the use of Spanish even in the home. The Church initially went along with the regime and played a repressive role both politically and socially, but there was also a progressive and pro-Catalan element in the Church, and Montserrat, the spectacularly-located Benedictine monastery outside Barcelona, was a shrine of Catalanism throughout the dictatorship. The monastery served as a hiding-place for dissidents and a meeting place for the regime's opponents. In 1963, the monastery's abbot, Aureli María Escarré, hit the world's headlines when he was forced into exile for expressing his opposition to Franco.

Another Catalan to get into trouble with the regime was a doctor called Jordi Pujol. He was imprisoned in 1960 for allegedly organising the singing of a nationalist song, *El Cant de la Senyera*, in the Palau de la

Música during one of Franco's rare visits to Catalonia. On release from jail three years later, he set about founding a Catalan bank which would promote investment in the country. Jordi Pujol was elected president of the Catalan government in 1980.

Towards the latter years of the regime, political opposition became more organised. The Assemblea de Catalunya was founded in 1971. All Catalan parties were represented in this clandestine organisation which struggled for "Amnesty, Freedom and Self-Government", in the words of its most repeated slogan. The song of Lluís Llach, *L'Estaca* (The Stake), became the symbol of

that period. Franco finally died in his bed on 20 November 1975.

Evolutionary spirit: Democratic opponents to the regime were basically divided between those who wanted *ruptura* (radical change) and those favouring *reforma* (pragmatic evolution). The present status of Catalonia in the Spanish state, a semi-autonomous region within a constitutional monarchy, can largely be put down to the fact that the evolutionists came out on top.

Forty years of fascism had left their mark on Catalonia: much of the coastline had been spoiled by tourist speculation; its leading politicians had disappeared and fear of another *coup d'état* had not been dispelled (a fear which was to be justified by the attempted *coup* of 23 February 1981, when armed Guardia Civil occupied the parliament building in Madrid); finally, the heavy industrialisation of the region, which although now enjoying a higher standard of living than any other part of Spain, faced the same sort of economic crisis the Republic had had to face in the 1930s.

Between 1960 and 1975, industrial development had attracted more than two million people from poorer regions of Spain to come and work. Francesc Candel's *Els Altres Catalans* (*The Other Catalans*, published in 1964) describes the plight of these newcomers, many of whom reached Barcelona without any knowledge of the language or cultural make-up of their new land. Nearly all were forced to live on run-down estates in what is called Barcelona's "red belt".

But the late 1970s, after the death of Franco, were also a period of renewed hope. On 11 September 1977, Catalonia's national day, the largest demonstration in the country's history demanded home rule. The Catalan language was coming back, to be taught in all schools. Democracy was beginning to bear its first fruits in the new city councils. Newspapers in Catalan were displayed on the news-stands alongside porno magazines. Priests were challenging the official Church line. The political parties were recovering their place in society. There was a buzz of optimism in the air.

Autonomy guaranteed: The pressure Catalans and Basques brought to bear on the state was largely responsible for the invention of the formula of the "State of the Autonomies" which now defines Spain. A policy of *café* *per a tots* ("Coffee for everyone"), has meant the somewhat artificial division of Spain into 17 "autonomous regions and nationalities". Catalan and Basque national rights have been swept under the carpet by a policy of "fair-play-for-all".

Under a new regional statute (1979), Catalonia has been granted a share in routine administration, but the power it had traditionally aspired to in such decisive areas as public finance, energy and transport is as distant as ever. On the other hand, pragmatists will point out, it has a parliament, a government, publishes 4,000 books a year, and has excellent TV channels in Catalan.

Since 1986 Spain has been a member of the European Community and a single European market is bound to affect Catalonia. The European high-velocity train is to be extended as far south as Barcelona and the Generalitat has been active in encouraging foreign investment. President Pujol makes frequent "state" visits to countries as disparate as China, Hungary and Argentina. In the late 1970s a crisis of the traditional textile industry caused most concern. At the beginning of the 1990s the key issues are the future of the region's agriculture, its transport system and power production, as well as some serious environmental problems.

Olympic fever: In October 1987, when the International Olympic Committee announced the decision to celebrate the 1992 Olympic Games in the Catalan capital, Olympic fever erupted. Money began pouring in and, by the end of the 1980s, Japan was investing more in Catalonia than in any other region in Europe. Hotels began to be built, through-roads constructed and after years of meagre investment the Spanish government budget allocation for cultural infrastructure in Catalonia shot up.

Since the death of Franco, one thing at least has certainly returned to its rightful

place: the Catalan cultural world. This is evident in the arts, architecture, design, literature, music and the theatre. Productions of Els Joglars, Els Comediants and La Fura dels Baus have been staged throughout the world; a Catalan National Theatre is to be built; the Liceu opera house is flourishing, publishing is blossoming.

As for Catalonia's continued aspirations, one either has to take the view of the writer Josep Pla that "Catalans are very much interested in their own country, but fail to believe in it", or that of the 19th-century poet Joan Maragall: "Catalonia is a country that is playing the waiting game."

<u>Left</u>, pride in the country. <u>Above</u>, Jordi Pujol, charismatic Generalitat president.

What is a Catalan? Jordi Pujol, the man who has dominated Catalan politics since the death of Franco, says that a Catalan is a person who lives and works in Catalonia with a view to permanence. His view is generous and all-embracing, but the situation is far more complex and difficult to define.

Catalonia, being one of the richest parts of Spain, has been absorbing huge numbers of immigrants, most of them from the south of Spain, for more than a hundred years. Even the tramps in Jean Genet's *The Thiefs Journal* came to Catalonia "because it is rich".

Throughout the latter half of the 19th century and until the civil war, Barcelona experienced a number of economic booms followed by slumps. The boom during World War I was followed by a particularly serious downturn, for example. Thus the thousands of immigrants who flocked into the city lived precariously, constantly unsure not simply of their identity, but of their economic future.

Yet, like immigrants anywhere, they preserved what culture they brought with them. Now, you can travel through the huge satellite towns which surround the city of Barcelona without ever hearing a single word of Catalan, or meeting a single person who considers himself or herself to be Catalan. The bars in Cornellà, for example, will play flamenco music and the clientele will clap their hands to its beat.

Catalans, on the other hand, have no interest in flamenco music—or in spending time in bars, for that matter. Catalans see themselves as a separate culture and a separate tradition, rather than a separate race. This is an important distinction: up to and beyond the civil war, the children of immigrants who learned to speak Catalan were, to a large extent, accepted as Catalans, and their children even more so. But since the 1960s, which saw an incredible volume of immigration into a vibrant and industrialised Catalo-

nia, the distinction between Catalans and non-Catalans who live and work in Catalonia with a view to permanence has become more pronounced.

Separate cultures: The immigrants went to live in new towns in the suburbs; they seldom came in contact with the Catalan language, or the idea of the Catalan nation. Their economic future was so precarious as to prevent them from investigating the surrounding culture. There was no Catalan used on television or radio until after 1975, nor

were there newspapers in Catalan, nor was Catalan used in the schools. Thus another culture grew in the suburbs of Barcelona, Girona, Tarragona, Lleida and other urban centres such as Reus which was Spanish-speaking, working-class and, invariably, left-wing.

Everything was in place for a serious confrontation between cultures, once the Catalans sought public support for the Catalan language. One of the reasons why this didn't happen—it happened earlier in the century when immigrants became virulently anti-Catalan—was the strength of the Communist Party in Catalonia in the 1970s; the

Preceding pages: wine sellers from Raïmat; mushroom contest, Prades. **Left**, Carles Comós of the Platja d'Aro Big Rock restaurant. **Right**, participant in the annual Sitges veteran car rally.

Communist Party was led by Catalans and supported autonomy for Catalonia. Thus in the early days after the death of Franco, the cry at the demonstrations was for amnesty, autonomy and freedom. Support for Catalonia was seen as part of the general support for democracy.

There is now a greater awareness among the immigrants of the Catalan identity and culture. Because of television, radio and the education system, the number of people who speak Catalan in Catalonia is rising by 20,000 every year. But still only half the population of Catalonia speaks the language though a majority claim to understand it.

The friction between Catalans and non-occupied country, a country occupied by Catalans, who are becoming, in their view, increasingly powerful and arrogant.

Catalans are seen as being interested only in money; they have a reputation for being mean. They are blamed for not being open, and for sticking together.

Catalans, in turn, dislike Spaniards for not being as productive as they might be, for being fickle in friendship (a Catalan friend, they say, will always stand by you). They hate bull-fighting—the very idea of it seems to give them the creeps. The macho ideal, in general, does not obtain among Catalans; they don't shout at women in the streets. The sort of openness and propensity to sing and

Catalans is more noticeable among the professional classes. In 1981, 2,300 "intellectuals and workers" living in Catalonia signed a manifesto which complained bitterly about the increasing use of the Catalan language and the denial of rights to those who spoke only Spanish.

Catalans are generally disliked throughout Spain. Thus for those who come from outside and happen to work in Catalonia, the idea that their children should have to learn Catalan in school, and that two out of the three television stations are in Catalan, is absurd, and offends their rights as Spanish citizens. They see themselves as living in an dance and play the guitar, which foreigners associate with Spain, cannot be found among the Catalans.

They see themselves as Europeans, rather than Spaniards. This is, perhaps, the most crucial aspect of their self-image. They are proud that their language has no Arabic sounds; they are proud, too, of Catalonia's Jewish heritage. They are proud of their European heritage and are proud that the city of Barcelona has such a rich classical musical tradition.

More than anything, they are proud of their bourgeois traditions; they see themselves as closer to Geneva than Seville. The middle classes took no part in either world war, nor, to any large extent, in the Spanish civil war. In Barcelona, the middle classes have grown to distrust the old quarter, and they tend to live above the Gran Via. They holiday in the same place every year, always in Catalonia, although they may travel at other times to France or Italy or England. But they will never go on holiday to any other part of Spain. They work hard; in Catalonia there is a fundamental belief in trade and business success, as in very few other places.

The quintessential Catalan, then, will be reasonably well-off, will lack the swarthy features associated with Spaniards, instead will, perhaps, have blue eyes or blond hair.

went into a sort of internal exile. The Catholic religion is not a powerful force in most Catalans' lives. The Catalan character, in all its manifestations of bourgeois culture, can be seen at its most intense at the Saturday evening concerts in the Palau de la Música off Via Laietana in Barcelona. That deep seriousness, that addiction to European culture, that unSpanish way of talking and relating are all in evidence as well as that old Jewish combination of bourgeois culture and business acumen. Many outsiders see the ethos of the Catalans and the Jews as very close indeed. The Catalans themselves are pleased about this: witness their celebration of the Jewish quarter in Girona.

He or she will be personally quite conservative and sober in dress and deportment, will like opera and classical music, will go skiing in the winter and will spend the month of August among his or her extended family either in the mountains or on the coast, usually the same place every year. It will be common for six Catalans to share a bottle of wine over dinner and not even finish it.

The quintessential Catalan will, in some deep way, despise Spain and all that it stands for. Throughout the Franco years, Catalans

Left, off-shore oil-rig worker, Tarragona. **Above**, market gardener on his plot.

And yet it would be very wrong to view the Catalans as an entirely middle-class phenomenon. There is a large artisan and shopkeeper class, not just in every village in Catalonia, but in the cities as well, which is also Catalan-speaking and which shares many of the traditions of their more bourgeois brethren.

Conservative heart: The two classes meet without any difficulty at the weekly celebration of the *sardana*, the demure Catalan national dance, or at the festivals which take place in each village. They are the bedrock of the support which Jordi Pujol's Convergència party has in Catalonia. The party is staunchly nationalist and supportive of business; it has no left-wing tendencies or any support among trade unionists.

Pujol's deputies, both in the Corts and in the Catalan parliament, are Catalans: that is, not just people working and living in Catalonia with a view to permanence, but Catalan-speakers, born in Catalonia, usually of Catalan parents, who feel themselves to be Catalans, and feel their identity as separate to the Spanish identity.

Oddly enough, the public representatives of the socialist and communist parties (both of which have separate organisations in Catalonia) are Catalans as well, although they represent a large group of voters who

were not born in Catalonia and do not feel themselves to be Catalan.

Thus the public representatives have Catalan names. The most typical Christian name is Jordi for a boy and Montserrat for a girl; Núria for a girl is also typical. The American composer Arnold Schoenberg called his daughter Núria when he lived in Barcelona in the 1930s; the footballer Johan Cruyff called his son Jordi when he lived in Barcelona some 50 years later.

The surnames tend to have that very clipped guttural sound which characterises Catalan. Pons, Puig, Pujol. Or else they end in an accented vowel: Miró, Dalí, Barceló,

Gaudí. It is possible to find Catalans called Sánchez or López, but it is not common.

So far we have listed three types of Catalans: those who live in Catalonia, but come from outside, the middle classes and the artisan classes. The final group are in some way the most important. They, too, are hard-working, solid and nationalistic. They are the farmers who own their own land.

There are no vast estates in Catalonia, as there are in Spain, and there is no great tradition of the absentee landlord living it up in Madrid while the farm-workers on the estate are underpaid. Also, Catalan tradition has it that one son inherits everything (which is why a great number of Catalans went to Cuba in the 19th century); this means that holdings tend to be viable and profitable.

Most middle-class and artisan-class people in Catalonia are descended from farming backgrounds. This may partly explain the solidity and the common sense for which Catalans are known. The traditional *masies* are large but roughly made, the houses of strong farmers rather than lords.

The farmers can be seen at their best at any of the weekly fairs in the villages: the Hotel Europa in Granollers, less than an hour by train north of Barcelona, plays host to them every Thursday morning from about 9 o'clock until noon. The Catalan spoken here is much richer and rarer than the Catalan which can be heard in Barcelona. The food which they eat on market day, too, is extraordinary: *la cuina de la misèria*, the food of misery, it is called, being made up of lungs, or brains, or kidney, or liver.

Sense and chaos: The Catalans' common sense is called *seny* in Catalan, and there is an opposite side to it known as *rauxa*, which came to the fore during the civil war. In Catalonia, often the two elements combine: *seny*, for example, gives us the skilful artisan; and *rauxa* gives us Miró, Dalí and Gaudí. Such artists began with superb draughtsmen's skills and knowledge of materials, *seny,* and built on them with vast imaginative resources, working all the time towards an appreciation of the artistic possibilities of chaos, *rauxa*, which their fellow Catalans are constantly careful to keep in check as they go about their business.

Left, schoolchildren, Tarragona old town. Right, postman, Sant Pere de Ribes.

VERDAGUER: FATHER OF MODERN CATALAN

Visitors arriving in Catalonia for the first time may imagine the Catalan language to be a Pyrenean dialect which has managed to survive, albeit in a derelict condition, like Irish, Provençal or Aragonese. But Catalan, a tongue without a state, is today spoken by more than eight million people and has such a lively tradition that it boasts more poets per square mile than any other country in Europe. The use of Catalan has been officially recognised in the European parliament in Strasbourg, and it is the host language of the 1992 Olympic games. Considering its history of banishment and repression, most recently for two generations under Franco's regime, the language has proved remarkably durable.

Romantic rediscoveries: Catalan literary culture 150 years ago had become little more than a joke. Though still spoken, no serious writer would have considered using the language which had been officially outlawed by the Bourbon's Decreto de Nueva Planta, issued in 1716. But in the mid-19th century, a romantic movement in Europe was looking back to lost cultures. In Provence, Frédéric Mistral was rediscovering the region's literary heritage; in Britain, the Pre-Raphaelites were reconstructing the courtly life of King Arthur, and in Italy, the Risorgimento was rousing the nation.

In 1830, Bonaventura Aribau wrote a poem called *Oda a la Pàtria* which is traditionally seen as the starting point for the romantic movement in Catalonia; but its early writers caused little excitement. Lo Gayter (The Piper) del Llobregat produced a stilted, Castilianised balladry, while amateur poets tried their hands at Catalan verse in a rather humdrum modern version of the Jocs Florals. These were the annual poetry competitions of the medieval troubadours of Catalonia and the Languedoc, exhumed in 1859 and re-enacted each year, in which flower prizes were awarded for the best poetic works.

In the end it was largely due to the efforts of one man, Jacint Verdaguer, that Catalan literature was put back on the map. Through his energy and ability, the literary prestige of the Catalan language passed from refutable to reputable in three decades. Authentic and linguistically sound, his poems were everything the romantic Barcelona-centred literary circles had dreamed of. He had a remarkable ear for popular language and a unique ability to express it. He gave Catalan the status it had been deprived of for more than 200 years.

Verdaguer was born in a humble home in Folgueroles near Vic in 1845. The poverty of his father, a quarry worker, and the devoutness of his mother pushed him towards the church somewhat against his will. He was robust and healthy-looking, clean shaven with penetrating blue eyes, and he had a pugnacious and competitive spirit which he showed as a young seminarist when he used to challenge his companions to barefoot races across corn stubble.

His earliest literary efforts were satirical verses, which an aristocratic fellow student, Jaume Collell, persuaded him to abandon in favour of serious religious and epic poetry.

Left, the library in Puig i Cadafalch's Can Amatller in Barcelona. **Right**, the popular literary priest Jacint Verdaguer.

He was only 20 when he stormed on to the Barcelona literary scene at the Jocs Florals. At the prize-giving ceremony he dressed as a peasant with a *barretina*, the traditional, sock-shaped red woollen hat. The impression he made on the city's bourgeoisie was indelible. He became immensely popular, too, and along with the playwright Angel Guimerà he was the leading figure of the Renaixença, Catalonia's renaissance.

His fame grew even more when he became the family chaplain to the millionaire Marquis of Comillas in Barcelona's Moja Palace in the Rambla. He wrote two epic poems: *L'Atlàntida*, which was set to music by Manuel de Falla, and *Canigó*, which has been described by the leading Spanish scholar Menéndez y Pelayo as the finest 19th-century poem in all Spain. These are some lines from his patriotic poem, *Enyorança* (Yearning):

> Sabéssiu lo català,
> sabríeu qué és enyorança,
> la malatia dels cors
> transplantats a terra estranya;...
> ...aqueix mal que sols té nom
> en nostra llengua estimada,
> aqueixa veu dels ausents,
> aqueix sospir de la pàtria
> que crida sos fills llunyans
> amb amorosa recança.

(If you knew Catalan,/ You would know what yearning was,/ The affliction of hearts/ Transplanted to foreign lands;.../ ...That malady that only has a name/ In our beloved language,/ The voice of those departed/ That sighing for the homeland/ Which calls the distant sons/ With loving sorrow.)

Verdaguer was widely published: 100,000 copies of his *Oda a Barcelona* (Ode to Barcelona) were distributed among the city's school children. He was an avid traveller and he met and was praised by popes, grandees and monarchs. But his life ended tragically. In contrast with the glamour of the palace life he was made to lead, Verdaguer was very much a man of the people. He came to believe that through exorcism, evil could be uprooted from society. It was this practice, and his championing of the oppressed in a period of crisis and violence, that resulted in his being defrocked. This public humiliation produced an enormous scandal which divided Catalan society into two bitterly opposed camps.

It led Verdaguer to write *En Defensa Pròpia*, a remarkable series of articles attacking the bourgeoisie and Bishop Morgades of Vic who had defrocked him. Even today they stand out as a startling piece of prose. But although Verdaguer was pardoned for his disobedience, he was soon to die in extreme poverty at Quinta Joana, the house of an admirer in Vallvidrera, just to the west of Barcelona.

This house is open to the public, and you can see his library and the bed where he died of tuberculosis, aged 57, during an anarchist uprising in June 1902. But his popularity was still so great that when his death was announced, the fiercely anticlerical anarchists ceased fighting, entered the churches and rang the bells.

Verdaguer legacy: Verdaguer had sparked off the rebirth of Catalan literature, but it was Pompeu Fabra, a figure associated with the later Modernists and the foundation of the Institute of Catalan Studies in 1907, who gave the language its definitive vocabulary and grammatical style. Fabra is to Catalan what Ben Jonson had been to English two centuries before. The "Fabra" is a household institution, found on the shelf of every Catalan, be they lawyer, farmer or worker.

The Modernists were attracted by the *fin-de-siècle* fever sweeping Europe. In direct contrast to the rather reverent, conservative Renaixença, which had promoted the ideals of "Love, Fatherland and Faith", the Modernists wanted Catalonia to have a fully emancipated European culture and they aspired to their own Ruskins and Maetterlincks. Gaudí and Picasso owed much of their inspiration to this movement, and a look at the poems of Joan Maragall (1860–1911) or the novel *Solitud* by Víctor Català (the pseudonym of Caterina Albert, 1873–1966) will satisfy any doubts about the standard of the movement's literature.

Catalan has now almost fully recovered from the Franco regime. The language emerged out of the dictatorship with authors such as Josep Pla, Manuel de Pedrolo and Mercè Rodoreda at their peak. Pla and Pedrolo are among the most prolific authors of the 20th century, while Rodoreda is the author of Catalonia's finest contemporary novel: *La Plaça del Diamant*.

Josep Pla (1897–1981) was something of an *enfant terrible*. He came from a farming family in Palafrugell and he was rarely seen without his black farmer's beret. He was pithy and somewhat eccentric, and is known to have thrown dishes out of restaurant windows if they were not to his liking. His books were varied, ranging from descriptions of Russia and New York, things, places and people Catalan, particularly his native Costa Brava.

The books he published were largely based on notes he jotted down on his endless walks around the country. For many people, these books were to be the only contact they were to have with written Catalan during the Franco period. They made him the widest read and most controversial writer of his

war society. *La Plaça del Diamant* is the name of a square in the Gràcia district of Barcelona, though when the book was published in English in 1975, it was called *The Pigeon Girl* and in America it was titled *The Time of Doves*.

Other modern writers would not or could not publish during the Franco years, with the result that, after 1975, manuscripts waiting in drawers suddenly found their way to publishing houses. This was certainly true in the case of Manuel de Pedrolo, a jack-of-all-trades who since then has produced *avant-garde* plays, political essays and a steady flow of novels, including science fiction and detective stories. He is also author of *Me-*

time. The fact that he was never awarded the Premi d'Honor de les Lletres Catalanes (Catalonia's most prestigious literary prize) may be put down to the fact that, although he wrote some of the finest pages of Catalan 20th-century prose, it was considered unsuitable for a man who had not condemned the Franco regime to be given the prize.

Mercè Rodoreda (1909–83) is one of several Catalan women writers to have come to the fore since the war and her novels give a woman's view of Catalan wartime and post-

Above, nationalist aspirations for the 8 million people who speak Catalan today.

canoscrit del Segon Origen (Second Draft of a Typescript) which has sold more than a quarter of a million copies. Other popular writers include Quim Monzó, Montserrat Roig, Pere Gimferrer and Baltasar Porcel.

Roots of the language: Catalan is a fully-fledged Romance (Latin-based) language comparable with French, Italian or Romanian. Its development owes more to the Languedoc in southern France than to anything in the peninsula, and political independence for 735 years of its 1,000-year history helped it take firm root. It is spoken beyond the modern political confines of the semi-autonomous state, and though one may need a map to check the popular saying that it can be heard "from Salses to Guardamar, and from Fraga to Maó", it is easier simply to say that it is spoken in Valencia, the Balearic islands, North Catalonia (in the Roussillon, southern France) and in the town of L'Alguer in Sardinia.

The earliest Catalan text is in the form of sermon notes, known as the *Homilies d'Organyà*, dating from the 12th century. A hundred years later the language began to enjoy great prestige. In other European cultures there are constant references to medieval legal tracts such as the *Consolat de Mar* and the *Usatges*. There were also the *Cròniques*, four extremely important his-

torical chronicles written by different authors, the most notable of whom was Ramon Muntaner (1265–1336). Muntaner followed Roger de Flor's Almogàver campaigns to Turkey and Greece describing their adventures vividly, if somewhat freely.

Catalan literature was well established by Muntaner's time. It had been given an enormous boost by the extraordinary writer and traveller, Ramon Llull (often written Lully or Lull in English). Llull (1232–1315) was born in Palma, Mallorca, and although his name is less well known than Chaucer's or Dante's, his influence on western philosophy and literature was profound.

He was the first to challenge the exclusive use of Latin in religious literature and he made Catalan the first Romance language to be used in its place. As a missionary, he was bitterly opposed to the crusades, favouring the conversion of infidels by persuasion. As a literary figure, he became one of the great translators and linguist of medieval Europe.

As one of the driving forces in the Renaissance, his fame spread throughout Europe. A department of the Sorbonne in Paris still bears his name. Llull's *Book of the Order of Chivalry* was one of the first and most influential to be published by William Caxton in 1478. And one of the most prized items in the old chained library at Merton College, Oxford, is a collection of six of Llull's treatises.

Llull has been called the father of the modern novel for his work *Llibre de Blanquerna*, an extraordinary book which is a fine portrait of the period. However, another major precursor of the modern novel is *Tirant lo Blanch*, written in Catalan by the Valencian Joanot Martorell (1414–68). The book was highly praised by Cervantes, who called it the "best book in the world". Martorell, a courtier, visited England to seek the intercession of Henry VI in a family feud, and the first 98 chapters of *Tirant* are based on the legend of Guy of Warwick. One episode in the book inspired Shakespeare's *Much Ado About Nothing*.

Completing a triumverate of early Catalan writers, is Ausiàs March (1397–1459), regarded as one of the three finest poets of the early Renaissance, alongside Dante and Petrarch. His brilliant combination of vivid images and humanist concepts, expressed in verse that makes the most of the monosyllabic nature of the language, make him the most profound, impressive and permanent of Catalonia's long succession of poets. This is from his poem *LXXXV (Leixe la sort)*:

Mas jo vull ço que natura no té,
e desig més que jo no pusc trobar,
volent que res no pogués empatxar
lo meu delit que per Amor me ve.
But I yearn for what nature has not,
and desire more than I can acquire,
hoping that nothing shall make me tire
of the delight love holds in store.

Above, the spoken word kept Catalan alive during decades of repression. **Right**, the prolific writer Josep Pla at Calella.

In common with the rest of Spain, Catalonia has a great many festivals. They can be picturesque, boisterous and noisy, solemn and mysterious, or they can simply be days when people dress in their best, enjoy large family lunches, meet friends at the evening *passeigada* and dance *sardanes* in the square. Whichever they are, the accent is always on participation of people of all ages.

Apart from *La Diada*, the Catalan national day on 11 September, most fiestas (*festes* in Catalan) are religious in origin, but since the death of Franco their religious aspect has been minimised in most cases and most places, although locked churches are usually opened and extra masses are said. Banks and businesses will close on official holidays but in tourist resorts, in the summer season, shops and exchange bureaux normally stay open, the season being too short to turn away business.

Music: Every town and village has its own saint and their days are celebrated each year with a *festa major*, "the main fiesta". These vary from place to place, but have at least two things in common: they always culminate in a dance, which rarely begins before 11 o'clock at night or ends before four in the morning. Often held in the open air, they feature loud, cheerful bands, and dancers are refreshed by *cava* and beer sold from giant ice bins behind trestle tables decorated with the Catalan flag.

The other common feature is the *sardana*, the slow and intricate national dance, which takes place earlier in the day. These dances are also a regular event at summer weekends in many towns and *aficionados* will travel miles to attend events when a good *cobla* (band) is playing. During the summer there are also *sardana* marathons called *aplecs*, which can last for up to three days.

Catalans are very fond of music and proud to have produced such international figures as the opera singers Montserrat Caballé and Josep Carreras. Summer music festivals take place in many picturesque and otherwise

under-used buildings—castles, monasteries and churches.

One of the most famous is at the castle of Peralada, in the province of Girona, a fairytale place when open-air concerts feature top performers in both classical and light music festivals. Another is the beautiful monastery of Santes Creus in Tarragona, where classical and sacred music are performed. A jazz festival is held annually at Terrassa, and Barcelona's Palau de la Música Catalana in Carrer Amadeu Vives hosts a number of festivals each year.

Larger than life: Another typical feature of Catalan fiestas is the leading role played by giants and bigheads (*gegants* and *nans* or *capgrosses*). The giants are huge, papier-mâché figures built on to a frame which, when supported on the shoulders of a volunteer, hidden beneath the voluminous skirts, will be some 15 ft (5 metres) high. The figures walk in stately procession through the streets, then whirl into a dance when the festival reaches its peak. Giants always come in couples: a king and queen, lord and lady, sun and moon or shepherd and shepherdess complete, at times, with baby. Bigheads, as the name suggests, are gigantic papier-mâché heads, sometimes amusing, sometimes grotesque, worn by dancers in fancy dress. Giants are treated with great respect, while bigheads play the role of jesters or attendants.

Most towns have their own giants, some of which are stored away when not performing but others can be seen guarding the foyer of their local town hall. There are some particularly good ones in Tarragona, with a splendid king and queen and also a handsome black couple known simply as *los negritos*. The present examples were made in the 1850s, but there are records of Tarragona giants as early as the 15th century, when the first ones were built by the blacksmiths' and carpenters' guilds—the guilds, or *gremis*, being the originators of most giants. Tarragona also has six pairs of *nans*, led by a splendidly dressed captain who also dates back to the mid-19th century.

Traditionally, the giants' progress in any fiesta is accompanied by a small band of

Preceding pages: Maundy Thursday Dance of Death, Verges; September St Mercè giants, Barcelona. **Left,** June *xiquets* at Valls.

wood and brass instruments called *grallas* and a small drum, the *tabal*, which play haunting, mesmeric music. Olot, a busy market town in the Garrotxa region, has a strong folkloric tradition and is the home of some very illustrious giants which can be seen annually at the *festa major* on 8 September, parading with bigheads and *cavallets*, gaily decorated little hobby horses.

Christmas: Patron saints' days apart, there are many fiestas which are celebrated throughout Catalonia, although usually with a strong local flavour, and a few which are specific to one place. Christmas is low-key here, being mainly an occasion for family feasting and mass for churchgoers.

the Gothic cathedral is filled with stalls displaying hand-made Nativity scenes and biblical figures. At Bagà and Sant Julià de Cerdanyola, both in Barcelona province, Christmas Eve is celebrated by a torchlight procession called *La faia-faia*.

New Year is also principally a family affair, although dances are usually held in towns and social evenings in smaller villages. Traditionalists swallow a grape for every stroke of the clock at midnight to ensure good health and prosperity throughout the coming year.

The Three Kings: Epiphany, on 6 January, is a bigger celebration. Known as the *Dia dels Reis*, the Day of the Kings, it is the time when

One of the few public Christmas festivities is *El Pessebre Vivent*, the Living Crib, which is best exemplified at Bàscara, a medieval village just off the N11 in Girona province. Most of the population takes part in enacting the Christmas story in the narrow village streets and the scenes are performed daily throughout Christmas Week. Castellfollit de la Roca, a village perched on the edge of a volcanic cliff, also has an impressive Living Crib, and La Pobla de Montornes in Tarragona performs the nativity scenes in the chapel of La Mare de Deu. In Barcelona, the Santa Lucia Fair is held during the week preceding Christmas, when the area around

children receive their presents. The handsomely costumed figures make their rounds of the neighbourhood, on foot or on horseback, tossing sweets to the crowds before distributing their gifts in the local recreation centre. In many seaside towns the kings arrive by boat, accompanied by a retinue, and their coming is celebrated by a lavish and noisy firework display.

Tossa pilgrims: In Tossa de Mar, on the Costa Brava, a large and very local fiesta is the next event on the calendar. The *Pelegri*, or pilgrimage, is held on 20 January, St Sebastian's Day, to give thanks to the saint for protecting villagers from a plague in the

14th century. The pilgrim is selected from a long list of local men, and to be chosen is considered a great honour.

After a solemn mass at 7 a.m. the pilgrim begins his silent walk, followed by a large crowd of townspeople, many barefoot, to the *ermita*, or chapel, of St Sebastian near the town of Santa Coloma de Farners, some 25 miles (40 km) away. At designated spots he and a group of dignitaries are given hospitality in private houses while his followers eat picnics and rest their weary feet in the countryside. The next day he retraces his steps and the *pelegri* ends, as it began, with a mass.

Carnival: The next big event in most places, *carne-vale*, the farewell to meat, used to be a

Carnival. The best places to join the celebrations are Roses in the Empordà and Sitges, a lively, cosmopolitan resort to the south of Barcelona, and the nearby, more provincial town of Vilanova i la Geltrú.

In Sitges, festivities begin the weekend before Ash Wednesday and usually last a week. Cornestoltes officially opens a week of parades, dances, puppet shows and concerts. The gorgeous costumes and sheer dedication to enjoyment have made Sitges Carnival an international event. It has a strong gay element, but this is far from exclusive and the events can be enjoyed by anyone who has the stamina to stay up most of the night and begin again the next day.

huge and licentious occasion in most Catholic countries, the last opportunity for indulgence before the 40 lean days of Lent. Nowadays, when Lenten sacrifices are not taken so seriously, Carnival is not so riotous. But Shrove Tuesday is still an occasion for masked balls and fancy-dress parties and shops display a wonderful selection of masks and costumes during the preceding weeks. Many places hold colourful and noisy processions, often headed by Cornestoltes, a symbolic figure representing

Carnival ends with the burial of Cornestoltes in the Passeig Marítim, which is celebrated with a huge castle of fireworks. In nearby Vilanova, festivities last for a fortnight and end with the "burial of the sardine" on Ash Wednesday.

Holy Week: *Semana Santa*, the week preceding Easter, and the Easter weekend itself is one of the most important festivals in Catalonia. Maundy Thursday and Good Friday were until recently treated publicly as a time of real mourning, with all businesses closed and radio stations playing only solemn music. It is taken less seriously now, but many towns and villages hold processions

<u>Left</u>, **Living Crib tableau, Corbera de Llobregat.**
<u>Above</u>, **a local beauty, Roses Carnival.**

The Sedate Sardana

Nothing more instantly suggests Catalonia than the sight of a circle of *sardana* dancers. The national dance is for everyone, and a weekend never goes by—or even, in summer, a day—when people aren't somewhere knotting the coloured ribbons of their espadrilles ready to step into the squares or promenades for the dance.

When the music starts, friends hold hands to form circles, placing any bags they are carrying in the centre of the ring. Anyone can join in simply by slipping in between two people (though not between a man and the woman on his right). The circles grow like replicating cells as the tune moves on.

If Catalans' enthusiasm for this pastime does not show on their faces as they hop and step first in one direction, then the other, it is because they are concentrating on counting every bar from the moment the music begins. Even if they join a circle half way through, they must know how many bars have already been played, otherwise they may have the ignominy either of not knowing when the short, sedate steps change to the bouncy long ones, or of ending up with one foot in the air when the music stops.

The *sardana* is not a folk dance; it is far too popular to be called that. Nor, in its present form, is it very old. As participants hold their hands high and step this way and that, it is easy to be reminded of the dances of Greece but the *sardana* was not given its present shape until the 19th century when the dance, from the Empordà region, was grafted on to an older tradition.

This older dance used to be held outside churches after certain services. These were presided over by the priest and accompanied by a three-man band playing bagpipes, cornet and pipe and drum. Changes were made by Pep Ventura whose father came from Roses, though Pep was born in 1817 in Andalucía where his soldier father was temporarily stationed. They returned to Roses when he was two, and four years later he went to live with his grandfather in Figueres where he learnt to play simple reed flutes.

As his influence grew, he began experimenting with the local *cobla* or band. In this he was greatly influenced by Antoni Turon, a native of Perpignan, who had developed an oboe-like instrument called the *tenora*. Ventura banished the bagpipe and adopted Turon's innovation of adding brass instruments and creating a two-section band. The city museum in Girona shows the development of these instruments, from the large recorder-like pipes of the shepherds to the silver-plated *tenores* of the great players.

Ventura lived at the time of the Renaixença, when Catalonia was rediscovering its identity, and he was vehemently opposed to using any music from outside the region. Instead he adapted popular Catalan songs (some *sardanes* are sung), as well as composing many tunes of his own. Among his most famous is El Cant dels Ocells, which the cellist Pau Cassals often played.

Completing the line-up of innovators was Miquel Pardas, from Torroella de Montgrí, who choreographed the music. A plaque in Torroella's square commemorates the first *sardana*, which was danced there in 1844.

Today's *cobla* is made up of 11 players. The leader, seated, plays a *flabiol* (a three-holed pipe) and taps out the rhythm on a *tabal*, a small drum strapped to his elbow. The players of the woodwind *tenoras* and smaller *tibles* are also seated. Standing behind them are the brass players on *trompeta*, *fiscorn* and *trombó*. A *contrabaix*, or double bass, completes the band. The idea is that the woodwind instruments assume a kind of soprano role and the brass takes the tenor; in a continual dialogue, the woodwind asks questions and the brass replies. Each tune lasts just over 10 minutes, and in an *audació*, which is a normal performance, there will be half a dozen tunes. An *aplec*, on the other hand, involves three or four *cobles* playing 24 tunes and lasts all day.

For a number of years La Principal de La Bisbal has been recognised as the top *cobla*. They celebrated their centenary in 1988 and are the official band of the Generalitat de Catalunya. Accordingly they are in demand throughout the summer and have had invitations to play in Holland, Germany and the USSR.

on these two days, in which legions of Roman soldiers precede robed figures carrying floats depicting the crucified Christ and weeping Virgin, while drummers beat an eerie accompaniment. Local people join the processions, some barefoot, although it is now rare to see penitents on their knees, once a common sight.

Barcelona and Girona have particularly impressive ceremonies, centred around their ancient cathedrals, and winding with difficulty through narrow, medieval streets. Barcelona's procession is dominated by the figures of Christ of the *Gran Poder* (great power) and the Macarena Virgin, replicas of the Sevillian figures. In Cervera, in the prov-

very convincingly as skeletons dance through candle-lit streets accompanied by little ghosts and ghouls, carrying clocks whose hands point to five to twelve, to indicate that mankind's time is nearly up. Such dances were common in the 14th century when the country was ravaged by plague, but today are performed only in Verges, the home town of the folk singer Lluís Llach who sometimes joins in the procession.

Easter weekend everywhere in Catalonia is a big family holiday, with people heading for the coast and the countryside. Restaurants are full of family parties and patisseries display cakes intricately decorated with marzipan flowers and Easter chicks.

ince of Lleida, an impressive Passion Play is enacted by local people in the specially constructed Gran Teatre de La Pasió on each Sunday during March and April. Passion Plays also take place at Esparreguera and Sant Vicenç dels Horts, in the province of Barcelona.

Perhaps the most unusual event, however, is held in the village of Verges (Girona), where a Passion Play in the village square on the evening of Maundy Thursday is followed by the traditional solemn procession and the Dance of Death. Macabre figures dressed

Above, *sardana* dancers, Volcanic Park, Olot.

St George (Sant Jordi) is Catalonia's patron saint as well as England's, and his day is celebrated with books and roses. The rose is, of course, the symbol of the saint, and the book has been grafted on, as this date is also the anniversary of the death of Cervantes. Shakespeare was born and died on this date, too, but the English are not as keen on honouring writers or saints.

Even quite small towns and villages will set up stalls in their *rambla*, or their main square, where local organisations, both commercial and charitable, sell books and red roses, which men will buy for their mothers, wives or girlfriends. In Barcelona, where the Rambla between the Plaça Cata-lunya and the port is the permanent site of book and flower sellers, it is particularly festive, and an exhibition of prize-winning roses is held in the Sala Sant Jordi at the Palau de la Generalitat (home of the Catalan parliament).

Dragons and flowers: Corpus Christi, a moveable feast dependent on the liturgical calendar, is also an important public holiday. In Berga, in the province of Barcelona, the ancient and impressive ritual of Patum the Dragon takes place. The festival culminates with the dance of the devils, grotesquely dressed and carrying exploding fire crack-ers, and the appearance of Patum, the mon-

the first Sunday in Lent; and during the first week of October an international festival of horror films takes place in the town.

Country customs: On the Sunday before Carnival the festa dels traginers, the carters' festival, a colourful event paying tribute to an old country trade, is celebrated in Balsar-eny, in the province of Barcelona.

In Ripoll, a small town centred on a mag-nificent monastery and known as the "cradle of Catalonia", a wool festival takes place on the third Sunday in May. Shepherds in tradi-tional costumes, complete with red baretti-nes—the stocking caps which country people once habitually wore—bring sheep in from the hills to present shearing displays

strous, fire-spitting dragon. Several towns have flower festivals, such as Sitges, where streets in the old part of town are transformed by flower carpets, intricate tapestries made largely of carnations, which remain intact all day until judged by an elected panel, then yield a wonderful perfume as they are crushed beneath the feet of the evening Corpus procession and the parade of giants. A national carnation exhibition is held on the same day and the flowers later offered to the Virgin of Vinyet.

Sitges specialises in unusual festivals, most of them of fairly recent origin. An International Antique Car Rally is held on

and sell the wool. In what is presumably the remnant of a fertility ritual, a wedding is then celebrated. Usually it is a symbolic one, but sometimes a local couple are actually mar-ried in the monastery's church and the fes-tivities are then even jollier. Castellar de N'Hug to the west of Ripoll is another area where sheep have always been important to the economy and here they celebrate sheep dog trials on the last Sunday in August.

Whit Sunday is celebrated in many parts of Catalonia. A colourful parade and a dance of *els cavallets*, little hobby horses, with giants and bigheads takes place at Sant Feliu de Pallerols in the Garrotxa region, and the village of Ridaura, near Olot, performs the *ball de gambeto*, an ancient folk dance, on the same day.

St John's Day, 24 June, is celebrated throughout Catalonia as a national holiday, with magnificent bonfires and firework displays in most places on the previous evening—an ancient celebration of the summer solstice which the Church found easier to legitimise than to stamp out. In Valls, to the north of Tarragona, the 24th is the best day to see the *castells*, human towers of specially trained young men in national costume, known as *els xiquets*, which are a part of several Catalan festivals.

If you miss seeing them in Valls, the *cas-*

age) just outside the town and taken out to sea in a beautifully decorated fishing boat, accompanied by a flotilla of small craft full of pilgrims. Back on shore a dance, believed to be of Arab origin and called the *almorratxes*, is performed in the square and after general feasting and enjoyment the saint is returned to her resting place.

The year's end: Autumn is a lean time for fiestas, apart from purely local ones, but *La Diada* is celebrated everywhere on 11 September with parades, giants, fireworks and *sardanes* and rousing choruses of *Els Segadors* (The Harvesters), the Catalan national song. Many villages hold wine festivals when the grapes are harvested in the

tellers also put on a very good display at the *festa major* in Vilafranca del Penedès in the last week in August, when a dragon, an eagle and a dance of the devils are also part of the festivities.

A month later, on 24 July, Lloret de Mar, on the Costa Brava, celebrates the festival of Santa Cristina, its patron saint who, according to legend, was thrown into the sea tied to a mill wheel, and her body later discovered by fishermen. The statue of the saint is removed from the beautiful *ermita* (hermit-

Left, *festa major* in the Gràcia district of Barcelona. **Above**, a sunny-faced "bighead".

second half of September. L'Espluga de Francolí, Tarragona, has a typical one, the *festa de la verema*, on the third Sunday in the month.

The day dedicated to Barcelona's patron saint, the Verge Mercè, is 24 September, but she merits a whole week of festivities and plays host to giants and bigheads from all over Catalonia. All Saints' Day, 1 November, is an important public holiday, a day when chestnuts, cakes and sweet wine are the traditional foods (see *The Country Kitchen*), but it is purely a family and religious celebration.

And that brings us back to Christmas.

Romanesque architecture is one of the great glories of Catalonia. Ranging from tiny rural churches through modest convents to great abbeys and cathedrals, to say nothing of domestic and military examples, it is represented within the Catalan borders by over 2,000 buildings.

The style known as "Romanesque" (which the British prefer to call "Norman" from its introduction by their conquerors) flowed directly from the design and layout of the Roman basilica after the conversion of the Roman Empire to Christianity. During the Dark Ages this stream went underground, to emerge in the reign of Charlemagne, King of the Franks from AD 771 to 814 and first Holy Roman Emperor from 800. In its first phase, running approximately from AD 800 to 1000, the style is often called "Carolingian", though the term "pre-Romanesque" is preferred in Catalonia, which had liberated itself progressively throughout the 9th century from the Frankish Empire.

Virtually all Christian building in Spain was contingent on the repulse of the Islamic invasion, which was unleashed on the peninsula in 711 and swept right up into France until it reached Poitiers in 732. From this high point it fell back over the succeeding centuries on to the Rivers Ebre, Douro and Tagus before contracting within its last refuge, the Moorish kingdom of Granada.

In its wake Christian colonisation and church-building followed fast. Much of this was monastic and primarily Benedictine, stimulated by Charlemagne and his successor, Louis the Pious, with the object of spreading the unique Benedictine amalgam of the practical and the spiritual to all corners of the Frankish Empire.

Some Benedictine foundations date from the early 9th century. Initially they relied on the relative security of the mountains; then they spread down to the foothills and coastal plains. But during the first phase of expansion they were contained, on the whole,

Preceding pages: apse from Santa Maria d'Aneau, painted in the early 12th century. **Left**, the richly decorated portico of Santa Maria in Ripoll. **Right**, 12th-century Majestat Batlló.

north of Barcelona's river, the Llobregat, along which the frontier lay. South of this was a no-man's land in the present winegrowing region of Penedès, until the Ebre basin was firmly repossessed in the mid-12th century.

It is usual to date Romanesque proper from AD 1000. The characteristic features of "first Romanesque" churches were their thick rubble walls, small windows, the semicircular arch over windows and doors and then, increasingly, the barrel vault, shaped

like the top half of a tunnel, which made its first appearance in Catalonia at Santa Maria in Amer, near Girona, dedicated in 949.

Most of these churches were tiny, hardly larger than a chapel: such is Sant Quirze de Pedret, near Berga, which preserves the earlier Mozarabic feature of horseshoe arches, indicating that it was the base of a very small and precarious community before the region was fully secured for Christendom. But others were on a grander scale, such as Cuixá, now under elaborate restoration, and the lofty Sant Martí del Canigó, both on the French side of the modern border. The latter (1001–26) has tunnel vaults on two levels, in crypt and nave—a remarkable feat for the period—and a splendid tower. The style was spreading its wings.

Oliba and Ripoll: One of the most energetic promoters and propagandists of the style was Oliba, abbot both of Cuixá and Ripoll and later Bishop of Vic. Oliba, brother of the Count of Cerdanya, was a personal friend of Pope Benedict VIII and of the abbots of the great French monasteries of Fleury and Cluny. He was therefore at home in the worlds of international diplomacy and learning. His library at Ripoll became famous for its works of history, poetry, astronomy, mathematics and music. From here Arabic numerals spread north into Europe.

During his reign at Ripoll (sometimes called "the cradle of the race"), which lasted from 1008 to 1046, Oliba replaced the earlier, humbler structure with a great church, dedicated in 1032. This had become a ruin by the 19th century and the present building, with the exception of its celebrated portico, is merely a faithful reproduction. Even so, the barrel-vaulted nave with double aisles and long transepts, each containing three apses on either side of the main apses, give a good idea of the scale and solemnity of the grand church of Oliba's time.

Ripoll is square-ended, with the exception of the bulges made by the apsidal chapels.

Curiously, there is no Romanesque example in Catalonia of the Cluniac layout of a semicircular ambulatory opening radially on to chapels housing saintly relics. This design was largely directed at the pilgrims on the route to Santiago de Compostela, who would circulate round the chapels as if they were exhibition stalls. Catalonia had no international pilgrim trade and the hard-headed Catalans were not much interested in the cult of relics.

If Catalan Romanesque differed from that of the northern pilgrim route, so too is it distinguished from the large parish churches in and around Avila and Segovia. These are remarkable for their elaborately carved porch-arcades, in which municipal councils and early parliaments were held. With one or two exceptions, these are not found in Catalonia, where Moorish raids continued into the 11th century, whereas the later churches of Castile did not begin to rise until the Moorish threat had been confined well south of the Tagus.

Though Catalan Romanesque lacks the grace-notes of these arcades, it gained in assurance throughout the 11th century, producing a number of impressive churches. One of these is Sant Viçens, located inside the castle of Cardona and consecrated in 1040. The main features are the massive piers; great barrel vault, dome on squinch arches, three apses and delicate crypt; there is also a raised gallery for the castle folk. Used as a prison in the civil war (1936–39), it was whitewashed and deformed by various accretions but now its lineaments have been laid bare by the zeal of state architects, who have stripped it back to its bones.

Another great building of the period is the ruinous monastery of Sant Pere de Rodes. Superbly sited on a bluff above El Port de la Selva, with two towers overlooking the indigo sea, it is yet another monument to the redoubtable Oliba. It flourished mightily from its consecration in 1022 until about 1300 when it entered a long decline. The restorers have now moved in. It is to be hoped that they will respect one of its most original characteristics, which is the underpinning of the main apse by a crypt with

Left, wood Madonna from Ger in the Cerdanya. **Right**, the cloister of La Seu d'Urgell, with capitals by a Roussillon craftsman.

94

rough columns resembling the roots of an enormous plant.

Lombard influence: Cardona and Rodes are both religious buildings of the fortress type. As the Reconquest progressed and the threat of Moorish raids faded away, a more sophisticated phase of Catalan Romanesque came to the fore. The basic solidity of the Romanesque ground plan remained but the carving of archivolts over doorways and of capitals in nave and cloister became more elaborate. There was also a proliferation of so-called "Lombard bands" on exterior surfaces.

The latter feature was imported by teams of builders from Lombardy who entered Catalonia via Provence and Perpignan. The contemporary peasant, though the modern traveller requires a key to decipher them.

The paired columns which were common in cloisters (sometimes forming larger clusters at the corners) were capped by twinned capitals, which also provided ample scope for carving. Here formalised birds and animals or geometric patterns (some influenced by Cufic lettering, others reminiscent of Celtic strapwork) were mingled with biblical scenes. The main intention may have been to instruct, but the effect was to provide a rich counterpoint to the austerity of the principal buildings.

Mature Romanesque: The style reached its maturity in Catalonia in the 11th century. A

"band" is really a shallow, false arcade in which brick or stone pilasters stand out a little from the wall, forming a recessed panel capped by single or multiple semi-circular arcs. The panel may be plain or have a window set in it. In towers it acts as the frame for window embrasures on short columns called *ajimeces*.

Though stone carving became richer and more varied, its purpose was didactic and iconographic rather than decorative. For example, the portico at Ripoll contains more than 100 human figures and beasts drawn from a number of biblical episodes that would have been easily interpreted by a fine example is Sant Pere de Galligants in Girona, founded in 1131. The nave capitals are topped by grand scenic capitals. The main apse is decorated inside with engaged columns and flanked by two lesser apses. The capitals of the cloister (1154–90) are highly varied.

The same assurance of a style at its peak is to be found in the cathedral of La Seu d'Urgell (1131–82), with its graceful semi-circular east end incorporating a charming arcaded gallery looking out over the lush vale of Urgell; also at the monastic church of Sant Joan de les Abadesses (consecrated in 1150) near Ripoll, which boasts five apsidal chapels—the central one is adorned on the outside with an elegant blind arcade.

These are all fine buildings. Yet perhaps the greatest pleasure to be derived from the Romanesque is to find an excellent specimen in a rural setting. In fact, these abound but there are two Pyrenean valleys where the works of God and Man come together to particularly happy effect: the Vall d'Aran on the border with France and the valley of the Tort with the villages of Taüll and Boí.

In the Vall d'Aran, frequently snow-bound, slate-hung spires are the norm and there are delightful examples at Salardú and Arties. In the Tort Valley the outstanding architectural features are the splendid six aspiring, all the greatest towers in Catalonia are Romanesque: to those of the Tort Valley may be added Sant Pere de Rodes, *el cloquer* of Vic Cathedral (these all square) and the octagonal towers of Sant Pere de Galligants and Sant Pere de Ponts. It is as if Romanesque masterbuilders, constrained in their interiors by the demands of structural solidity, found some kind of release in the upward thrust of their bell-towers, while Gothic architects were able to give full rein to their aspirations in their vaults and were thus less concerned with external gestures.

Museum treasures: Though the main impact of the Romanesque style in Catalonia, as elsewhere, is made by its buildings, it is

and four-storey tower-belfries of Sant Climent and Santa Maria de Taüll, faced on the opposite slope by their five-storey rival at Erill-la-vall. With the subtle arrangement of their columned windows, increasing in height and width as they go up, these are very sophisticated exercises in design, with the added advantage of a superb setting.

It is interesting to note that, though Gothic architecture is generally considered more

Left, early this century wall paintings were stripped from churches in the Boí Valley, crated up, carried by mules to Barcelona and restored in the Museum of Catalan Art, **right**.

important to remember that Romanesque art was not confined to construction. There is also the whole range of fittings, paintings and images with which the churches were furbished. For these we must, in the main, turn to the museums, in which Catalonia excels: ever since the 19th-century Renaixença the Catalans have been thirsty for cultural as well as financial enrichment.

It would be wrong, however, to conclude that the country churches were pillaged by greedy curators for the benefit of the urban bourgeoisie. The great riches of the museums are due to the poor condition and virtual abandonment of many of these churches, especially the smaller and more remote ones. This made it imperative to remove their artistic contents, not least their frescoes, to places of conservation and safe-keeping.

The Modernist architect Puig i Cadafalch, author of the major history of Catalan Romanesque architecture, was much involved in the foundation of the Romanesque section of the famous Museu d'Art de Catalunya in Barcelona, which contains the finest collection of Romanesque art in the world. Frescoes from Sant Quirze de Pedret, Santa Maria de Taüll and many another church without cult or congregation have found a safe haven here, along with paintings on board, altar fronts, carved images and iron-

work—all beautifully installed and well displayed with good wall maps of their period and provenance.

Whether frescoed or on panel, Catalan Romanesque painting is linear, Byzantine in its modelling, accentuating formalised folds of clothing and strongly outlining limbs and features to achieve its form. Like stone carving, its aim was didactic and its means iconographic. But it was also boldly coloured and covering, as it often did, almost all the wall surface of a small church, its effect must have been overwhelming. We may like the stripped starkness of what we see today, because we idealise the simplicity of an

earlier age, but that is to leave out of account most of the thrill and glamour of the medieval Church, glowing from every wall. After harsh days in field or forest, it must indeed have seemed the threshold of another world.

There are two other museums which are essential to a full appreciation of the Romanesque period in Catalonia. The diocesan museum of Solsona takes the prize for presentation outside Barcelona and is no laggard in quality, with more frescoes from Sant Quirze de Pedret and Sant Pau de Casserres; there is also a fine reredos from Sant Jaume de Frontanyà.

Though less well displayed, the episcopal museum of Vic is an absolute *must*. The 12th-century murals from Sant Sadurní d'Osomort and Sant Martí del Brull are outstanding, as is the rich collection of paintings on wooden panels, to say nothing of the great, gaunt, unpainted Descent from the Cross from Erill-la-vall. Founded earlier than Barcelona's museum, this is a treasure house not to be missed.

Gothic touch: There is an important footnote to the Romanesque in Catalonia in the shape of the "transitional" style. Such 13th-century churches as the old cathedral of Lleida and the parish church of Agramunt, with their tentatively pointed arches, remain fully within the Romanesque tradition as far as layout is concerned and tend to run back to mother for their archivolts and tympana a century or more after the Cistercians introduced their Gothic revolution.

At Lleida, where the vast cloister was begun in 1286, Romanesque capitals launch Gothic tracery. At Poblet, Romanesque capitals combine with a Gothic arcade well into the 14th century. Even the great Cistercian monasteries themselves could not make a clean break with the past.

The conclusion must be that the Romanesque style, in its strength, simplicity and gravity, accorded so well with the Catalan character that Catalonia was loath to lose it and clung to vestiges of it long after it had been superseded elsewhere. This had a profound effect on the tardy development of the Gothic style which, when finally established, was almost as sober and restrained as its predecessor.

<u>Left</u>, altar front from Lluçà in Vic's Museum. <u>Right</u>, Sant Climent de Taüll, Vall d'Aran.

Entering Catalonia from the south, drivers on the national road, the N340, will pass by the sturdy Roman Arc de Barà. From the north, arriving on the motorway from France, they will stop at the border by the modern monument created by Ricardo Bofill. In between they can see 2,000 Romanesque buildings, half a dozen great Gothic cathedrals, a liberal scattering of Modernist mansions and the latest showcase buildings for the Olympics. Catalonia is architects' country, and though it attracts both students and practitioners, few are more aware of this tradition than Catalans.

Talk of the town: Barcelona is both a magnet for talent and a source of inspiration, and Catalans are particularly proud of their capital city and of the men who built it. Although its beautiful buildings belong to a dynamic European tradition, there are few European cities where the man in the bar can reel off the names of the top local architects and also give an informed opinion on the buildings currently under construction.

In the late 1960s, Ricardo Bofill had the following of a guru and students flocked to his cement-factory atelier on the outskirts of the city. Today the top architects are familiar faces in newspaper and television reports: people such as Alfons Milà who, together with his partner Federico Correa, is responsible for the best of the modern blocks that pepper the city's tree-lined Diagonal. Milà, cheery and avuncular, has popularised the image of the architect as the ordinary man.

Or perhaps the talk is of the "new Barcelona" and how much of it is due to Oriol Bohigas, an architect whose slightly donnish appearance belies a sharp political mind and an immense creative vision. Or of one of Bohigas's partners, English-born David Mackay, who cheerfully admits his intense dislike of Gaudí's Sagrada Família.

Interior designers are also popular personalities, and no new night club in the city or in the top holiday resorts can afford not to hire

one of them to come up with something startling. Among the names most in demand are Alfred Arribas, who can create Space-Age fantasies, and Javier Mariscal, creator of the Olympic mascot, Cobi, whose bright and bouncy cartoon style epitomises the joyful side of the Catalan character.

Modernism and modernisers: Perhaps the popularity for modern architecture stems from Modernism, the turn-of-the-century style which so successfully blended the contradictory ingredients of Catalonia's

long cultural tradition. Antoni Gaudí (1852–1926), Josep Puig i Cadafalch (1867–1957), Lluís Domènech i Montaner (1850–1923) and the other followers of Modernism created buildings which combined the anarchic Catalan free spirit with the cautious realism of the bourgeois industrialists who commissioned them. They affected factories, farmhouses and holiday villas and, together with enthusiastic municipal architects, they left every town in Catalonia with examples of the style.

During the political upheavals of the 1920s and 1930s this approach was rejected as a compromise. The battle lines between

Preceding pages: Palau de Sant Jordi, Montjuïc, by Isozaki. **Left**, Ganchegui's Parc d'Espanya Industrial helps the city breathe. **Right**, a Modernist mansion, Casa Serinya, Cadaqués.

Modernism and the new modernisers were drawn up in 1929 when the exhibition complex at Montjuïc was built for the Barcelona Fair. Approached between two towers up the wide Passeig de Maria Cristina, this was Puig i Cadafalch's last major work and it was berated for being too pompous. Nearby, in the Avinguda Marques Comillas, was another building commissioned for the fair: the sleek, geometrical German Pavilion by the Bauhaus director Mies van der Rohe (1886–1969). Critics pointed to this as the signpost to the future.

The radical philosophies of the Republican government of the 1930s attracted the most original of Catalonia's architectural faculty and a pioneer in modern building design. After Franco's death he returned to Barcelona to design the art gallery housing the work of his old friend, Joan Miró, in Parc de Montjuïc and it demonstrates what a talent was lost in the intervening years.

Sert had escaped the constraints of "National Escorialism", the official architecture of the Franco regime which tried to ape the austere monumentalism of Felipe II's 16th-century palace outside Madrid. Fortunately, Catalonia was out of favour with Franco, and though its architects had to work within strict confines, by and large it managed to avoid any major impositions. Only a few daring spirits managed to break down the barriers

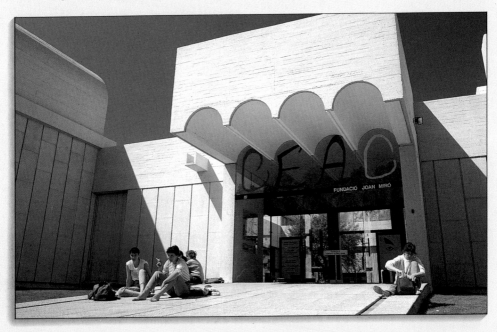

minds. Among them was Josep Lluís Sert (1902–83), who drew up numerous housing schemes which would sweep away the hierarchies of the old Barcelona and produce a new democratic city. It was a Utopian concept, of an architecture which would improve the lives of the people, and it was the philosophy of GATCPAC (Grup d'Artistes i Técnics Catalans per el Progres de l'Arquitectura Contemporània), in which Sert was a leading light.

Franco's victory in 1939 robbed Catalonia—and Spain—of Sert's talents, for he went into exile to America, where he became dean of the Harvard University architecture and create genuinely modern buildings. In 1954 Josep Coderch (1913–84) designed an apartment block on Barcelona's Carrer Almirall Cervera which combined an irregular and asymmetrical facade with such traditional touches as wooden louvre windows. It is a style much copied these days (and rarely bettered) but it was considered dangerously radical at the time.

Another daring spirit of the mid-1950s was the Lleida-born architect Josep Maria Sostres (1915–84) who designed the Hotel Maria Victoria in the Pyrenean resort town of Puigcerdà. The building is unashamedly modern, but its scale and the careful use of local materials ensure that it nestles comfortably into its rural setting.

Sostres was also responsible for the mould-breaking Casa Augustí in Sitges. Disarmingly simple in concept, it is an object lesson in the use of space. In nearby Caldetas, Coderch built the Casa Ugalde and these two villas became models for hundreds of weekend homes all along the coast, though none has yet matched the simplicity of the originals.

Sostres and Coderch were part of the Barcelona Grupo R. This loose cluster of architectural talents aimed to keep alive the ideals of GATCPAC and to maintain contact with the architectural revolution taking

the Plaça de la Font. The following year he designed the law faculty at Barcelona University with the unmistakably clear lines of Mies van der Rohe.

But the building that really hit the headlines was the Col.legi d'Arquitectes in Plaça Nova, opposite Barcelona Cathedral. Built in 1962 by the architect Xavier Busquets, it caused quite a stir. A sign of the changing times was Picasso's involvement. Though still refusing to visit Spain under Franco, he designed an exuberant frieze which surrounds the first floor with dancing, singing and music-playing figures.

The Barcelona School: After democracy had returned to Spain and architecture finally

place in the rest of Europe. Much of their activity had to be conducted in a clandestine atmosphere and there were few opportunities to put theory into practice, but the proposals which the group developed had a profound influence on later generations.

Occasionally there were surprises. In 1957 Alejandro de la Sota, an architect in Tarragona who had been following the rules of "historic" architecture, produced the straightforwardly functionalist town hall in

Left, the gallery designed by Sert for his friend Miró after years in exile. **Above**, Barcelona waterfront bar interior created by Mariscal.

shook off the shackles of officialdom, the modern movement in the rest of the world was suffering from a crisis of confidence. In Catalonia the old Utopianism was losing ground to the "new realism" of the Barcelona School, a group of architects who emphasised the need to use the lessons of Catalonia's considerable heritage when meeting modern demands.

The driving force behind the school was Oriol Bohigas and his partners Josep Martorell (they were both born in Barcelona in 1925) and David Mackay, an English architect who was born in Eastbourne in 1933 and who had become firmly established in the city. They had been designing unpretentious, even cautious buildings, using modern methods and materials, but few really outstanding works date from this time.

Their approach typified a general architectural tentativeness which had no sweeping grand designs. And though this might not have produced any startling buildings, it did mean that the historic centres of Barcelona, Girona and other Catalan towns did not suffer the wholesale redevelopment which has proved so disastrous elsewhere in Europe.

Sadly, the same cannot be said for some parts of the Catalan coast. The tourist boom fuelled a construction craze for high-rise horrors and impoverished parodies of

beings"—made for outstanding architecture. The fantastic honeycomb of the Walden 7 housing complex in St Just Desvern has become a local landmark. So, too, has the headquarters of his Taller de Arquitectura located in a former cement factory next door.

In Andorra, his Pont de Sant Meritxell religious centre is not only a building; its linear structure allows it to form a path, viaduct and bridge linking a beautiful valley. By the French border post on the motorway over El Portus Pass, his Parc de la Marca Hispanica is a monumental pyramid which pays homage to Catalonia's history. But apart from these there is little of Bofill's work to be

Andalucían *haciendas* and Ibizan *fincas* jostling for sea views. One saving grace about many of these buildings is that their short life span will ensure demolition sooner rather than later.

Although architecture was emerging cautiously with the arrival of democracy, one architect had already begun to set the pace. Ricardo Bofill, who was born in Barcelona in 1933, had burst upon the scene in the late 1960s with a restless and imaginative breathlessness that was obvious in his buildings. His personality—"somewhere between the realms of pure dream and an instinct to make a living by astonishing his fellow human

found in Catalonia, since he now spends most of his time working abroad.

The new space makers: It is Oriol Bohigas and the "new realists" who have made the greatest impression on current Catalan architecture. Pleasing examples of the Martorell-Bohigas-Mackay marriage of traditional styles with modern needs are the housing at Avinguda de la Meridiana in Barcelona and in Mollet. But it was their blueprint for new public spaces, adopted by the city council, that has had the lasting impact. Thanks to what Mackay describes as "careful surgery that allows the city to breathe again", Barcelona has created a profusion of squares, gardens and parks which are appreciated by both visitors and residents.

Two outstanding examples are the Parc Joan Miró in Carrer Tarragona and the Parc d'Espanya Industrial in Carrer de Muntadas near Sants railway station. The Miró park, designed by Solana, Quintana and Gali, is dominated by the sculptor's extraordinarily joyous *Dona i ocell* (Woman and bird). Fabulous, other-worldly creatures feature in the Parc d'Espanya where the Basque architect Luis Peña Ganchegui has created an artificial lake surrounded by staircases and grassed areas and guarded by 10 slim towers which serve as both lighthouses and lookout

points. These spaces, which are central to Bohigas's view of the city, have been given over to people's pleasure rather than sold to developers for profit, and they express the vitality of a modern city while remaining a pleasure to wander through.

Some of the real excitement and creativity of modern Catalan architecture is to be found inside the buildings. Behind some of the most unprepossessing facades are the interior designs, furniture, fabrics and graphic

Left, Ricardo Bofill's landmark Walden 7 housing complex and, **above**, his Pont de Sant Meritxell religious centre in Andorra.

art which have made Catalonia something of a design Mecca. But perhaps this is no more than a continuation of the tradition of Modernism which held that the interiors of their buildings should be as expressive as the outside fabric.

Since the 1980s there has been a flowering of Catalan design, shown in the magnificent interiors of bars, shops, restaurants and private houses. In Barcelona highlights include glossy, high-tech clubs such as Nick Havana in Carrer Rosello, or Velvet in Carrer Balmes, jokey interiors such as the Marbeye bar in Avinguda Tibidabo and Hollywood revivalism at Il Giardinetto restaurant in Carrer La Granada. Also notable is the surrealist fantasy of Louie Vega, a discotheque in Calafell on the Costa Daurada where the designer Alfred Arribas has created a stage set from *The War of the Worlds*, with sumptuous bars, dizzy staircases, a water cascade and jet plane crashing through its walls.

Arribas is a talented interior designer as well as an architect, as is Oscar Tusquets, who designed the eccentric, Italianate Belvedere Georgina near Llofriu (Girona), a private house with a pavilion to accommodate a car. Tusquets also refurbished the interior of the Modernist Casa Tomás in Carrer Mallorca for the Barcelona furniture firm of BCD, and he is also now widely regarded for his furniture.

Architects' Olympics: The siting of the 1992 Olympic Games in Barcelona gave a further lift to the architectural imagination at which Catalonia excels. Necessary infrastructure work has been transformed into works of art even when the architects or engineers involved are foreigners who have been invited to take part. Among them are Arata Isozaki from Japan, responsible for the Palau de Sant Jordi in Monjuïc, a building with a gleaming vaulted roof; Vittorio Gregotti from Italy has superbly restored Pere Domènech's original 1929 Olympic stadium; and Santiago Calatrava has built a beautiful edifice on Carrer Bac de Roda which is part sculpture, part bridge.

There are also works by Richard Meier, I.M. Pei and other international practitioners. And if they weren't household names in Catalonia a few years ago, they will soon be as hotly discussed in the bars and restaurants as Gaudí, Puig, Sert, Bofill, Bohigas and the rest.

Picasso, Miró, Dalí and Tàpies: the four names dominate any discussion of modern art in Catalonia. All four have been at odds with Catalonia, politically or culturally; all four, in the main, made their reputations elsewhere; all four have museums dedicated to their work in Catalonia.

They seem to have nothing else in common. They are individualists who went their own way; their art is uncompromising, deeply original. And yet all four arose from a set of cultural circumstances, and an important line can be traced between each of them and trends in Catalan painting.

The two founding fathers of modern Catalan painting are Ramon Casas (1866–1931) and Santiago Rusiñol (1861–1932). Both were sons of rich families and both became guiding spirits in the loose movement known as Modernism, which can be defined, in the words of the critic Cristina Mendoza, as "a common search for something new" in Catalonia in the last decade of the 19th century and the first decade of the 20th.

The work of both painters dominates the Museu d'Art Modern in the Parc de la Ciutadella in Barcelona. Although the influence is clearly French, neither is an Impressionist; their work is closer to Whistler, say, than Renoir. Both found a subject and stuck to it, particularly in their later years: Casas as a portrait-painter and Rusiñol as a painter of gardens. Yet, along the way, they painted some remarkable compositions. Casas's two political paintings, one of a policeman on a horse charging a crowd, another of a public garrotting, are powerful and dramatic. Rusiñol's portrait of Eric Satie depicts a drab, bohemian setting, a *fin-de-siècle* atmosphere notably absent from other Catalan paintings of the time.

The importance of Casas and Rusiñol lies perhaps more in the atmosphere they created in Barcelona than in the work they did. What they brought home with them from Paris, which they visited constantly and lived in from time to time, besides a style of painting

Preceding pages: Dalí Museum, Figueres. Left, Casas's 1901 drawing of Picasso, aged 20. Right, *Dona i Ocell*, Miró Park, Barcelona.

which emphasised light and mood, was a sense of the cosmopolitan world beyond the Pyrenees. They became leaders, trend-setters.

Barcelona at the end of the 19th century was a world in a constant state of flux and growth in which a huge explosion occurred in the visual arts. A new generation emerged; this time the sons of shop-keepers, officials and farmers became artists. They all began to frequent a bar, Els Quatre Gats, based on Le Chat Noir in Paris, which was set up by Casas

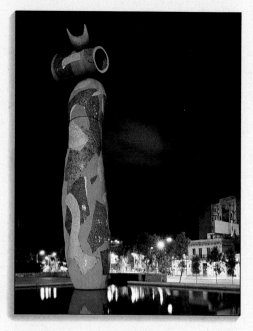

and Rusiñol, among others, and housed in one of the best examples of Modernist architecture in Carrer Montsió, which is now a restaurant.

Picasso's Catalan roots: Els Quatre Gats was where Picasso had his first exhibition, of drawings of figures from the artistic and bohemian life of the city in the manner of Ramon Casas. This was where Picasso spent his evenings between 1899 and 1904 when he was in Barcelona. His family had come to the city in 1895 when he was 14, and he would spend most of his time here until 1904, returning for summer sojourns in 1906 to the village of Gósol in the north of Catalonia and in 1909 to Horta de Sant Joan in the province of Tarragona; his last extended stay in the city was in 1917, when he came with the Russian Ballet.

The Picasso Museum in Barcelona is a collection of work from Picasso's development. It shows paintings and drawings from his childhood in the south of Spain, then records the family's move to Barcelona (they lived on Carrer de la Mercé, near the waterfront), where he painted the roofscapes and streetscapes of the city as well as portraits of his parents, and a great deal of academic studies from his time at the Llotja, where his father taught art.

His career up to 1904 was typical of every

century both began to paint women in states of solitude and desolation.

Nonell's work, like that of the other painters Picasso left behind, including Joaquim Mir (1873–1940), a remarkable landscape painter, is housed in the Museu d'Art Modern. In the same building there is only one Miró, a work which the painter himself rightly considered minor. In the years when the gallery could have bought Miró's work, he was politically suspect. The later rooms of the museum are full of examples of Noucentism, a movement which sought to replace the excesses of Modernism with classical distance and refinement.

Miró, unlike Picasso, was Catalan through

artist of his generation in Barcelona, enough for him to be considered a Catalan painter up to that point. The similarities between his early career and that of his Barcelona contemporary Isidre Nonell (1873–1911), for example, would be uncanny were they not both adhering to a general prevalent pattern of work and movement.

Both studied at the Llotja and soon rejected its dry academicism; both felt liberated by extended stays in the Catalan countryside; both went to Paris; both exhibited in the same gallery there, lived in the same building, later had a studio in the same building in Barcelona; at the beginning of the

and through. His father came from a village in Tarragona, his mother from Majorca. Both his grandfathers were artisans. The family lived off Carrer de Ferran in the centre of Barcelona, near Miró's father's watch shop. His mother and Picasso's mother, who lived nearby, were friends. Miró also attended the Llotja, but the teachers there were not impressed by his talents and he went instead to study as an accountant. Later, after a breakdown, he studied at a private academy and at the Cercle Artistic de Sant Lluc where the ageing Gaudí was among his fellow students. (Miró, unlike Picasso, admired Gaudí.) Here he tried to draw with great difficulty; his main interest, even then, was colour.

He began to spend a great deal of time at his parents' summer house at Mont-roig, near the sea, south of Tarragona. His work from this period is housed in two rooms of his Foundation on Montjuïc, overlooking Barcelona. It was only later, in Paris, that his free-flowing style, using surreal shapes, flat colours and musical images, was developed.

Throughout his life, Miró had a great talent for friendship. In Barcelona he became friends with the ceramicist Josep Llorens i Artigas, with whom he later collaborated. He also became friendly with the Dadaist Francis Picabia, who spent some of the

World War I years in Barcelona, and who encouraged Miró, as did the gallery owner Dalmau who gave Miró his first exhibition.

Miró was desperate to go to Paris, still the art capital for Catalan painters. When he first went there Picasso's mother gave him a cake to take to her son. He became friendly with Picasso, 12 years his senior, and Picasso bought work from him (as did Hemingway) and spoke about his work to art dealers.

His museum, Fundació Miró, is also a testament to friendship: to his friendship

Left, pop studies of Miró, Picasso and Dalí.
Right, Tàpies's public *Homage to Picasso*.

with Joan Prats, whose father also owned a shop in the city centre, who collected Miró's early work and presented it to the Fundació. The architect who designed the cool, white Rationalist building was also a friend, Josep Lluís Sert, who designed Miró's studio building in Mallorca as well. The best work in the Fundació building is late Miró, paintings like *The Fireworks Triptych*, full of Miró's personal calligraphy and iconography, surreal, naive, suggesting an underworld of electricity, dream, memory, imagination; moving from dark, atavistic nightmare to whimsy and humour.

Miró established himself in Paris in the 1920s and 1930s, returning to Catalonia only on the outbreak of World War II. He supported the Republicans in the Spanish civil war, exhibiting his own protest painting beside Picasso's *Guernica*. He settled first in Mallorca, in 1942 he moved to Barcelona, and from the mid-1950s he lived near Palma in Mallorca, but he remained implacably opposed to the regime, and on several occasions joined in protests against Franco. After Franco's death, he designed posters for Catalan causes.

Help for Dalí: In the 1920s Miró helped Salvador Dalí a great deal, visited his studio, wrote to his father recommending a career as an artist for his son, sent his agent to look at Dalí's work. Dalí was born in 1901, eight years after Miró, in Figueres, a market town north of Girona. Whereas Miró was quiet, retiring and self-effacing, Dalí was the great playboy of Catalan art.

He, too, first exhibited with Dalmau in Barcelona, although he had been to Madrid to study painting. He, too, came to see Paris as the capital, the place which Picasso and Miró had conquered and he wanted to conquer as well. Both painters helped him, paved the way for him, offered him introductions. Picasso said that his imagination reminded him of "an outboard motor continually running". Through Miró he met the leading Surrealists, with whom he would later quarrel.

Unlike Miró and Picasso, Dalí was prepared to accept Franco's regime. After the civil war, with his wife Gala, who had previously been married to the Surrealist poet Paul Eluard, he returned to Catalonia from America where he had made his name. He lived at Portlligat, near Cadequés, later at a castle near Girona. In his last years, when he was ill, isolated and lonely, he lived in his museum, where he is now buried.

The museum in Figueres is more a set of installations by Dalí than a collection of his work. It is a theatre, with Dalí playing all the parts, rather than an art museum. He makes jokes with every object he can find, from espadrilles to corn, to television sets to car tyres and ancient statues.

Common background: What do they have in common, then, these geniuses of modern painting? Is there anything particularly Catalan about Picasso, Miró and Dalí? Why should three such important figures in the development of contemporary art have spent

time, which made it possible for them to develop as artists. No one from their class had emerged as artists in the previous generation. They were, to a certain extent, created by the economic boom in Catalonia.

The second reason has to do with the nature of Catalan society, which is firmly based on the work of the individual farmer and the independent artisan, which gave life to political liberalism and anarchism, but also to a fierce sense of the uncompromising individual, someone working and thinking alone. Gaudí as architect comes to mind; Casals as cellist.

The third reason has to do with heritage. All three artists in their years in Catalonia

their formative years in the same place with only 20 years between them?

There are three main factors worth considering. The first is economic: in the years when all three were growing up, as Catalan industry expanded, there was enormous political and cultural ferment: Barcelona became the main centre for anarchism in Europe. Architects became the main innovators throughout Catalonia, trying all new available methods. Nothing was settled or fixed. Growth was followed by slump. All three, Picasso, Miró and Dalí, came from the same kind of background, and were subsidised by their parents for a certain length of

came in contact with Romanesque art, of which there is a fine and extensive tradition in Catalonia. Here the human figure becomes symbolic, the figures in *Guernica* are oddly reminiscent of figures in a Romanesque wall painting; and here too paint is used for its own sake, flatly, as decoration, as in a Miró painting. Miró used to say that the Romanesque tradition went through his veins, like blood.

The spirit of Tàpies: One of the most fascinating figures from this period is the Barcelona art critic Sebastià Gasch, the first critic to write about both Miró and Dalí, who became a friend of both and a supporter of *avant-garde* work in the city—including the drawings of Federico García Lorca, which were also exhibited at the Galería Dalmau.

In the 1940s Gasch wrote to the father of the young painter Antoni Tàpies, just as Miró had done to Dalí senior, advising him that his son had considerable promise as a painter. Tàpies came from a cultured, Catalan, bourgeois background in the city.

He became the heir to Miró in the 1950s, using paint to explore problems of matter and the human spirit. He, too, was aware of the specifically Catalan nature of his work. The profound knowledge of the materials he employed and his attitude towards mysticism were both ascribed to his Catalan iden-

Eixample in the middle of Barcelona. One of the painters whom he has invited to exhibit in his new Foundation is the young Catalan painter Miquel Barceló, who is now the best known painter of the younger generation. Barceló's work is figurative, but the figure is always tentative, isolated, ghostly, although drawn with immense skill. As a painter he seems more interested in the atmosphere around an object. His work from Mali, which he exhibited in 1989 in one of the fashionable galleries along Carrer del Consell de Cent, was full of haze and heat, the objects were distant, curious shapes. He is likely to become an extremely important painter.

There is one object in Barcelona which

tity. Like Miró and Picasso, he stood apart from the regime, and created work that, in his words, "could create a general revulsion for the regime". Like his two predecessors, and indeed Dalí, he felt free to invent his own style, to paint like no one else has ever painted, using new materials, new ideas. He was concerned, like Miró, about how little of his work had been seen in his own city, because of Franco. His foundation, which includes work by other artists, but mainly houses a collection of his own work, is in the

Left, Miró's unmistakable touch. **Right**, Dalí and Gala (centre), sovereigns of Portlligat.

seems to sum up the uncompromising energy of these Catalan painters of the past hundred years. It is a monument designed by Tàpies to pay homage from the city of Barcelona to Picasso. It is situated along Passeig de Picasso, by the edge of the Parc de la Ciutadella. It is a huge glass box, in a pool of water, with an old dresser, old sheets and a stack of chairs inside and iron grids running through them, and indecipherable messages written on the sheets. It is, in its strange way, a monument to the human capacity for making images, for thinking up something new and extraordinary, at which Catalonia has excelled over the past century.

The Raventós and the Pagés families, owners of the massive Codorníu Group, have a curious ritual. Once a week, all the members of the family in the company headquarters on the Gran Via in Barcelona meet in a room and have a blind wine tasting. In front of each person there are six glasses containing six different wines. These tasters put them in order of preference, giving six points to the wine that they like most and one to the one that they like least. At the end of the tasting the points are added up to see which has been the favourite one of the day.

To the visitor it is a fascinating ritual. Family members appear from every department—oenological, commercial, legal and administrative—and sit down alongside the two great patriarchs of the family, the two Manuels, Raventós and Pagés. There is a good deal of family banter, a cheerful exchange of light-hearted insults. Then they all disappear to their respective offices. There is a lot to be done and the Catalans are well-known in Spain for their hard work.

For the visitor it can also be a rather frightening experience because two of the six wines are always produced by the company. Rate them fifth and sixth and it can be embarrassing, to say the least. But the families seem genuinely interested in outside opinions. It is all part of a continuing process of education and self-appraisal, an interest in how the international wine industry is developing and seeing how their own wines are currently shaping up against tough international opposition.

Both families are steeped in wine and no member more so than Manuel Raventós who has been the managing director of the group since 1969. Today he is a large man in his sixties, his white hair closely cropped in a crew-cut. He sits massively in an armchair, fidgeting with a cold, empty pipe and talking English in slow, measured tones, stumbling at times for the right word but determined to find it. In the local *Who's Who* his interests are listed as gastronomy, tennis and detec-

tive novels. But there is little doubt as to what his abiding passion is.

The first fizz: The Raventóses can trace their ancestry in the wine industry back to 1659 when Miquel Raventós married Maria Anna Codorníu, who came from a family that had been producing wine for over a century. But it was not until the second half of the 19th century that they had a decisive influence on the region's wine industry. Josep Raventós, Manuel's grandfather, travelled extensively throughout the wine regions of France and

was particularly impressed with the wines of Champagne. Back in his native Penedès, south of Barcelona, he imitated their production methods and, in 1872, opened the first bottle of sparkling wine to be made in Spain.

Josep's wines achieved local fame. But it was the vision of his son, Manuel, that built the foundations of the Codorníu empire today. When Manuel took over the family firm in 1885, he launched a massive programme of expansion, replanting extensive areas of vineyard that had been decimated by the phylloxera—a louse that attacks the roots of the vine and came close to extinguishing the European wine industry in the second half of

Preceding pages: Cabernet sauvignon grapes, Torres vineyard. **Left**, Penedès harvest. **Right**, Manuel Raventós, of the *cava* family.

WHICH WINES TO TRY

The hub of the Catalan wine industry lies a few miles south of Barcelona in the Penedès Denomination of Origin (roughly the equivalent of the French *appelation contrôlée*) and is centred around the two wine towns of Vilafranca del Penedès and Sant Sadurní d'Anoia. This is one of the most advanced wine regions of Spain and vast quantities of white wine flows from its high-tech wineries every year.

Much of it goes into the production of sparkling wine but, in recent years, there has been a revival of interest in still wines. These are usually a blend of the famous Catalan grape troika: the Macabeo, which gives acidity, aroma and resistance to oxidisation to a blend, the Xarel.lo, which contributes body and colour, and the Parellada which adds freshness, aroma and fruitiness. When cold fermented and released within a year of the harvest these grapes can produce thoroughly "modern" wines, low in alcohol, fresh and fruity and with a refreshing cut of acidity.

The Penedès is also at the forefront of Spain's viticultural revolution and an increasing number of growers are planting imported, "noble" grape varieties such as the Chardonnay. Although usually only added in small quantities to a blend, it gives elegance and finesse. If you want something a little more interesting, therefore, look closely at the label before buying.

Much the same can be said for the region's reds. Many of them are blends of the local Garnatxa, Ull de Llebre (also known as the Tempranillo) and the Carinyena. These can produce worthy wines, big, characterful and hearty. But the addition of Cabernet sauvignon, considered by many as the king of the world's red varieties, makes the wine longer-lasting and more complex. Look out for Torres's Gran Coronas and their splendid—and expensive—Etiqueta Negra, the reds of the Raïmat estate in Lleida and, more difficult to find, the Cabernets of Jean Leon.

The Penedès, however, is probably best known for its *cava* sparkling wines, quaffed in copious quantities in the province's *xampanyeries*. *Cava* is produced by the *méthode champenoise* in which the wine undergoes its second fermentation in bottle and is universally accepted as the best method of sparkling wine production in the world. Because of the region's climate and the grape varieties used, *cava* is a very different wine to Champagne, warmer, earthier and less acid and complex. But it is generally regarded as one of the world's great sparkling wines. Names to look out for, apart from the two giants Freixenet and Codorníu, are Segura Viudas, Juve y Camps, Rovellats, Parxet (from a "boutique" winery in the Denomination of Alella to the north of Barcelona) and, perhaps the greatest of them all, the Chardonnay of Raïmat.

Outside the Penedès, Catalonia has five other delimited regions and, although their wines are not as widely sold, some of them are worth seeking out. To the north of Barcelona there is the Empurdà-Costa Brava centred around the historic town of Peralada which produces mostly sound but uninteresting reds but has two specialities: *vi novell*, a young, light red; and Garnatxa, a sweet dessert wine.

And then there is the postage-stamp Denomination of Alella where the Co-operative produces interesting, traditional oak-aged whites, while Parxet offers outstanding wines usually made from imported varieties, mostly Chardonnay and Chenin Blanc, as well as *cava*.

The other three Denominations—Tarragona, Terra Alta and the Priorat—are in the southern part of the region. The first produces vast quantities of everyday quaffing wine, most of it white and uninteresting, although the house of De Muller does make some good sweet dessert wines. The last two, up in the mountains behind Tarragona, produce red wine, big in body, deep in colour and high in alcohol.

Of the two, the Priorat is the more interesting. This is an area of quite outstanding natural beauty with deep gorges and steep hillsides to which the vines cling like mountaineers. Its wines—go for those from Scala Dei and Masia Barril and ignore the co-operatives—are almost black in colour and can reach a mule-stunning 16 percent in alcohol. In Spain, these extraordinary and almost unique wines have achieved a cult status.

the 19th century and the early years of the 20th. He built the huge Codorníu cellars in Sant Sadurní d'Anoia, designed by the Modernist architect Josep Puig i Cadafalch; today, they are a national monument (well worth a visit and open to the public).

This investment led him to the brink of bankruptcy. But he had judged the situation correctly. The Catalan bourgeoisie, increasing in numbers and affluence on the back of the region's industrial revolution, needed a wine to celebrate their success. And Manuel Raventós provided them with one of which they could justly be proud. By 1894 Codorníu was being exported to Cuba and Argentina and, three years later, it replaced

which his father bought in 1914. And, during his lifetime, he has seen a desert, described in the deeds of purchase as "3,000 hectares with a castle and one tree", turn into what has now been declared a "model agricultural estate" by the Spanish government, with its own railway station and workers' village, 2,000 hectares (5,000 acres) of cereals and fruit trees and 1,000 (2,500) of vineyard.

He has seen the building of the Rondel cellars in the small town of Cervello. He has seen the acquisition of Masia Bach, a well-respected estate producing still wines in Sant Esteve Sesrovires; it had been built in the early part of the 20th century by two cotton barons. And, finally, in 1989 he presided

Veuve Clicquot as the sparkling wine served at official banquets. Today 90 percent of Spain's popular *cava* sparkling wine is produced by Codorníu and the other big wine houses of Sant Sadurní d'Anoia, the main wine-producing town of the Penedès.

The Raventóses have not rested on their laurels. The present Manuel was born in 1922 in the *casa senyorial* or château on the Raïmat estate outside the city of Lleida

Left, Miró's label design could not be used on the open market because it included the French copyright word Champagne. **Above**, Codorníu's, Manuel Pagés with the house *cava*.

over an earth-breaking ceremony in the Napa Valley, the first step in the building of a brand new winery to produce sparkling wines in California, an initiative that will convert Codorníu into a massive multinational with feet on two continents. In 1989 he was also—together with his cousin Manuel Pagés—in the Soviet Union, making preliminary investigations into the possibility of a joint venture in Moldavia.

Curiously for a man in his position, Manuel Raventós is a retiring, private man. Loved and respected by his employees, many of whom have followed their fathers and even grandfathers into the firm, he is seldom in the public eye. His influence on the whole Catalan wine industry might be enormous but he is by no means seen as a well-known figure internationally.

The Torres family: No greater contrast to Manuel Raventós could be found than Miquel Torres Jnr. Both belong to families with deep roots in the wine industry; both have a burning mission to raise the image of the wines of their region. But they belong to different generations and are as different as chalk and cheese.

Miquel Jnr is not yet the head of a wine dynasty. His father, also called Miquel and as often a foe as an ally in his son's career, is still firmly in control of the family firm. But,

invariably available for interview, highly intelligent and educated and refreshingly willing to admit and discuss past mistakes.

Although the Torres family have been growing grapes in the Penedès for generations, it was Miquel Snr who laid the foundations of today's multi-million dollar business. Things could well have been easier for him. He inherited the business from his father when he was only 23. Already driven by a boundless ambition, he realised that the future lay not in buying wines, blending them and selling them to other firms but in marketing them under his own brands.

Just a few years after he took the driving seat, however, the civil war broke out and he

if one had to pick one towering Spanish figure on the international wine scene, it would undoubtedly be Miquel Jnr. His wines command immense respect. And few other men in the world produce such a variety of wines combined with such a consistently high level of quality.

Torres is a surprisingly small man, lightly built and usually casually dressed. With dark glasses to cover the piercing blue eyes, he could easily melt into a crowd. But he never does. He (and other members of his family) has an almost uncanny sense of public relations, an extraordinary ability of getting into the limelight. He is a journalist's dream:

was dispossessed, control of the firm passing to a workers' committee. Then there was the day in 1937 when the surging Nationalist army that was driving the Republicans against the border bombed the family *bodega* in Vilafranca instead of the neighbouring railway station. Seeing over half a million litres of wine gush out of the shattered vats and pour out into the street, Miquel Snr is said to have sat down on the pavement and cried.

After the civil war, the Torres family reconstructed the firm with typical energy and determination. The fall of France in 1940 created a massive vacuum for wine in the

United States, an opportunity which Miquel Snr, with the help of his wife Margarita, was quick to exploit. Those early "Spanish Chablis" and "Burgundies" laid the foundations for the firm's success in America where, today, it sells more than a million bottles a year. When World War II ended, Miquel Snr packed his Renault car with samples and headed for Eastern Europe, markets which Margarita still looks after today.

The 1940s and 1950s, therefore, were years of recovery, growth and success. But, in the early 1960s, the firm still bought its wine from local producers, blended it and resold it. The next step, the one that would transform the firm into one of Europe's lead-

ing wine producers, was masterminded by Miquel Jnr. After attending the University of Barcelona, Miquel Jnr went up to Dijon to study oenology. Travelling around the wine regions of France, he began to make his plans. The future, he decided, did not only lie in making your own wines but in growing your own grapes. Only with complete control over every stage of production could the desired quality be achieved. So, in 1963, the firm made its own first fermentations under Miquel's supervision.

Left, the Torres family in Miquel Jnr's farmhouse home. **Right**, fermenting bottles.

Throughout the 1960s and into the 1970s the family began to buy up estates and plant them with the vines they believed would thrive in the different soils and climates. Today they still buy in grapes and crush them in their high-tech winery near Pachs. But their top wines, the "estate" range which includes brands such as the "Black" and "Green" labels and the Milmanda Chardonnay, are all made from their own vineyards.

This programme of dynamic expansion transformed the firm's wines. In a famous blind tasting held in Bordeaux, for example, the 1970 "Black Label" outpointed some of the Médoc's greatest châteaux. It established Miquel Jnr as one of the top wine makers in the world. But the price that the family was to pay was a high one.

Family conflict: As the estates were purchased and replanted to Miquel Jnr's specifications, as he delved ever deeper into the mysteries of blending wines from different grape varieties and experimented with different ageing methods, as his international reputation grew, so too did the tension between him and his father. At virtually every turn the young oenologist from Dijon seemed to clash with the powerful, dictatorial patriarch of the family. Today, for example, Miquel Snr insists that the introduction of foreign, "noble" grape varieties was his idea. In reality Miquel Jnr pressed ahead with the plan in the teeth of his father's opposition. The growing tension brought constant arguments. Finally, in 1983, Miquel Jnr left for a year's sabbatical to pursue his studies in Montpelier. It was even whispered that Miquel Snr sacked his son during a particularly heated exchange.

These two extraordinary characters now seem to have worked out a *modus vivendi* and, outwardly at least, peace reigns over the firm. Miquel Snr, the company's life president, looks after its commercial and administrative side from the headquarters in Vilafranca. Miquel Jnr lives with his German-born wife, Waltraud, in a farmhouse near Pachs surrounded by vineyards. He is in complete control of the technical side of the business and supervises the running of the Chilean subsidiary and the new vineyard planted in California. He seems to publish a wine book every year. And every year both his reputation as a wine maker and that of his wines grows even greater.

Traditional Catalan cooking has a definite country flavour. It is one of the most original of Spain's regional cuisines and it is typical of the Catalans themselves, who have always had a strong sense of their own identity.

The cuisine is eminently Mediterranean. Culinary skills were passed on by the Phoenicians, Greeks and Romans and the first Spanish cookbook, one of the oldest in Europe, is the *Llibre de Sent Sovi,* written in Catalan by an unknown author in the first half of the 14th century.

Regional variety: Sweeping down from the green and rugged Pyrenees to the beaches of the beautiful Costa Brava and the golden sands of the Costa Daurada, Catalonia is a mixture of mountains and plains which makes the climate and agriculture very varied. There are two well-defined cuisines: one built around the fish dishes of the coast, based on the bounty of seafood found only in the Mediterranean, the other characterised by the more solid, sturdy preparations of the inland areas. In the Pyrenees the cooking is warm and comforting.

The wealth of the cuisine relies on the wide range of produce available, from alpine mushrooms (especially the unique, delicious *rovellons*) and herbs collected and grown in the Pyrenees to the rice, fruit and vegetables of the fertile Ebre river valley in the south. The classic Mediterranean trilogy of olives, vineyards and wheat dominates; other basic staples are fowl, veal, baby goat and, above all, pork, whose fat has been used as a cooking element throughout the centuries. There is also a lot of game, from small birds such as partridge and quail to rabbit and hare, dove, duck, goose (a speciality) and even deer.

Historic influences: One of Catalonia's main gastronomic centres is L'Empordà (Ampurdán in Castilian), based on the ancient Greek city of Empúries in the dramatic Costa Brava. According to the gastronomy historian Manuel Martínez Llopis, it has the finest and most elaborate of all Spanish cuisines. The Roman influence came when Tarragona was established as the capital of

<u>**Preceding pages**</u>: ingredients for an *escudella*.
<u>**Right**</u>, country meals taste better out of doors.

their Spanish empire, Hispania, and remnants of other ancient cuisines, such as the Arabic and Jewish custom of using lemon, honey and cinnamon in certain dishes, can still be found.

Traders from the Far East introduced a variety of other spices, and pasta arrived in Spain via Barcelona when Naples, Sicily and Milan belonged to the count-kings of Catalonia-Aragón. Roussillon and Provence, part of Catalonia for 500 years, share similarities in their cuisines.

Basic ingredients: There are six primary flavouring ingredients in Catalan cooking: olive oil, garlic, onions, tomatoes, nuts (almonds, hazelnuts and pine nuts) and dried

pounded with a mortar and pestle, then added to the preparation while the cooking is in progress. *Picada* is used as a thickening and flavouring agent, and can be seen as a complement to *sofregit*.

3. *Allioli*, an emulsion of pounded garlic and olive oil traditionally mixed together in a mortar, is one of the most widely used sauces in Catalan cooking. It is served with grilled meats or fish and is also used to enliven the flavour of a dish by stirring in just a spoonful at the end.

4. *Romesco* today is a sauce that evolved from a fish dish, *romesco de peix* (fish stew), typical of the Tarragona area where there are lots of almond groves. A favourite accompa-

fruits, particularly raisins and prunes. And there are four traditional herbs: oregano, rosemary, thyme and bay leaves.

There are also the following five basic prepared flavourings:

1. *Sofregit* (*sofrito* in Castilian), meaning long sautéing, consists of onion and tomato slowly sautéed in olive oil, sometimes with garlic, peppers or other ingredients. It is used as a basis for many dishes and sauces.

2. *Picada,* which literally means "pounded", is usually a mixture of garlic, parsley, nuts, toasted or fried bread, and sometimes saffron or other spices. These ingredients are traditionally ground or

niment to grilled fish and vegetables, it is usually a paste of toasted almonds, garlic, sweet red peppers or *nyores* (a type of dried, mild red pepper), bread and tomatoes. No two versions are ever quite the same.

5. *Samfaina* is a mixture of onion, tomato, pepper, aubergine and courgette, cut into small pieces and sautéed in olive oil. It is served to accompany meats, fowl, fish, especially cod (*bacallà*) and even fried eggs or as an omelette filling.

A very basic utensil in the Catalan kitchen is the mortar and pestle. Despite the availability of such modern conveniences as blenders and food processors, it is still frequently used to grind nuts and spices, as in *picada*, or to prepare sauces such as *allioli* and *romesco*.

Romesco: Because of its importance in Catalan country cooking, this sauce deserves a chapter on its own. Truly indigenous to Catalonia, it comes from around Tarragona. The city holds an annual festival dedicated to its preparation at the beginning of summer, the prime season for the vegetables essential to the sauce. The winner of the competition is awarded the title of *Mestre Major Romescaire*—Major Master Romesco-maker.

Originally *romesco* was not in fact a sauce but a fisherman's dish which was made all along the coast from Vilanova, 20 miles (32

monds, red pepper, garlic, onions, tomatoes, herbs and spices and, most important, a good, fruity olive oil.

Many restaurants serve a little bowl of *romesco* as well as *allioli* without being asked for it and both sauces are sometimes blended together. On its own, *romesco* is especially good with grilled dishes, which Catalans love cooked outdoors on open fires, but you may find it served with salads, pasta, rice, or as a dip with breadsticks or croutons.

Grandmother's pot: *Escudella i carn d'olla* is the most typical Catalan dish, one of the family of boiled meals in a pot, which includes French *pot-au-feu* and Italian *bollito misto*. In the old days it was the staple meal

km) south of Barcelona, to Valencia. They prepared it when out at sea, using the lesser-quality fish from the day's catch (naturally saving the best to sell) and improving the flavour with a strong sauce. Later on, the sauce came to be made separately, and today it is served mainly to accompany grilled, poached or deep-fried fresh fish.

However, purists still maintain that *romesco* is not a sauce but a dish. Either way, it is always based on the primary Catalan flavouring ingredients: hazelnuts or al-

Left, La Boqueria fish stall. **Above**, the staple *pa amb tomàquet* with lashings of olive oil.

for those who lived in the country; some families might have had it five or six days a week. A special *escudella* was reserved for Christmas Day, and it is still a classic Catalan Christmas dish.

The idea is to simmer meats and sausages with vegetables. The broth is then served as a first course with pasta—traditionally the large shell pasta or *galets*. The entrée will be the meats and vegetables. On Christmas Day—if you can believe it—the turkey course then follows.

Turkey is seldom otherwise eaten in Spain, but it is traditional at Christmas. An old recipe is to stuff it with a delicious and

MUSHROOM MANIA

Catalonia has one of Europe's strongest mycological traditions. *Bolets*, from the Latin *boletus*, is the Catalan name for wild mushrooms (*setas* in Castilian) and these gastronomical delicacies are an important part of the region's life.

Mushrooms appear for only a short time after rainfall, usually following a dry spell. Most come up in the autumn, although several strains of field mushrooms arrive in the spring. Of more than 400 different kinds found in Catalonia, some six dozen are edible. Of those, the most common is the *rovellon*, followed by *ceps*, *rossinyols*, *fredolics*, *llanegas*, *moixerons*, *cama secs*, *martinencs* and *mirgolas*. Often cooked in soups and stews, they can also be served by themselves as *tapes* or hors d'oeuvres, sautéed with garlic in oil.

Monday morning coffee breaks in the autumn often revolve around the weekend's expeditions ("Three baskets full of *rossinyols*… I could have filled the whole Jeep") but favourite hunting grounds are a closely guarded secret. *Boletaires,* or wild mushroom buffs, tend to know all or nothing about the forest fungi; experts abound and there is much to be learned.

As an iron rule, however, if there is any doubt about a mushroom's identity, do not pick, taste or even temporarily mix it in with edible *bolets*. Guides to wild mushrooms are available in bookstalls everywhere, but when starting out it is advisable to accompany somebody who knows what they are doing.

Experts are also unanimous in advising *boletaires* to distrust all folkloric tell-tale signs said to prove the poisonous or edible qualities of the fungi: silver spoons or rings turning black, beads of milky fluid, skin pealing away from the cap or umbrella—none of them is foolproof.

Once you get to know them, however, the differences seem obvious. Nevertheless, mortal mistakes occur: a restaurant in Madrid poisoned a customer a few years ago and during 1987, a year of uncommon mycological bounty in Catalonia, there were several fatalities.

Many species are available in the town markets and on stalls set up by the roadside. Getting to know them in the markets helps in identifying them in the field, and indicates their availability in the wild. If a kilo of *rovellons* is selling for more than 1,000 pesetas, you will be lucky to come across any in the countryside: if they cost less than 500, you stand a good chance, although at that price you might as well buy some, too.

Like hunting or fishing, wild mushroom gathering is a great way to discover some remote and deeply satisfying countryside. *Bolets* offer a mystic communion with nature, and if they are left unpicked, within a day or so they will become part of the rich, musty decay of the forest floor.

For collecting, experts recommend stiff wicker baskets rather than plastic bags, and a small penknife for cutting the stalk just above the *mycelium* or base, which is essential to the regeneration of spores and the ecology of the forest floor. Montseny, the Empordà, the Pyrenees and nearly anywhere moist and below the frost line, especially piney hillsides, are *bolet* habitat. South-facing slopes are recommended when it is wet; northern faces or deep north–south valleys when it is dry.

Bolets will, however, sprout nearly anywhere when the conditions are right. *Moixerons* have been spotted on the grass verge of the Diagonal in Barcelona; a *camperol* can appear on the back seat of a Jeep; and one wild mushroom fanatic swears that he knows a woman who found a *Phallus impudicus* (a remarkably priapic mushroom which sprouts and disappears within a few hours) actually growing in her laundry.

There is a magic aura surrounding wild mushrooms: the excitement of the hunt, the aromatic forest floor, the pleasure of cooking and savouring the taste of the woods themselves. Dried mushrooms, which can be bought all year round, last for years.

There is a real magic, too, in the *Amanati muscaria*, the fairytale mushroom with a red cap and white spots. Pyrenean shepherds were said to have enjoyed its hallucinogenic effects, while the Modernist architect Antoni Gaudí, who was a religious mystic and man of the forest, was rumoured to have been *tocat del bolet*—touched by the mushroom.

very Catalan combination of prunes, apricots, apples, raisins, pine nuts and sausages. Before turkey came from America, a rooster (*gall* in Catalan) was used, a tradition that dates back to the 13th century.

Notable desserts: *Postre de músic*, "musician's dessert", is one of Catalonia's simplest desserts—nothing more than a mixture of dried fruit and nuts. The name comes from the times when musicians, usually young and poor, travelled around the countryside. They were not paid much but always got some food, and if their music was really good they were given a treat: raisins, filberts, almonds, pine nuts—whatever the farmer had on hand. Another traditional des-

central iron circle in the wood stoves used in the homes. These stoves had iron tops made of separate concentric circles and you would take out with a handle as many circles as were necessary to fit the size of your pan. The central circle would be about 3 inches (7.5 cm) in diameter, and this was used to burn the sugar top, just touching the surface so it would caramelise. These days such iron plates are sold commercially in Spain but you can also use a flat metal spatula heated on a gas stove or open fire.

Caramelising is frequently used in Catalan country cooking, whether to line a flan mould or to add colour and flavour to a savoury dish. Caramelised apple and coco-

sert is a tart of pine nuts over *cabell d'angel*, or angel hair, a filling used very often for sweets. *Cabell d'angel* is spaghetti squash (a pumpkin-like vegetable) slowly cooked with sugar until it caramelises and turns into a jam of dark gold threads.

Crema catalana is a delicious custard which appears on nearly every menu. The nicest thing about it is the caramel on top, which is made by sprinkling sugar over the custard and burning it with a red-hot iron plate. In the old days it was done with the

Above, *pa de forn*, country bread baked in a traditional wood-fired oven, in Girona.

nut flans are two recipes that are especially delicious.

Breads and pastries: *Pa amb tomàquet* (literally, bread with tomato) is a Catalan staple. This is bread, usually large slices of a crusty country loaf, rubbed with tomato and sprinkled with oil and salt; it is usually served at country-style restaurants instead of plain bread. Sometimes it is accompanied by anchovies (those from L'Escala on the Costa Brava are the best), cold local sausage or cured ham.

Another staple in the Catalan diet is *coca*, a name given to a number of different breads or pastries. These can be either savoury or sweet. Savoury ones have a bread base and are traditional in the northeastern regions of L'Empordà and Maresme. Usually long and oval, these *cocas* are often toasted, rubbed with half a fresh tomato or with garlic, and sprinkled with olive oil and salt. They are sometimes topped with local produce such as herring or anchovies, peppers, pitted olives, eggs, *pernil* (cured ham) and *botifarra* (black or white sausage).

At any traditional restaurant, *coca del Maresme torrada amb tomàquet* (Maresme toasted *coca* with tomato) is served with your meal instead of bread. In the old days, this plain bread *coca* or *coca de forner* (baker's *coca*) was also called *pa de torn* or

"return bread", because the baker might give it in return for purchase and payment instead of change.

Sweet *cocas* are used in a very different way, for breakfast, midday snacks or dessert. Usually covered with crystallised fruit, pine nuts and sugar, most of them have a religious connotation and are made for a particular *festa*. Perhaps the best known is *coca de Sant Joan*, eaten on St John's Day, 24 June. When covered with crystallised fruit and sugar they can be a little too sweet, but those with only pine nuts and sugar are always delicious.

Tortells are a most popular dessert. Shaped like a doughnut, they are filled with anything rich and sinful—whipped cream, chocolate, custard cream. Like *cocas*, some *tortells* have religious ties. A memorable one is the *tortell de Sant Antoni*, eaten on his feast day, 17 January. He is the patron saint of animals and all over Catalonia farmers take theirs to the church, where they are given *tortells de Sant Antoni* after they have been blessed.

Tortell de reis is probably the one *tortell* also eaten elsewhere in Spain, where it is known as *roscón de reyes*, the *reyes* being the Three Kings of Epiphany on 6 January. This tradition dates back to the 15th century in both France and Spain. It is still traditional to hide a dried fava bean, a symbol of good luck, inside the filling. There may be a little prize or treat hidden there too, usually a tiny white ceramic piece in the shape of something silly like a duck or a shoe.

Panellets ("little breads"), are delightful cookies typical of autumn because they use yams or sweet potatoes. They are traditional on 1 November, All Saints' Day, an important date for those whose name is not in the registry of saints, for that is when they celebrate their saint's day.

Where to eat: Although Catalonia is one of the Spanish regions where home cooking is best, there is also a wealth of restaurants, with more than 10,000 eating establishments in Barcelona alone. The oldest of them, Can Culleretes, dates back to 1786. It was originally a chocolate house, similar to a coffee shop. Patrons would go there in the afternoons and drink hot chocolate with rolls or with sweets.

Many of the best restaurants reflect the best of Catalan country cooking; some have taken an old country dish and introduced a new twist and flavour of their own. Good examples of this are Jaume de Provença, Agut d'Avignon, Cal Isidre, Azulete and many others which specialise in *cuina de mercat*, or market cuisine. Their secret is that every morning their chefs go to the best market in Barcelona, La Boqueria, and personally select the produce for the day's menu. Located in the Rambla, La Boqueria displays an array of the most wonderfully fresh produce. It can be the most unforgettable memory of a trip to Barcelona.

Above, a snail feast in Lleida. **Right**, autumn fireside treats of yams, chestnuts and pastries.

TEXTILES COME INTO FASHION

For more than 150 years Catalonia has been a place where Spaniards have come to find work. It was here, in textile factories beside the Ter and the Llobregat, and, particularly, just outside Barcelona in Terrassa and Sabadell that the Spanish industrial revolution began, bringing new wealth, spawning other processing industries and planting acres of workers' housing estates.

Today the region still produces more than 90 percent of Spain's textiles and controls around 30 percent of its large-scale clothing manufacture, but their relative importance in the local economy has slipped considerably. Construction is booming, technological parks for automation, electronics and computing are spreading fast and investment pours in to these sectors (Catalonia took one-third of all foreign investment in Spain and 70 percent of Japanese capital in the late 1980s). But relatively little has gone into textiles or clothes manufacturing. Between 1987 and 1989 more than 60 factories went to the wall and the trend is continuing.

To try to break out of the downward spiral, manufacturers are looking towards Catalonia's talented designers. Given the Catalans' fame for linking art with commerce and their respect for the decorative arts, it is curious that the alliance has never been forged before. In the 18th century, when Barcelona was forced to burst out of its city walls by the calico workers, who set up workshops all along the Maresme coast, the famous Escola de Llotja was founded to prepare them for their job. But since the 1830s, when hydraulic and steam-driven machinery was imported from England and the cotton industry really got under way, the design element has received scant attention.

Even the textile barons who commissioned many of the great Modernist factories and workers' communities and who were so meticulous with their own interiors, by and large gave textiles a miss. In Barcelona's excellent fashion and textile museum, the Museu Tèxtil i d'Indumentària (Carrer de Montcada 12–14, opposite the Picasso Museum), there is a splendid roomful of Modernist dresses but, indicatively, all the styles and fabrics were imported from Paris.

To a large extent, the same pattern has held true throughout this century. Barcelona became the Spanish capital of the industry, where most foreign manufacturers still have their base, but very little fashion has originated here. It simply arrived here before it arrived in other Spanish cities from Paris or Milan or London.

The industry's new interest in fashion has been triggered by economics rather than the rediscovery of design in the post-Franco era. As the growing flood of EC imports and low-cost competition from Portugal and the Far East make their impact, survival rather than safe profit is at stake and design has suddenly come into its own as a sales tool.

"It was the entry into the Common Market in 1985 which really marked the beginning of a change in attitudes," says Isabelle Clerc, who works for Promostyl, the leading French fashion forecasting consultancy. "Before that, it was hard to persuade people to spend money on a designer rather than a copyist. Now, for the first time, good original design is considered essential."

More precisely, design is being looked on as a catch-all solution which can, at a stroke, add value, move products upmarket away from the new competition and carve out new export markets. And while the pace for Spanish street-style is now set elsewhere—Ibiza, Valencia and Madrid at the start of the 1990s—Barcelona's much-hyped reputation for visual flair provides the perfect wagon to which such design consumerism can be hitched.

Bourgeois styles: It is hard to pinpoint a distinctive Barcelona look. "Yes, there is a very strong awareness of clothes," says

abdication in 1931, it followed the court. As a result the women's clothes were much less grand. Pedro Rodríguez [1917–78], the Catalan couturier, always used to say that *les senyores* dressed much more simply in Barcelona than in the capital."

Although Rodríguez is less well known than the two great Spanish couturiers—Catalan-born Mariano Fortuny (1871–1949) and Basque-born Balenciaga (1895–1972), who both made their names abroad—he is generally recognised as an important influence on later generations. The fluid Mediterranean simplicity that can be seen in his clothes, so very different from the classic Spanish severity, is also evident in the work

Heidi Speilhagen, a fashion importer. "But it's essentially very bourgeois—label-conscious, elegant and rarely outrageous—and it's about dressing rather than fashion. The most important thing is to dress in the same way as the others in your circle and to be seen to do so. Coco Chanel's maxim that it's better to be underdressed than to stand out says it all."

That low-key elegance goes back to the 19th century. "Society in Barcelona was very different from Madrid," says Rosa Martin i Ros, director of the Museu Tèxtil i d'Indumentària. "Here it was rich and bourgeois while in Madrid, up until the king's

of the younger ready-to-wear Catalan designers who began to come through in the late 1960s. They included Toni Miró, nicknamed the king of Barcelona fashion, whose shop Groc! was the first anti-establishment boutique, and Margarita Nuez and Roser Marcé, both of whose flourishing companies began as small family operations.

Together with a younger generation, which includes Pedro Morago, Jordi Cuesta, Chu Uroz and Lourdes Vergara, these designers put Barcelona on the European fashion map for the first time. Today it is rivalled, some would say overtaken, by Madrid, which has Spain's biggest stars, Sybilla and

Adolfo Domínguez. Top Spanish designers, such as Purificacion García, have been attracted to working here and Gaudí Hombre, the Barcelona ready-to-wear men's show, is now second only to Milan, and the women's fashion and textile fairs increasingly pull in foreign buyers.

And, although Barcelona doesn't yet have a particular image—as, say, Paris does for head-to-toe sexiness or London for witty eccentricity—a certain style is beginning to emerge. Toni Miró's description of his clothes as Mediterranean, "combining classical beauty with the spirit of Spain", is generally apt.

"It's a very self-conscious, stylised look,"

but attitudes are harder to change, especially in the smaller black-market companies which rely on outworkers beavering away in small workshops and front rooms.

"Our textile and clothes sector is thought of as commercially aggressive but, in reality, it needs to be far more so," argues Esther Allegre from CIE, the cotton manufacturers' association. "Many companies are still the classically Catalan family outfits—old-fashioned and too small to have marketing, let alone export departments. Likewise, many of the designers, who could not survive without the family's labour, need to take on a more commercial outlook."

Central government has been trying to

says Heidi Spielhagen. "Nothing is left to chance. The clothes are comfortable and wearable, but not extreme—they have to be elegant."

Family workshops: While the designers are beginning to deliver, the vital links with bankers, manufacturers and distributors that have made Italian fashion such a success story in the past 20 years are still missing. The subsidised Plan de Reconversion for updating machinery and retraining staff in the 1970s helped modernisation at one level,

<u>Left</u>, Toni Miró, the king of Barcelona fashion. <u>Above</u>, salesgirl in a city boutique.

show the way with controversial five-year Plan de Intangibles, through which more than 80 billion pesetas have been poured into subsidies for designers, fashion and textile shows at home and abroad and (trickier) selling the idea of design as an important, if intangible, asset to the manufacturers.

How long it will take industry to make its own initiatives has yet to be seen. There are many stories about the difficulty young talent still has in finding the right kind of support. Generally the designers blame the manufacturers' conservatism, the manufacturers blame the designers' lack of commercialism and everyone blames Spanish retailers for playing safe. There are a few shining examples of enterprising manufacturers and producers who saw the light some years ago, and are now enjoying handsome profits.

Success stories: Perhaps the most obvious example is Nicky Bosch, a textile manufacturer who has been working closely with local designers like Toni Miró since the 1970s; his company evolved the wrinkled look—called *arrugada* in Spain—which Adolfo Domínguez made fashionable around Europe, and his clients abroad include most of the top Paris designers.

In the same way, Jumberca, manufacturers of industrial knitting machinery, who started developing design software for knit-

ting patterns in the 1970s, now control an astonishing 70 percent of the world market. This fusion of technology and design may well be a hallmark of Barcelona fashion in the future. Likewise, there are producers and financial backers who have taken a leap into the dark with design and come up trumps. The street-sportswear launched by Basi in the mid-1980s, sold under the label Armand Basi, now appears in hip fashion magazines and shops around the world. More recently, Roser Marcé picked up a cool £10 million from a Catalan investment company, initiated by the Generalitat, which was scouting for local talent with high profit potential.

Significantly, they rated design alongside computer technology as one of the hottest investment opportunities in Catalonia.

But perhaps the most important step forward has been the expansion of the Escola de Disseny, a school of textile design at Sabadell. Increasingly, the manufacturers have become aware that lack of opportunity is one of the main reasons why ideas and designers haven't bubbled up more freely in the past. So, realising the urgent need for properly trained designers with practical understanding and creative flair, the textile industry has linked up with the state to fund a four-year design course with university standing.

Many people argue that the school should have been within a university rather than an independent, private venture. But at least it is a start. In the past most designers have had to learn their art on the job—Miró trained as an architect, Jordi Cuesta began as a model, Roser Marcé studied music—or, more recently, have gone abroad to study, which is hardly likely to encourage distinctively Catalan design. Perhaps by the mid-1990s, after the results of the Escola de Disseny have begun to show, state and industry will invest in a fully fledged fashion course.

There is a more general feeling, too, that the industry's problems are precisely the boost needed by Barcelona to fulfil its potential as a fashion capital. "Learning to walk on real ground within the tough European market can do nothing but good," says Heidi Spielhagen. "Having to compete on equal terms with imported fashion will push the designers and manufacturers to come up with new ideas and in the end, that will produce stronger home-grown fashion."

Where to see and buy: Until the Catalans hit the European catwalk, the best places to track them down on home ground are in Barcelona's Bulevards Rosa, a series of fashion malls with small shops that offer a blend of established and younger designers such as Chu Uroz, Lourdes Vergara, and José Font and Luz Díaz. Or try the hipper nightclubs, such as Otto Zutz or Central Ciudad, where you can observe local style against the backdrop of the stunning decor which sets the standards for which the fashion industry must now reach.

Left, innovative designer Purificacion García. **Right**, window shopping, Barcelona.

REVISTA DE S'AGARÓ

ESTIU 1936

TOURISM ON SPAIN'S FIRST "COSTA"

Ever since the first Catalan "tourists" ventured out of Barcelona in the late 19th century, the resorts along the rugged and beautiful Costa Brava have catered for demanding visitors. And even if some of those resorts—Tossa, Lloret or Sant Feliu, for example—appear to have been transformed into extensions of Germany, Britain or France, they remain the favoured holiday destinations of the average Catalan, as well as visitors from the rest of Spain.

Dotted in the hills and mountains above the 10 miles (16 km) of stomach-churning coast road between Tossa and Sant Feliu de Guixols, nestling amongst the rocks and pine trees and with superb views over the Mediterranean, are the second homes and weekend retreats of thousands of the more prosperous inhabitants of Barcelona, Girona and even Madrid. But the real money, the 15 percent of Catalonia's economy earned from tourism, comes from the 15 million annual visitors to the region, most of whom at some point go to the Costa Brava.

For more than 30 years there had been uninterrupted growth in the number of tourists arriving in Catalonia, first with the "boom" of the 1950s and then with the concentrated development of the tourist sector launched at the beginning of the 1980s. By the end of that decade, however, the authorities began to confront the predicted but nonetheless unwelcome fact that fewer holidaymakers want to come here.

After years of catering to the whims and considerable economic power of the big package-tour companies, the resorts and authorities are being told that the quality of service, amenities and accommodation, which they have pared to the bone to keep prices down, are now unacceptable. The mass package-tour market will never again be on the level of the boom years, and, slowly, the authorities are learning to adjust.

The likely result will be fewer hotels and restaurants at the bottom end of the market, and a distinct improvement in the quality and

level of service and attractions on offer to the visitor. In return, the authorities hope that those who do come to the Costa Brava will have more money to spend.

Some hopes are being pinned on low-cost travellers from the Eastern bloc to take the place of the missing British, German and Dutch visitors who have found alternative holiday destinations. The first few hundred, as invited guests, began to arrive as the first blocks of the Berlin Wall came down. At the other end of the market, many of the larger

properties on the Costa Brava are starting to be snapped up by the increasing number of Japanese companies setting up in Catalonia.

Exemplary resort: Popular both with the comparatively recent arrivals and with two generations of visitors from the rest of Europe and the United States is the highly original resort of S'Agaró, which is described by the Catalan government as "the most intelligently designed tourist phenomenon of the entire Costa Brava, and an example to be followed by other towns". Extremely well served by facilities offering a variety of water sports, golf and horseriding, in addition to two of the most beauti-

Preceding pages: Malgrat holiday flats. <u>Left</u>, S'Agaró in its fashionable heyday. <u>Above</u>, a 1959 guest at La Gavina, Elizabeth Taylor.

ful beaches of the Costa Brava, this small and relatively undeveloped resort is a complete contrast to nearby Sant Feliu and La Platja d'Aro.

Dominating the area, in many senses of the word, is a hotel with a fascinating past, the Hostal de la Gavina. Even though a single room without breakfast runs to around £100, while the "Royal Suite" in high season goes for a cool £500, it is worth visiting just to take in a piece of the Costa Brava's recent history.

The hotel started life as the project of a wealthy Catalan industrialist, Josep Ensesa, who in 1923 spent some of the profits he had made in producing flour and tartaric acid—the fizz in fizzy drinks—on a large plot of

Conca—and employed several devices to make it inaccessible for vehicles or even bicycles, as it still is today.

S'Agaró grew steadily in the next few years, attracting a select band of visitors away from the delights of Monte Carlo or Deauville. Though retaining a somewhat eccentric reputation, the Costa Brava's exposure to the outside world really began during the early 1930s, especially after Madeleine Carroll, the British film actress and star of *The Thirty-Nine Steps*, bought a house on the coast and married Bob Heiskell, the publisher of *Life* magazine. The artistic fraternity was also developing a fad for the rugged coast, many of them visiting the

land nestling between the two popular beaches (which, like all beaches in Spain, remain public). Overlooking the two bays, Ensesa built a small hotel with 15 rooms, bringing in a friend, the Girona architect Rafael Masó, to design the original Gothic-style building. The other friends and business acquaintances who decided to build their own villas on the land, named by the industrialist S'Agaró after the Agaró stream that runs through the area, were obliged to design them in the same style as the original hotel. Finally, Ensesa cut a beautiful promenade, almost a mile long, into the cliffs linking the two bays—Sant Pol and Sa

famous illustrator and artist Josep Maria Sert at his house near Palamós.

Like many of his fellow industrialists, Ensesa exiled himself to France for several years during the civil war, escaping the attentions of the unpredictable anarchist movement. This part of the Costa Brava was one of the last in Catalonia to be taken by Franco's troops. Just after S'Agaró fell, on 10 February 1939, the war in Catalonia was over, and by 1 April resistance in the interior of Spain was finally crushed.

On his return from exile, Ensesa was ordered to change the name of his hotel to *gaviota*, the Castilian equivalent of *gavina*, meaning sea gull. But the wily and confirmed nationalist unearthed a dictionary showing that *gavina* exists in both languages, and he was allowed to retain the original name.

Left in relative peace, Ensesa decided to undertake major work on his hotel to modernise and extend it. Following the death of the original architect, Masó, his collaborator this time was Francesc Folguera, who had made his name contributing to the Poble Espanyol, the re-creation of villages from throughout Spain built for the 1929 Barcelona International Exhibition.

Folguera gave the hotel its present austere and classical appearance, and extended it to

fashionable tag. La Gavina, with its special reputation among the more "popular" resorts launched in the major tourist boom of the 1950s, naturally attracted the richer and more fashionable visitor. It gained brief worldwide notoriety at the end of the 1940s, at least in the popular press, when Ava Gardner, enjoying a fling with a well-known bullfighter, Dominguin, during the making of *Pandora and The Flying Dutchman*, was pursued to La Gavina by her husband-to-be, Frank Sinatra. Out of season, other film stars made their base at the hotel. Among them were Orson Welles, when he was starring in *Confidential Report* (known as *Mr Arkadin* in the US) in 1954, and, five years later,

56 rooms and 16 luxury suites. Ensesa had a passion for collecting antique furniture and fittings, and each of these rooms and suites decorated around these period pieces has its distinctive style. The main entrance lobby is a masterpiece of good taste and architectural innovation. But it is the visitors who give La Gavina its particular caché.

As the rich of Europe regained their taste for travel after World War II, the Costa Brava began to recapture its exclusive and

Left, the elegant, 5-star Hostal de la Gavina, founded by Josep Ensesa, **above**, is a contrast to modern developments **right**.

Elizabeth Taylor and Montgomery Clift, while making *Suddenly Last Summer*.

Ensesa also started a series of prestigious summer concerts, held in a villa he had built nearby, the Senya Blanca, which housed an amphitheatre and featured a loggia overlooking the Mediterranean. Further influences on the resort's British "connection" were due largely to two other men.

The first was Dr Josep Trueta, who exiled himself to Britain after the civil war, and developed his radical new treatment for war injuries, first practised in Spain and then on the war wounded in London and Oxford, where he was awarded a University Chair.

He returned regularly to Catalonia on holiday, when he would visit S'Agaró. In peacetime he treated lesser injuries suffered by members of the British royal family, Winston Churchill and Aristotle Onassis. Word of the resort's beauty soon got round.

The other key person involved was a journalist on London's *Daily Telegraph*, Cedric Salter, who was a friend of Toby O'Brien, a leading spokesman for the Conservative governments of the 1950s and 1960s. Between them, Trueta and Salter brought many prominent members of the party to S'Agaró. Selwyn Lloyd, who held various ministerial posts, visited La Gavina every summer for 15 years and developed a passion for the area. In 1989, a key meeting of European Community Finance Ministers was held there, a reminder of its rich political history.

The tartaric acid factory has now closed down, unable to compete with synthetic methods of producing it, but La Gavina remains in the family's hands. Josep Ensesa, the son of the original owner, now in his seventies, continues to own the hotel. He is married to Dr Trueta's niece, Carmona.

Just 650 ft (200 metres) from La Gavina, another hotel, the S'Agaró, is part of the effort now being made to develop the sophisticated tourist image of the area. Its prices are slightly more accessible than those of its older competitor, and the surroundings of this renovated hotel, in a building owned by one of Ensesa's two daughters, are in a classical style combined with modern facilities. Operated by a consortium which includes a Catalan Member of Parliament, Anna Balletbó, the S'Agaró is fast developing a reputation for drawing the leading lights of the country's economic and social life to its shaded gardens and fine tables.

In the end, though, most visitors to the area stay in the rather more reasonably priced hotels of nearby Sant Feliu or La Platja d'Aro, and visit S'Agaró's beaches for the day, or travel to some of the beautiful villages just a few miles inland. Both La Gavina and the S'Agaró close at the end of October, and re-open in time for the Easter Week rush. But the two beaches—and the villas and streets of S'Agaró itself—are there to see and enjoy all the year round.

Right, Lloret de Mar, the package tourist's paradise and the busiest resort on the coast.

148

Catalonia is a place for outdoor activities all the year round. Its geographical and climatic mix, its beaches, mountains, rivers and forest, are all natural places for recreation and sport. From late May to mid-September even Barcelona seems to be just another seaside town, squeezing a working week from a busy schedule of beach activities. Autumn is the time to hunt wild mushrooms, and from December to April weekends are marked by massive migrations to ski resorts in the Pyrenees. Palm trees grow along the coast; but in parts of these mountains, just two hours away, the snow never melts and midsummer nights can keep campers deep in their down sleeping bags.

Because the activities are so numerous, they cannot be geographically defined. Fishing, for example, extends from the depths of the sea to the tarns and streams of the high Pyrenees; the red-legged partridge can be hunted from the 7,000 ft (2,150 metres) treeline to the flatlands of Lleida; watersports range from seaside windsurfing to white-water kayaking; hang-gliders take off from the mountain tops and pot-holers scramble around underground.

Sometimes the activities make surprising combinations. A "Cerdanya double", for example, might include a morning ski at 8,000 ft (2,600 metres) in one of 13 ski stations within 40 minutes of Puigcerdà (either in France, Andorra or Catalonia), followed by grilled lamb chops next to the Segre on the river valley floor and an afternoon spent fly fishing in one of Europe's finest trout streams.

Tricky peaks: Climbing and hiking both have a large and dedicated following in Catalonia. International expeditions arouse great interest in the local press and the sport is taken seriously by mountaineers venturing among the trickier peaks of the Pyrenees. Most climbers, however, are simply sightseers who don't want to risk life and limb, and the region is rich in spectacular peaks and ranges which they can scale without dangling from pitons or suffering more than

Preceding pages: downhill at Baqueira-Beret. Left, cross-country skiing in Andorra.

blistered feet. Climbs and excursions vary in difficulty and originality; but the more remote and challenging the peak, the greater the rewards of solitude and scenery. Montseny, north of Barcelona, is networked with approaches and trails; the hike from Núria across the Pyrenees to La Molina is more difficult; and the climb from Prat d'Aguiló above Martinet in the Cerdanya up to the top of the rock wall of the Cadí makes the River Segre look no more than a silver thread curling along the valley floor.

Tourist offices, even on the coast, should be able to provide local walking guides. For more ambitious excursions and mountain treks, Ediciones Alpina publishes a series of

and illuminated Roman columns, the remains of the city's acropolis, Mons Taber. The CEC also has a library open to the public with maps and guidebooks for every imaginable excursion.

Gun law: Hunting provides wonderful opportunities to see some of Catalonia's wildest and most beautiful country. Armed with only a dog, a friend and a camera, going after the mere sight of an *isard* (chamois) or *perdiu nival* (snow partridge) inspires the spirit as well as the appetite.

There is nothing to prevent any visitor from joining in the shoot. Registered firearms, accompanied by the appropriate documents and permits from one's own country,

maps to areas such as Montseny, Puigmal, Núria, Serra del Cadí and the Vall d'Aran. In Barcelona the Llibrería Quera (Carrer Petritxol, 2) specialises in *cultura excursionista*, and can provide guidebooks, itineraries and military maps covering every square metre of the hinterland.

Throughout the mountains there are stone refuges (*refugis*) which are looked after by the Centre d'Excursionista de Catalunya. These are simple buildings offering shelter for the night and a fireplace to cook on. The CEC's headquarters in Barcelona is just off Plaça Sant Jaume, at Carrer Paradís 10, and is worth a visit to see the superbly restored

can be lawfully used. The difficult part is finding the place to go, for virtually all Spanish hunting lands are privately leased (visitors will soon notice how much land is marked with *caça* signs). This important detail is best solved by going directly to the local hunting and fishing associations and inquiring about available land to lease. The provincial hunting federations of Barcelona, Tarragona, Girona and Lleida are an important link to these rod-and-gun clubs and can usually direct you to a local "Associació" able to lease or lend land for the day or days you would like to hunt.

The hunting season is from October to

March and it varies slightly from year to year and from province to province. Fifteen-day licences can be obtained from Medi Natural (Carrer Sabino d'Arana, 24), Barcelona, or from the local associations.

Perhaps the finest hunting—certainly the finest eating—in the region is the famed red-legged partridge, which takes off like a rocket and looks after itself well. A feast of redlegs and dry *cava* is delicious. Rabbit is also exquisite and much-hunted. Doves migrating from central Europe to north Africa come in different shapes and sizes (*torcáz*, *tórtola* and *tordo*) and are popular game. In Tarragona's Delta del Ebre wetlands migrating ducks are plentiful, while

pressure. They can be hunted most of the year with the normal licence and local permission to use the land. Wild boar have been known to flourish as close to Barcelona as the Collserola and it is not unknown to see hunters getting off the Metro stations in central Barcelona on their way home from the nearby hills.

Fishing: Fishing in Catalonia can mean spear or deep-sea fishing in the Mediterranean, bait-casting from beaches, big-river trout angling or fly fishing in clear mountain streams.

Sea fishing goes on all the year round and is licence-free. The fresh-water season lasts from late March (normally the 19th) until the

woodcock (*becada*) are found in the Empordà around late November.

Big game: *Capra hispánica*, *muflón* and *rebeco*—different species of mountain goat —can be hunted in special reserves by submitting an application to the Direcció General del Medi Natural a year in advance and winning the subsequent draw. There are special quotas for foreign applicants. Easier to hunt are wild boar which are becoming more numerous despite intense hunting

Left, *Capra hispánica*. <u>Above</u>, Sunday rabbit hunter, Cap de Creus. <u>Right</u>, the new sport of *puenting* in Gerri de la Sal, Lleida.

end of August and two-week non-resident or season licences are available at local fishing associations, some tourist offices and the Medi Natural in Barcelona.

Two of the most important fresh-water fishing centres are at Ponts on the Lleida-Seu d'Urgell road and at Bellver de Cerdanya. Both have excellent public and reserved sections on the Segre.

Trout streams in the Vall d'Aran and in the Cerdanya are dependent on snow run-off and other seasonal conditions. The flow often remains low and clear at the start of the season before the thaw, when low water temperatures and scant insect hatches keep trout activity to a minimum. In April and the first half of May the peaks release a flood, making the rivers high, muddy, fast and unpredictable and all but unfishable. During this period it is best to seek out some local brook less affected by the run-off. In August the waters are usually too low and warm, and trout metabolism is slowed by a reduced oxygen level.

By far the best stream and river angling takes place between mid-May and mid-July, with the very best around the summer solstice. On St John's Eve, each Pyrenean village has its own bonfire, some lit by torches brought down from the highest peaks, and it is not unusual to leave the stream as late as 11

Barcelona's *escullera* or breakwater, and affiliates along the coast from the Delta del Ebre up to the French border. These centres do not specialise in boat charter but they are extremely helpful about the local boating scene.

There are races off the coast all the year round in Optimist, Cadet, Europa, Star, Vaurien, 420, 470, Snipe, Laser, Windsurf, Finn, Hobie Cat, Soling, Tornado and cruising-class craft. José Luis Doreste, the Olympic gold medallist in the Finn class in Seoul in 1988, has been one of the most visible of the crews and skippers preparing here for the 1992 Olympics in Barcelona.

The Catalan *patí* (skate) or *patí a vela*

p.m. The sulphur yellow *ephemerella* mayfly is the typical hatch of the *Nit de St Joan*. It gives excellent visibility long after dark when the towns' festivities are beginning.

Sailing: Maritime Catalonia is a world of its own. Here the seafarer sails, as the late poet and editor Carlos Barral wrote in his *Catalunya des del Mar*, "in the shadow of the old Catalan admirals of the Middle Ages and the sheer rock cliffs of the coast".

That coast is nearly 300 miles (480 km) long and its ports and beaches offer a full range of waterborne activities. The Federació Catalana de Vela (Catalan Sailing Federation) has its school on the port of

(sailing skate) is a locally created and designed one-man catamaran. Tillerless, rudderless and guided by weight distribution, the *patí* has been compared to an "unbridled horse" in winds of Force 4 and over. But in light winds, according to Jorge Lamarca, perennial national champion in the class, any experienced sailor should be able to manoeuvre this 17 ft (5.2 metre) enigma.

Masnou, 30 minutes north of Barcelona, is an important centre for buying, selling or chartering craft, including the *patí a vela*. Roses is the capital of windsurfing, while Castelldefels is an important Hobie Cat base, especially during the winter. Other small craft are popular at all of the 36 clubs and marinas, though boats are more easily come by from October to June than in the summer. The larger clubs are open all the year round and the Associació Nacional de Crucers (National Cruising Association) in Barcelona can be helpful in suggesting itineraries and arranging charters.

Winter sports: From December to May, there is excellent skiing in the Vall d'Aran, La Cerdanya, and in the Vall de Ter above Camprodón and Setcases. Including the neighbouring Pyrenean ski resorts in France and Andorra, there are some 30 alternatives, clearly more *pistes* than most enthusiasts can cover in a lifetime.

in Spain or Andorra because of government subsidies. The trick is to find out, by asking around and eavesdropping in bars, where the snow is abundant and the skiers are not (although spots bruited about as useless often turn out to be just fine, and empty). The Puigcerdà tourist office supplies information, as does the travel agency El Touring in the centre of town.

In the Cerdanya, La Molina and Masella are the ski areas on the Spanish side of the border and, 30 minutes from Llivia or Puigcerdà, they are no closer than Porte, Font Romeu or Puigmal on the French side. The absence of snow and the higher-priced lift tickets often make the offer from France

Andorra offers six winter-sports stations, all within an hour of each other: Ordino-Arcalis, Arinsal, Grau Roig, Pal, Soldeu-El Tarter and Pas de la Casa. Near the French border, Pas de la Casa is on the N20 between La Vella and Puigcerdà and it usually has the most snow. On the other hand, it is often overcrowded.

The French Pyrenees—Chambre d'Aze, Els Angles, Puigmal, Font Romeu, Porte-Puymorens, Puigvalador and Formiguera—are somewhat less expensive than ski areas

<u>**Left**</u>, **endless activity provided by the sea.**
<u>**Above**</u>, **trout fishing in the River Segre.**

and Andorra more attractive; but certainly, if the snow is on the Spanish side, that will be the place to go.

Probably the most spectacular skiing is found in the Vall d'Aran where Baqueira-Beret, the Spanish royal family's favourite, is the top choice. Other good areas include Boí-Taul, La Tuca, Llessui, Port Aine and Super Espot.

The ski areas above Ripoll in the Ter Valley, Núria and Vallter 2000, Catalonia's easternmost slopes, are sometimes the only ones with snow. Artificial snow is becoming indispensable and only a few places have yet to install snow-making technology.

Nordic skiing is also available at Aranser, Beret, Bonabe, Lles, Sant Joan de L'Erm and Tuixén-La Vansa as well as on the French side at Porte-Puymorens, Font Romeu and Pyrenees 2000. Most of the other ski areas also have cross-country sections.

Another speciality in the Pyrenees is mountain skiing, using skins and trekking over high fields and peaks. While the advantages of this approach include no lines or lift tickets, it can be dangerous and guides are recommended.

There are also excellent ice-skating rinks at Andorra la Vella, Puigcerdà, and in Font Romeu. Although the best artificial ice is in Font Romeu, there are high ponds and lakes with natural ice which, used with caution, can be incomparable. Ice hockey games can be seen in Puicerdà and Font Romeu, and there are even old-timers' ice hockey clubs which would be more than happy to let a visitor suit up for a game of shinny.

Weekend snow reports are published every Friday in *El País* newspaper. In Barcelona the Centre Excursionista de Catalunya can also be helpful in confirming published information, as can the Federació Catalana de Sports d'Hivern.

Other activities: Almost anything people do on land, ice or snow, in the air or on and under water can be done in Catalonia. The Olympic movement, a booming sense of economic optimism and Catalan curiosity have made everything possible in this new leisure-time society. Ultralights buzz over Puigcerdà, gliders drift over the Penedès; there is hang-gliding, sky-diving, para-sailing, as well as cycling, horseback riding, kayaking and water-skiing. "Para-penters" leap off cliffs wearing parachutes while other thrill-seekers throw themselves from bridges after attaching themselves to elastic leashes in a sports speciality known as "puenting".

On a less exotic note, squash and tennis courts are widely available to the public, while golf courses are found in and around Barcelona, in Puigcerdà and on the Costa Brava, and are on the increase.

Catalonia's triangle—mountains, sea and plains—placed within reach of six million intense Mediterranean inhabitants is proving to be a sure formula for outdoor specialities of nearly infinite variety.

Right, rafting on the Noguera Pallaresa.

Catalonia is a classic corner of the Mediterranean, where the mountains come down to the sea. On a clear day skiers at Vallter 2000 in the Pyrenees can see the fishing fleet in the Bay of Roses, while visitors to Montserrat might on one side glimpse the mountains of Aragón, and on the other the BalearicIslands way out to sea. There are peaks and ranges all around; there are plateaux and coastal plains; and the agriculture, the flora and fauna are as diverse as the landscapes would have them be.

The region is the size of Maryland, half way between the sizes of Scotland and Wales. This may not sound vast, but it is not easily conquered and some effort is required to seek out its deepest secrets. Roads tend to run north to south, following the rivers that come down from the mountains. Travelling across country, east to west, can involve tortuous winding roads, but such is the price of discovering some fabulous scenery.

The less adventurous may easily be rewarded, too, for behind the coastal resorts, not far from the bright bustle of Barcelona, there are numerous places which are imbued with the distinct flavour of Catalonia, places where men play *boules* in dusty squares beside Romanesque churches, where women sit on balconies sewing, where dogs bark at shadows in the shade, and where the Mediterranean light fills the mountains and farmlands with a warmth you will want to bottle and take home.

Since the middle of the 19th century the region has been divided into four administrative provinces, named after the provincial towns, and, although local administration is shifting more and more towards the 41 *comarques* (small counties), this guide is written province by province. The two most northerly are Lleida and Girona, which share the Pyrenees. In between them is the province of Barcelona, reaching only as far north as the pre-Pyrenees. South of Barcelona and Lleida is the province of Tarragona. The small co-principality of Andorra is included, too, since it borders Lleida, faces south and has Catalan as its official language. Place names are all in Catalan.

Preceding pages: snowy peaks of the Pyrenees in the Alt Urgell; the monastery of Sant Pere de Rodes, Alt Empordà; wine harvest, Penedès; sun and sea on the Costa Brava. **Left**, wedding at Tarragona Cathedral.

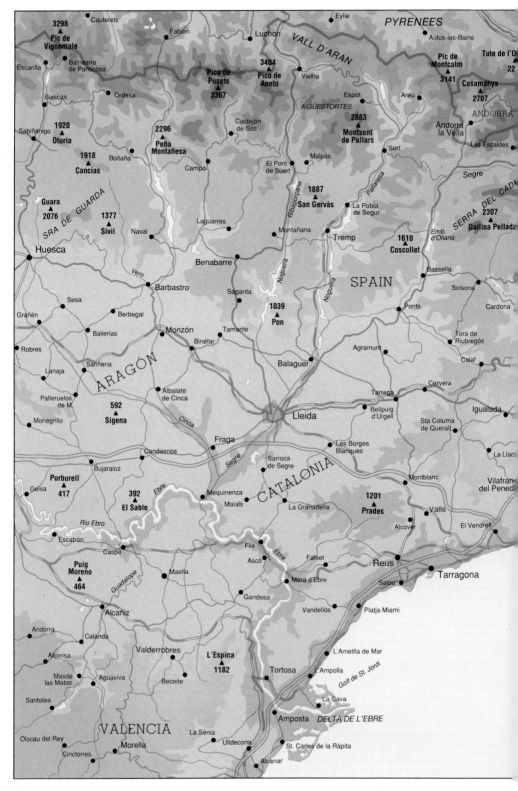

Catalonia

25 miles/ 40 km

Portbou
Estagel
Perpignan
Sournia
Millas
Madres
▲
2471
Thuir
Boule D'Amont
Argelès
Port-Vendres
FRANCE
Collioure
Banyuls
Pic du Canigou
▲
2785
Amélie-les-Bains
ont-Romeu
Mont Louis
La Jonquera
Portbou
Puigcerdà
Cap de Creus
Cadaqués
Puigmal
▲
2913
Camprodón
Figueres
Roses
Castelló d'Empúries
Guardiola de Bergueda
Ripoll
Olot
Fluvià
Banyoles
L'Escala
Viladamat
Torroella de Montgrí
St. Gregori
Girona
Ter
Emb. de Sau
Prats de Lluçanès
Anglès
Cap de Begur
St. Hilari Sacalm
Cassà de la Selva
Palafrugell
Navars
Vic
Sta Coloma de Farners
Llagostera
Palamós
Moià
St. Feliu de Guíxols
SRA DE MONTSENY
St. Feliu de Codines
St. Celoni
Tossa de Mar
Lloret de Mar
Manresa
Blanes

Costa Brava

Granollers
Calella
Terrassa
Arenys de Mar
Mataró
Sabadell
Meresme
torell
Badalona
St. Feliu
Barcelona
Hospitalet de Llobregat
astelldeféls
El Prat de Llobregat (Airport)
Sitges
ova i eltrú

Costa Daurada

171

LLEIDA PROVINCE

Lleida is both the least known of Catalonia's four provinces and the only one that sits squarely inland without even a sniff of the sea. These two factors no doubt account for the generally held impression of the province as a collection of dusty towns on far-off plains, not worth the trip from the coast. In reality, anyone unfamiliar with Lleida could never claim an intimate knowledge of Catalonia.

It is twice as big (4,659 sq. miles, 12,028 sq. km) as any of the other three provinces and its population is less than half. To the north, it touches Andorra and France; to the south and east, Catalonia's other three provinces; and to the west, it lies against Aragón.

The discerning traveller who heads for Lleida's plains and hills will be rewarded with some of Spain's finest touring country. The province contains within its boundaries Catalonia's only national park, its most prestigious ski resorts, best preserved Romanesque churches and some of its most idiosyncratic towns. From spectacular gorges to glorious alpine scenery and from parched plains to the lush Vall d'Aran, Lleida never ceases to impress. With some justification, its inhabitants argue that, in its diversity, Lleida is the most Catalan province of all.

Its culture has been forged out of successive occupations by Iberians, Carthaginians, Romans and Visigoths. Dotting the more southerly parts are hilltop castles, usually of Moorish origin, for the Moors remained in the lower-lying areas longer than they did in much of the rest of Catalonia. Beside them lie the medieval monasteries, chapels and cathedrals that celebrate Ramon Berenguer IV's 12th-century Christian Reconquest.

The dance of darkness and light and the inextricable interweaving of the military, political and ecclesiastical are nowhere more poignantly played out than in Lleida. Touring the province you realise that every cathedral cloister has served as a barracks and nearly every chapel has been razed. Even the inhabitants of the Pyrenees, enjoying both unprecedented wealth and contact with the rest of Europe, like to remind visitors that their land was a battlefield for exiled guerrillas who continued to fight Franco's troops.

The very different conditions on the plains and mountains have produced two distinct cultures and industries. The Pyrenees now rely almost exclusively on tourism while the agricultural plains have developed factories that transform their almond, fruit, cereal and olive crops into juice, jam, wine and oil. Bottling, packaging and canning plants are the new fortifications surrounding most towns.

The main lines of communication run north to south along three roads which follow the three main rivers coming down from the Pyrenees. These are: the **Noguera Ribagorçana**, on the border with Aragón; the **Noguera Pallaresa**, in the centre; and the **Segre**, to the east, which catches both rivers and takes

Left, Bosc de Conangles, Ribagorçana. **Right**, mountain farmer.

their waters on to fill up the Ebre flowing through the province of Tarragona in the south.

Embattled capital: Eighty-five miles (136 km) west of Barcelona, the provincial capital of **Lleida** (pop. 110,000) is the gateway to Aragón and a six-hour A2 toll-road drive from the Atlantic ferry port of Santander. It has cold winters and parched summers and, in spite of its 4,000-year history, the blossoming culture of the coast seems by and large to have passed it by. It is a sober town with little evidence of an entertainments industry, though students do their best to add zip in the dive bars along the Carrer de Sant Carles.

Lleida's favourite claim is that it has suffered more sieges and persecutions for Catalonia than any other city. Girona might make the same claim but nonetheless it is indicative of the proud frontier mentality that still exists. Pompey and Caesar chose to fight out their civil war here; its Moorish governor, Lope ibn-Muhammad, slew Catalonia's founder, Guifré, in a battle nearby;

Napoleon's brother Joseph engaged in rape and pillage at the end of a year-long siege; and, most recently, the city was razed during the civil war.

Perched on a hilltop, rising above walls first erected by the Romans, is the immense old cathedral, **La Seu Vella**, dominating both the city and the plain and casting off its crumbling, beleaguered aspect at night under gentle, flattering illumination. Its construction was begun in 1203 and the layout follows the pattern of a basilica, with three naves, typically wide cross-vault and five apses facing east.

But the cathedral has not been in use since 1707, when Felipe V converted it into a barracks, as part of his retribution on Catalonia for supporting the Habsburgs during the War of Succession. As a result, of all Catalonia's ravaged cathedrals, Lleida's is unquestionably the barest, creating in the visitor a melancholy which is deepened by an awareness of the terrible vandalism it has suffered over the centuries. The high altar has vanished, 14th-century

Fun at a sardana aplec.

paintings in the presbytery are unrecognisable and the chapels that skirt the vast nave are in a similarly poor state. One of the apses, used to store gunpowder, has blown up three times.

The cathedral's Romanesque-Gothic cloister, however, is perhaps the loveliest in Catalonia. Like the cloister at Vic, one of the south-facing portals is open on both sides, providing a panoramic view over the southern plain through which the Segre flows.

Alongside the cathedral are the ruins of the Moorish castle, **La Suda**, later a residence of the kings of Catalonia-Aragón, which Joseph Bonaparte blew up on his departure. The rest of the city flows round the base of the hill like a moat, and its denizens, rather than skirt the hill to reach destinations on the other side, take a lift over the top from the Plaça de Sant Joan.

The **Catedral Nova** was built in the lower town in the second half of the 18th century. A cold, neo-classical building, it has never really won the hearts of the people but it contains some fine Flem-ish tapestries and the city's most celebrated statue, the Virgin of the Bruise—legend says it was so named when a master craftsman, jealous of his apprentice's work, took a hammer to the Virgin's head.

Opposite the cathedral in the Carrer Major is the 15th-century Gothic **Hospital de Santa Maria** which now houses the archives of the Institute of Lleida Studies and the **Archaeological Museum,** containing one of the most important Roman and pre-Roman collections in Catalonia.

The Carrer de Cavallers, off the Carrer Major, was once Lleida's most desirable residence, as can be seen from its fine mansions. A convent has been converted into the **Museum of Modern Art**, containing works by Jaume Morera and other local painters. The Carrer Major leads next to the imposing 13th-century town hall, the city's finest example of late Romanesque secular architecture. The building, once the city jail where the condemned were held before being deposited in the River

Lleida Cathedral cloister.

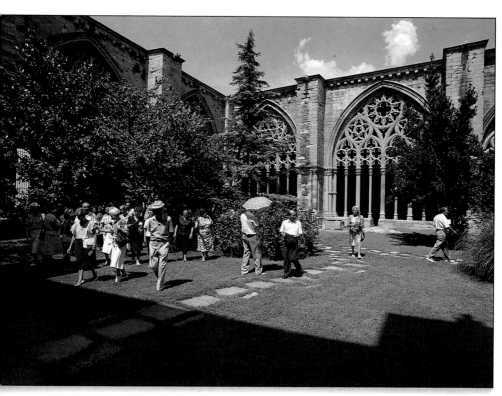

Segre wearing a necklace of boulders, now houses the **Museum of Archaeology and History**.

Other sites worth visiting are the 13th-century Romanesque church of **Sant Martí**, which provides a fitting setting for the **Museum of Medieval Sculpture** (Ronda de Sant Martí), and the transitional church of **Sant Llorenç** (Plaça de Sant Llorenç), behind which is the **Museum of Medieval Painting**.

Wine detour: A westerly 9-mile (14-km) drive on the N240 towards the border with Aragón leads to **Raïmat**, part of the Codorníu wine empire and one of Spain's most important estates. The workers' village lies below a 17th-century castle (originally Moorish) from which the vineyards stretch as far as the eye can see. At the beginning of the century it was a wilderness but Don Manuel Raventós Domènech, with the help of the Catalonia-Aragón canal, transformed it into a model agricultural estate (see *Wine Dynasties*).

The old winery was designed in 1918 by Joan Rubió i Bellver, a pupil of

Gaudí, and its entrance-way was the first in Spain to be constructed of reinforced concrete. The typical Modernist preoccupations with red-brick, ribbed arches and stained glass remind one immediately of the main Codorníu estate in Sant Sadurní d'Anoia, built by Puig i Cadafalch. Opposite is a new winery designed by Domingo Triay and opened in 1988. Its neo-classical triangular marble pillars and glass mirror wall create an impression of a topless pyramid.

North of Lleida, the C1313 heads out through the city's ugly industrial sprawl to **Balaguer**, capital of La Noguera *comarca*. Like Lleida, Balaguer is dominated by a church of considerable girth, the 15th-century Gothic **Santa Maria**, which stands quietly assisted by the metal street-lamp supports and telephone terminals chipped into its façade. Sharing the skyline is the 13th-century **sanctuary of Sant Cristo**, the patron of the city, and between the two churches are part of the old Moorish fortifications and castle, the **Castell Formós**, later used as the residence of the counts of Urgell.

Balaguer is an odd town. A dirty warren of streets, inhabited by a large resident gypsy population, lead down from the Santa Maria to the best shops and squares located in the Carrer Major, Carrer d'Avall and the vast arcaded Plaça del Mercadel. Modern colourful patisseries and delicatessens rub shoulders with bizarre shops selling uncertain products which seem locked in a time warp beneath their Gothic arcades.

The ugly modern sector is confined to the eastern bank of the river where only the long, characterless Passeig de l'Estació redeems the industrial spillage. The **monastery of Sant Domènec** has a fine Gothic cloister and it nestles by the upper bridge opposite the vastly over-starred *parador* (national hotel). The town's major **museum** has a variety of pottery, ironwork, sculpture and glass from around the *comarca*.

Lake land: From Balaguer, the speedy C417 heads due north, following the River Segre and offering some dramatic views, but the L904 provides a diver-

Festival character.

sion to the northwest which is rewarded by a chance to see the ancient abbey of **Bellpuig de les Avellanes**, marvellous views from the **Ager Pass** and the fine collegiate church of **Sant Pere** in **Ager** itself. The road re-joins the C147 near the 11th-century church and castle of **La Baronia de Sant Oisme**. The country around here is favoured by speleologists (those who like to clamber through chasms and caves), hikers and climbers.

The drive continues alongside the Noguera Pallaresa, through the **Pas de Terradets** honeycomb gorge and along a string of man-made lakes which are truly spectacular. A good place for lunch is the Hostal del Llac, overlooking the **Embassament** (reservoir) **de Terradets** with the Serra de Montsec providing the backdrop at **Cellers**. Plans are afoot to turn the whole Montsec range into a protected park. Lunch can be followed up with a detour a few miles up the road to **Guàrdia de Noguera** to visit the ruins of the 10th-century **Mur Castle** and 11th-century church of **Santa Maria**.

Tremp, capital of the *comarca* of El Pallars Jussà, is situated in a large plain and has both a modern bustling commercial centre and old quarter surrounded by what remains of the medieval walls. Don't miss the **Tower of Forques** and the 9th-century **parish church** (restored in the 17th century). Monday is market day. Just outside town, beside the **Embassament de Sant Antoni**, stands the medieval town of **Talarn** which has fortified walls, ancient houses and castle remains.

At the top of this reservoir is **La Pobla de Segur**, surrounded by orchards and running an important hydroelectric industry. From here the C144 goes on a 30-mile (50-km) switchback to **El Pont de Suert** on the border with Aragón. Just before the tunnel that leads into the town, the ruins of the 8th-century monastery of **Lavaix** literally rise from the waters of the **Embassament de Escales**, which flooded the area. The town itself is an interesting mix of old and new (the modern church was built in 1955) and produces rather

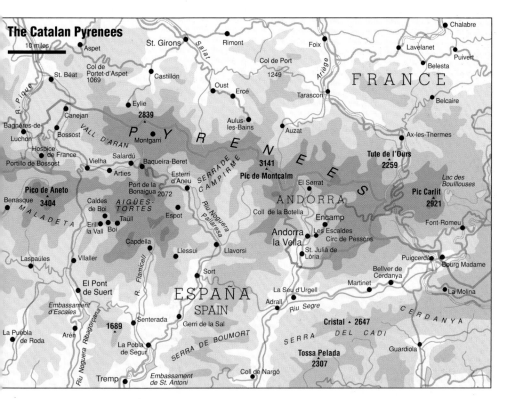

The Catalan Pyrenees

lovely blankets that can be bought cheaply.

Romanesque gems: A short distance beyond Pont de Suert on the C144, a right turn leads alongside the Noguera de Tor up the **Boí Valley**. This valley should not be omitted from anyone's itinerary as it boasts the finest collection of Romanesque churches in Catalonia. Every hamlet has its cluster of medieval homes nestled round a 12th or 13th-century parish church. At **Barruera** there is also a camp site (open 1 April–30 Sept) and a tourist information office.

Particularly noteworthy are the churches of **Santa Eulàlia** at **Erill-la-vall** and **Sant Climent** at **Taüll**, a mile above **Boí**. Both boast exquisite six-storey campaniles. Santa Eulàlia wins by a head but it is Sant Climent that has become something of a shrine, attracting especially large numbers of visitors since it was converted into a museum. Its original, celebrated fresco of the Pantocrator is in the Museum of Catalan Art in Barcelona but there is a faithful reproduction in the central apse. Gracing the main square in Taüll is a larger 12th-century church, **Santa Maria**.

Aigüestortes Park: The Boí Valley is the latest area to go ski crazy and one hopes that its distinctive character will not be buried under the anonymity of new resorts. Its chances of survival are improved by the valley's other major claim to fame, as a gateway to the bordering **Aigüestortes Park**. This is the only national park in Catalonia (see *Pyrenean Wildlife*) and one of only nine in the whole of Spain. At the head of the Boí Valley is the thermal springs and spa of **Caldes de Boí** where many walkers on this side of the park base themselves at the four-star Hotel Manantial, soaking their aching limbs in between sorties into the park. The path into the park is just a mile away and reached either on foot or by "jeep taxis".

The park has both demanding and undemanding walks, dramatic scenery, wild boar, Pyrenean chamois and golden eagles. In spring it is coloured by red mountain rhododendron, yellow

Raft festival, Noguera Pallaresa.

gentian and wild lilies. The flow of water continues its recurring mantra, cascading in waterfalls over gnarled rocks, rediscovering old courses over man-made paths and gathering again and again in the deep, still waters of the tarns. Dotting the park are eight *refugis* for moderate overnight stops.

Aigüestortes means "tortuous waters", a description which encompasses the 200 lakes, waterfalls and torrents that twist and turn below the park's mountainous peaks on the southern slopes of the Pyrenees. It is located at the junction of five mountain ranges and covers 40 sq. miles (105 sq. km). The two valleys, **La Vall de Boí** and the eastern **La Vall d'Espot**, are connected by a walkable pass. To visit both valleys by road, however, means taking a 62-mile (100-km) detour back down the valley, up the N230 and through the 3-mile (5-km) **Vielha Tunnel**, along the **Vall d'Aran** on the C142 and over the **Port de la Bonaigua** to **Espot**.

The base for walking tours on the eastern side of the park, Espot is split into two distinct hamlets, **Salou** and **Obago**, from the bad old civil war days when the Nationalists, appropriately enough, lived on the right bank of the river and the Republicans on the left. Simmering jealousies, rivalries and unforgiven crimes continue to bubble below the surface, kept under control by the amazing bonding qualities of the pesetas the national park attracts. The town itself (pop. around 350) has a good deal of charm, with its typically Pyrennean parish church, rustic, bare-brick homes, sheep pens filled with domestic deer and pervading wood smoke.

On the park's eastern flank the major walks all start out from **Lake Sant Maurici**. To the north a necklace of lakes lead up to **Agulles d'Amitges**—*agulles* means "needles" and it gets its name from the prismatic effect of its splintered mountain peaks. The most dramatic alpine scenery, however, is to be found in the south, skirting the darkest and highest tarn, **Estany Negre**.

Salt beds: From Espot a road of more potholes than tarmac descends 4 miles

Lazy days of summer, Lleida.

(6 km) to another beautiful lake, **Embassament de la Torrassa**, and the C147, which follows the course of the Noguera Pallaresa river. Some 8 miles (13 km) south of Sort, a bridge crosses the river and disappears into the medieval alleyways of **Gerri de la Sal**. The town takes its name from the terrace of salt beds on its north side. In spite of the plentiful salt springs in the Catalan Pyrenees, this is the region's only extraction project.

Nestling in the steep wooded hills of the nearby **Collegats Gorge** is the abandoned 12th-century **monastery** of **Santa Maria**, which is usually open. Inside, the three tall naves are flooded by a warm orange light filtering through the upper windows, but the frescoes on the ceilings of the three apses are in poor condition. The drive back down to La Pobla de Segur through the gorge is sublime.

From Sort the C146 to **La Seu d'Urgell** is a 33-mile (52-km) rollercoaster over a high pass offering fine views and car sickness. This town of 10,000 inhabitants is 6 miles (10 km) from Andorra to the north, and 15 miles (24 km) from the Cerdanya to the east. It was made a bishopric by the Visigoths in the 6th century and its lengthy history as an episcopal see has been interrupted only by a brief period of Moorish rule.

It is a quite extraordinary town. From its ancient grain measures and bizarre shop fronts under Gothic arcades, to the magnificent cathedral, cloister and museum, Seu d'Urgell is both the Catalan Pyrenees' most important town historically and also the most fascinating for the visitor. Ancient and dingy, it has never had its medieval buildings sandblasted or wrapped in mothballs but instead it has been allowed to breathe unselfconsciously.

The **old quarter** has a cluster of outstanding buildings: private homes of the Borxi family and the Anti-Pope, Pere de Luna, and the Casa del Pelegri. The 19th-century **Episcopal Palace**, with valuable archives, is the residence of the Bishop of Urgell, who is also Co-Prince of Andorra. The fine state of the **cathedral** remains a wonderful tribute to the Lombardic workmen who built it and also to the staggering egotism and perseverance of the great medieval churchbuilders. Three cathedrals were consecrated on this site within 300 years, the present one being completed towards the end of the 12th century. Above the central doorway is a frieze of gruesome monsters that are overcome by the Church Triumphant. On the exterior walls of the side aisles, and encrusted in the arches and columns inside, are the Romanesque "bread rolls" of Dalí's museum in Figueres.

The imposing interior, which follows an Italian model unique in 12th-century Catalan architecture, consists of three aisles and a large transept whose rear wall has four of the five apses embedded in it. The 124-ft (38-metre) nave is unusually high (68 ft/21 metres), creating an overall impression of grandeur, strength and endurance. The beautiful central apse houses the revered Romanesque statue of Santa Maria d'Urgell.

Piped church music plays in the 13th-century cloister, which is particularly **Gerri de la Sal, the salt centre.**

peaceful and harmonious and in a good state of preservation. In the western portico are the entrances to the sublime, purple-stoned 11th-century **chapel of Sant Pere** (also known as Sant Miquel) and the excellent **Diocesan Museum** (where a nasty glass *mirador* or view point rudely interrupts the continuity of brick above the cloister). Among the treasures inside are the first map ever made of the Pyrenees and a most beautiful 10th-century copy of the *Apocalipsis* by Beatus of Liébana.

The *parador* is one of the better ones, despite its lack of view and lowly three-star status. It is worth a visit to see the extraordinary hanging gardens that have been created out of an old cloister. Nearby is an impressive 19th-century red-brick seminary, still in use. A market is held in the town on Tuesdays and Fridays.

Segre Valley: The River Segre is joined by the Valira at La Seu d'Urgell, and the two fast-flowing rivers are becoming increasingly attractive for white-water sports. It is the chosen site

for the Olympic kayak events. The C1313 follows the Segre south and after 15 miles (24 km) reaches **Organyà**, which offers further evidence of this region's historical importance, for this is where the *Homilies*, the first known written Catalan, came from.

The Segre spills into the **Embassament d'Oliana**, and just beyond this reservoir the L301 leads off to **Solsona**, past **Castellar de la Ribera**, which has attractive castle ruins and an 11th-century church, **Sant Julià de Ceuró**, one of 90 Romanesque churches in the *comarca* of El Solsonès. The fortifications of its capital, Solsona, have seen better days but still manage nine towers, a moat and three gateways. In the 16th century it was an episcopal see and a prosperous city.

Inside the city walls are fine mansions of the nobility and the 12th-century **cathedral** which has three finely arched vaulted naves, three apses, Baroque facade and a Romanesque statue of the Virgen del Claustro. The **Bishop's Palace** has an important

Cerdanya mare in the snow.

Diocesan Museum containing prehistoric and medieval exhibits.

The C1313 continues to follow the Segre, and after 8 miles (12 km) reaches **Ponts** and its 11th-century church. Nearby are the ruins of the Benedictine priory of **Santa Maria de Gaulter**.

Generalitat's birthplace: The L313 heads east across country for some 25 miles (40 km) through a succession of small villages that lead eventually to the hillside town of **Cervera**. Reconquered by Berenguer Borrell from the Moors in the 11th century, it was self governing during the 13th and 14th centuries and was awarded the status of city in 1702, which it still retains despite its present population of only 6,444. It was here that Felipe V built a university after closing Catalonia's other universities following the War of Succession. A four-day fair is held here in September.

Cervera is a reasonably important trade and industry outpost. The **Museu Duran i Sanpere** has a fine collection of 16th-century pottery and Iberian and Roman exhibits. Also worth taking a

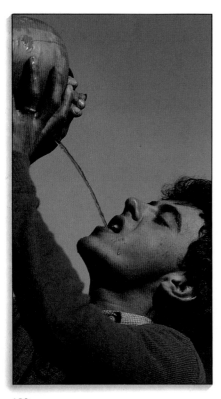

look at are the 18th-century **Paeria** (town hall), the transitional churches of **Santa Maria** and **Sant Antoni** and the **medieval quarters** around the Carrer Major and Carrer de les Bruixes. One house on the Carrer Major is of particular historical importance: this was where the Generalitat de Catalunya was established in 1359 and, 10 years later, the marriage contract between Fernando of Aragón and Isabel of Castile was signed.

The Urgell plain: Nearby is the town of **Tarrega** (pop. 11,000), located in the fertile plain of Urgell. It is an important commercial centre but it also has a thriving arts scene with schools of music, arts, crafts, dance and drama, and a theatre festival in September. There are some fine civic buildings, such as the 17th-century town hall, an archaeological museum, park, castle and Monday market.

To the south on the C240 is **Verdu**, which has medieval castle remains and a Gothic church. But it is best known for its pottery industry. Its traditional earthenware is black and its pitchers once supplied most of Catalonia. The delightful medieval village of **Guimera**, centred around the remains of a castle and fortifications, lies nearby, as do the Gothic monastery of **Vallsanta** and the convent of **Vallbona de les Monges** (one of the "Cistercian Triangle": Poblet is just a few miles away in the next province, see *Tarragona* chapter). Heading back towards Lleida, the only other town of any size is **Les Borges Blanques**, which is renowned for its olive oil. The town has a sprinkling of attractive 18th-century mansions, a Tuesday market, an ethnological museum and an important olive festival in December when the olives are picked.

The 19th-century **Canal d'Urgell** flows through the town and on to Lleida on the final leg of its 155-mile (250-km) irrigation route, which began on the Segre near Ponts. From the moist mountains, it has arrived where it is needed, on the dry, inhospitable plains best visited in spring when the almond groves carpet the land with their blossom.

Left, a long, refreshing drink. Right, La Seu d'Urgell in the last century.

VALL D'ARAN

The jagged peaks that snarl protectively around the Vall d'Aran kept this high valley isolated for centuries. With no link to the outside world until 1924, when the corniche road over the 6,560 ft (2,000 metres) **Bonaigua Pass** (C142/C147) was completed, this extreme northwest corner of Catalonia remained virtually cut off from the rest of Spain. Travel beyond the valley continued to be daunting during winter until the **Túnel de Vielha** was blasted under the mountains in 1948.

Driving through this passage is formidable even today: enormous ventilators rust and drip, and a line of overhead lights show nothing but grey cement for 3 miles (5 km). Emerging from the grim tunnel is a revelation. Suddenly there is the beautiful narrow valley stretching ahead for 30 splendid miles (50 km).

Inaccessible for so long, the Vall d'Aran is genuinely rustic. The local dialect, Aranese, is a variant of Gascon, and much closer to Provençal than to Catalan. Most of the locals also speak Spanish, Catalan and French. More than three dozen small villages, built of granite and slate, cluster around 12th-century Romanesque church towers. These hamlets are woven with a network of streams, often frozen in the winter months. Shaggy white Pyrenean shepherd dogs romp in the cobbled streets beneath carved wooden balconies and trails lead from the hamlets, through beechwoods and pine, up to the high meadows, frequented by cross-country skiers, hikers and horse riders.

Royal ski resort: At the eastern edge of the Vall d'Aran, walled off by the very tallest peaks, is Spain's foremost ski station, **Baqueira-Beret**. Baqueira is 9 miles (14 km) east of the main town of **Vielha** (Viella in Aranese) on the C142 and Beret is up a turning on the left. The multi-storey hotels and apartments are dwarfed by the mountains. Most are modern versions of the traditional stone-and-slate, stepped-gable buildings, accented with carved wood.

Baqueira has steep chutes through the firs and there is a helicopter service to distant summits for the chance, at a price, to cut the first tracks on a pristine mountainside. Afterwards, tired muscles can be soaked in thermal springs, discovered by the Romans.

The Baqueira-Beret crowd consists of avid skiers and the families of sporty Spanish socialites and is surprisingly uncosmopolitan. Many drive up from Barcelona, while others cross the French border just 25 miles (40 km) away. The Spanish royal family have a chalet in Baqueira village and ski during the season as frequently as duty permits, from December to April.

Cosy restaurants: At night, the entire valley takes on an exuberant quality as sunburnt skiers descend to seek taste thrills. Baqueira sophisticates, independent Nordic skiers and intermediates who prefer the smaller local resort, **Tuc-Betrén**, just outside Vielha, are all ravenous by 9 p.m. To cater for them, clever entrepreneurs have turned farmhouses in many of the villages off the

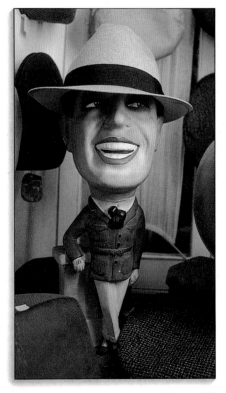

main road into split-level restaurants. **Arties**, about 3 miles (5 km) west of Baqueira, has two of the most innovative restaurants. Casa Irene, which faces the *parador* (state hotel), sets the standard with its house speciality: duck with truffles. Basque seafood is best at Patxiku Kintana. Wine lists everywhere feature the best Spanish vintages alongside some French labels.

Summer idyll: Although the Vall d'Aran has obvious appeal for snow sports enthusiasts, it is not just a winter resort. In summer the meadows come alive with butterflies which hover like levitating wildflowers, and ramblers pick pocketfuls of raspberries and wild strawberries. Climbers, hikers, hunters and anglers come to cool off, and many head into the hinterland on horseback or in Land-Rovers, whose engine noises are drowned by the sound of 100-ft (30-metre) cataracts.

Architecture buffs who want to check out the Romanesque churches in the valley will be intrigued by the border village of **Bossost**, on the Spanish side of the western **Portilló Pass**. Small votive chapels close to the village, near the banks of the Garonne river, are rather austere in comparison to the fine 12th-century Lombardic church. Hefty round pillars support the vaulted roof and the two portals are carved deeply. One shows the Creator with his handiwork, the sun and the moon.

Moving on to **Vielha** in search of further Romanesque treasures may be disappointing. The parish church of **San Miquel** holds the Mig Aran Christ, a wooden image from the 12th century, and the octagonal belfry and carved doorway are impressive. Yet the honky-tonk of a resort town is beginning to intrude on this pretty *comarca* capital, and the plate-glass and bright signs detract from the scenery. The traffic clogs at the junction of two main roads and the smell of diesel pervades. Nonetheless, there are still spires and slate roofs, and the merest sprinkling of snow brings a solemn beauty to Vielha.

The tourist centre here can advise which of the forest tracks will be pass- **Vielha, the valley's main town.**

able by car during your stay. There is also a riding school close by which can arrange excursions. Also within easy reach are examples of Romanesque or early Gothic churches at **Gausac**, **Vilac**, **Betrén**, **Betlan**, **Escunhau** (Escunyau) and **Casarilh** (Casarill).

These heavy hewn stone buildings, many with a separate campanile, resemble those of Lombardy. Frescoes cover the smooth inside walls, and light for the worshippers enters through side lancets. Stained glass came later, with the Gothic influence.

Near the **Bonaigua Pass**, beyond Baqueira, **Salardú's** ancient church of **Sant Andreu** is constructed over the ruins of an even earlier castle, and there are traces of fortifications ringing the pretty village. The tall bell-tower dates from the 13th century, but the detailed wooden crucifix inside was carved nearly 100 years earlier. Neighbouring **Unya** and **Tredòs** also have distinguished religious architecture, but hiking above Unya past the ghost town at **Montgarri** to the sanctuary and cascade is more inspiring. Every 2 July, the hermitage holds a traditional *romeria*. Salardú is also the base for an exhilarating hike to a mountain lake, the **Llacs Colomers**. The **Llacs Saburedo** are reached from Tredòs, where there is a little hot spring.

Seasonal variations: The Vall d'Aran is a holiday spot with tremendous social cachet, but the winter season is a bit tricky. By mid-March, snow coverage is pretty certain on every run, and the slopes won't be mobbed. Try to avoid Carnival Week in February, when the slopes teem with French schoolchildren. Easter Week is the height of the season, so book early and be prepared for price hikes.

Four remote refuges are open for use during most of the year and there are four camping sites. The best restaurants close for at least part of May and June, and again in November. If you need solitude, this is the time to come, though it is apt to be muddy. Off-season, choose early September to coincide with the *festa major* in Vielha.

Dog days of summer, Vielha.

ANDORRA

For a long, silent millennium since, legend claims, it was founded by Emperor Charlemagne in gratitude to local folk for guiding his army through the mountains, Andorra was forgotten territory. This craggy outpost of 181 sq. miles (468 sq. km), with Europe's highest and most remote capital, was snowblocked for half the year.

Wedged below the 7,900-ft (2,400-metre) Envalira Pass between France and Spain, belonging to neither but with a topographical and commercial tilt towards the south, tiny Andorra woke up in the mid-20th century to its potential as a tourist attraction and a tax haven. Today, no one has to make a tax return. The only direct personal tax is the *foc i lloc* (hearth levy) which, even in the most exacting of the country's seven small administrative parishes, amounts to little more than 5,000 pesetas (around £25).

Andorra has one of the world's oldest constitutional documents, dating from 1278. Four elected representatives from each parish make up the General Council of the Valleys which sits in the Casa de Vall, a 16th-century fortified mansion in the old quarter of the capital, Andorra la Vella. Here, too, justice is dispensed much as it was in the feudal past. The judge investigating a murder, for example, three times exhorts the body to disclose the culprit's identity. Finally he says: "The corpse that does not answer is truly dead." Andorra's political and electoral systems are seeded with similar curios, which have prompted calls for reform.

In the 13th century, as a result of squabbles and marriage pacts on either side of the watershed, suzerainty of this co-principality was divided equally between the Spanish bishop of Urgell and the successors of the counts of Foix, a title which has now passed to the presidents of France. The price of independence is a nominal annual tribute of the equivalent of a few pounds sterling paid alternately to each co-prince.

Both French and Spanish currencies are legal tender (although the Andorran government calculates its finances in pesetas) and the official language is Catalan. Conversion tables to pesetas are stuck on petrol pumps that tot up in francs. The *postes* box stands next to the yellow tub for *correus*, but no stamp is required for internal correspondence. Andorran television relays three channels from France, two from Spain and TV3 in Catalan. The national flag splices red with yellow with blue.

Andorra's 46,166 inhabitants (first subjected to official census in 1989) have one of the world's top life expectancy rates and one of Europe's highest *per capita* incomes. Immigration doubled the population between 1975 and 1990 and less than a quarter now qualify for coveted Andorran nationality. Although widely recognised internationally, by an historical quirk the principality has never been accorded full statehood. Even today, Andorran passports are not valid in Japan. More than 54 percent of the population are

Preceding pages: Pas de la Casa, last stop before France. Left, winding over the border at the fiendish Envalira Pass. Right, pastoral scenes shoppers fail to find.

Spaniards running businesses for which they are allowed their own doorplates only if they have been resident for more than 20 years. A growing expatriate community—among them about 1,000 Britons—is colonising the La Massana Valley. Many are former residents of Spain who have resettled out of reach of post-Franco tax reforms.

Shopping scrum: At least 70 percent of all businesses is devoted to retailing. Shops squashed along the valley floor at the confluence of the North and East Valira rivers are the goal of the majority of the 10 million visitors who come here throughout the year. They see the principality as one huge, tax-free bazaar and the most adventurous reach only as far as the larger stores' top floors.

Despite enormous variety, most goods are little cheaper than across the borders, but the coachloads still flood in. Sacks of sugar, drums of dried milk, Dutch cheeses, French aspirins, umbrellas from Taiwan, designer trainers, cigarettes and booze—all are scooped up in bulk and carted off, downhill, past Customs, together with (sometimes declared) cameras, watches and electronic hardware.

Top shopping is concentrated around Avinguda Meritxell in **Andorra la Vella** and Avinguda Carlemany in the neighbouring town of **Escaldes**. Hiper, Escala and Andorra 2000 stores are good territory for bargains, but a scrum. Pyrenees is larger and more exclusive, with French labels in both food and clothes departments. The Papereria Sol stationery shops are packed with novelties. There are sanity-saving car parks adjacent to the leading stores.

In **Sant Julià de Lòria** and **Pas de la Casa**, close to both frontiers, there are supermarkets for final purchases before joining the exit queue which, at peak times in high season (either sunny or snowy), can last four hours as cars are individually inspected at Customs. Shops are open from around 9.30 a.m. until 8 p.m. each day and only selected boutiques close after lunch on Sunday.

Mountain peace: Way above that high-street scrum, the other face of Andorra

The bustling shopping streets in Escaldes, centred around Avinguda Carlemany.

unfolds: the high land, glorious unspoilt country the masses do not penetrate and casual passers-through barely raise their eyes to see. Here is trout fishing, climbing, trekking and other summer pastimes amid glacial lakes and peaks with profiles as sharp as cut crystal. With snow from December to April, there is fine skiing on 124 miles (200 km) of *pistes* at five stations. Roads run to the very foot of the slopes, making exploring easy all year round.

After Easter, alpine flowers poke through melting snowdrifts to signpost walking country *par excellence*. First to show are the Pyrenean buttercup, the pink-belled soldandella and the spring gentian. Andorra's national emblem, the white *grandalla* or poet's narcissus, swathes meadows at the end of May. In June up to 350 species of flora from both the central and eastern Pyrenees run riot over pastures, valleys and rock screes.

Two *grandes routes* traverse the country without dropping below 4,265 ft (1,300 metres). GR7 runs through the dramatic **Cercle de Pessons** bowl of

lakes in the east, then crests on the southern rim to follow the ancient mule track down the Madriu torrent to Escaldes, a hot-water spa even in Roman times. Still inaccessible to cars, the **Madriu Valley** is a haven for ptarmigans, capercaillies, snow finches, ring ouzels and golden eagles.

The GR11 enters from France by the **Tristaina Peak** in the northwest, skirts the glacial lakes in its lap and tumbles with the headwaters of the North Valira below the Arcalís snowfield to the hamlets of **El Serrat** and **La Cortinada**. Here, the chapel of Sant Martí, with fine frescoes, is an outstanding example of local, Romanesque architecture. The route then climbs away to the sweep of the **Coll d'Ordino**. These are hikes for seasoned walkers.

Rudimentary overnight facilities can be had at 21 upland refuges. Maps and full details of these and less strenuous excursions are available from computerised tourist information booths in the main village of each parish.

Nudging Andorra's western border is

Stores offer variety, but prices are not much cheaper than in either France or Spain.

the saddle of **Coll de la Botella**, which tops the Lleidan valley of **Setúria**, and **Canòlic**, above the only road to the Spanish hamlet of **Os**. This is country for nature lovers, facilitated by tracks trodden by smugglers for centuries.

Around Sant Julià, tobacco plants grow on meagre pockets of fertile soil missed by the raking fingers of the Ice Age. Andorra makes licensed American and British brands from imported leaf and local cultivation. But now there are fears that revised EC Customs agreements may send the profitable tobacco industry up in smoke.

Kitchens and gardens: Tucked under Andorra's northern ridge is the lovely **Sorteny Valley**. This wild rock garden is the domain of little, peaty frogs and cropping horses which are wintered in the old stone *bordes* where homesteaders lived on the upper floor, warmed by the animals' body heat and dropping fodder down into the mangers below. Many of these stables have been converted to restaurants featuring chops seared on a hot slate—*a la llosa*. The

best of the *bordes* do offer authentic local fare in agreeable surroundings but others, seeing easy money, can lay scant claim to kitchen expertise.

The lie of this land, split by valleys and gorges, has traditionally dictated the characteristics of the cooking. Rough, honest ingredients such as herbs, forest mushrooms, root vegetables, trout, capons, hogs and game are staples of hearty recipes like thyme soup, a hefty vegetable fry-up called *trinxat*, *bringuera* brawn, cured ham with honey and vinegar, jugged hare, venison and wild boar, and a robust stew of pumpkin or dried eel (from the days when carriage of fresh fish was out of the question). There is also *escudella barrejada*, dolloped from a cauldron of vegetables, noodles, meatballs, blood sausage and rabbit that was the peasants' midday meal, left to cook itself.

Nowhere in Andorra has the Gallic influence been better employed than in the clutch of restaurants catering for more sophisticated palates. Several are headed by French chefs. Fresh *foie gras*, *primeurs*, *langoustes*, *filet mignon* and fine cheeses and wines contribute to truly *haute cuisine* at establishments such as Versailles or Chez Georges in Andorra la Vella.

With the threat of 1992 and the abolition of border controls, the Andorran government has embarked on a major programme to attract tourists. Projects, either in hand or under survey, include a third customs post (at **Setúria**) to decongest Spanish traffic, a tunnel under the fiendish **Envalira Pass**, an airport and a tobacco museum. Joint capital is financing the ski centre of **Els Cortals d'Encamp**, due for completion for the 1992 season. The most ambitious project involves building a luxury resort on **La Comella** plateau, to the east of Andorra la Vella. From the village square, lifts will run up to a new ski station spread over 22 sq. miles (56 sq. km) that is designed to become Andorra's leading ski area. When eventually linked to slopes in the parishes of Encamp and Canillo, it will be possible to whoosh from Spain, over the shoulders of Andorra, right into France.

Left, rural spire. **Right**, crumbling crucifix, Sant Joan de Caselles.

197

From snowy peaks to riverine valleys, from lush mountain meadows to the rugged rocks that tumble into the sea, the Pyrenees are the home of the most varied wildlife in Spain. There are hungry raptors, unique butterflies, basking snakes, playful goats and even, very occasionally, brown bears.

The area marks the northern range of many Mediterranean species and the southern limit of many European and even sub-Arctic ones. It is a key spot on the main west European migration route for birds of passage, and more than 15 different birds of prey breed here. In spring and summer a wealth of wildflowers includes several species of mountain orchid.

In spite of the proliferation of ski resorts, winter weekend hunters and summer hikers, the Catalan Pyrenees remain relatively unspoilt. There are other constant dangers, such as forest fires and excess felling, but the gradual abandonment of *masies* (farmhouses) and the arable land around them is making the areas of natural habitat larger and more woody.

The Catalan Pyrenees are one of the few areas in Europe where naturalists can get a real feeling of "discovery". Some lesser-known species' ranges may be plotted; hitherto unrecorded butterflies or orchids may still be found. For instance, it was only recently that breeding dotterel (a red-breasted wader) and Tengmalm's owl were discovered here. There is plenty to see for casual nature lovers as well as those who have done their homework. Information, reading material and local nature associations can all help.

There are several nature reserves in the Catalan Pyrenees. Their legal status ranges from "National Park" (Aigüestortes), where conservation regulations are very strict, to "Natural Parks" (Cadí-Moixeró, Zona Volcànica de la Garrotxa), "Hunting Reserves" (La Cerdanya, Vall Cardós, Vall Farrera, Tossal de l'Orri, Vall d'Aneu, Vall d'Aran) and "Natural Landscape Areas" (Pedraforca), where the degree of conservation is not so intense. Because of the relatively recent introduction of environmental policies, many of the parks are still subject to enlargement. Ecological groups are constantly pressing the Catalan government to create more parks and expand existing ones.

Aigüestortes: The Vall d'Aran is the only north-facing valley in Catalonia. The river that runs up the valley (the Garonne) flows out into the Atlantic at Bordeaux. The valley is verdant and rainfall is three times greater than in the Empordà 105 miles (170 km) to the east. Fine pastures, beech and mountain pine forests predominate, but the area suffers from intense year-round tourism.

Just to the south of the Vall d'Aran is the Parc Nacional de Sant Maurici i Aigüestortes, one of the most interesting nature reserves in western Europe. Sub-alpine mountain pine and fir forests are often carpeted with splendid rhododendron bushes which produce a marvellous pink summer bloom. Peaks

reaching 7,500 ft (2,300 metres) are dotted with scree and alpine meadows and beneath the twin granite peaks known as Els Encantats (the enchanted orbs), the spectacular symbol of the park, is the beautiful Estany de Sant Maurici.

As in other Pyrenean areas, the legendary chamois (*isard* in Catalan) may here be seen on the scree or among the rocks on slopes above 3,825 ft (1,500 metres) in summer, descending to 3,280 ft (1,000 metres) in winter. It has short horns that stick vertically upwards with a graceful backward hook at the tip. Its head is white-ish yellow with two dark face patches which reach from the snout to the eyes and ears, giving it a masked appearance. It is just over 3 ft (1 metre) long, less than 1 metre tall and is entirely vegetarian.

The chamois is a playful creature. It can be seen sliding down snowy slopes and scrambling up again to have another go. Although once rare, reserve areas were created for its safe reproduction in the upper Núria, Cardós and Farrera valleys in the early 1970s. It is now doing very well and seems to be spreading into lower areas, suggesting that, as in the case of the brown bear and the wolf (now extinct in the Pyrenees), it has only lived in high mountain areas because of persecution. The chamois' relative, the Spanish mountain goat, is found only in the Ordesa Park in neighbouring Aragón.

The protection of the rare brown bear is more difficult. In severe winters, bears come down to the valleys on either side of the frontier in search of food. They have been known to take calves and are seen as vermin by many farmers who will not hesitate to shoot them on sight. Government compensation has as yet proved ineffectual and numbers of bears have dwindled to about 20 in the whole Pyrenean area. Little more than a handful are now to be found in Catalonia and, unless strict measures are introduced, they will suffer the same fate as the wolf.

One splendid species that you are more likely to see is the bearded vulture. Although there are reckoned to be only

Preceding pages: a chamois or *isard*; vipers and whip snakes provide food for eagles. **Left,** the Tengmalm's owl.

about 40 pairs in the whole Pyrenean range, Aigüestortes is a regular breeding site. The species is distinguished from other vultures by its flight silhouette: a black, diamond-shaped tail and dark wings which are more slender than those of the more common Griffon vulture. In contrast to the tail and wings, however, the body is a pale buff colour, and the face, in good sunlight, will be seen to be white.

The "bearded" effect should also be visible to those with good binoculars. It resembles a huge falcon as it glides along the mountain tops, barely moving its wings. It breaks open bones by dropping them from a great height on to rocks, feeding on their marrow, hence its name in Catalan: *trencalòs* (bonebreaker). The rugged mountainsides and cliffs of the Pyrenees are its last stronghold in Europe.

Although until only recently it was thought that the range of the Tengmalm's owl was limited to northern Europe and the Alps, the discovery of breeding birds at various sites in the Pyrenees has proved otherwise. Its very secretive habits, and the fact that it calls only when snow makes its haunts inaccessible, had enabled the species to be overlooked by birdwatchers in its high pine and fir forest habitat. Now ecologists are busy checking its range, seeking the Generalitat's protection for the woods it breeds in and putting up nesting-boxes.

Butterflies are another speciality of the Pyrenees. Some interesting and beautiful species live high up in the mountains. *Zygaena osterodensis*, a rare black-and-red species, is present up to 5,500 ft (1,700 metres) and is active in June and July. Two species of *Parnasius apollo* are to be found, ranging from 2,500 ft (760 metres) up to the alpine meadows at the summit. The spectacular swallowtail flits through the valleys.

The Cadí-Moixeró: Farther to the east is the Cadí-Moixeró Natural Park. The Cadí mountains, which run parallel to the Pyrenees, are geologically different from the main range but the limestone

Bearded vulture.

cliffs of their north face make them no less impressive. The Cadí massif, breached by a tunnel, acts as a great divide between the marvellous Cerdanya Valley, which resembles Switzerland, and the rugged, pine-clad Berga area. Along with Aigüestortes, this is a large and well-known Pyrenean park, but it is drier here and more suitable for Scotch than mountain pine.

The Cadí is an overlap zone which north European and Mediterranean species both enjoy. In this sense, the Cadí is an excellent place to observe the two kinds of chough found in the Pyrenees: the common chough, which can also be seen in parts of Wales, and the rather more exotic southern European alpine chough.

The common chough is a bird that appears to be declining in Europe. Several Oxford college shields depict choughs on college towers, suggesting that, as in some southern European cities today, the species used to breed on towers in England. These days, choughs are almost always associated with cliffs and ravines, not necessarily at great altitudes. They breed in crannies on the rock face. The jet-black common chough has red legs and a fine red beak. It is larger than a blackbird but smaller than a carrion crow. Its most distinctive feature is the gruff pealing call it utters on the wing. In the Cadí, chough have to watch for the aggressive peregrine falcon that also breeds on the cliff.

Alpine chough are normally seen above the 4,900-ft (1,500-metre) mark. They also breed on cliffs, but outside the breeding season they are often seen on pastures on mountain tops or even near villages on the lower slopes where they come to scavenge for food. The alpine chough is about the same size as the common chough and it also has red legs, but its bill is yellow. The colour of the bill and its almost absurd warbling chirp of a call, which one would associate with a much smaller bird, distinguish it from the common chough.

Another beautiful cliff-loving bird seen both here and at many other Pyrenean sites, is the intriguing wallcreeper. **The green lizard, found everywhere.**

Limited to mountain areas in southern Europe, it descends to lower, rocky areas in winter. It is slightly bigger than a treecreeper, and prefers rock faces to trees. It is slate-coloured above and has ruby-red wings with black-and-white tips. It has a strange butterfly-like flight and flutters its wings incessantly when seeking food on rock faces. It utters a weird, ascendant warble when on the wing. The wallcreeper breeds in crannies in mountain cliff faces and buildings above 5,400 ft (1,650 metres).

In the Cadí, as in other areas of the Pyrences, there is a great difference between the vegetation on the *solanes* (sunny, south-facing slopes) and the *obagues* (shady, north-facing slopes). The tree-line is about 1,000 ft (305 metres) higher on the sunny side, and fir and mountain pine forests don't start to appear until around 5,500 ft (1,700 metres), reaching 7,200 ft (2,200 metres). On the cooler, damper, north-facing slopes, the tree line is at the 6,300-ft (1,900-metre) mark, and pine and fir forests are found between 4,800

The large, loud black woodpecker.

and 6,300 ft (1,460–1,900 metres). Chestnut and beech forests will stretch further down the north-facing slopes, while ilex woods, often stunted by excessive felling, will cover the lower south-facing slopes.

It is in the remoter fir and mountain pine forests that the remarkable black woodpecker is found. It is Europe's largest woodpecker, half as big again as the green woodpecker, and its startling black plumage and red head are unmistakable, though it will be more often heard than seen. Its strident alarm call, normally given on the wing, is similar to the green woodpecker's, though it is shorter and slower. The loud drumming of its bill on tree trunks—to mark its territory—is also a thrilling sound. When heard for the first time, it is difficult to associate the noise with a bird.

The large, chicken-like capercaillie shares the habitat of the black woodpecker, preferring solitary high mountain woodland with little or no human disturbance. It is best seen during the breeding season in May, when the cock bird utters a soft, rather guttural "tick-up, tick-up" sound which accelerates and ends in the popping noise of a bottle being uncorked. The slate-coloured male is quite aggressive. The female bird is brown. A large dark forest fowl hurtling excitedly through the undergrowth is how the bird normally appears. Its population in the Pyrenees seems to be recovering after decades of over-hunting.

Núria and Freser-Setcases: Further east, beyond the Toses mountain pass, is the Núria Valley, famous for its sanctuary and hunting reserve. The reserve, which covers 78 sq. miles (202 sq. km) of mountain habitat, was created in 1966 to protect the endangered chamois. The preservation of the area has led to the recovery of many mountain species, and despite the existence of a ski station and the disturbance caused by the constant flow of pilgrims to Núria, it is possible to see chamois here throughout the year.

To the north of the reserve is the formidable Puigmal peak, almost 9,000 ft (2,750 metres) high. In summer three species of beautiful blue gentians appear on the mountain. If you are lucky, you may see snow finch above the 6,000-ft (1,800-metre) mark: look out for the flashes of white visible when the grey-brown sparrow-sized bird flies. It breeds in holes in walls and cracks in rock faces. In harsh winter conditions it will come to lower areas, turning up on bar terraces and camp sites in search of breadcrumbs.

You may well put ptarmigan to flight while walking on the higher slopes. The remarkable thing about this partridge-like bird (indeed in Catalan they are known as *perdiu blanca*, "white partridges") is that it changes colour from season to season. In summer it is largely grey-brown with red "eyebrows", and in winter it is mostly white. Its white wings remain constant, however, making it immediately identifiable against green or grey mountain backdrops in summer, while in winter the unchanged black edgings on its tail will enable you to spot it against snow. The overall change in colour is to provide seasonal camouflage against its major enemy, the golden eagle.

As in Scotland, the Pyrenean golden eagle is the monarch of the air. But his kingdom has to be shared with other large raptors: Bonelli's eagle, the short-toed eagle and three species of vulture. In general, the golden eagle is to be found in the high mountain areas, whereas short-toed and Bonelli's eagles and bearded, Egyptian and Griffon vultures will be found at lower altitudes, too. The Bonelli's eagle, which often makes an untidy nest on relatively low cliff ledges, is another enemy of the ptarmigan. But the short-toed eagle—the only large bird of prey which is white underneath and hovers—feeds exclusively on snakes, making it a summer visitor.

To feed on snakes in Pyrenean areas such as Núria means preying on vipers (*Vipera aspis*) and the distinctly marked western whip snake (*Coluber viridiflavus*), both of which live up to 6,000 ft (1,800 metres). The Pyrenees are the southern limits of the viper and it can

Red squirrels are common in the woods.

often be seen sunning itself on stones in the summer months. Among other reptiles is the rough-skinned Pyrenean brook salamander which is endemic to the mountains and lives in clean streams and ponds. The large green lizard is also to be found up to the altitude of 4,500 ft (1,370 metres).

The valley of Núria is an important summer grazing area. Thousands of sheep from the Catalan lowlands are brought up in late spring to feed in the Núria pastures, descending again before the winter snow comes on. A century ago up to 300,000 head were herded up to this part of the Pyrenees every year. Now only a few thousand sheep are brought to pasture here and this has had a detrimental effect on the vulture population.

The Garrotxa Volcanic Park: The largest volcanic area in the Iberian peninsula is in the Garrotxa, in the province of Girona. In 1982, the Catalan government made a 47 sq. mile (121 sq. km) nature reserve in the area around some 30 extinct volcanoes. Grey basalt is the predominant stone in the area, and it can be seen in the colour of local farm walls. Castellfollit de la Roca, a spectacular village on the road between Girona and Olot, is perched on a cliff which is what remains of a giant lava flow.

Although the Garrotxa is well removed from the Atlantic winds' humid influence, it has a higher yearly rainfall than other surrounding areas. In Catalan the town of Olot is often referred to as *l'orinal de Catalunya* ("Catalonia's chamberpot"). The rainfall, combined with rich volcanic soil, gives rise to exuberant vegetation such as the *Fageda d'en Jordà*, a legendary beech wood on the road to Santa Pau. The 19th-century poet Joan Maragall wrote a famous poem about it:

Si vas pels volts d'Olot, amunt de pla,
trobaràs un indret verd i profond
com mai cap més n'hagis trobat al
món.
(If you go to Olot, above the plain, you'll find a profound green haven such as you've never found in the world.)

One of the species that breeds in the woods is the red squirrel. Although heavily hunted in the past, it is now quite common, as it is in most Pyrenean woods. In Catalonia there are no grey squirrel. Wild boar are also common in the mountains, although periodic bouts of swine fever affect the population.

The Santa Margarida volcano, between Olot and Santa Pau, is well worth a visit. Several nearby volcanoes, such as the Croscat, have been severely disfigured by open-cast mining, but this volcano has a perfect round crater with a small chapel in the middle. The vegetation covering the external part of the cone is extraordinarily lush.

The Garrotxa is something of an exception; behind these volcanic lands the summits of the Pyrenees in the Alta Garrotxa look barren and pale. From the Vall d'Aran to the beautiful rugged cape of Cap de Creus, the lush mountain scenery gradually gives way to drier, rockier Mediterranean landscapes. The changing face of the Catalan Pyrenees allows a rich variety of wildlife, and there is always something to see.

A bright burnet moth on a thistle.

GIRONA PROVINCE

Lying along the Pyrenees against Catalan France and running down the wild Costa Brava, the province of Girona could be described as Catalonia's heart. In the foothills is Ripoll and the monastery of Santa Maria, the "cradle of Catalonia" consecrated in AD 888 by Guifré (Wilfred the Hairy) and for several centuries the emergent nation's spiritual home.

Of the four provinces, Girona is the most blessed by nature, having the best of both mountains and sea. It has two beautiful plains, the Cerdanya and the Empordà, and its natural parks include the mountainous Cadí-Moixeró, the volcanic region of Olot, the wetlands of Aiguamolls and the Medes Islands, the first protected marine area in Spain. There are some 500 Romanesque buildings, and its delightful capital of Girona, too often associated with the corrupted parts of the coast, is frequently overlooked.

The Cerdanya: "You have here a whole countryside as broad as a small English county might be, full of fields and large enough to take abreast a whole series of market towns," wrote Hilaire Belloc in *The Pyrenees* (1909). The Cerdanya, lying 4,000 ft (1,200 metres) above sea level, is the Pyrenees' largest plain. It centres on the Segre, a fine trout-fishing river, and its verdant landscape is broken by Lombardy poplars and a few farming hamlets. Mountains on all sides rise to nearly 9,000 ft (2,900 metres), making it a centre for summer walks and winter sports.

The plain forms a figure of eight, narrowing in the middle as the mountains crowd in on **Bellver de Cerdanya**. This attractively set town is the centre for information for the **Cadí-Moixeró natural park**, and the tourist office at the bottom end of the town provides information on serious walks and four-wheel-drive car hire.

A lane up past the tourist office leads to **Talló**, the "cathedral of the Cerdanya". In a land of humble churches, it was designated a cathedral by a bishop of Urgell, hiding from the French Count of Foix who had occupied his monastery at La Seu.

The farms of the Cerdanya are distinctive, introspective buildings with high doors and slate roofs, huddled together to form hamlets. Cattle are led in and out for milking and iron pens once used for holding the *euga ceretana*—the Cerdanya mares—for shoeing still stand in some village lanes. Horse riding is a popular activity and there are stables at **Prats**, **Prullans** and **Guils**. Few of these communities have central squares or communal cafés, though the hilltop village of Meranges 6 miles (10 km) above Bor, possesses one of the province's most famous restaurants, Can Borrell, where jugged *isard* (the chamois mountain goat) is sometimes on the menu.

Perched on a pimple of a hill at the top of the plain is **Puigcerdà**, capital of the Cerdanya and the border town. It has three principal parallel shopping streets selling leatherware, cakes, cheeses and

souvenirs, and there is a Sunday market abundant with the region's fruit and vegetables. The town was knocked about quite a bit in the civil war. Only the tower of its fortified church of Santa Maria remains. Outside the newly built town hall there is a viewing spot which shows why Puigcerdà has been dubbed the "balcony of the Cerdanya".

The enclave of Llivia: Just beyond Puigcerdà, along a 4-mile (6-km) "neutral" road, lies Llivia, a 5 sq. mile (13 sq. km) piece of French Cerdanya still in Spanish hands because the 1659 Treaty of the Pyrenees ceded 33 villages to France, neglecting to make mention of towns, which Llivia certainly was. It is this curiosity perhaps more than anything else which brings visitors, for there is nothing too startling about the town. Its old part consists of little more than a church and 14th-century fortified tower. The church possesses a compelling crucifix and the acoustics attract international players to summer music festivals.

Opposite is a small **museum**, a rarity

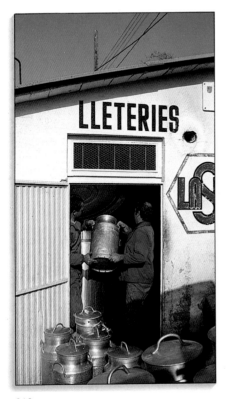

in this corner of Catalonia, built around the artefacts of an apothecary's dating from the early 15th century. There are a handful of Roman remains, too, for the town of Julia Llivica was built here by the Romans on the Strata Ceretana, their highway through the valley to the interior of Spain.

The main road through Llivia is lined with pristine modern chalets and apartments, and many new second homes have been built on the Cerdanya plain around **Alp** and **Urtx**, following the opening of the Cadí Tunnel in 1986, connecting Bergueda and the province of Barcelona. These serve ski stations such as **La Molina**, the most popular and longest standing in Catalonia.

The Freser Valley: From Cerdanya, the N152 twists precariously above the Rigart for some 45 minutes of low-gear driving through pleasant alpine scenery of pine forests, of anemonies, lady orchids and enamelled burnet moths before reaching **Ribes de Freser**. This is a small mountain town with a number of hotels catering for walkers and hikers, for whom the tourist office beside the church provides itineraries and maps.

From Ribes a "zip" train runs every half an hour up to the sanctuary of Núria, a breathless, vertiginous 20-minute journey to the head of the Freser Valley. It is better, however, to drive to the train's first and only stop, at **Queralbs**, which is as far as the road goes. This is a pretty little mountain village where Jordi Pujol, the president of Catalonia, takes his summer holidays. Sant Jaume is a beautiful slate-roofed 10th-century church which, unusually, has a porch of six arches.

After Queralbs, there is nothing for it but to take the zip train on up to **Núria**. With a café, accommodation and a huge restaurant, the sanctuary has the look of a 19th-century institution, but it pales into its stunning surroundings where hikers, back-packed and booted, take off for serious walks. In front of the sanctuary is a lake where hired boats row around wading cattle in summer and where skaters waltz in winter.

Cradle of Catalonia: From Ribes the road south follows the Freser, past stone

The dairy in Prullans.

bridges, waterfalls and the Ribes mineral water bottling plant. Increasingly lining the road are aqueducts and *colonies*, 19th-century settlements built for the iron workers of the valley. Now only in **Campdevànol**, just north of Ripoll, is there any metallurgical industry.

Ripoll was once famous for its *farga catalana*, a forge used in the smelting process which harnessed the power of falling water. It was invented here in the 11th century and was used right up to the present one. A plaque from the American Society of Metals on the door of the town's museum attests to the impact it had, not just on Europe but on the Americas, too.

This museum, in the 11th-century church of St Pere, is enchanting. It explains the area's importance as a manufacturer of firearms and nails, and through a variety of artefacts gives an insight into the lives of the local people, especially the shepherds. The town has a wool festival in May.

Ripoll has a certain shabbiness, with tenements rising above the Ter, where it is joined by the Freser. Its town walls were destroyed by the French, and floods have swept away some of its more recent history. Yet it has an honest air and it has cause for great pride in its **monastery of Santa Maria**.

The original church on this site was built by Reccared, the first Visigothic king to convert to Catholicism. It was sacked by the Moors and then rebuilt by Guifré el Pilós who, along with several subsequent counts of Barcelona, was buried here. The monastery was brought to fruition in the 11th century by the powerful Abbot Oliba and it became a place of inspiration and a centre of learning where Arab mathematics and astrology filtered over the Pyrenees into the West.

The church's astonishing portal was carved under Oliba's guidance and is a jewel of Romanesque architecture. History has otherwise not served the church well. The incendiary anti-clerics of the 19th century burnt all but the porch and the charming cloister, and this century's civil war destroyed much

Cerdanya cowgirl.

FOUNTAINS AND SPAS

Catalonia is a land of hot and cold running water. A small region where the terrain tumbles from 9,500 ft (2,900 metres) to the sea is bound to be rather wet. After heavy rain or when the snow melts, streams crash in such torrents it is impossible to hold a conversation on their banks. Yet, by the time many of the smaller rivers have completed their short courses to the coast, the water has disappeared, leaving dry beds; these are the *rambles* which so many towns and villages have turned into their main streets.

Although the summer sun can suck the rivers dry, much of the water escapes underground and is sometimes channelled back to the surface in generous and constant spouts. Every small village is based around a *font* and on Sunday nights weekend visitors can be seen queuing to fill up their rows of plastic containers, not necessarily because their own supply is unpalatable, but because the countryside's springs are thought to be both healthy and pure. Throughout Catalonia these natural waters, sparkling and still, are bathed in and bottled, used for communal open-air laundries and taken as a cure for all sorts of ills.

Some of these waters are hot, coming out of the ground at a steady temperature of up to 70° C (157° F), which, of course, delighted the Romans. They soaked in hot baths from the coast to the Vall d'Aran, where après-skiers at Baqueira-Beret still enjoy them today. The towns where they built their thermal centres bear the name *caldes*: examples, complete with remains, are at Caldes de Malavella near the Costa Brava, and in Caldes de Montbui, northwest of Barcelona, where the baths were in use until the mid-14th century.

Spas were exclusive, aristocratic places when they again came into vogue in the 17th and 18th centuries; but when the bourgeoisie took a fancy to them in the 19th century they grew in popularity and style. Perhaps the most famous is Vichy Catalan in Caldes de Malavella. It is a huge hotel with grounds stretching down to the railway station, and augmented by a Noucentisme bottling plant. Vichy Catalan was the first of Spain's bottled waters, registered in 1893, and it has become such a household staple that people often ask for a "Vichy" when they simply want fizzy water (*aigua amb gas*).

There is a second spa hotel in Caldes de Malavella, Balneari Prats, which is nearly as large, while not far away at Santa Coloma de Farners is the quieter Termes Orion. At Caldes de Montbui there are four spa hotels, which are less imposing, but older, quieter and most attractive. Termes La Salud dates from 1674 and is Catalonia's oldest spa, and Termes Solà has been run by the same family since 1680. The newest of the region's spas is Hotel El Manantial in the Pyrenean valley of Boí in the province of Lleida, built in 1957.

Each spa's waters have particular properties which are believed to be beneficial for different ailments. Vichy Catalan, for example, has mineral-rich, sodium-bicarbonated waters which surface at 60° C (140° F) and are recommended for rheumatism, and for digestive, respiratory, circulation, kidney and urinary tract complaints.

Visitors can, however, enjoy the hotels' splendours without having to take the waters or follow any dietary regime. In fact, good cooking is often promoted by the hotels as much as the proffered cures. There are also some spa hotels, such as the Montagut near the Ribes mineral water plant, which have stopped providing health treatment altogether but remain elegant places to stay.

Most of the spas have a full back-up of medical facilities, but people merely wishing to take the local waters are more likely to head for Montseny, the humid mountain range between Barcelona and Girona. At its centre is Sant Hilari Sacalm, which likes to be known as "La Font de Catalunya" on account of 100 springs found in and around it. This is a friendly town that has scant need of cafés; instead, the social centres are the plastic sofas of the hotel lounges and their large dining rooms. At midday and in the evenings, visitors and locals stroll along to the two main fountains, Font Vella (which is commercially bottled) and Font de Ferro where they bring out their cups and eyebaths, exchange pleasantries, drink deeply and hope for good health.

of what remained of the interior ornament after the rebuilding.

The upper Ter: Pausing briefly for a perusal of a great junk emporium on the outskirts of town (cow bells, bicycles, marble sinks, masses of woodwormed furniture), the C151 leads out of Ripoll to **Sant Joan de les Abadesses**. This little town, centred on a crumbling, rural square, has the finest Romanesque site in the province. The monastery of Sant Joan was a gift from Guifré to his daughter Emma, the first abbess, and it retains a feeling of solace.

The small museum beside the elegant cloister is worth a visit, but the crowning glory is a remarkable altarpiece in the church, a 12th-century wood Calvary which a visitor may easily mistake for a modern carving. In fact, one of the crucified robbers has been replaced since it was burnt in the civil war, and it is hard to spot the difference.

The road opposite Sant Joan leads 3 miles (5 km) up to the former coal-mining village of **Ogassa**. The mayor, Ramon Tubert, who presides over the Can Tal-Lara restaurant, decorated to look like a working mine, will recount tales of bygone lawlessness in this curious mountain community.

The C151 continues along the Ter's banks, past one of its numerous hydroelectric power stations, to **Camprodón**. This is one of the richest-looking towns in the province, full of grand mansions and shops of pastries, cheeses and meats, and as self-confident as any border town, which it virtually is. It has a monastery (consecrated AD 948) and a typical 12th-century bridge which straddles the crashing Ter. Inexpensive trout-fishing licenses can be bought at the tourist office.

Two roads lead north from the town, the one to the northwest ends at the ski resort of Vallter 2000 and the source of the Ter. En route are the villages of **Llanars**, which has a charming rose-covered church containing a fine 12th-century painted altar front. The next village is **Setcases**, meaning six houses, but there are more than that number of restaurants alone here now. Food is

12th-century Calvary, Sant Joan de les Abadesses.

wonderful in any one of them. In spite of the tourism that skiing has brought, Setcases remains a pretty mountain village of dogs, cats and cows.

The northeast road out of Camprodón leads to **Molló**, the **Coll d'Ares** and France. The land flattens out rather blandly and Molló is not really worth a detour, in spite of a good campanile to its church. Better, if one has a couple of hours, to take the long winding road down into the exquisite haven of **Beget**. Fewer than two dozen people live in this delightful village centred around the only Romanesque church in the province which still has its interior intact. The key is kept by the cobbler's widow. Surrounded by Italianate wall paintings and Moorish decorative work is a 12th-century crucifix of enormous dignity.

Garrotxa: The Garrotxa is a land of volcanoes, green conical hills and basalt outcrops. These produce a distinctive landscape in such dramatic scenery as the escarpment on which the village of **Castellfollit de la Roca** perches above the Fluvià. This is the region's principal river, and it rises to the southwest, in the lovely farmlands of the Vall d'En Bas. Houses in villages such as **St Privat d'En Bas** and **Els Hostalets d'En Bas** typically have wooden balconies decked with flowers.

These farmlands were painted by Josep Berga and the Vayreda brothers Marià and Joaquim, and other members of the 19th-century painting school founded in the region's capital, **Olot** (pop. 50,000). The Ecole de Belles Arts, which was set up in the 18th century to feed ideas to the local textile industry, still exists in the Carmelite monastery, as does Art Christià, the factory making church statues which the Veyredas and Berga began. It is situated in Carrer Veyreda, near the Veyreda family home. The **Comarcal Museum** in the 18th-century Hospice has a good selection of the artists' work, as well as sculptures by Miquel Blay, whose beautiful damsels support balconies in the main street, the Passeig Miquel Blay. Known locally as the Files, this is where the Monday market is held.

On the outskirts of town, on the Santa Coloma road, is the **Casa de Volcans**, set in a small park. This gives out information for the volcanic region which lies to the east of the town. The pretty medieval village of **Santa Pau**, on the GE524, is a centre for the natural reserves, but the tourist office there is generally closed. Santa Pau, nevertheless, is a good base (visit, too, the old-fashioned general store on the way into the village). There are a number of walks nearby, including the **Santa Margarida** crater, the **Fageda d'En Jordà** beech woods and the extraordinary **Croscat** crater, excavated for its pumice and cinders.

The Garrotxa used to be part of **Besalú**, one of the counties created in Charlemagne's Spanish March. The county town still exists and it maintains a medieval flavour. It has a dramatic entrance, with a fortified bridge over the Fluvià, and two excellent churches, St Vicenç and St Pere, which was part of a Benedictine monastery that was destroyed in the last century, leaving a dusty square behind. The extremely

Spring flowers in the mountains.

helpful tourist office in the arcaded square gives St Pere's opening times, and the key to the *mikwah*, unusual Jewish baths discovered in the 1960s by a man digging over his allotment by the river. The town has two good antique shops worth a browse.

Banyoles: Eastwards from Santa Pau and south from Besalú, the road converges on the turquoise-blue waters of Banyoles, chosen as the site of the 1992 Olympic rowing events. This unusual lake, fed by warm underground springs, is 5 miles (8 km) round and its peaceful northern banks are shaded by willows—a good place to picnic when the weather blows up on the coast. On this same shore is the perfect, golden-stoned Romanesque church of **Porqueres**, which is invariably open.

Banyoles itself has the air of a Victorian resort: ferry boats with goose-neck prows, a lakeside café with pin-ball machines, giant carp to feed and piles of wonderfully awful souvenirs. There are good large restaurants around the lake but the town is set back from it, centred around a colonnaded square of some 40 arches. The Victorian air is maintained by a museum created by Francesc Darder, a local Barnum-and-Bailey figure and former director of Barcelona Zoo who invented a new method of embalming corpses. There are five rooms of weird and exotic stuffed animals and even an African warrior.

The **Pia Almoina**, the almshouses, have an interesting prehistoric collection which includes a jawbone 100,000 years old, one of the earliest pieces of evidence of man on the peninsula.

Figueres: This working town is capital of the Alt (high) Empordà, with a large Thursday market divided into two parts: food in the canopied square just off the bottom of the Rambla, clothes and hardware up by the park. Narcis Monturiol, an inventor of the submarine, is the town's second most famous son: its most famous, **Salvador Dalí**, built his museum in the old theatre among the attractive car-free lanes around the town hall. It is the most visited museum in Spain after the Prado, and queues

Old-fashioned summer fun, Lake Banyoles.

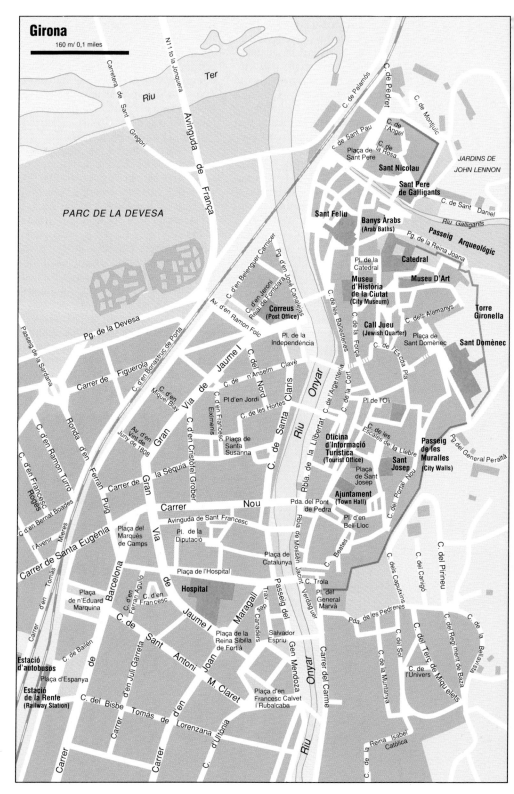

Girona

160 m/ 0,1 miles

N11 to la Jonquera

Riu   Ter

PARC DE LA DEVESA

Carretera de Sant Gregori

Avinguda   de   França

Pg. de la Devesa

Passeig de la Sardana

Carrer de Figuerola

C. d'en Bonastruc de Porta

Ronda d'en Ferran Puig

C. d'en Ramon Turró

C. d'en Francesc Rogés

l'Avenir

C. d'en Bernat Boades

Carrer   d'en Tomás   Mieres

Carrer de Santa Eugènia

Ronda d'en

Via de Gran

Av. d'en Vint de Juny de 1808

C. d'en Miquel Blay

C. d'en Cristófel Grober

la Sèquia

Carrer de Gran

Carrer   Nou

Avinguda de Sant Francesc

Plaça del Marquès de Camps

Pl. de la Diputació

Plaça de l'Hospital

Hospital

Via   de   Barcelona

C. d'en Ferran Aguiló

C. d'en Francesc

Plaça de n'Eduard Marquina

Estació d'autobusos

Plaça d'Espanya

Estació de la Renfe
(Railway Station)

C. de Balién

C. del Bisbe

Carrer   d'en

Carrer   d'en Juli Garreta

C. de Sant Antoni M. Claret

Joan   Maragall

Via   de   Jaume I

Plaça de la Reina Sibilla de Fortià

Tomás   de   Lorenzana

C. d'Ultonia

Carrer

Carrer

Plaça d'en Francesc Calvet i Rubalcaba

Salvador Espriu

Passeig   del   Gen   Mendoza

Trav. Canadera

Sep

C. Trola

Pl. del General Marvà

Pda. de les Pedreres

Riu   Onyar

Carrer del Carme

Plaça de la Reina Isabel Catòlica

C. d'en Belenguer Carnicer

Pg. d'en José Canaleias

C. d'en Jeroni Real de Fontciara

C. d'en Bonatruc

Av. d'en Ramon Folc

Correus
(Post Office)

Pl. de la Independència

Via   de   Jaume I

C. del Nord

C. de n'Anselm Clave

Pl d'en Jordi

C. d'en Francesc Eiximenis

Plaça de Santa Susanna

C. de les Hortes

C. de Santa Claris

Riu   Onyar

Rbla.   de   la   Llibertat

Rbla. de Mossén Jacint Verdaguer

Beates

C. de les Ballesteries

C. de la Força

C. de l'Argenteria

C. de la Cort

C. de les Escales de la Llebre

C. de l'Escóla Pia

Pl de l'Oli

Pl de l'Oli

Oficina d'Informació Turística
(Tourist Office)

Plaça de Sant Josep

Sant Josep

Ajuntament
(Town Hall)

Pda. del Pont de Pedra

Pl. d'en Bell-Lloc

Plaça de Catalunya

C. de Palamós

C. de Sant Pau

C. de l'Àngel

C. de la Rosa

Plaça de la Rosa

Plaça de Sant Pere

Sant Nicolau

Sant Pere de Galligants

C. de Sant   Daniel

Sant Feliu

Banys Àrabs
(Arab Baths)

Riu   Galligants

Passeig   Arqueológic

Pg. de la Reina Joana

Pl. de la Catedral

Catedral

Museu d'Història de la Ciutat
(City Museum)

Museu D'Art

C. dels Alemanys

Torre Gironella

Call Jueu
(Jewish Quarter)

Plaça de Sant Domènec

Sant Domènec

Pg. del General Peraltá

Passeig de les Muralles
(City Walls)

C. del Pirineu

C. del Canigó

C. dels Caputxins

C. del Sol

C. de la Muntanya

C. de l'Univers

C. del Terç de Miquelets

C. del Regiment de Baza

C. de la Bellavisa

C. de Pedret

C. de Montjuic

JARDINS DE JOHN LENNON

C. del Portal Nou

Riu   Onyar

218

lengthen in summer, although it is open all day. Also worth a visit is the **toy museum** in the old Hotel Paris in the Rambla.

Just to the east of Figueres, off the C252 to Llança, is **Vilabertran**, a small village with a charming 12th-century Augustine monastery where concerts are held in summer. Its simple church is an ideal setting for chamber orchestras.

The wine route: Some of the best summer concerts in the area are held in the grounds of the castle of **Peralada**, just past Vilabertran. Liza Minelli and Sammy Davis have appeared here and Josep Carreras made a comeback performance in front of the royal family. A guided visit to the castle is worthwhile: inside are huge old wine barrels bound by oak roots, a large ceramic collection and Spain's largest private library. A gambling casino operates in the castle and seems rather out of place in this dusty medieval town.

Peralada, the birthplace of the great Catalan chronicler Ramon Muntaner, is famous for its wines, particularly its sparkling whites and pinks, made by the Champagne method. The regulated Empurdà-Costa Brava wine comes from several nearby villages, from **Villajuiga** to **Espolla**, which have co-operatives. The largest producer is the Oliveda company in **Capmany**.

Girona: The provincial capital has a population of around 90,000 and provides a dukedom for the heir to the Spanish throne. It is the first city the traveller—and the invader—encounters on Spanish soil when coming over the Pyrenees' lowest, eastern pass. For that reason, it has been sacked and besieged more times than it cares to remember, its most heroic defence being against the French in 1809 during the War of Independence.

In spite of the ravages of history, the city has retained an impressive medieval heart, centred around the cathedral and Jewish quarter, and no monument in these shady, cobbled alleys is hard to find. The old town looks down on the River Onyar from ochre tenements and footbridges lead across to seek out its secrets. The cathedral tower and the

spire of the collegiate church of Sant Feliu pierce the skyline and both invite immediate investigation.

A Baroque flight of 96 steps rises to the imposing west front of the **cathedral,** which is sombre, serene and very grand. Inside, Catalan barrel vaulting reaches a climax in its nave, built by Guillem Bofill in 1416, which is exceeded in width only by St Peter's in Rome. An unusual *baldachin* (canopy) covers the altar and a copy of a marble throne made for Charlemagne (he undoubtedly never came to sit in it) is kept behind the altar. The **cathedral museum** is compulsory, if only to see the exquisite 12th-century Tapestry of the Creation and a very colourful Beatus produced in AD 975.

Sant Feliu is high Gothic, dating from the 14th–17th centuries, and probably built on the site of a former necropolis, which provided eight Roman sarcophagi in the presbytery wall. The city's principal church also has a mausoleum to General Alvarez de Castro, who defended Girona in a seven-

A JEWISH INHERITANCE

What is striking about the Jewish legacy in Catalonia is that there is one at all, since Judaism was officially banished in 1492 and remained proscribed for nearly 400 years. For centuries many local families—Desmestra, Sabarra, Falcó—had no idea of the Semitic roots of their family names.

Well over 100 towns and villages in Catalonia had Jewish communities. Some—Juia, Vila-juiga—are named after them, while many others carry Jewish street names. At Besalú a *mikwah*, a ritual bath for menstruating women, is one of only three known in Europe. No synagogues remain (the one boasted of at Vilajuiga is not authentic), and the Jewish districts were incorporated into the old parts of towns, such as Barcelona's *barri* Gòtic around Carrer Sant Domingo de Call—*call* is the Catalan word for a Jewish quarter—and around Girona's Carrer de la Força. These cities have most evidence of their Jewish history: outside their old walls both have hills called Montjuïc, former Jewish burial grounds.

Jewish families were neither numerous nor exceptionally wealthy, but they had been arriving steadily in Catalonia since the Diaspora. After the Moorish capture of Girona in AD 890, 25 families were allowed to

take over some of the buildings near the cathedral, then a monastery, which the clergy had just hastily vacated, and they thereby founded one of Spain's most important *calls*.

Tolerated by the Moors, Jews also enjoyed special privileges under subsequent Christian rulers. Count Ramon Berenguer III (1093–1131) was the first to entrust the treasury specifically to them. Soon they were accorded a degree of autonomy and given special protection in return for taxes paid directly to the royal exchequer. This caused some resentment, which was inflamed by intermittent bouts of anti-Semitism.

Increasingly ostracised and even physically attacked, they were driven deeper and deeper into their *calls*. Finally they were expelled from the peninsula by Fernando and Isabel, the Catholic Monarchs who drove the last Moors out of Spain. (Like other monarchs, Fernando had employed Jewish advisers at court and some historians believe he was himself part-Jewish.)

Although Judaism was again permitted under liberal 19th-century laws, it was banned once more by Franco. In 1976, two years after the dictator's death, a romantically inspired citizen bought up a chunk of the Jewish *call* in Girona and chipped away at its fabric. He began to unravel the warren of rooms and passageways which the *call* had finally become, when windows, doors and whole alleyways were sealed off. An inventive romantic, he called it the Isaac El Cec (Isaac the Blind) centre, after a cabalistic Jew who had in fact never set foot in Spain, but had lived in Montpellier in southern France.

After taking over the centre in 1987, the local authorities, with help from the Center for Hebrew Studies in New York, opened it to visitors and as a centre for learning. They would like, eventually, to change its name to the Nahmonides Centre, after a real resident of the *call* who was important in the spread of the mystical philosophy of cabalism which had taken hold in Languedoc. Moses ben Nahaman became the grand rabbi of Catalonia and scored a notable victory in the Disputation of Barcelona in 1263. This was a famous public debate, held in the Palau Reial Major, in which he successfully defended Judaism against the heated attack of a Dominican friar, Pau Cristià.

The Isaac El Cec Centre is now a major site on Girona's tourist map. To walk around it, or simply have coffee in the Courtyard of the Rabbis, is to get some idea of the extraordinary life the 300 or so Jews who lived here must have led, cooped up in their ghetto, going out perhaps only once a month through the single doorway on to the outside world in the Carrer Sant Llorenç.

More doorways, windows and alleyways may yet be opened up. In the meantime, to get a deeper insight into this area, it is best to visit in May during the flower festival, when privately owned apartments and houses push open their huge wooden doors to reveal their patios, balconies and courtyards, which are the secrets of Girona's medieval heart.

month siege during the War of Independence, helped by a company of local women, the heroines of Santa Barbara, who are also represented.

Beside the cathedral a gateway leads the former Via Augusta out of the old city. Condemned prisoners took this route to their execution and a niche in the arch holds the Virgin of Good Death. Just beyond is the church of **St Pere de Galligants** (St Peter of the Cock Crow), completing a triumvirate of churches which is hard to beat. It now houses the **archaeological museum**. A room above the cloisters has many interesting Bronze Age artefacts, while the cloisters themselves contain a number of *steles*, inscribed stones from the Jewish burial ground on Montjuïc.

From St Pere de Galligants, the **archaeological walk** along the top of the old city walls begins, broken around the former university building, where the coat of arms of the Habsburgs can still be seen over the main door. It was closed down by Felipe V, Spain's first Bourbon king. In 1988 work began to improve and considerably expand the present university, which will involve building on the old site.

The **Arab baths** are also worth a visit. These public baths were built in the late 12th century, long after the Moors had left Girona. But they are beautifully proportioned rooms, taking their lines from Romanesque and Mozarabic architecture. The **Museum of Art** is essential visiting. It is excellently laid out, and has some fine Romanesque church ornamentation, showing how rich the interiors of such grand monasteries as Crüilles must have been. Gothic is also well represented, with some fine paintings and an outstanding Calvary from Mestre Bartomeu, who is said to have introduced the Gothic style to Catalonia.

The whole of the old city is a pleasure to walk around, and it cannot be conquered in less than a couple of days. There are good restaurants, galleries and shops. In the **Rambla de la Llibertat** booksellers whose shelves are piled high attest to the reading habits

Students and shade seekers in Girona's Rambla de la Llibertat.

of the Catalans. On special days shop-keepers take their wares out on to the streets and set them on trestle tables.

On the other side of the river, in the "19th-century" town, there are several examples of Modernism by Rafael Masó (1880–1935)—Girona's principal exponent. His work can be seen in buildings such as **Casa Batlle** in Carrer Nou, topped with yellow owls. Girona has a permanent market on weekday mornings near the Plaça Catalunya, and a weekly Saturday market, which in summer is held beneath the cool of the tall plane trees in the **Davesa**, Catalonia's largest urban park.

Cork country: To the east of Girona lies the Baix (lower) Empordà, still farming country, but more rolling than the plain of the Alt Empordà. Towards the south the hills rise to the woody Gavarres. In the heart of this ancient woodland, in a peaceful glade of cork oaks, is the **Cova d'En Daina**, an arrangement of pagan stone for some prehistoric rite. The woods are now mostly hunting land—although cork, once a major industry, is still extracted from the oaks to provide stoppers for Champagne. Bark can be seen piled up in yards at today's principal centre, **Cassà**.

The industry once employed half the working population of **Palafrugell**; it now employs around 400. Palafrugell is a pleasant but rather uneventful town which grew up when Barbary pirates chased the coastal inhabitants inland. Today it provides the back-up services for the adjacent Costa Brava resorts. This was the birthplace of the prolific writer Josep Pla (1897–1981) and the local library has his collection of books, taken from his home, a beautiful *masia* or farmhouse nearby at **Llofriu**, still owned by his family.

Historic villages: Pla is commemorated on the *mirador* of El Pedro, the high point of the medieval town of **Pals** 5 miles (8 km) north of Palafrugell. Pals is one of several medieval enclaves in the area, and the best restored. It used to be a port in a rice growing area (rice is still grown, and sold retail, nearby on the Riu Daró at Molí de Pals). Topped

Town bar, Palafrugell.

by a distinctive, round clock tower, this is a pleasant town to wander through, with the bonus of good restaurants, as is nearby **Peratallada**. Though not quite as grand, Peratallada is in many ways more interesting, not least because of its castle, first documented in 1065, which until recently was open to the public.

A third place of interest in the immediate area is **Ullastret**, an important Iberian site 3 miles (5 km) north of Peratallada. Set out like a park, it overlooks the flat land that was once a lake. In its small museum are many finds, including fragments of the Iberian alphabet.

There are several small Romanesque churches in the area, plus the delightful 10th-century, pre-Romanesque church at **St Julià de Boada**, which was used as a cow shed until the 1970s. On the southern side of the C255 Girona road are three further medieval villages: **Monells** was a fortified market town and once the most important in the area, **Sant Sadurní** is worth a brief coffee stop; and **Crüilles** has a pleasant café in its square. In any case, drivers need to turn off the road towards this village in order to pass back under the same road to reach **St Miguel de Crüilles**, one of the great Benedictine monasteries, in full Romanesque flight, though now in disrepair and acting as a magnificent dovecote.

Ceramics: Monells' importance has long been overtaken by **La Bisbal**, the capital of the Baix Empordà and the former residence of the bishops of Girona. It is also the largest of three ceramic centres. The main through road is lined with three dozen shops selling decorative ware; a pottery school (Escola de Ceràmica La Bisbal), running short summer courses, is situated up at the back of the town next to the monastery of Sant Sebastià. If you ring the bell one of the Franciscan noviciates may show you around.

Quart, just south of Girona towards Sant Feliu, also makes ceramics from local clay mixed in baths by the roadside. The town's speciality is green or black glazes which attempt to emulate bronze. A third centre is **Breda**, just south of the fortified town of **Hostalric**. Here the ceramics are mainly plain, inexpensive earthenware for which Spain is justly renowned. The Romanesque belfry on Breda's church is promising, but the cleric with the key is a hard man to pin down.

The Guilleries: Behind Breda lie the Guilleries, moist mountains of Spanish chestnuts and myriad springs. The principal towns are **Arbúcies** and **Sant Hilari Sacalm**, where four-wheel-drive vehicles can be hired. Apart from the many fountains which bring visitors here all year round for their health, Sant Hilari has a thriving wood-turning industry, though you must knock on the small factory doors to see the wares, since no examples turn up in the local shops. The shops are otherwise small and quaint and hung with the many herbs and infusions enjoyed by the health-seeking visitors. The less healthy may care to drink the local Ratafia, anise-flavoured with a mix of a dozen or so of these herbs. The Guilleries lie on the edge of the Montseny ridge, in the province of Barcelona.

A potter in Quart.

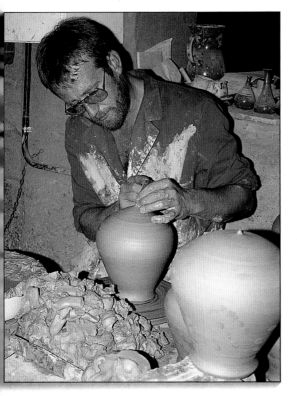

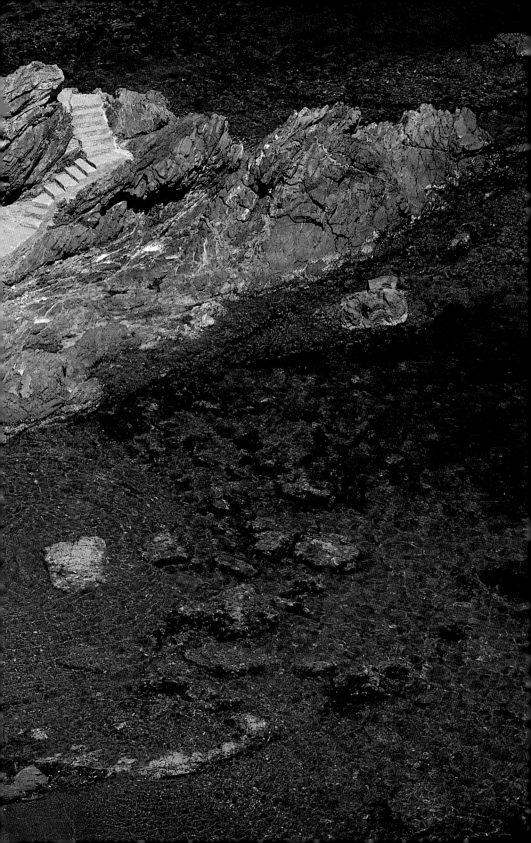

THE COSTA BRAVA

From the French border to the beaches of Barcelona, Catalonia's northern coastline is a rugged place of sheer cliffs, secret coves, pine-backed bays and a good many miles of golden sand. Two-thirds of the way down the coast, a small river, the Tordera, runs into the sea, dividing this littoral into two administrative and geographical parts. North of the Tordera is the **Costa Brava**, which belongs to the province of Girona; south of it is the **Maresme**, in the province of Barcelona. They are two quite distinct places.

The Paris-to-Barcelona railway line comes over the border from France at Portbou, continues a few miles south to Llança, then hurries inland to Figueres and Girona before a line branches off to the coast alongside the Tordera. From there it stays on the coast to the capital, giving fine views for the passengers, but leaving the resorts of the Maresme cut off from the sea.

Bypassed by the main road and the railway, the secrets of the Costa Brava (which means "wild coast") have therefore to be ferreted out, and, although nowhere is undiscovered, there are plenty of out-of-the-way beaches and coves, some of which can only be reached by boat or on foot.

In July and August tourists multiply the local population some 20-fold but the developments, the high-rise and package-hotel resorts on this 125-mile (200-km) coast have been contained and there are still many delightful *platjas* (beaches) and *cales* (coves) to seek out. The worst excesses of development has by and large taken place where there are expanses of beach and flat land: at Santa Margarida in the Bay of Roses, at Sant Antonio just south of Palamós, at Platja d'Aro and at Blanes, the town furthest south.

Portbou to Cap de Creus: The N114/C252 coastal road from Perpignan in France winds slowly over the last granite fingers of the Pyrenees and is a route to take only if you have time. It crosses the border with little formality, twists around Cap Falcó, then drops down into **Portbou**, stuck tight into the back of its small bay. Dominating the top of the town are the shunting yards where different gauges mean that cross-border passengers must change trains.

Portbou has the confident air of a frontier town, a small harbour with a handful of fishing boats, a couple of seafront restaurants and a good bar, the Esport, which serves cheap *raciós* (portions) of seafood and generous glasses of wine.

The road twists up out of Portbou, then drops down to **Colera,** a thin and uneventful town wedged into a slightly smaller bay. But the view soon opens up across to the great hump of **Cap de Creus**, the Pyrenees' last exertion before they fall into the sea. Like a number of other towns on the coast, **Llança** is in two halves: the port and the inland town, both now reaching out to embrace each other. Fish are auctioned in the port each weekday evening, and restaurants such as the Miquel serve up good *bouilla-*

Preceding pages: small cove at Portbou. **Left**, Cadaqués. **Right**, Roses.

baise: the French are the predominant foreign holidaymakers.

Urbanisations crowd around most of the coves on the road to **El Port de la Selva**, a fishing port facing west, safely tucked into the crook of a bay. Shallow waters and a sandy seabed make it a good place for small children to swim, though detritus from visiting anchovy trawlers can sometimes intrude. Windsurf boards go hell for leather when the Tramuntana blows.

From the southwest corner of the bay, a road leads up to the monastery of **Sant Pere de Rodes**, a 20-minute first-gear-only drive (an easier route runs inland up from Vilajuiga). Magnificent as much for its position as for its architecture, this is one of Catalonia's grand pieces of Romanesque. Though plundered and ravaged (its Bible is in the Bibliotèque Nationale in Paris, some artefacts in New York), it was once very powerful and by AD 934 its Benedictine abbot was beholden only to Rome. Half a mile away, near the car park, are the remaining few walls of its local

village where the bell wall of the pretty little church of **Santa Helena** still pricks the skyline. It is best to drive up, leaving enough energy for the 30-minute climb to the remains of the **castle of Sant Salvador** above. From this 2,200-ft (670-metre) vantage point, a 360-degree view takes in Mt Canigó and the Pyrenees, the vast Empordà plain, the great scimitar sweep of the Bay of Roses, and the extremities of Cap de Creus.

An 8-mile (13-km) road from El Port de la Selva leads to **Cadaqués** on the far side of Cap de Creus, the most easterly town in mainland Spain. Cadaqués seems to live in a time warp, trapped in the 1960s when it was at its trendiest. It is a pretty village, whitewashed, cobble-stoned, dripping with jasmine. Young people still come here to drop out, but the village also has an air of sophistication, confirmed by the little boutiques and architect-designed interiors of the old fishermen's homes.

Overlooking the town is the huge Baroque church of **Santa Maria**, which has a hideously over-gilded altar. On the seafront are some Modernist buildings, such as Casa Serinyena, a blue-and-white painted Dutch-style house. Nightlife is lively in summer and there is an outdoor cinema season. The town's small art gallery is not over-impressive, though the **Perrot-Moore Museum** does better with several of Dalí's works. There is also a gallery on the first floor of the fine seafront **casino** where the old men mix with the young.

The name of Cadaqués has been inextricably linked with Salvador Dalí, who made his home with his wife Gala in two knocked-together fishermen's cottages about a mile (2 km) to the north in **Portlligat**. This is a remarkably unspoilt haven, where fishermen's boats are painted, unusually, green and black. The Hotel Portlligat is the only new building in the place, built with thin slices of granite like the drystone walls which terrace the olive groves on the surrounding hills. It has a sea-water swimming pool open to non-residents, with a restaurant and small apartments, used mainly by divers.

Bijou streets beneath Santa Maria, Cadaqués.

The Costa Brava

16 km/ 10 miles

Other coves can be reached by walking north, passing first by the *Capitainarie*, the bizarre chunk of coast Dalí's Irish-born agent, Perrot-Moore, has claimed for himself. A driveable road leads to the barren rocks and **lighthouse** on the extreme of the cape, and continues round to the north side and the **Club Méditerranée.**

The Bay of Roses: Early traders rounding Cap de Creus would head for Empúries towards the southern end of the Bay of Roses, an 11-mile (18-km) sweep of golden sand which was then a delta of lakes, marshlands and lagoons. **Roses**, at the top of the bay, was the Greek Rhodes and up until the last century it was primarily a strategic port. Its 16th-century castle, **La Trinitat**, was destroyed by the French in 1794; its fortified **citadel** was again attacked in the War of Independence until saved by the arrival of the buccaneering English admiral, Lord Cochrane.

Reduced to a pretty fishing village, Roses was a favourite holiday resort of the English in the 1950s. Though still an important trawler port, it is skirted with supermarkets and entertainment centres from large night clubs to go-kart tracks and aquatic parks. Should a visitor find him or herself stuck here, it might be better to press on round the cape to the twin **Canyelles bays**, where good restaurants include the interesting-looking Roc Chez Paquita.

Just outside Roses is the skyscraping new resort of **Santa Margarida**, and next to it the equally modern **Empúriabrava**, a local "Venice" where the manicured gardens of white villas run down to 20 miles (30 km) of canals formed by the Muga's delta. Being a purely modern invention, it has no real heart, but it has everything the tourists, mainly German, may want; nearby are riding stables and a small flying club.

Building such a place on an otherwise apparently useless marshland may have seemed a good idea in the 1960s when it was begun, but a more enlightened view has since prevailed and the neighbouring wetlands of **Aiguamolls** have now become an important nature reserve.

Typical pine-backed beach between Tossa and Sant Feliu.

This Natural Park, founded in 1983, straggles over 18 sq. miles (47 sq. km) of marshy land. By far the larger part of it lies on a former lake around **Castelló d'Empúries**, but the main information centre, which needs to be visited first, is on the road between Castelló and **Sant Pere Pescador**, an agricultural town in the heart of a fruit-growing area.

The centre gives out maps for walking through the park and there are several hides from which one may glimpse some of the 300 or so species which alight here, 90 of them nesting. They include the garganey duck (*Anas querquedula*), which the park has adopted as its symbol.

The ruins of the Graeco-Roman city of **Empúries** lie towards the south of the Bay of Roses behind the renovated hamlet of **St Martí**, which has a small church and a shady square where two cafés and two restaurants do good trade. In this idealistic, rural setting among umbrella pines, by the blue sea and golden sand, these few acres of mosaic floors and foundation stones hardly seem likely once to have been the major western Mediterranean port of the Greeks, a town which eclipsed all others in what is now Catalonia and whose nearest rival was Marseilles.

The Iberians were here first, protected by 3 miles (5 km) of perimeter wall; when Greeks from Phoecia arrived, the two lived uneasily together in separate enclaves. Then the Romans came, under Scipio, setting foot in Spain for the first time to quell Hannibal's ambitions. The Visigoths were also here, and then the Christian counts of Empúries who were finally chased off by pirates and settled a few miles inland at Castelló d'Empúries, where they built a cathedral the pope refused to recognise. There is a small museum on the Empúries site and the guide book is a good investment.

The church of **Santa Maria**, the would-be cathedral in Castelló, 2 miles (5 km) from the sea, was consecrated in 1064. Part Romanesque, part Gothic, its nave is like a great baronial hall, so redolent of the Empordàn counts one

The beach bar crowd.

WHEN THE WIND BLOWS

In a fanciful poem, Joan Maragall called the Empordà "The Palace of the Winds". Beneath the long, hazy wall of the chill Pyrenees and beside the warm blue Mediterranean, this most north-easterly corner of Catalonia is a climatic enclave. It can seem the most peaceful place on earth as the golden light of late summer afternoons gives way to crimson sunsets of biblical proportions, but this spacious "palace" also invites trouble from the turbulent air. And of all the eight winds which can whistle around it, none is more respected than the Tramuntana.

This is a dry, north wind and it seems to come straight off the snowy heights of Mt Canigó. It sweeps every drop of cloud and moisture from the sky and arrives out of the most perfect blue day, enraging the sea, rattling doors and windows and whipping washing lines clean away. From the cliffs of Portbou down to Cap de Creus, birds are blown from their flight, pines are permanently cowed and people struggle hard to remain on their feet. It howls over the Empordà plain and down the Costa Brava, softening its cry by the time it has reached the Tordera river and defining the "wild" coast as well as any geographical landmark.

There is no rhyme or season as to when it will blow. Fishermen have their theories, some saying that it only happens a dozen times in a year, and if it has used up its allocation by August it will not blow again until January. But the Tramuntana has proved too elusive to be pinned down by scientific inquiry.

When it comes, it generally lasts two or three days, but it can on occasion blow for more than a week, forcing large ships to seek the shelter of the coast's bays, keeping fishing boats inshore and allowing sea creatures a brief respite from their nets. Weather reports usually warn of its imminent arrival, but it can still catch navigators unawares. To become suddenly embroiled in such a storm is a nightmarish experience, and if it bears down on a balmy summer's night, the dawn will invariably reveal one or two boats reduced to matchwood on a jetty or the shore. In his book *Viva Penelope!* Kendall McDonald recalls a time when he and a friend came ashore at Tamarin, having been caught in a Tramuntana storm. Both of them were shaking so much they were unable to raise their glasses of brandy to their lips, but had instead to sip from the glasses where they stood at the bar. The old sailors in the bar were not surprised: they had seen the effects of the wind on seafarers before.

Like the Mistral, its French counterpart in the Gulf of Lyons, the Tramuntana can keep up its din so long it threatens to disturb all reason. Unlike in France, where crimes of passion may be blamed on the Mistral, the Tramuntana is tempered with no such excuses, though some believe it has helped form the character of the Catalans. The rocks and stones of Salvador Dalí's paintings are precisely those he saw around Cap de Creus; but his mind and his talent were not just shaped by the landscape, they were also scoured by that unhinging wind.

In *Gatherings from Catalonia* (1951), the English journalist John Langdon-Davies took the point further. "The Tramuntana," he wrote, "is largely responsible for certain clarities and brutalities of the Catalan temperament. It is the enemy of sentiment and romanticism. It is the moving spirit of classicism... It explains the flourishing of Romanesque art in Catalonia and it explains why Catalan Gothic remained so virile, never sacrificing strength to grace."

Opposing the Tramuntana is the Garbi, its counterpart in every respect. A warm, moist, "romantic" wind from the southwest, it chops the sea into small, spray-tufted, superficial waves. The further south one goes, as the Tramuntana's effect wanes, the more the soporific Garbi predominates.

The other winds—the northeasterly Gregal, the easterly Llevant, the southeasterly Xaloc, the southerly Migjorn, the westerly Ponent, the northwesterly Mestral—all figure in local lore and can everywhere be seen in wind roses glazed on to tiles, sundials, bowls and plates. But none of these has the Tramuntana's reputation of striking with a ferocity that can take the most seasoned sailors by surprise.

can almost hear the sound of their boots on the flagstones. Around the doorway are the 12 Apostles, sculpted by the Italian Antonio Antigoni at the beginning of the 14th century.

At the southern end of the Bay of Roses, a mile (2 km) south of Empúries, is **L'Escala**, an important fishing port until relatively recently. Its reputation for salted anchovies continues, though most of them are not caught here. They are worth buying by the jar from the factories, shops and garages around the town. (Bone and wash them thoroughly, soak in olive oil for at least 24 hours, and serve with a splash of vinegar.)

The mouth of the Ter: The Bay of Roses has a smaller mirror image to its south, centred on the mouth of the River Ter and the sandy Platja de Pals. At the north is **Estartit**, a cheery holiday spot of go-karts and bars. Its sandy beach, stretching south, is collecting new apartment blocks every year. From the port there are glass-bottomed boats to take visitors out around the **Medes Islands** (see *Diving* chapter), a former

pirates' lair, and up the high-cliffed coast towards L'Escala. It is not always easy to see through the glass, but the trip has a variety of rewards, including a diversity of birdlife, from cormorants and petrels to blue rock thrushes.

The 1,014-ft (309-metre) **Montgrí massif** forms the cliffs between L'Escala and L'Estartit. A sudden barrier of limestone, pockmarked with caves where Palaeolithic man lived, the massif divides the high and low Empordà. The road between the two resorts skirts this high land, passing through **Torroella de Montgrí**, a quiet and ancient small town which is worth a leisurely day's exploration.

From this erstwhile port, in 1229, the family of the lords of Torroella set out under Jaume I (the Conqueror) to snatch the Balearics back from the Moors. The royal palace of these times, the Palau des Reis d'Aragón, was on the site of the present Mirador in the Passeig de l'Església, an elegant building refurbished by the Girona Modernist architect Rafael Masó.

Sun-hat seller, Estartit.

Trouble nearer home caused the building of the great square **castle of Montgrí** on the top of the massif. Jaume II (1291–1327) built it to keep an eye on the troublesome counts of Empúries. The long walk up to the castle is not recommended under a summer sun. The **Museu del Montgrí i del Baix Ter** in the Casa Pastors, 31 Carrer d'Església, is mainly concerned with local flora and fauna. Torroella's sombre Gothic parish church holds summer concerts which have attracted Yehudi Menuhin and other celebrities.

Past the marshlands of the **Ter estuary**, the sandy beach swoops south to the **Platja de Pals**, a wide beach which rises in maram-grassed dunes towards a good golf course where the main hazard is the Tramuntana. The beach is enjoyed by campers and the owners of new villas, but it is somewhat overshadowed by the giant red-and-white masts of Radio Liberty, for whose American staff the golf course was built.

Rugged rocks: The Platja de Pals terminates at **Cap Begur**, and from here to **Cap Roig**, a distance of no more than 10 miles (16 km), there are some 200 coves and beaches, capes, grottos and islands. This is the heart of the Costa Brava, and its small pine-backed beaches and craggy cliffs are the face it likes to show to the world.

From north to south, the *cales* (coves) grow larger. The northern ones are reached from **Begur**, a quiet inland town built with money brought back from the Americas and topped by a crumbling 14th-century castle last used in 1810. From here the roads run down in rivulets to the sea. The most northerly cove is **Sa Riera**, followed by **Aiguafreda** and **Sa Tuna**, none of which is big enough to sustain much more than a basic tourist life. Twin bays follow, those of **Fornells** and **Aiguablava**; they are the most captivating.

The English writer Rose Macaulay was here in 1949, gathering material for her book *Fabled Shore*. She wrote: "Between the sea and the little creeks of white sand and the shadowing pines and the paths that climb the wooded mountainside, the mellow days slide like sun-warmed apricots that burst with ripeness, the nights, chirring with crickets and lapping waves, lit by an amber moon and huge bright stars, by glinting fireflies among the trees and the candling of the fishing boats in the bay, the nights must surely be like purple figs for sweetness."

The *parador* at Aiguablava is modern, white and rather out of place, but this is made up for by the Aigua Blava Hotel opposite Fornells, run by Xiquet Sabater, one of the characters of the coast who built up the business from the wartime ruins of his family home. The restaurants in both are very good.

Tamariu is the last and the biggest of the coves which can be reached from Begur. Long a favourite with English holidaymakers, its fishermen have given up their cottages for summer rentals and abandoned the sea to inflatables and runabouts. But it is still a pretty place. There are two attractive grottos nearby but they can only be reached by boat. Tamariu is the most northerly resort visited by the *Cruceros*

Festival time, Palafrugell.

excursion boat in summer, which comes up the coast from Calella on the Maresme coast.

Just as Begur protected the fishing villages to the north, so **Palafrugell** protected those to the south. It is said that the town was built in a hurry by the inhabitants of **Calella de Palafrugell** and **Llafranc** who were fleeing pirate invasions. Today both are attractive resorts with a gentle air, connected by a pleasant cliff walk, Avinguda del Mar.

Their seafronts are quite different. Llafranc has a small port and a tree-lined seafront of hotels and restaurants, though these are by no means intrusive. Calella de Palafrugell is divided between two main beaches. The first, **Platja de Canadell**, has the air of a quiet Edwardian promenade. The second comes in two parts, **Port Bo** and **Port d'En Calau**, where whitewashed arcades, Les Voltes, lead attractively on to little sandy beaches.

Every summer Calella de Palafrugell holds a festival of *havaneres*. These songs were originally brought back by sailors from South America in the 18th and 19th centuries (hence Havana-res), and they have now been revived and embellished as tourist attractions.

At the southern end of Calella de Palafrugell the road climbs up to **Cap Roig**, where there is a beautifully sited botanical garden, designed and built up by a White Russian colonel, Nicholas Wievowski, and his English wife, Dorothy. If it is closed, ring the bell to be let in. Opposite Cap Roig lie the barren **Formigues** (ants) islands.

From the sea, Calella de Palafrugell and Llafranc seem unspoiled, but a drive to the lighthouse at **Sant Sebastià** reveals the development which, barred from the coast, has sprawled backwards into the hinterland. The trip to this 550-ft (168-metre) high spot is worth it for the spectacular all-round view and cliff walks high above the sea. Attached to the *ermita* is a café, restaurant and hotel built around a courtyard.

Maritime towns: From Palafrugell an outsized highway whistles 5 miles (8 km) down to **Palamós**. This breezy

The *parador*, Aiguablava.

port, where the sea seems greener than elsewhere on the coast, stages a number of national sailing events throughout the year. It has always been a major coastal town, though it was burnt to ashes by Barbarossa and his Barbary pirates in 1543 and 400 houses were demolished in Nationalist air raids during this century's civil war.

A music festival is held in July and August in **Santa Maria del Mar**, the 18th-century church which gives the town its distinctive skyline. A new home has been found for the **Museu Cau de la Costa Brava**, a maritime museum which has been closed for a few years. As one might expect, there are some good fish restaurants in Palamós, as well as one of the coast's best established hotels, the Tria. An overall tattiness gives the old town a friendly air, but nearby there is another example of development taking advantage of a fine beach.

Apartment blocks have sprung up at **Sant Daniel** to the south of the town, while 3 miles (5 km) further on lies the glittering concrete of **La Platja d'Aro**. Jam-packed in summer, home of magicians' conventions and *bierfests*, it boasts more discos per square metre than anywhere else on the coast. It is clean, tidy and efficient and there are benefits: a long sandy beach, a string of coves to the north, and good shopping, especially for leatherware. Big Rock, at a country house just inland is a restaurant with a large reputation.

Half a dozen coves run north from Palamós, starting with **La Fosca**, a pleasant beach for swimming and with some amenities. **S'Alguer**, the next cove, though sandless, is worth a visit. Here, beside pomegranate trees, is a small group of whitewashed cork workers' cottages, built in the last century when the pickings were so rich that people reputedly had to work only three days a week, and would spend their long weekends fishing on the beach. From this comes the story of *le niu* (the nest), a local Lenten dish made from cod's tripe and embellished by these bored workers into a real feast: it is still served

Elaborate sundial, Sant Feliu.

in one or two restaurants in Palafrugell.

Cork was also the principal export of **Sant Feliu de Guixols**, 8 miles (12 km) to the south, and a locomotive on the seafront is a reminder that this trade paid for its own railway to Girona. Until the arrival of foreign yachts and the building of modern marinas, this was indisputably the coast's most important maritime town. Though its sea links have now largely dried up, its handsome promenade and Modernist **Casino dels Nois** still give it a dignified air.

The town grew up around a **Benedictine monastery** and the monastic buildings that remain around the Plaça Monestir are a hotch-potch. The monastery was documented from AD 968 but the **Porta Ferrada** is all that remains of the pre-Romanesque building. The church is Gothic, **St Benedict's Arch** 18th-century Baroque, while the **Museu Municipal**, housing ancient and medieval local finds, is in a neo-classical wing.

"Plumcake" in Sant Feliu's patisseries is a sign that the English have been coming here for some time, but in the Rambla there is also one of the most famous restaurants on the coast, the Eldorado Petit. Above the town, to the south, is a fine look-out point beside the 18th-century *ermita* of **Sant Elm**.

Some 2 miles (3 km) to the north of Sant Feliu is the superior, man-made resort of **S'Agaró** (see *Tourism* chapter). A barrier prevents non-residents from driving around the estate in summer, but visitors on foot can gape at the size of the villas and walk round the Byzantine-Romanesque-Renaissance church built in the 1920s. The 30-minute cliffside promenade past the Hostal de la Gavina should not be missed. Take swimming things to enjoy the little coves and the unspoilt beach of **Sa Conca** at the walk's end. Coffee can be had on the terrace of the hugely expensive Gavina and some of the extraordinary beach-side follies on the sandy **Sant Pau** beach have been converted into cafés and restaurants.

The big resorts: South of Sant Feliu, the road twists and turns in classic Costa

Evening stroll, Blanes.

Brava style, dropping down into coves (campers sometimes get the best sites) and rising high on cliffs to which century plants, agaves and prickly-pears cling. In the midst of this switchback lies **Tossa**, one of the prettiest places on the coast and therefore one of the first to be "discovered"—in 1928 a regular weekly bus ran back and forth to Berlin. The attractions of this clean and tidy resort are its small cobbled streets and whitewashed houses and the **Vila Vella**, the 12th-century castellated old town at the southern end of the bay where the Snoopy bar and other restaurants have taken over the fishermen's traditional homes.

A visit to the **Museu Municipal** in the Vila Vella will show that in spite of such notable visiting artists as Marc Chagall, no art school emerged. Nevertheless, Tossa is rightly proud of the inspiration it has given many painters and each August a "fast painting" competition, in which competitors take just a day to complete a work, is a great attraction. In Tossa, as in most towns on

the Costa Brava, Roman remains have been discovered, but the large villa of Saliius Vital, which came to light earlier this century, has had to be closed to the public, who were looting it.

Tossa is not for the culture snob. The Wimpy bar on the seafront does terrific trade. Yet at the same time, and for not much more, visitors can have an excellent local meal cooked by Camilla Cruanas at La Bahia. The grandfather of the Wimpy Bar's owner was the captain of the last merchant ship to be built on Tossa's beaches to trade with South America, exporting oil and wine. There are no commercial vineyards in the area now: tourism is a more lucrative trade.

Lloret de Mar, 8 miles (13 km) south, was a similar fishing village where boats were built on the shore and vineyards covered the hills. Then package tours were invented and it is hard to imagine a place that has suffered more. It now has more hotels than any other resort in Spain. It also has scores of discos, night clubs, a casino and huge entertainment palaces. Like all the Costa Brava's resorts, however, there are still relatively unspoilt little coves within striking distance, especially **Santa Cristina**, beneath a small church to the south of the town.

Blanes, the southernmost town of the Costa Brava, was also one of the first package holiday destinations and has thus suffered a similar fate. Most of the development is to the south of the town, where high-rise hotels and apartments line the sandy beach but the old town has not escaped, and egg-and-chip signs line the pleasant promenade of Pau Casals. One reason to visit Blanes, however, is to see **Mar i Murta**, a fine botanical garden begun by Carlos Faust, a German industrialist from Hadamar who made his money in Barcelona. It has 4,000 specimens and is the home of the International Station of Mediterranean Biology.

Nearby is the ruined **castle of Sant Joan**, and from here there is a view south, past the high-rise buildings to the mouth of the Tordera river. The land is flattening out. The Costa Brava has ended and the Maresme begun.

Left, Modernist inspiration, Lloret de Mar. Right, boats and bathers, Blanes.

DIVING IN THE MEDES ISLANDS

Kendall McDonald describes his underwater experiences.

The iceberg of water which erupted suddenly from the sea was almost as high as the islands behind it. Cordite had stained it dirty-black. Less than a mile away, the explosion was so muted that it merely made the town of L'Estartit twitch in the middle of its *siesta*.

Three divers in a cave under one of the Medes Islands were closer and not so lucky. They thought their last moments had come as shock waves jabbed at their ear-drums. No one had thought to warn them of the Spanish navy's intention, on that September afternoon in 1989, to detonate an old wartime mine which had become tangled in nets just outside the marine reserve.

Long before those same divers, shocked but unhurt, had got back into their diving boat—almost, in fact, before the fine spray of the explosion had melded back into the flat of the sea—the fish came drifting and dying up to the surface. By early evening the town's small fishing boats had collected an unexpected harvest of more than 1,000 lb (500 kg) of prime fish.

If this sounds a strange way to start the story of one of the greatest marine conservation success stories in Europe, then it should be said that, if that same mine had been exploded only six years previously, it is doubtful if the fish casualties would have reached a tenth of that figure. The fact that so many were killed is a mark of the success of Catalonia's brilliant policy of establishing reserves around breeding grounds.

The Illes Medes reserve was the first to be set up, and it proved so successful that a second opened in early 1990. This is around three underwater pinnacles called Els Ullastres near Llafranc, 10 miles (15 km) further south.

The original idea for creating a marine reserve around the Medes came from divers. The CRIS Club (Centro de Recuperación e Investigaciones Sub-marinas) of Barcelona, Spain's first aqualung diving club, formed in 1952, pressed for the whole area around the islands to be made into a protected reserve and underwater park as long ago as 1974. But it wasn't until Catalonia had its autonomous government that the idea became reality. The reserve was set up by the Generalitat's agriculture and fisheries department, and the regulations were finalised on 29 April, 1985. These stated:

1. There was to be a protected zone of 240 ft (75 metres) around the Medes.
2. Inside that zone there was to be no fishing of any kind.
3. Nothing living, animal or marine growth, was to be taken from the zone.
4. Diving was permitted, but there was to be no night diving.
5. Inside the zone the speed limit was three knots.
6. Anchoring of boats where they might cause damage was prohibited.

To make sure these instructions were obeyed, regular inspections would be carried out by the *Elisenda*, a boat be-

Left, Calella diving school, a base for the new Ullastres reserve. **Right**, diving off the Medes Islands.

longing to the Direcció General de Pesca Marítima.

Although the new regulations were welcomed by divers, they were not liked by the professional fishermen of L'Estartit and other nearby fishing communities. It had always been their right to fish the Medes as and when they wanted, just as their fathers and grandfathers had done. Now, at the stroke of a pen, they had been deprived of their ancient fishing grounds. The proposals to create a marine reserve raised great local anger and many forecast the demise of the fishing industry in the area. In fact, the reverse has happened.

Slim catches: In the 1950s, there were fish everywhere. Spearfishing was popular, but had not yet become the plague that it was soon to be, even though Spain was one of the first countries to ban its use with aqualungs. While spearfishing deprived the shallow depths of all the big fish, the local professional industry was overfishing the main food fish to satisfy the vast numbers of tourists arriving on the Costa Brava from all over Europe.

Catches from the small inshore boats became smaller and smaller, not always in quantity, but in fish size. Crews who fished pots for lobster went out further and further in search of fresh grounds and they were soon complaining that they were out so far that cruise liners were chopping off their pot buoys.

You didn't have to be a fisheries expert to see the size of lobsters in the keep tanks of the big hotels diminish. Divers watched the fish in depths down to 100 ft (30 metres) dwindle, until diving some parts of the Costa Brava was like being in a garden which had no flowers. Areas which had once been alive with life were still dramatic, but now they were also dreary, with only the occasional small fish to be seen. Among amateur divers the word went round that the Mediterranean was "finished" and "fished out"—even though it had been the birthplace of their sport, with Jacques Cousteau's first aqualung dives in the south of France in 1943.

It was not only the fish life which diminished in those 30 years. Precious red coral, used in jewellery world-wide, had been fished along the coast of Catalonia from man's earliest days and intensely from the early 18th century. The Medes were good hunting grounds for the coral fishermen, but their crude tangle-tackle dragged from a boat could not reach the real coral treasure of the islands. Great sprays of it hung from the roofs of the underwater caves and mouths of the tunnels which honeycomb the Medes.

That rich harvest was left for the first aqualung coral fishermen to collect. And it didn't last long. Soon even the red-and-yellow fans of gorgonia were on sale in the souvenir shops and when that was gone, it was replaced by shells and coral which had never seen the Mediterranean, but had been imported by the ton from some luckless Far Eastern reef.

There is now overwhelming evidence that Catalonia acted just in time. That evidence is clear to see as soon as you dive the Medes today. I had stopped diving Costa Brava waters in 1974. My **Coral is beginning to grow back.**

242

logbook noted that last dive: Cap Begur, 16 August, depth 60 ft (20 metres)— and to a general description of the site, added "very few fish", and "very little life", phrases which had appeared too often on my logbooks' pages for previous years. It was not a deliberate termination of my Costa Brava diving. I just drifted away to other parts of the world where there were plenty of fish to be seen and photographed. But on 13 September, 1985, I came back.

Fish soup: The diving boat called *Paraquay* moored up between the most southerly islands of the Medes group, Tascons Petits and Carai Bernat. I had heard divers' stories that "the fish are back". But divers, like fishermen, always exaggerate. Or so I thought as I rolled backwards from the gunwhale into the calm sea. From the moment my entry bubbles cleared and I sank gently down, I realised I was dropping through layers of fish. It was like diving in a fish soup. I reached the seabed at 60 ft (20 metres), looked up, and in wonderful visibility saw the mirror of the surface high above. But the mirror soon clouded and disappeared under a huge umbrella of fish.

Nearest to the surface were blue-grey sheets of sardines, flashing silver in places where they mixed with a mass of anchovies. Hanging down like chandeliers of silver with black bands, sparkling in the sunbeams, were the triangles which all divers call sars, but which are technically white bream. Swooping down from this happy hunting ground came the silver-grey shapes of big bass, making a pass and then turning back to inspect me again.

Other hunters powered through the shoals close by: dentex, big ones with their distinctive, steeply curved foreheads looking for all the world like sea billy-goats about to butt. It was amazing that dentex, normally the most elusive fish in the Mediterranean, should come so close.

Down on seabed level, the little violet "sea flies", or chromis, danced over the weed. And keeping just a little distance from me were shoals of goldline bream

Fish like this grouper are getting bigger.

with their body-long stripes flowing like molten gold over the rocky outcrops. Wrasse, big and small, swam in and out and under my fins. Grey mullet zoomed up towards the surface. In just a few moments under the Medes, I had seen more fish than I had on any dive since the early 1950s.

More was to come. As I turned to fin further down the slope on which I had settled, my wife, who was diving with me, thumped me on the arm and pointed downwards. For a moment I found it impossible to take in what she was showing me. For there, lying on some rocks, was the biggest grouper I had ever seen out in the open. Merou, cernia, dusky perch, call it what you like, that fish was gigantic. Four feet long, he (or she) must have weighed in the region of 80 lb (36 kg). Dark brown, flecked with lighter, almost yellow patches, he wasn't afraid of divers and stayed put as we approached even closer. As I boggled at the sight, another, almost as big, glided into view and settled down near him. Within moments we had four groupers around us.

Since that date I have returned again and again to dive the Medes. The fish have multiplied, and so have the divers. The groupers have got bigger and fatter and are now totally fearless of divers who feed them by hand. There is even a growing school of barracuda.

The word of the Medes miracle has spread far and wide among divers. There are now five separate organisations available to those who want to dive the islands and eight of the traditional big Catalan fishing boats are involved in what amounts to an almost continuous shuttle between the fishing port and the islands, a distance of just under a mile (1.5 km). For the non-diver, there are glass-bottomed boats to see the fish.

Those who want to dive the Medes come from far and wide. Every dive boat is a babble of the tongues of the Western world, with German, Belgian, Dutch and English predominating. This boom has brought a great deal of money into the town of L'Estartit, which is especially welcome because the diving does not stop when the summer tourists have flown home. Modern dry suits have put paid to the cold-water barrier. Tony Murray, who runs Unisub, the longest-running dive business in the area, says that there are sometimes only two or three days a year when the weather stops the boats going out.

However, the real success of the Medes reserve is not just the diving. The Medes have always been a breeding ground, but now, with the Catalan government's protection, that breeding ground is becoming one giant nursery for fish. Local fishermen realise the wisdom of the conservation and see the results in their catches which are improving year by year from areas well away from the of the reserve. Red coral is returning, too, in clefts in the sheer walls of the island bases, which are being repopulated with lobsters.

A second reserve: It is this all-round success story which led to the setting up of Catalonia's second marine reserve in 1990, once again in an area much loved by divers for its dramatic scenery and fish life. It has long been known as a breeding ground, but this, of course, has not prevented over-fishing in the past. The Ullastres are about 100 yards from each other. The first plunges from 40 ft (12 metres) below the surface to 100 ft (30 metres). The second goes from 26 ft (8 metres) to 137 ft (42 metres) and the third from 26 ft (8 metres) to 177 ft (54 metres). The marine reserve is a circle around Els Ullastres of some 200 yards in diameter. Most growth—gorgonia and corals—is on the northern side.

Experts on diving the Ullastres are Emili Agusti and his wife Lotti, who run the Triton Diving Centre in the Plaça dels Pins in nearby Llafranc. They regularly run divers out in their boat to the pinnacles to see the groupers, barracuda, black corbs, bass, giltheads, congers and moray eels, which make these rocks their home.

It is too early yet to say whether Els Ullastres will be as great a success as the reserve around the Illes Medes, but with the same complete ban on fishing I expect to be diving in the same fish soup within just a few more years.

The waters around the Medes are clear, safe for first-time divers and full of interest.

THE MARESME

El Maresme, a coastal strip as well as a *comarca* of Barcelona province, is also called the Costa de la Maresma and, confusingly, is sometimes described either as being part of the Costa Brava or part of the Costa Daurada, the coast to the south of Barcelona. But the Maresme is a quite different place.

For the whole 35 miles (56 km) of its shoreline, from the end of the Costa Brava just south of Blanes to the beaches of Barcelona city, the villages and towns have been cut off from the sea by both the railway and the main N11 road. In spite of the spreading of beaches with added sand, the building of new marinas and the promise that the trains might one day be diverted, the continuous rush of traffic sets the tone for the whole coast.

Growing business: The Maresme is Barcelona's back garden: flower fields, vegetable patches and glinting greenhouses can be seen immediately on arriving in the *comarca* at **Malgrat de Mar** in the north. Acres of tomato plantations lead down to the sea where cafés offer cheap *paella* and snacks. Nearby is a huge **marineland**, which is a combined park and aquatic zoo.

Malgrat has an unprepossessing old town surrounded by apartment blocks which follow the coast down to **Pineda de Mar**, which in turn merges into **Calella de la Costa**. The town is twinned with Heidelberg; a tile plaque outside the tourist office, put up in 1985, commemorates 30 years of German tourism. The small **Museu-Arxiu Municipal**, with tiles, textile machinery and local historical finds, is in the Carrer de les E. Pies.

The resort of **Sant Pol de Mar** quite literally stands out from the rest as it is based on the site of a 12th-century monastery perched on a hill overlooking the sea. There is not a lot to the town, reached by turning off at the large Hotel Gran Sol which has a bridge spanning the main road, but the houses are attractive and hibiscus is effusive. Beyond is

Canet de Mar, a place of camp sites and apartment blocks. **Arenys de Mar**, the next town, has character. In the Carrer de l'Església are two good museums, one devoted to mineralogy, the other, the **Museu Mares de la Punta**, is one of the finest lace museums in Europe. Its six rooms exhibit examples going back 400 years. Through a shop window in the same street children can be seen learning this largely neglected local craft. The parish church has a vastly overdone Baroque altar.

On the far side of the subway, beneath the railway and the road, is a pleasant, sheltered marina, a fishing fleet and a fish market. At one of the good restaurants, such as the Posit, you can sit outside and try local dishes such as whole fish baked in salt.

The town is centred around a *rambla*, and 3 miles (5 km) inland the twin village of **Arenys de Munt** lies on the same empty riverbed which gives the whole place a shady, dusty feel. There is an old lace shop, the Navarra, and bars such as the Caliu offer cheap meals.

Left, summer clothes shop in Calella. **Right**, scene from Sant Pol: rail travellers have the best view of the Maresme.

Inland routes: As is often the case, the villages in the hills just behind the coast offer attractive prospects, and one can take one's pick of pleasant restaurants on the inland road between Sant Pol and the Maresme's capital, Mataró. **Sant Iscle de Vallalta** has a couple of acceptable restaurants in the Hostal Martí and Can Bosch. On the road between Arenys de Munt and **Sant Vicenç de Montalt**, an attractive town with several grand houses, is the Restaurant Tres Turons, set among pines with a terrace which has a view of the distant sea.

Back on the coast, the next resort south of Arenys de Mar is **Caldes d'Estrac,** a chic little oasis for a stop on a journey. The sheltered beach of coarse yellow sand is fine for a swim, its seafront houses are elegant and there is a snack bar in a shady square. The Colon is a dominant four-star restaurant, but Raco de Peix has much more character and has an excellent restaurant with a variety of food in different price ranges.

Commercial capital: The main town of the Maresme, **Mataró**, is 6 miles (10 km) further south and although its beaches are as wide and golden as anywhere on this coast, Barcelona's suburbs seem to be growing. Mataró is a commercial town, but it has no historic port, though recreational boating facilities are proposed: harbour arms are springing up along the coast, as they have at **Premiá de Mar** and **El Masnou**, the crowded ports to the south.

Mataró's 17th-century church of Santa Maria is worth a visit for its paintings by Josep Lluís Sert. The town's most famous son is the great Modernist architect Puig i Cadafalch, who left his mark with the Casa Coll i Regas in Carrer d'Argentona. Later on, he built a summer house 2 miles (3 km) inland at **Argentona,** in the Plaça de Vendre, as well as the town's other grand mansion, the Can Gari. There is also a fine interior to the swish El Raco d'En Binu restaurant—though, like other inland towns, Argentona has cheaper places to eat.

Wine and roses: Beside the main road at **Vilassar de Mar**, just south of Mataró, is the **Mercat de Flor y Planta Ornamental de Catalunya.** This is one of the largest flower markets in Europe and, although it is open to visitors from 3–6 p.m. on Mondays, Tuesdays and Wednesdays, business is only for those in the trade. All around Vilassar, particularly up towards the small dormitory town of Cabrils, the fields are full of flowers, produce and garden centres. The **Zoo Maresme** in Cabrils is little more than a large pet shop.

One last town worth a visit before being swallowed by the capital is **Alella,** a mile (2 km) inland from El Masnou. This is the centre of the smallest wine-growing Denomination of Catalonia. Several *bodeges* sell a variety of its products, and the two main wine houses are in the middle of the town. The Duran is a big, busy café which sells inexpensive meals and there are a couple of smarter places such as the Los Tisos restaurant (evenings only) by the road leading to El Masnou.

Shortly after El Masnou, a large and efficient pleasure-sailing port, the N11 starts to slow down in Barcelona's seaside suburbs of Badalona.

Left, learner windsurfer looking for a second wind. **Right**, fishing from boats, Arenys de Mar.

BARCELONA CITY

If epithets like "glamorous", "exciting" and "stimulating" have become clichés when applied to Barcelona, it is for only one reason. They happen to describe the feelings it arouses in so many travellers.

Dead would he be of soul whose pulse did not quicken on first sight of the broad **Passeig de Gràcia** with its hexagonal, peacock-blue paving slabs embossed in patterns of spirals and swirling tendrils. Or at the tessellated pavements and fountains of the **Plaça Catalunya**. Or strolling under the plane trees of the **Rambla** or along the city's great arteries, the **Gran Via de les Corts Catalanes** and the 6-mile (10-km) palm-tree-lined **Diagonal**.

With a population of 3 million, Barcelona is Spain's second city. It is also the capital of Spanish Catalonia.

This now has its own government, the Generalitat, and its own parliament, while its ancient language is in official use. Welcome as all this is, to a people to whom being Catalan is more important than being Spanish, they are small steps on the road to total independence. This is not a sentiment they are at much pains to hide. King Juan Carlos, on a visit to the city, was greeted with catcalls, though it was later pointed out that they were directed less at him personally than at the government from Madrid he symbolised.

One ground on which the Catalans claim uniqueness is through their culture. Certainly in sheer raw statistics, Barcelona can challenge most European capitals. It has 40 museums and art galleries, 14 theatres, 130 cinemas, 100 dance halls, two bullrings and an opera house. Not that its vibrant artistic life is to be confined within the walls of buildings. It sometimes feels as if the entire population is caught up, either as spectators or as performers, in a monumental piece of street theatre.

Barcelona is Spain's principal port as well as the centre of the Barcelona Economic Area, a region extending into French Catalonia and inhabited by some 15 million people. As one discovers driving through the outskirts, it is highly industrialised. Besides considerable pollution, its factories generate a high density of fast, impatient traffic and attempts to relieve it with a tortuous one-way system make it a severe test of temper and nerves.

This means that, unless it is essential, you may find a car an encumbrance. On the other hand, the city is too big to be explored entirely on foot. Luckily, there is a clean, modern, cheap bus service and an easy-to-use Metro system.

The Eixample: It was the rise of industry which led to Barcelona's exponential growth in the mid-19th century. The bourgeoisie, whose entrepreneurial dynamism had been its driving force, wanted to see their success reflected in a great city. Their enlightened patronage stimulated the Renaixença, or rebirth, exemplified by Modernism, the specifically Catalan form of Art Nouveau. This is often taken to be synonymous with architecture's *enfant*

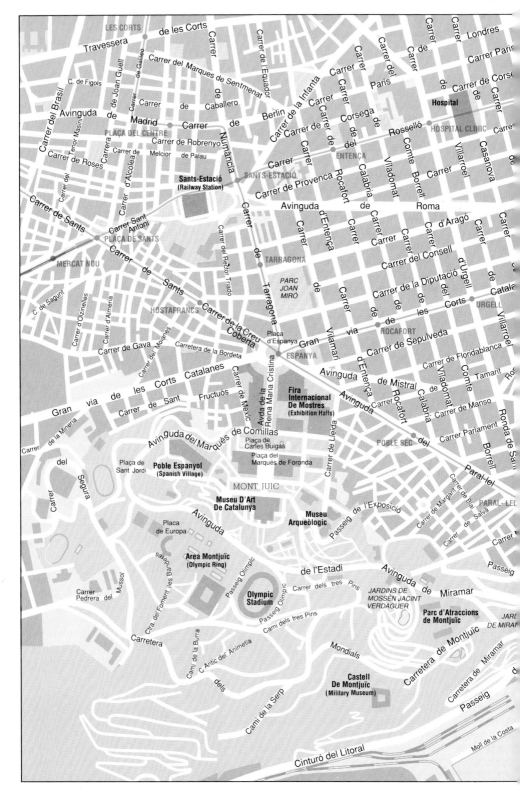

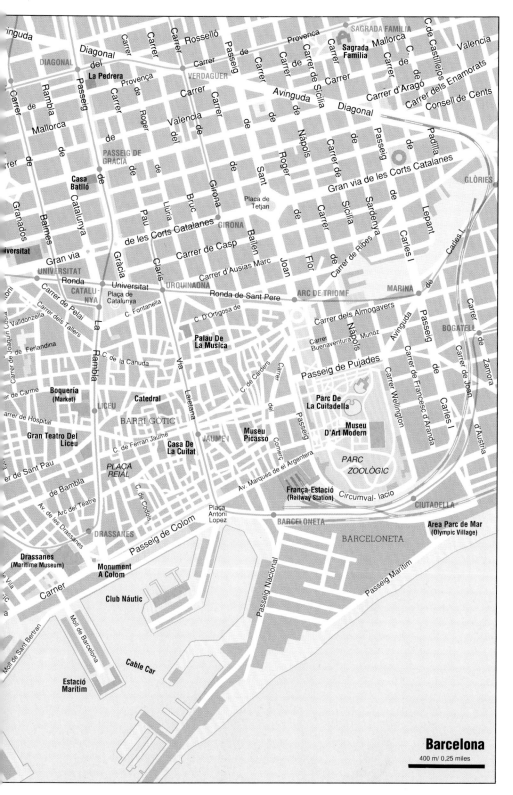

Barcelona

400 m/ 0.25 miles

terrible, Antoni Gaudí (1852–1926). He was undoubtedly a seminal figure, but it was another Modernist, Ildefons Cerdà, who, when the city burst its ancient walls, presided as a genius over the creative town planning which brought the **Eixample** into being above **Plaça Catalunya** and the old town.

The grid plan, responsible for some of the world's most boring urban developments, succeeds triumphantly here, largely due to wide boulevards and splendid street furniture. Look at the elaborate seats and wrought-iron lamp standards by Pere Falqués in the **Passeig de Gràcia**, or those paving slabs by Gaudí.

There are also the magnificent buildings, which owe much to the bold use of such materials as glass, timber, wrought iron and, most strikingly, ceramics. Modernist architects were not past decorating their structures with broken tiles, even bits of household crockery. The effect is often reminiscent of the Moorish architecture further south.

The work of the principal archi-tects — Lluís Domènech, Josep Puig, Josep Vilaseca, Salvadori Valeri, Josep Prat and Manuel-Joaquim Raspall — can be seen not only in grand buildings but also in quite modest shopfronts. Look out, for instance, for the **Papere-ria Teixidor**, the **Filatelia Monge**, the **Bar London**, the **Panaderia Sarret**, the **Farmacia Bolós** and the **Farmacia Viladot**.

Two of Gaudí's most remarkable buildings, the **Casa Batlló** and **La Pedrera** (which can be visited), are in the Passeig de Gràcia. His most famous and controversial work, the unfinished Temple of the **Sagrada Família**, is just north of the Avinguda de Diagonal.

Further to the north is his **Parc Güell**, named after his friend and patron, Count Eusebi Güell and intended as a garden city on the British pattern but uncompleted at his death. The house in the grounds, bought by the architect in 1905, has been turned into the **Gaudí Museum**, with drawings, plans and examples of furniture by the architect.

South of the Diagonal, in the Sants

Gaudí's Sagrada Família.

district, is the football stadium and **Parc de l'Espanya Industrial**. Though its Basque architect, Luis Peña Ganchegui, claimed to have conceived it as "a modern Roman baths", in reality it is an opportunity for a city, where so much belongs to the past, to show its hi-tech side. Wide tiers descend to a central boating lake overlooked by 10 slim, lighthouse-like towers with observation platforms and pods of floodlights. It has modern sculptures, including a huge dragon by Andrés Nagel which is also a children's slide.

Opposite Sants railway station is **Plaça dels Països Catalans**, a modern development where highly ingenious fountains produce domes of water.

Nearby, too, is a park which is named after the Catalan artist Joan Miró (1893–1983). Its pool, a great, glass-like plain, provides a setting and mirror for the artist's sculpture, *Woman and Bird*, and round it are gardens and playgrounds.

The Rambla: The southern corner of the **Plaça Catalunya** gives on to one of the world's most renowned thoroughfares, the **Rambla**, lined on either side with hotels, smart restaurants and elegant boutiques, as well as many truly splendid buildings. The name so evokes the words "ramble" and "amble" to English ears that it comes as no surprise to find ambling is what half the world seems to be doing there.

The Rambla is something of a misnomer, for, though the whole forms one continuous pedestrian precinct, thoughtfully provided with seats, there are actually five *rambles*, leading down to a statue of Christopher Columbus and the port.

Nearest to the Plaça Catalunya is the **Rambla de Canaletes**, a draught from whose fountain will, it is said, ensure your return to the city. It is also the place where the Barcelona's football supporters gather to analyse and criticise the latest game.

Next comes the **Rambla dels Estudis**, until the 18th century the site of the city's university. It is now usually known as the **Rambla dels Ocells** (the

Flower seller in the Rambla.

rambla of the birds), and here one can buy an albino canary, a brightly plumed parakeet or a tortoise, a tropical fish or a guinea pig.

Forming the corner with **Carrer del Carme** is the **Betlem Church**, built in the 17th and 18th centuries and formerly a Jesuit convent, and the 18th-century **Palau Moja**, now the Department of Culture of the Generalitat.

From the Rambla dels Ocells, the noisy twitter of caged birds gives way to a brilliant kaleidoscope of the **Rambla de les Flors**, with its numerous stalls of dried and fresh-cut flowers.

Overlooking it is the **Palau de la Virreina**, the palace of the viceroy's wife. The lady in question is the 18th-century vicereine of Peru, then part of the Spanish Empire. It is now home to the city cultural service with a tourist information centre, postal museum and a collection of Italian, French, Dutch and Spanish masters assembled by Francesco Cambó.

A few doors on is the **Mercat de Sant Josep** or **La Boqueria**, a daily market aglow with piles of fruit and vegetables and where fish glint on marble slabs.

Behind the market, among the narrow, jostling streets, is the **Carrer de l'Hospital** and the **Antic Hospital de la Santa Creu**, established in the 13th century for the benefit of sick pilgrims. In the 18th century, it was taken over by the Royal Academy of Medicine and Surgery and it retains its chandelier-lit operating theatre. Its chapel is now an art gallery, showing different artists' work every month.

Next door to the chapel is a courtyard with benches and orange trees and a porch at its far end leading through a passage to the left of which is a galleried and arcaded cloister. In the days when the Santa Creu was a hospital it was in these pleasant squares that convalescing patients took the air.

The passage itself emerges in the Carrer del Carme, where an ambitious development project is converting its former religious establishment, the **Casa Caritat**, into a cultural centre for Catalonia. Here, too, are a number of

The daily food market in the Boqueria, on the Rambla.

unpretentious restaurants, popular with the locals, where you can eat an excellent *paella* and drink a bottle of wine at a surprisingly moderate price.

If you continue down the Rambla, you will next come to the **Rambla dels Caputxins**. Here, at café tables, you can relax over an al fresco drink or meal and perhaps read the newspaper, local or international, bought at one of the numerous kiosks.

It is dominated by the **Gran Teatre del Liceu**, Barcelona's impressive 19th-century opera house. Worked into the pavement here is a circular design of bold blue, yellow, cerise and white by Joan Miró.

Opposite, forming the corner with **Carrer Cardenal Cassaas**, is Caixa de Sabadell (a savings bank) with a strange facade of Chinese and Japanese motifs, including a glowering dragon hanging, gargoyle-like, over the street. A few yards further on, the smokey **Café de l'Opera** is said to have been the haunt of Casanova.

The name "Caputxin" comes from the Capuchin monastery replaced in the last century by the broad **Plaça Reial**. The square's fountain and towering palms are overshadowed by a quadrangle of four-storey ochre-coloured buildings which have seen better days and, though a delightful spot for a meal, it now attracts some shady characters.

On Sundays, however, you will find huddled groups in intense numismatic or philatelic negotiation, while its arcades are filled with the stalls of stamp and coin sellers. Among them you may well find a pile of Roman *denarii*, to say nothing of the currency of an earlier age—Palaeolithic and Neolithic worked flints.

In the **Carrer Nou de la Rambla**, on the opposite side of the Rambla, is another Gaudí building, the **Palau Güell** (also open to visitors). Part of the building is a theatrical museum which can be visited only by appointment.

The last expanse of the Rambla is the **Rambla de Santa Mònica**, named after the 17th-century convent which is a temporary home for the **Museum of**

Opera singer Alfredo Kraus in a Liceu dressing room.

CHOCOLATE MAESTRO

Dubbed the "Mozart of Chocolate" by French gastronomers, Antoni Escribá is universally acknowledged as the master of the art of chocolate sculpture. Some of his more spectacular creations have included a life-size statue of the footballer Maradonna and another of Michelangelo's *David*, a cake for 10,000 people drawn into a banqueting hall by a horse-drawn chariot, the Sagrada Família modelled and baked as bread, and a live mermaid coated with chocolate scales. The ultimate accolades have come from other Catalan masters: Miró called him a wizard and Picasso swapped a painting for one of his sculptures. But it is the quieter, everyday work in which Escribá seems to take most pride.

"When people ask how long it took me to make something," he explains, "I tell them a few hours and 40 years of professional experience."

During that time, he has perfected a technique for printing photos or line drawings on bread and chocolate, developed formulas for all kinds of diabetic confectionery, written the standard work on chocolate sculpture and, last but not least, run the two family *confiteries* in Barcelona on Gran Via and the Rambla, with the help of his wife and sons.

Although the Catalans may not leap to mind as a race of chocolate-makers, Escribá's talents are firmly rooted in local tradition. For two centuries after the cocoa bean arrived from the New World, Spain held the European monopoly, and the best chocolate—for drinking only—was made in its Trappist and Cistercian monasteries; at Poblet the monks indulged their passion in a hall now called La Xocolateria.

Now there is chocolate on most festive occasions and even savoury dishes include it. *Llangosta à la catalana* and *conil à l' empordanesa* are considered among the region's great specialities and have graduated to expensive restaurant menus. But it is the *pastisseries* and *confiteries* which are the mainstay of Catalan chocolate making. In the weeks running up to Easter, their windows become showcases for *mones*, elabo-

rate chocolate scenarios which range from Baroque religious retables to witty jokes on topical themes.

Since the war Escribá has developed his technique so that he could build up the abstract elements—cones, columns, pyramids and so on—into anything from a Wild West show to a miniature Modernist building.

"The key to it all was tempering the melted chocolate to change its molecular structure, which I worked out under a microscope with the help of a geologist friend", says Escribá, "and, of course, working quickly enough to make it commercial. My father insisted on that."

At the end of the 1950s, he began to demonstrate his ideas abroad. "The thought of a Spaniard telling the Swiss how to sculpt chocolate was rather like someone from Switzerland coming here with revolutionary bullfighting theories," says Antoni Escribá. But the sceptical were soon convinced by the speed and spectacular effects of his work.

Of course, imagination was the real key to his success. "Inside I am a sculptor," he says, "and that is what I would have been if family circumstances had not decided otherwise."

He first discovered his flair for sculpture working with wood and stone at the School of Arts and Crafts, the Llotja, where he was soaked in the exuberant local Modernist tradition. Among strong direct influences, he singles out Miró, who became a friend. "He taught me to keep a certain restless, childlike curiosity and a healthy sense of doubt. But obviously there is something much broader than that. Barcelona has always been a part of the creative culture of the Mediterranean, a cradle for artists, and I grew up inside that."

A firm believer in the Catalan spirit of family enterprise, Escribá has already begun handing over the kitchen to the fourth generation: his sons Christian the *pastisser*, Joan the chocolate maker and Jordi the ice-cream maker. "To me, a family trade also represents the development of a craft," he says. "Now my sons have gone beyond me. That is the way it has always worked in our family and that is the way I think it should be. Teachers produce students, but a *maestro* should produce *maestros*."

Contemporary Art until it moves into the permanent one now being prepared for it in the Casa Caritat. A former bank building houses the **Museu de Cera** (the wax works); besides figures of celebrities, it has its own very macabre Chamber of Horrors.

The Rambla is at its liveliest in the evening or on a Saturday afternoon, when knots of men are gathered round chessboards, or on Sunday as the devout leave Mass. This is when you are most likely to encounter its buskers. They can range from a British rock duo or a group of flute-playing Andean Indians to such home-bred products as the woman who imitates bird-calls and the tiny whitened-faced figure in full evening dress, top hat and lavender gloves who remains motionless until someone tosses a coin into his bag when he springs into the gyrations of the automaton he resembles.

At any time, though especially on feast days, you may come across a ring of hand-holding youths and girls solemnly dancing the intricate steps of the *sardana,* the Catalan national dance some believe to date back to the time of the Greeks.

The waterfront: The Rambla ends at the **Monument a Colom** (Columbus Monument), floodlit at night. The people of Barcelona, much given to superlatives, will be quick to tell you that this is the highest monument to Columbus in the world. A lift inside will take you to the top for a view over harbour and city.

Nearby is the **Reials Drassanes**, the 14th-century shipyard which has a high timber roof supported on rounded stone arches. It is now the **Maritime Museum**. The star exhibit is a life-size copy of the *Real*, in which Don Juan of Austria sailed to victory at the Battle of Lepanto in 1571, thereby halting the Turkish conquest of Europe. Its displays show shipping down the ages and there are collections of figureheads and navigational instruments.

From his pinnacle Columbus points toward a replica of his *Santa Maria* in the harbour and it is from here that the

ferries for Ibiza leave as well as the *golondrinas* which will take you on a trip round the port.

Northeast of the monument is the seafront promenade of the **Passeig de Colom**. Among its buildings is the **aquarium** and a stock exchange, the **Llotja**, which has operated on the site since the 14th century.

The church of **Santa Maria del Mar**, a century older, is also known as the Riverside Cathedral and has a special place in the city's heart. Its impressive interior is often used for such secular purposes as concerts of classical music and jazz. In the Middle Ages, when Barcelona was a great port, it was in this area that both the merchants and the crews who manned their ships lived cheek by jowl. Facing the church are the old lists where tournaments were held and where public executions were carried out under the Inquisition.

Barceloneta: The Passeig de Colom will take you to La Barceloneta, the man-made peninsula built as protection from the sea. Its **Passeig Nacional**, the harbour-side street, and the streets giving off it, are another restaurant area and at its end is one of the two towers of the cable-car system from which you can get splendid, if vertiginous, views of port and city.

The beach: The Passeig Nacional also goes down to the beach, but the wider expanse of the Platja de la Barceloneta can be reached through the side streets and is a reminder that, among other things, Barcelona is a seaside resort. If you eat or drink at its cafés which tout for your custom you may find yourself being serenaded by a guitarist.

The beach itself is kept cleaned and raked, but if you go there early enough you may come across discarded syringes, reminders of one of Barcelona's seamier sides – as a drug centre. But the scene is changing fast and much of Barceloneta has been pulled down to make way for the Olympic Village.

Ciutadella: Inland to the northeast is the **Parc de la Ciutadella**. The *ciutadella* (citadel) was built in 1716 by Felipe V to keep an eye on the turbulent

The city port, heart of a once great maritime nation.

Catalans. It has been replaced by a public garden which, besides pretty walks, a boating-lake and a concrete mammoth, houses Barcelona's **Zoo** and the Catalan **parliament**.

Nearby is the **Museum of Modern Art** with works by Casas, Mír, Nonell and other artists well worth discovering. Also within the precincts of the park are the **Geological Museum** and the **Natural History Museum**.

Its southwestern side is bound by the **Passeig de Picasso**, renamed after one of the city's adopted sons. It was here that Tàpies erected his *Homage to Picasso*. Though the master would surely have approved of this extraordinary fountain, in which water flows round a glass cube containing old chairs, sofas and steel beams, he is more conventionally celebrated in his own museum about 300 metres to the southwest.

Carrer de Montcada: This narrow street of Gothic mansions, once the homes of aristocrats, lies off the Carrer de la Princesa, between the park and Via Laietana. Arches in the facades give on to cool patios. Often these are decorated with plants, though a few have been reduced to builders' yards.

The **Picasso Museum** is in two of the finest buildings, the 14th-century palaces of Berenguer de Aguilar and Baró de Castellet. You can get an idea of their original splendour from one of the rooms which has been kept deliberately free of paintings, giving an uncluttered view of marble floors, gilding and elaborate ceilings.

On show in the main rooms are drawings, engravings and etchings tracing Picasso's development from a young artist in the city, with weeks spent in Sant Joan de la Horta, to such well-known works as *The Sick Child* from the Blue Period (1904) and *The Harlequin* (1917). *Las Meninas*, his "variations on a theme" by Velázquez, are in a separate gallery and there is an exhibition of his dazzling and witty ceramics donated to the museum by Jacqueline Picasso.

A few doors down the road, in another 14th-century palace, is the **Textile and Costume Museum**, showing fab-

rics and fashions from the 16th to the 20th centuries.

The *barri* Gòtic: Next to this area and roughly delineated by the Via Laietana, the Passeig de Colom and the Rambla, is the 1,000-year-old walled city, the ***barri* Gòtic**. Its centrepiece is the Gothic **cathedral of Santa Eulàlia** which stands on what was once the site of the Roman Temple of Augustus, four columns of which remain.

Incidentally, if you turn your back to the west door of the cathedral and look across the Avinguda de la Catedral, you will see another memento of Picasso, the sgraffito of dancing figures on a frieze around the modern **Col.legi d'Arquitectes**.

The present cathedral dates back to the 13th century with some 19th-century additions. Inside are carved and painted stalls and a white marble choir-screen illustrating the martyrdom of Santa Eulàlia, the city's patron, whose relics are in the crypt. The side chapels contain Gothic altarpieces and marble tombs. A museum is in the chapter-house with an impressive 15th-century *Pietà* by Bartolomé Bermejo and altar-piece panels of the same period. But, whatever you do, don't miss the cloister, a shady quadrangle surrounding a garden of ferns, tropical plants, soaring majestic palms and a family of geese, descendants of a flock which has lorded it here for centuries.

Behind cathedral and cloister is a network of medieval alleys and courtyards, such as the **Plaça de Ramon Berenguer el Gran**, with a sunken garden, and the **Plaça del Rei**, on whose steps Queen Isabel and King Fernando were said to have greeted Colombus returning from his successful voyage to the Americas.

The **Museum of the City of Barcelona**, telling its story from its foundation by Phocaean Greeks in the 11th century BC, is at the opposite end. The remains of a 4th-century basilica and the walls of a Visigothic palace excavated beneath the cathedral are also now in the museum.

As you explore this area keep your

Roof-top view of the most important commercial city in Spain.

eyes open for those arches, often quite unassuming, which lead into a pretty patio or garden. Examples are those of the **Frederic Marés Museum**, opposite the north door of the cathedral, with its orange trees, and the **Casa del Ardiaca**, the archdeacon's house, with its blue and white tiles and its palms, now used as the **Municipal Institute of History**. It is particularly worth seeing in spring and summer when its fountain, gallery and arcaded windows blaze with flowers.

The Frederic Marés Museum occupies the four floors of the former palace of the counts of Barcelona, later kings of Aragón. Besides Roman sculpture, Iberian *ex-votos* and Punic terracottas, it features a uniquely Spanish art-form, painted wood statuary, going back to the 10th century.

A little further on, the area opens up into the **Plaça de Sant Jaume**. This was the site of the forum, or market place, and the point at which the two main streets of the Roman city met. As well as trade, the forum was always a centre of political life, a tradition continued in the two magnificent buildings facing each other across the present square. They are the **Palau de la Generalitat**, seat of Catalonia's government, and the **Casa de la Ciutat** (city hall).

Both contain treasures. There are richly ornamented rooms and an orange tree patio on the upper floor of the Palau de la Generalitat, while a star-vaulted arch crosses **Carrer Bisbe Irurita**, linking the building with the canons' residence, today the home of the president of the Provincial Council. The Casa de la Ciutat has a Chronicle Chamber decorated by the painter Josep Maria Sert (1876–1945).

From the southern corner of the Plaça Sant Jaume you can return to the main shopping area, via the **Carrer de Ferran** which leads back into the Rambla. To continue the exploration of the older area, take a narrow street at its southern corner; this leads to the **Carrer de Boqueria**, where any of the alleys off it link with two adjacent squares, the **Plaça Sant Josep Oriol** and the **Plaça**

Left, the cathedral's Santa Rita chapel. **Right**, a *sardana* in front of the Generalitat.

del Pi, named after its lone pine tree. This could be called Barcelona's Montmartre and at its centre is the Bar del Pi, where Tomás Martí has reigned host for the past 30 years and is portrayed in most of the scores of paintings covering its walls. An open-air art show is held in Plaça Sant Josep Oriol on Saturdays and Sundays and there is a Thursday flea-market in both squares .

Montjuïc: Barcelona is dominated by three hills, **Vallvidrera**, **Montjuïc** and **Tibidabo**. The first is primarily a residential area and, though it contains several interesting Modernist residences, it is the other two which are most likely to lure the traveller.

Once a military strongpoint, Montjuïc is nowadays given over to pleasure and its hilltop fortress, the **Castell**, is now a **military museum**. You can reach Montjuïc by taking the cable car from the harbour or, if you suffer from fear of heights, you can take the Metro to Espanya or Paral.lel stations. It is a mile or so of uphill trudge from Espanya on foot, but an antique London double-decker bus will take you to the top free of charge. It stops by the two towering red-brick pylons in the Plaça d'Espanya.

From Paral.lel a funicular — there is direct entry from the Metro station — will deliver you to Montjuïc's large amusement park, which also has an open-air theatre.

In 1929 the hilltop site was chosen for the Barcelona World Fair. Its German Pavilion was designed by the German Bauhaus architect Mies van der Rohe and it was for this building that he produced his famous Barcelona chair. His original building, later demolished, has recently been reconstructed as **El Pavelló Barcelona**.

But other former pavilions have provided the city with a legacy of buildings it has put to good use as art galleries and museums. The **Museum of Catalan Art**, in the dominant Palau Nacional, has one of the world's finest collections of Romanesque art which should on no account be missed. Gothic art is also well represented and there are paintings

The Palau Nacional, where Catalonia's finest art treasures are kept.

by El Greco, Tintoretto, Zurbarán and Ribera.

The successive strata of Catalonia's evolution are portrayed in the **Archaeological Museum**, in the former Palace of Graphic Arts. Among outstanding exhibits are motifs from Greek mythology, derived from a similar work in Pompeii, and the Circus Games mosaic.

The most recent addition to the complex is the **Joan Miró Foundation** by the contemporary Catalan architect, Josep Lluís Sert. It houses 290 paintings and 3,000 drawings by the artist. From time to time exhibitions of contemporary art are held here and various rooms attached to it are used for film shows, as a children's theatre and for recitals and concerts.

One of the most striking exhibits of the 1929 Fair was the **Poble Espanyol**, intended to illustrate the variety of traditional Spanish architecture. Each street and square typifies a region, so by taking a stroll round and buying a set of postcards, you can impress friends at home with your knowledge of Spain.

Besides bars and restaurants serving the drinks and foods of each region, craft shops offer their products. Inevitably much is tourist kitsch, but it also has some good items, including pictures, tapestry, prints, shoes, tiles, leatherware and wood carving, though there are few bargains.

If you're anxious to save your pesetas you will probably find anything from a medieval joust to a miniature carnival going on in its central **Plaça Mayor**. And, all else failing, you can always go and watch the craftsmen at work. The glass-blowers are particularly fascinating. The price of your ticket entitles you to visit the **Museum of Popular Arts and Industries** and the **Museum of Graphic Arts**. Before making a special trip, it is a good idea to check they are open as their opening hours tend to be arbitrary.

Tibidabo: This is the highest of Barcelona's hills, reached by taking the blue tram from **Passeig de Sant Gervasi** to the funicular station. The hill is capped by the church of the **Sagrat Cor**,

The 1992 Olympic stadium behind the Palau Nacional on Montjuïc.

a piece of neo-Gothic erected in 1911 with a giant Christ on its topmost tower.

Beneath is a big amusement park and what is perhaps its greatest attraction, a **Museum of Automata**. Besides 19th-century toys, many of them highly ingenious, it has several examples of penny-slot machines.

Pedralbes: On the outskirts of the city is the wealthy suburb of Pedralbes which can be reached by bus or by taking the Metro to **Palau Reial**. The *palau* is the palace and surrounding park given by the city to King Alfonso XIII in 1920. Based on Italian Renaissance designs, its contents include specially imported tapestries, furniture and chandeliers.

It also houses a **carriage museum**. Two other museums are devoted to ceramics from Arab to modern times and to the decorative arts with examples of porcelain, clocks and gold and silver work. Among its most fascinating exhibits is a collection of engagement rings going back to the Visigoths.

On the Avinguda de Pedralbes is Gaudí's **Pavellons Güell** with its dragon-gate. But the jewel of the area — and, indeed, of the city — is undoubtedly its 14th-century **Pedralbes Monastery**, burial place of its founder Queen Elisenda, consort of Jaume II. It is one of the finest surviving examples of Catalan Gothic.

The chapter-house, infirmary, kitchens and refectory can be visited, and among its greatest treasures is the chapel of Sant Miquel with splendid murals by the 14th-century Catalan artist Ferrer Bassa. It opens on to the tranquil cloister where a garden of cypresses and palms is surrounded by three storeys of elegant arches balanced on slender pillars.

Nightlife: Barcelona has a nightlife unrivalled by many capitals. Obviously there are good restaurants — like the rest of Spain, the city tends to eat late — but there are also cinemas, theatres and an opera house, the Liceu, presenting a mainly classical repertoire. Besides discotheques and night clubs, there is a music hall, La Belle Epoque, with a

Tibidabo, high above the city: fun for families on Sundays.

spectacular nude show. The lower part of the Rambla has a number of sex bars and strip shows but, unless you have a reliable personal recommendation or a guide, they are best avoided.

Apart from its other diversions, Barcelona is at its most glamorous by night when its buildings and its fountains are floodlit. The great, stunningly illuminated fountains of Montjuïc, showpiece of the 1929 Fair with their great domes and shafts of water reaching heights of 165 ft (50 metres), are an entertainment in themselves.

Well worth a visit after dark is the Poble Espanyol. The main buildings are floodlit, spectacular firework displays take place on the slightest excuse, and in the bars and cafés you can hear music from flamenco to jazz. Also, if you possibly can, take a look at the buildings, patios and courtyards of the *barri* Gòtic at night.

But a word of caution: in spite of increasing prosperity over the past decade, like all Spain, Barcelona has many pockets of deprivation. You won't need to go far to encounter your first beggar, male or female. There are always several in the Rambla and usually at least one and sometimes several in the porch of every church.

It is also, of course, a big port city. This combination means that it has its share (and perhaps rather more than its share) of crime. In particular, be wary of the pickpocket and the bag-snatcher. These menaces, once largely restricted to the red-light district round the ***barri*** **Xines** on the south side of the lower part of the Rambla, have recently been extending their activities.

When going round the city after dark women should leave their handbags in the hotel safe and avoid wearing expensive jewellery. Both men and women should carry only cash for immediate needs and, if possible, leave behind them such items as passports or travellers' cheques.

Beware, especially, the young man who tells you you have a stain on your clothes and offers to clean it. It is a thief's ruse.

Los Caracoles, one of the *barri* Gòtic's best known restaurants.

BARCELONA PROVINCE

Stretching from the capital of Catalonia and the coasts of the Maresme and the Costa Daurada to the foothills of the Pyrenees, the province of Barcelona, which touches each of the other provinces, is certainly worth exploring if only as an eye-opening antidote to the main tourist resorts and destinations.

In virtually every way, the province is dominated by the city, even though much of the 2,985 sq. miles (7,733 sq. km), and just under half of its 4.7 million population, have little in common with the more cosmopolitan city-dwellers and life of Barcelona itself. The River Llobregat, which ends up spilling its often very polluted water into the Mediterranean next to Barcelona, starts life infinitely cleaner in the far north of the province, near the charmingly named Castellar de N'Hug.

To the west of the province, the vineyards of the Penedès, artificially separated into two *comarques* in the 1936 territorial division, begin near Vilafranca, while to the east, the pretty and under-populated region inland from the Maresme coast provides much to divert travellers off the motorway between Catalonia and the rest of the world. This area is dominated by the city of Vic, which is by reputation the most conservative part of the country and often described as "the capital of Catalan Catalonia". Almost exactly in the centre of the province, and of Catalonia itself, lies Manresa, an important economic and cultural influence on its surroundings, which sits next to the confluence of the Cardener and Llobregat rivers.

As you would expect with a city the size and industrial importance of Barcelona, much of the immediate surroundings are scarred with the signs of economic development. But, once clear of the town, the complex of major roads make it easy to travel to other parts of the province. It is hardly worth stopping within about a 10-mile (16-km) radius of the city, except perhaps to visit **Sant Cugat del Vallès** to the northwest, not for the site of the main national television studios for the area, which is what most Catalans associate with Sant Cugat, but for the medieval monastery in the centre of the town, with its 13th-century walled cloisters.

Also very near Barcelona, at **Santa Coloma de Cervelló,** is the Gaudí-designed church in the **Colònia Güell**, difficult to find within this unprepossessing 19th-century industrial village, but well worth the effort (take N340 turn-off, junction 3 on A2). Within the naturalistic and dim interior, you can imagine being in a forest glade.

Wine region: To the west and south of the *comarca* of Barcelona lies the vineyards of the Penedès. For those with more than simply a taste for the end-product, **Vilafranca del Penedès**, 37 miles (60 km) from the city on the A7 or N340, is the biggest town in the area and it houses the **Museu del Vi** (wine museum) within the 14th-century palace of the kings of Aragón. Throughout this region, and technically into the pro-

Preceding pages: **Montserrat, Catalonia's stunning holy mountain. Left**, the town beneath the monastery. **Right**, drummer boy at a festival, Sant Pere de Ribes.

THE HOLY MOUNTAIN

Montserrat is the holy mountain of Catalonia. A long day's ride from Barcelona in the mid-19th century, it is now accessible in an hour or so by the autoroute to Tarragona, taking exit 25, which skirts Martorell and leads to Monistrol, from which a steep winding ascent leads up to the monastery. The name of the mountain derives from the jagged, serrated silhouette of its fantastically shaped sandstone and conglomerate spine rising abruptly to a height of 4,072 ft (1,241 metres). Though its first impact is that of a striking natural feature, its fame is due to the goddess who shelters under its crags, described by the English traveller Richard Ford in 1845 as "the great Diana of the Mountain".

Ford clearly aims at a pagan analogy and goes on to speak of "the radiancy of Hecate's image" which "dazzled all beholders". But the effect of the carved wooden image of the Virgin of Montserrat is not to dazzle but to calm and sooth.

The legend is that she was made by St Luke and brought to Barcelona by St Peter in the year AD 50. Then, it is said, she was hidden from the Moorish invaders in AD 717 and lost until her rediscovery by peasants in AD 880; on hearing of this, the local prelate, the Bishop of Vic, claimed her and sent for her, but she refused to move be-

yond a place on the mountainside known as the Santa Cava (Holy Cave, now accessible by funicular), where a shrine and chapel were built and served by nuns. In AD 976 the nunnery was converted into a Benedictine monastery, which in time became famous for its learning and the seat of a mitred abbot.

The present frigid Renaissance church was built between 1560 and 1592. The old monastic buildings were destroyed during the Peninsular War (1808–14), when Catalan guerrillas (*somatenes*) resisted the French on the sacred hill, until it was overrun in July 1811 by Suchet's troops. "The troops," wrote Ford, "amused themselves with hunting the hermits like wild goats in the cliffs, and, having butchered them, proceeded to the convent, plundered the altars, hung the monks, robbed even the poor pilgrims, and burnt the fine library."

Ruin and decay followed until the monks returned in 1874. A new facade was added to the basilica in 1900 and the cult began to flourish once more. The present barrack-like dependencies—incorporating the needs of a modern pilgrimage centre such as shops and restaurants—are of little architectural interest. The Virgin is the thing. Whatever predecessors she may have had, the actual image seems to have been carved in the 12th century and belongs to the celebrated category of "black Virgins", made of dark wood further blackened by smouldering candles. Of these, Our Lady of Guadalupe, patroness of the Hispanic World, is the high priestess.

Despite her ornate surroundings, the Virgin is no idealised doll. She is a mysterious mixture of the homely and the hieratic. Her oval face, with long nose, receding chin and frank gaze, is extremely human. She is often referred to familiarly as *la Morenita*, the dusky one. At the same time, the Child is formalised in His posture with His right hand raised in benediction, while she herself holds in her hand the orb of the world.

La Mare de Déu de Montserrat, to give her her full title, had a profound effect on a number of historical personages. St Ignatius Loyola had visions of her in the sky above the mountain and undertook a vigil in front of her, laying his sword on her altar and dedicating himself to her service, before founding the powerful Jesuit order.

Kings, soldiers and statesmen have professed a special devotion to the Virgin of Montserrat; their names are recorded on a monumental slab on the pleasant walk up to the hermitage of Sant Miquel. Nor should the monastery's importance to the Catalan sense of national identity be underestimated. The abbots of Montserrat were and are elected by the monks which has allowed the monastery to preserve a certain independence, even under Franco. After his death, in the hushed and hesitant interregnum, Montserrat celebrated the first service of national reconciliation. But if there were ever a return to political repression, the resistance would derive much of its inspiration from Montserrat.

vince of Tarragona, there are many wine producers to be visited, especially the Codorníu museum in **Sant Sadurní d'Anoia**, in order to develop a representative view of the area's main product.

Leather town: To the north, on the N11 Barcelona-to-Lleida road, is **Igualada**, best known as an important producer of leather goods—70 percent of Spain's leatherwear is produced here—as well as woollens and paper. Within easy range of **Montserrat** (*see opposite*), the town offers ample opportunities to buy its goods at very reasonable prices. And on the way from the monastery and mountains of Montserrat stands the village of **El Bruc**, which is famous in Catalan history as the site of fierce battles with the hated French troops of Napoleon, who were fighting their way to **Manresa** in 1808.

Legend has it that the French made a run for it after a local drummer boy sounded the alarm near Bruc. Echoing round the mountains, it was mistaken for the sound of a large opposing force. The myth has been equally amplified over the years, as the real battles which did occur between Napoleon's forces and the Swiss troops aided by Catalan militia proved one of the turning points in the War of Independence.

In spite of its actual geographical position, Manresa, about 50 miles (80 km) northwest of Barcelona, is considered the "heart" of Catalonia. The main town of the *comarca* of Bages, this is an area which has played a rich part in the region's history, in no small way owing to Manresa's important situation in communications between the different parts of the country. The town also lays claim to the origins of Catalonia's modern autonomous constitution, after the Bases de Manresa were drawn up there in 1892 by the Unió Catalanista. The Jesuits have also played an important part in the development of the town and province, especially in the Benedictine monastery of Montserrat.

Cardona, 20 miles (32 km) northwest of Manresa, has a fine *parador* sited in the 13th-century castle atop a hill dominating the area. It also has salt

Miles of walkable woodland in Montseny.

mines and an accompanying **museum** which, by arrangement, will reveal not just exhibits relating to the extraction of salt from the earth, but a fascinating collection of sculptures moulded from the area's main industrial product.

Industrial bases: Between Montserrat and Barcelona is **Sabadell**, an industrial suburb notable only for its important textile sector, giving the area its reputation as the "Catalan Manchester", and **Terrassa**, which is more interesting and has a longer history in more traditional textile production. The two towns have for long competed over the honour of being capital of the Vallès Occidental *comarca*, with Sabadell awarded prominence in 1936. At the beginning of 1990, however, the Catalan parliament awarded both towns the title of joint capital.

Terrassa holds a small advantage for the tourist, however, with its churches and monuments. Enclosed within the walls of **Sant Pere d'Egara**, built on the site of a Roman city which used to be the administrative centre of this part of

the country, are three churches—**Sant Pere**, **Santa Maria** and **Sant Miquel**— which all date back to at least the 7th century. The collection of buildings, now a national monument, is well worth the visit, especially as the churches are easily accessible by road or train from Barcelona.

To the west of the two towns lies **Caldes de Montbui**, the site of a spa and Roman baths which became fashionable in the 19th century when many distinguished people, among them Queen Isabel II (who reigned from 1833 until the 1868 Revolution brought her down), came to take the waters. These days, the visitors are slightly less distinguished and their interests are more mundane. The waters pouring out of the Font del Lleó are said to be the hottest in Spain and, once they have cooled a little, are believed to be excellent for arthritis, rheumatism and high blood pressure.

Montseny mountains: In the far east of the province of Barcelona are the *comarques* of Vallès Oriental and the Maresme. The chief attraction of the area, unquestionably, is the **Serra de Montseny**, a beautiful and impressive range of mountains which straddles the provinces of Barcelona and Girona. The designated Natural Park covers some 120 sq. miles (310 sq. km) of mountains, valleys and abundant fauna and flora, and provides some breathtaking drives—though it teems with visitors on summer weekends. The area is dominated by the **Turó de l'Home**, a mountain some 5,618 ft (1,712 metres) high and, slightly further north, by Matagalls, which stands at 5,288 ft (1,695 metres).

There are several pretty towns and villages dotted around the region, and much to offer people interested in Romanesque religious architecture. There are some 65 churches from the era in Vallès Oriental, although the capital, **Granollers**, is notable chiefly for its recently restored covered market, which dates back about 400 years (a market has been held here regularly since 1040). The **Porxada** covered market was almost entirely destroyed in

13th-century castle, Cardona.

276

a bombardment in 1938, when more than 200 people were killed as they attended the weekly Thursday market under its roof.

Furthest corners: The parts of the province furthest from Barcelona hold a certain interest, if only because fewer tourists want to strike out that far. They are wrong not to make the effort, as the heartland of Catalonia holds much promise. Alongside Bages the two largest *comarques*, by surface area but certainly not by population, are Berguedà and Osona, both of which touch on the foothills of the Pyrenees. The cities of **Vic**, at the centre of Osona, and **Berga**, in the middle of Berguedà, are equally the respective centres of activity in these "provincial" locations, and both have a rich tradition in the historical development of Catalonia.

Vic is considered a serious and upright place, and by reputation the girls of the city are thought of as very straight-laced, not to say prudish. But more important, and far safer to test, is Vic's reputation as a producer of *salchichón*,

the salami-style sausage renowned for its quality and meaty taste.

The religious significance of the city is demonstrated by its ample supply of churches—some 35 of them—and especially its magnificent **cathedral**, built at the end of the 18th century around the original 11th-century tower constructed by Abbot Oliba (1018–46). The interior of the cathedral was decorated—twice—by the prominent Catalan artist, Josep Maria Sert, once in 1930, and a second time after his designs were severely damaged by fire during the civil car. Sert was still working on the interior when he died in 1945, but the majority had been completed.

The cathedral provides one of the best reasons for visiting the city, together with the fine collection of mainly religious art and relics housed in the adjacent **Museu Episcopal**. Some of the collection comes from other parts of the country, but the majority has been gathered from the rich and traditional parishes of Vic and its surroundings.

The small towns and villages in the

Haymaking near Berga.

KEEPERS OF THE FLOCKS

The dull clunk of a bell around the neck of a grazing animal is one of the evocative summer sounds of the Pyrenees. Under blue skies, in meadows of emerald grass and yellow daisies, they are free to munch and amble from dawn to dusk with only their own bells to disturb them. Come the winter, they head down the valleys, escaping the snow and continuing the transhumance (seasonal migration) which has gone on since the first Celtic herdsmen arrived.

There was a time when shepherds and their flocks seemed to be constantly on the move, like those from Montaillou, a small village over the border in the French Py-renees. Emmanuel Le Roy Ladurie wrote a history of this rural community, based on statements taken by the Inquisition, which was investigating the Cathar heresy in the Languedoc. "The shepherd from the Ariège and the Cerdanya in the 14th century was as free as the air he breathed," he concluded.

The heretics from southern France found friends from Torroella de Montgrí to Lleida, the Ebre and beyond. "Without necessary chat," wrote Le Roy Ladurie of two of these shepherds, "they merely melted into the flood of migrants, shepherds, unemployed and misfits which the Languedoc call *gavaches* and which the ebb and flow of 'human transhumance' drove towards Iberia."

Today's transhumance is not such a great tide, but it goes on nevertheless. Only around 6 percent of the population works on the land and though livestock are reared throughout the region, they are mainly confined to the Pyrenees. In summer sheep and cattle are driven to higher pastures, and in winter snow forces them down into the valleys and plains. Cattle are sometimes taken by truck to the coast where they graze on the hills behind the villas while the herdsmen pass a few months by the sea.

There are still shepherds who are complete nomads. Some of those who bring their flocks to the marshlands of Aiguamolls in the Bay of Roses cannot sleep under a roof. They will eat their evening meal indoors, then step out into the night to bed down, even on the coldest days of winter (snow fell in 1986).

Catalonia is not dairy country. Milk comes from cattle in the Pyrenees, often from a local brown short-horned variety, though there is an ancient long-horned herd kept on the estate of the fairytale castle of Requesens, near the border at La Jonquera, which are not milked but kept just for their meat.

Good local cheeses made from cow's, sheep's and goat's milk do exist, but are not always easy to find. Some of the best come in unmarked wheels, perhaps wrapped in vine leaves, and should be eaten within a few days of being sliced. *Recuit* and *mató* are soft cheeses, sometimes made in individual earthenware pots, which are eaten with honey as a dessert and can be delicious. Butter is expensive and not commonly spread on bread.

Sheep are kept both for their meat and their wool, though their numbers have been rapidly diminishing, taking with them a rich way of life. Ripoll is a sheep town, as well as an industrial one, and it holds a wool festival, with sheep-shearing competitions, every May. The artefacts of its shepherds and the tale of their lives are well displayed in the charming Museu Arxiu Folklòric. Here are the signs of the leisurely time they had to carve collars, pipes and pocket sundials and to sew sheepskin coats, leggings and even umbrellas. Today, alas, says the museum's curator, Sr Grailles, young shepherds entertain themselves by listening to their pocket radios.

But, however modern the shepherd is and however unpastoral his aspirations, he needs the patience to train and keep a good working dog. At Castellar de N'Hug, 12 miles (20 km) west of Ripoll, at the source of the Llobregat, sheepdog trials are held every summer. These working animals come in various shapes and sizes—though they are not the shaggy black-and-white Pyrenean mountain dogs. Typically the *gos d'atura* will be a hairy, brown animal, a fast and wily dog whose social standing as a symbol of a nation was confirmed when the artist Javier Mariscal used it as the model for Cobi, the mascot of the 1992 Olympic Games.

area have an emphasis on agricultural production. **Rupit**, a village whose destiny lies in tourism, is worth a detour on the winding road north, the C153. Some of the houses in this much-visited village provided a model for part of the Poble Espanyol in Barcelona, which recreated typical Spanish villages for the 1929 International Exhibition.

Mountainous north: The northernmost part of the province is the *comarca* of Berguedà, with its capital, Berga, lying on one of the main routes from the south of the province into the Pyrenees and Andorra. A chilly and often wet climate makes it unattractive for sun-seekers, but the scenery, especially in the mountains, can be dramatic. In winter the attraction lies in the ski slopes of **Rasos de Peguera**, 8 miles (13 km) north of Berga and the nearest ski resort to Barcelona. A wide range of water sports can be practised at most times of the year, particularly at the **Embassament de la Baells** lake just northeast of Berga, a beautiful stretch of water fed by the River Llobregat. The river itself starts

"Tro", a typical sheepdog.

its long journey in the far north of the *comarca*, at **Castellar de N'Hug**, nestling in the mountains which rise to over 6,500 ft (1,980 metres) in this area, taking in part of the **Cadí-Moixeró Park**. The name of this village comes from the the Counts of Hug, who ruled in the Empúries until 1325, when their lands were confiscated by the Aragonese. A glass of water taken here, among the picnicking Catalan families, is likely to be far healthier than the same water taken from the taps of Barcelona once it has made its way to the coast, then been treated and re-treated.

For the view, not far from Berga lies the **Santuari de Queralt**, an austere-looking religious sanctuary which provides an astounding panorama of the mountains and valleys of Berguedà, and the distant mountains of Cadí.

The tunnel that pierces the Cadí mountain range is the longest in the region, and is the much-used gateway to Andorra and France or, as many inhabitants will tell you, to the northern parts of "old" Catalonia.

COSTA DAURADA

Escaping the sights and smells of the industrial suburbs south of Barcelona, the C246 Autovia de Castelldefels soon arrives alongside one of the longest (and probably the widest) beaches in Spain. This is the beginning of the Costa Daurada, the Golden Coast, which stretches from the capital of Catalonia to its southern limits beyond the delta of the River Ebre at Valencià.

The Costa Daurada's great expanse of beaches has long provided tourists from home and abroad with resorts catering for a wide range of tastes and requirements. The town of Sitges, well known among British travellers, was one of the first to attract tourists to this part of the coast, and with this influx, its reputation grew. Since then package tourists have been catered for in Salou, campers have found seaside sites and wildlife enthusiasts have discovered the Ebre delta.

At the start of the coast, outside Barcelona, the delta of the **River Llobregat**, with its woods, lakes and fens, is one attraction that is almost impossible to visit. Major works carried out near the airport at **El Prat** have made access to the area difficult, but worthwhile for dedicated nature lovers.

As you continue to drive carefully south along the highly dangerous dual carriageway, be ready to swing past drivers who have stopped to speak to one of the down-market prostitutes who ply their trade by the *autovia*. About 10 miles (16 km) out of Barcelona, pine woods and accompanying camp sites begin to dominate the scene on either side of the road. There are eight between the city and **Castelldefels** and they are of varying quality; but **Gavà** and, more especially, Castelldefels offer many good shops, bars and restaurants as well as the beach.

These two towns have been traditionally the most popular destinations for weekenders from Barcelona, who arrive by their thousands in cars, buses and trains throughout the summer—although the sandy beach, kept as clean as possible by the local authorities, never seems really over-crowded. Castelldefels has an ambitious plan to convert the rather haphazard sea front into a modern *passeig marítim* to replace the ramshackle *chiringuitos* (small bars and restaurants) with legally authorised and better-built facilities. The two resorts are worth a weekday trip if you are based in Barcelona.

A recently built yacht marina, **Port Ginesta**, lies just before the road begins to twist over cliff-tops towards Sitges, about 15 miles (24 km) from the city. Outside the port are several restaurants, both typical family and tourist establishments, and there are several bars and cafés in the marina itself.

The road to Sitges twists round and back on itself for about 10 miles (16 km), passing a very ugly cement works and a tiny but charming beach at **Garraf**, which has a row of gaily painted beach houses. And on the outskirts of Sitges sits the modern development of **Aiguadolç**, the site of another yacht marina in an attractive rocky setting, which is developing a certain "chic" for food and drink.

Carnival towns: It is worth approaching the next resort of **Sitges** by turning off the main road at Aiguadolç and passing the blocks of holiday apartments on the road into town. One of its smallest beaches, **Sant Sebastià**, is a pretty introduction to the town, with one or two good restaurants facing the sea. If you manage to park in the area, it's a short walk up to Sitges' parish church and museums, rewarded by a fine view over the sea and the main beaches.

An important commercial port in Roman times, when it was known as Subur, Sitges gained its present name in the Middle Ages. The town is a mixture of old and new buildings, of tourist traps and quality boutiques, and it is said to have been "discovered" by the painter, poet and playwright Santiago Rusiñol at the end of the 19th century. He bought two fishermen's cottages and converted them into an artistic centre, much visited by painters, writers and other leading cultural lights of the time. Now the

Preceding pages: Sitges seafront. Left, the beach at Garraf.

Museu Cau Ferrat, it houses Rusiñol's collection of paintings, including works by El Greco and Picasso, and Spain's largest collection of wrought-iron *objets*, as well as sculpture, arms, ceramics and photographs.

As one of the first tourist resorts of Catalonia, Sitges rapidly gained favour with prosperous citizens of Barcelona and elsewhere to build their weekend or summer residences. Beyond the old town, along the sea front, stands villa after villa built in different styles, some of them very attractive but all very expensive.

These days, the town is popular with a wide variety of tourists, especially during its annual pre-Lent Carnival, which has become an excuse for everyone—particularly the semi-permanent gay community, whom the authorities see no reason to discourage—to let his or her hair down. Sitges also celebrates several feast days during the year, and everyone is caught up in the noise and excitement as, on each of these occasions, processions wind up and down

through the old town. The many bars and restaurants, the majority based around the Carrer del Pecat ("Street of Sin", though its real name is Carrer Primer de Maig), do their best business during these festivals.

A few mile south of Sitges on the C246 are the unpromising outskirts of the area's main town, **Vilanova i la Geltrú**, a thriving fishing port and the third biggest harbour in Catalonia. This coast was visited regularly by the merchants and fishermen of Phoenicia and Greece, but the nucleus of the busy town, la Geltrú, with its narrow streets, dates back to the 11th century, while its surroundings grew up as it became an increasingly important industrial, agricultural and maritime centre.

Vilanova prospered from a cotton industry built on the gold from the Indies brought back in the 18th century and, in spite of modern competition from the Far East, cotton remains an important element in the local economy. The town also finds room, on its three beaches, to attract the tourist, especially with some fine restaurants to match its place as a fishing port.

A selection of museums includes the **Casa Papiol**, providing a slice of Catalan life from the beginning of the 19th century, and the 13th-century **Castell de la Geltrú**, which houses a collection of modern Catalan paintings and *avant-garde* art. The town has a rich cultural tradition, and in spite of first impressions on entering, it is worth time off to take in some of the museums, or to walk the old streets. The annual pre-Lent Carnival, one of the most popular in all Catalonia and among the first to be prohibited under the Franco regime because of its many incitements to nationalism, is always an explosion of colour, noise and flair.

Beyond Vilanova, the Costa Daurada plunges more deeply into package tourism, starting with **Cubelles**, the last resort in the *comarca* of Garraf and the southern boundary of Barcelona province.

Diversions and excursions: The hills of the **Garraf**, which are penetrated by minor roads starting near Barcelona, **Street market at Vilanova i la Geltrú.**

form a designated Natural Park (threatened by the construction of a new motorway) and provide a beautiful alternative to the busy coastal route. The countryside ranges from bare mountains and wooded land to the beginnings of the vineyards of **Penedès**. At **Sant Pere de Ribes**, just inland from Sitges, visitors can make their way to the **Gran Casino de Barcelona** and try their luck at the tables in a mansion built in 1918.

All the beaches of the Costa Daurada in Barcelona province can easily be reached by train from the capital. Avoiding morning, early evening and weekend rush hours, they are a preferable way of travelling. The railway continues to provide sea views all the way down the coast to L'Ampolla on the Ebre delta: the journey from Barcelona to Tarragona, halfway down the coast, takes little more than an hour.

Inland, the A7 from Barcelona (worth the toll if you are heading further south) catches up with the coast road at El Vendrell and both highways continue south to Tarragona and Valencia.

Tarragona's beaches: Since the 1960s much of the shoreline of Tarragona province has become a continuous ribbon of straggly tourist development. From **Cunit** in the north to **l'Hospitalet** in the south, the coastal villages and towns have grown tall and fat while the gaps in between have been plugged by camping sites, roadside eateries and *urbanizacions*. As a result, the coast road, once the noble Roman Via Augusta, is plain and often nightmarishly crowded. To cap all of this, first impressions may be prejudiced by the sensationalist British tabloid stories on typhoid in Salou (in reality, probably food poisoning contracted elsewhere) and the more serious scare following the nuclear accident at nearby Vandellós.

Despite the doubts cast by such reports the coast has many charms. Its main tourist enclaves are surprisingly old-fashioned and salubrious. They aim at the family crowd rather than the disco hordes of the Costa del Sol and, with 50 miles (80 km) of beaches, it is not hard to find some with little or no develop-

Rusiñol's Cau Ferrat in Sitges.

ment. In summer these are all busy, especially where there are camping sites; but by September, when the sea is still warm and the locals only drift back to the beach to take their lunch-hour or to fish in the evening, you often have the sand to yourself.

Distinct characters: Another pleasant surprise is the extent to which the resorts have each kept their own character. Between Vilanova i la Geltrú and Tarragona city, at **Calafell**, **El Vendrell** and **Torredembarra** (all popular with the French and Germans), family-owned villas and apartments are squeezed into the fishing quarter between the railway line and the sea. Calafell and Torredembarra both have small *cascs antics*, historic centres, but Sant Salvador, El Vendrell's *barrio marítim*, makes the most interesting resort.

Apart from the usual modern attractions—the wide, flat expanse of sand, a marina, seafront cafés and restaurants—there are relics of an elegant past: a splendid abandoned Modernist

spa-hotel and the **Museu Pau Casals**, housed in the celebrated cellist's old summer beach-house, which is well worth a visit even for those with no musical leanings, since Casals (1876–1973) accumulated a fine collection of paintings reflecting his ardent Catalan nationalism. Implacably opposed to Franco, he lived in exile from the civil war till his death in Puerto Rico, but his remains were brought back to the family tomb in El Vendrell in 1979. Concerts are held in a modern auditorium opposite the house.

Just inland from Sant Salvador there are further distractions: the quiet 18th-century village of **Sant Vicenç de Calders** or the safari park 5 miles (8 km) northwest on the C246 at **Albinyana**, where a French tourist was eaten by a lion called Marcos a few years ago (another wily tourist, safely locked in his car, took photographs and sold them to *Paris Match*).

In the evenings, the main town of El Vendrell makes a good break from the manufactured nightlife of the resorts: it is still remarkably as the English writer Rose Macaulay described it, with plazas, palms and "a casual Mediterranean *savoir vivre*". It also has an extraordinary Modernist altarpiece by Jujols in its angel-topped church (where Casals' father was the organist), festivals with local devil and stick dances and fire parades, and a good local nightlife along the small *rambla*.

Unspoilt spots: It is remarkably easy to find unspoiled pockets tucked in between the next few resorts going south: at **Roc Sant Gaietà**, reached through an *urbanització* by the Roman **Arc de Berà**; the windswept coast around Torredembarra; **Punta de la Mora**, once a look-out post against Algerian pirates, now a good place for bird watching; and **Tamarit**, where the beach and camp site, tucked under the cliff-top castle, are reached by a winding road through vegetable gardens.

Tamarit belongs to **Altafulla**, one of the most picturesque towns along the coast. It has a long history as a wealthy summer resort: 16 centuries ago the Roman governor came here to escape

The church, Altafulla.

the heat in a splendid villa (the excavations are open in summer, but the mosaics and statues are in the Tarragona museum) and seven centuries ago, the archbishops began using Tamarit as a summer palace. Since the beginning of this century, private villas have filled the old marshes behind the 18th-century *botigues de mar*, or fishermen's stores, which were built in the days of the contraband trade.

But tourism remains low key, thanks to the town's pride in its heritage. The main town, clumped around the privately owned medieval **Castillo de Montserrat**, has kept a seigneurial feel, with everyday small shops, no discos—they are banned—and only a small colony of English bars in among the rose-coloured stone houses.

Tarragona city: The beaches of the provincial capital are also remarkably unspoilt, largely because the *tarraconenses*, great sun and sea lovers themselves, are determined not to see their shoreline appropriated. There are four main beaches: **Platja del Miracle**,

a tiny city-centre bay which genuinely becomes a small wonder in the dramatic sunsets and moonlight; **La Rabassada**, which has a couple of cafés and is the fashionable young people's meeting place; **La Sabinosa**; and, finally, furthest out from town, **La Platja Larga**, a long stretch of blond sand with pines, a camping site and a nudist bay nicknamed "Waikiki" that can be reached only on foot.

The city itself is very much the daughter of Mare Nostrum. Originally built by the Romans both as a port and as a town of seaside relaxation, it embraces the Mediterranean, unlike Barcelona which has turned away from the sea. Symbolically, the Rambla Nova finishes at the steps of the splendid **Balcó del Mediterrani**, where the *tarraconenses* stroll on Sundays and evenings to *tocar ferro* (to "touch the iron" of the balcony) and get a whiff of the sea. (See *Tarragona Province* for a guide to the city.)

To the south the shoreline is swamped for several miles by the huge

expanse of Tarragona's industrial port, which has grown to the second largest in Spain since the petro-chemical complex and oil refinery opened in 1975. But the fishing quarter of **Serallo**, still in the town itself, has a lot of character, a working atmosphere and good, bustling restaurants (in summer try the old fishermen's club out on the quay).

Package-tour towns: Tarragona's two major resorts are **Salou**, 5 miles (8 km) south of the city, and **Cambrils**, 3 miles (5 km) beyond. Both offer package tours served by the charter airport at Reus, 10 miles (15 km) inland. In high summer, their palmy esplanades bulge at the seams and their cocktail bars throb late into the night, but at the end of the season they shrink back to surprisingly upmarket residential towns with smart shops, eating places (Cambrils has a trio of excellent seafood restaurants) and hotels which tick over quietly all year with the help of government-subsidised holidays for pensioners.

Despite problems with the British press and the off-putting approach from Tarragona through the sprawling, smoky industrial zone, the future of both resorts seems assured by the massive new American theme park planned for the Salou headland. If, as everybody hopes locally, the combination with sun and sand turns the park into a blockbuster then the Costa Daurada will probably seem more akin to Florida than Spain by the end of the century.

Miami Platja, 10 miles (15 km) south of Cambrils, and nearby **L'Hospitalet** are both uninspiring resorts packed with tall apartment blocks. Beyond them there is a break in the flat beaches where the distant hills curve round and drop down to the sea like the jagged line of a graph. Here small enclosed coves and creeks indent the shore. Some are frighteningly close to the nuclear reactors at Vandellós, but others, signposted through the *urbanizacions*—for example, **Cal Vidrell** and **Cal Mosques**—are beautifully private nooks and crannies.

In the centre of this rocky stretch is **L'Ametlla de Mar**, which, despite

Full beach: package tourists in Salou.

camping sites, yachts and a few souvenir shops, has kept the salty, wet atmosphere of a fishing village. Everything seems to be in miniature—the three beaches, the alleys of the town, the church—except for the port, which dominates the life of the village. Next to the quay are shops selling *efectos navales* and the open shed where the *abastos* (fish auctions) are held after the fleet comes back late in the afternoon. There are also stalls where the local housewives buy their seafood.

The Ebre delta: After L'Ampolla, the landscape changes abruptly again to the delicately balanced amphibious world of the Ebre delta. Jutting out into the sea like a gigantic fish head, it was first settled by the Arabs and then by the Knights Hospitalers, but remained largely barren until the Canal Dreta was built along the river's right bank in the mid-19th century.

Today the delta is nicknamed "the larder of Catalonia" and the land, governed by its own *junta*, is some of the most valuable in the region. Interspersed vegetable and rice fields, giant mirrors to the sky, bask under wide horizons and stretch down to huge expanses of golden white sand, the largest of which, the **Platja dels Eucaliptus**, resembles an ocean beach. Idyllic though it looks, there are drawbacks: a long walk before you start swimming and currents which need to be watched.

Inland, the scattered thatched *albarcas* have been replaced by modern houses and there is no trace of the traditional way of life which grew up around the rice fields, though a glimpse of how it once was can be seen in the museum at **Amposta** where there is an excellent permanent display. But the small towns in the centre of the delta keep a languorous, self-contained, southern feel, with whitewashed walls, flat roofs and dogs watching the world go by. At **Sant Jaume d'Enveja**, two pontoon ferries chug back and forth; they have the fascination of all boats which take you across a great river.

The main town of the delta, **Sant Carles de la Ràpita**, sits at the mouth of the southern **Port dels Alfacs**, the largest natural harbour in the Mediterranean. Carlos III (1759–88) had a grandiose plan to elevate it into a great port and his unfinished palace and the old customs house stand as amusingly overscaled monuments for such a pleasantly slow, small town. Tourism is less important than the land, boat-building and fishing; the fleet makes a fine sight as it sails home late in the afternoon.

A few miles to the south, on the border with Valencia's Costa Blanca and under the protectively lowering shadow of **Montsià**, the last spur of the coastal hill range, lies the small, elite resort of **Les Cases d'Alcanar**, a wealthy summer colony. Palmy villas overwhelm the fishermen's cottages and the occasional helicopter lands near the port. It has only a moderate beach but two claims to fame: very good fish restaurants (especially for *llangostins*) and a recently acquired curiosity value as the place where Lieutenant Colonel Antonio Tejero and his military chums came to hatch their plot for the failed parliamentary coup of 1981.

Summer chores, L'Ametlla de Mar.

BIRDS OF THE EBRE DELTA

Flying in or out of Barcelona airport on the southern approach, you are likely to see a huge silver trellis stretching out into the blue Mediterranean. This is the delta of the Ebre, Roman *Iberus*, the major river in the peninsula which has taken on its name.

Roman maps don't mention a protrusion into the sea at this point and Amposta, now a good 15 miles (25 km) upstream from the mouth, is shown as a seaport. The Ebre delta grew as a result of the sudden increase in alluvium in the river's waters. The erosion was caused by intense felling on the *meseta* (inland Spain) accompanied by the appalling *mesta* policy, begun in 1273, that resulted in widespread overgrazing by the royal sheep. A visit to the barren Monegros area in Aragón will give some idea of the destruction this caused.

The combined effect of the accumulation of alluvium, off-shore currents and winds have resulted in the creation of the delta—a huge system of channels, lagoons, sand bars and marshlands. Its inland part is largely agricultural, made up of 70 sq. miles (180 sq. km) of paddy fields and 40 sq. miles (100 sq. km) of fruit orchards. Fishing is lucrative: on the estuary's canals eels and giltheads are plentiful; lobster is abundant in the bays.

On the coastal strip there are large saline lagoons, dunes and wide tracks of wild marshland, where saltwort freely grows. Most of this area is included in the 27 sq. miles (70 sq. km) park. At the river's mouth long-shore currents push the silt deposits to either side, forming the **Trabucador** spit to the south and the **Fangar** points to the north. This makes the overall shape of the delta rather like a blunt arrowhead pointing out to sea.

The delta is flat and easy to visit. **Amposta** is a good base for the northern and southern sectors. Plenty of ferries cross the river at several points during the day. The roads are narrow but enable you to reach all the interesting areas of

n the exception of Buda
cars are not allowed. The
ve (*parc natural*) has two
n centres. One is at **Deltebre**
ther, the Casa de Fusta, is on
n bank of the **Encanyissada**
. Both supply maps and bro-
s on the reserve area.

northern sector: There is a fine
d leading from Amposta to Deltebre
rmerly called La Cava) and the
ark's central information centre. This
goes through paddy fields which are
flooded from May, when the rice is
planted, until harvest-time in October.
In dry winters the rice fields can look
barren but in summer the dense plants
often cover over the water. This is a
fundamental habitat for tens of thousands of wintering and migratory water
birds from the north of Europe.

A walk or drive along the Fangar
peninsula reveals the waters of the **Golf
de Sant Jordi** and a wealth of wintering
grebes, cormorants, eiders and other
ducks. Terns are sure to be diving into
the sea in search of fish. In winter you

can also look out for black-headed
Mediterranean gulls, which usually
wing their way across the bay in the
evening, on the way to their roost in
L'Ametlla de Mar.

A boat trip up the river from the
landing stage opposite **Buda Island** is
worth making. At dawn and dusk the
landing stage is a good place to see
thousands of birds—cormorants, cattle
egrets, little egrets, waders and even
squacco herons—flying to and from
roosts on the island. The boat trip goes
downstream to the mouth of the river
where you may be lucky enough to see
ospreys or otters. In winter the rare red-
necked grebe is often seen off the cape
area, which is made up of a series of
ever-changing sand bars.

In all the paddy-field areas, the black-
winged stilt is a common summer visitor. Its extraordinarily long red legs and
bill contrast with its black-and-white
plumage and it looks as if it belongs in
a Japanese print. When disturbed, it
rises up in the air and utters a repetitive
strident call, letting intruders know they

**Preceding
pages:** El
Garxal on the
Ebre delta;
worker's hut.
Below,
flamingo
flypast.

are not welcome. The edges of the paddy fields are the haunt of harmless but abundant viperine water snakes (*Natrix maura*) which slither off into the water as you approach, usually accompanied by a flurry of excited marsh frogs.

The egrets are another treat. The little egret is common again after recovering from the hat-plume craze of the 1920s, which brought it near to extinction. This elegant heron can now be seen tip-toeing across the shallows, like a white-suited Gene Kelly. The cattle egret, on the other hand, belongs in safari films. This species, which is spreading north from Africa, perches on the backs of horses, for want of rhinos, and pecks its mobile platform free of parasites. The cattle egret is a rather chicken-like bird, but it looks beautiful in the breeding season when it gets an orange hue on its head and back.

You will have to be luckier to see the rare squacco heron, which has the Ebre delta as one of its last breeding sites in the whole of the Iberian peninsula. The beautiful purple heron, a summer visitor, completes the list of large exotic water birds.

The southern sector: Whether crossing over from the north sector or coming straight out from Amposta, a good place to start a visit of this sector is the **Casa de Fusta** information centre, which has a collection of stuffed birds. A raised hide at this point gives a wonderful view out on to the **Encanyissada**, the largest of the delta's nine major lagoons. You may well see a marsh harrier—the delta's largest bird of prey—quartering the dense reedbeds in search of mice and small birds.

On the road to **Poble Nou**, to the east, is a bridge which is a good watching spot. There are high reeds on either side where reed-dwellers, such as the marvellous pink-and-black male little bittern, can be seen. Birdwatching experts can also get to grips with small brown warblers here.

The **Tancada** lagoon and salt pans, nearer the sea, are also good for birds, particularly breeding avocets, which

Birdwatchers scan the skies.

can be seen from the car. Their startling black-and-white plumage and upturned bill will be visible even to those without binoculars.

The grassy area between the lagoon and the sea is where you are most likely to encounter two delta specialities: the pratincole and the lesser short-toed lark. This particular lark is something of a connoisseur's piece, but the pratincole is fascinating for laymen, too. It is a cross between a swallow and a wader, although the Catalans call it the *perdiu de mar*, the sea partridge. The fact that this mixed-up beast tends to make its nest in cowpats does not make its classification any easier. However, the sight of this rare bird hawking for insects on summer evenings is unforgettable.

Punta de la Banya: This is the star of the delta in terms of wildlife. A huge and relatively inaccessible area of lagoons, saltings and dunes, it is skirted by the large, shallow **Alfacs Bay**, which is rich in food for birds. The Banya has also become vital after the disappearance of practically all other breeding sites for water birds on the Catalan coast as a result of tourist developments. The Catalan government's nature conservation authorities now restrict access to the most interesting parts of the Banya Point during the breeding season, although plenty can be seen from the perimeter areas and on the nearer salt pans.

The flamingo must be the most startling bird in Europe and the Banya Point is one of this species' few European breeding sites. Flights of up to 1,000 birds can be seen on the lagoons and salt pans. The pink sheen of their plumage in the hazy distance creates a tantalising effect, while the sight of migrating flocks against a backcloth of tourist apartments, makes a statement that is impossible to miss.

Apart from the flamingoes, the major attraction are two species of gulls. Bird-watchers come a long way to see the rare slender-billed gull. Its head is white and its long red bill makes it unmistakable. This species can only be found breeding at a handful of sites in Mediterranean Europe.

But it is the Audouin's gull, considered to be the rarest gull in the world, which is the real success story of the delta. This maritime gull—one of the few European gulls not to have been seduced by rubbish tips—bred only on a few rocky Mediterranean islands until not long ago. However, poaching and egg-collecting threatened its survival. Its remarkable adaptation to sandy nesting sites, particularly those of the Banya Point, seems to have ensured the species' future. In little more than 10 years, its breeding record here progressed from a handful of pairs to hundreds. The Ebre delta is now the Audouin's gulls' main breeding site in the world.

Terns also breed in their thousands here. Common terns, Sandwich terns, little terns and, recently, the rare Caspian tern, are a spectacle as they flash past, drop into the water and tend to their shrill-voiced young.

The ceaseless activity of these birds contributes to making the Banya Point one of the busiest and liveliest nature reserves in Europe.

Left, the odd pratincole. **Right**, weighing a heron.

THE CISTERCIAN TRIANGLE

"New Catalonia" sprang to life from the conquests of Count Ramon Berenguer III (1096–1131), who repopulated Tarragona and restored its ancient archbishopric; and of Ramon Berenguer IV (1131–62), who recovered the Ebre basin from the Moors. Fast behind these military successes came the Cistercian monks with their civilising mission and agricultural skills. They also brought the pointed arch, though the general feel and layout of their monastic churches differed little from the massive Romanesque buildings further north.

The three great Cistercian foundations of New Catalonia, sometimes called "the Cistercian triangle", are **Poblet**, **Santes Creus** and **Vallbona de les Monges**. All are easily accessible from Tarragona. Vallbona is the most distant but should not be missed.

From **Tarragona** the N240 leads via **Valls** and **Montblanc** to **L'Espluga de Francolí**, from which it is but a short run to the royal monastery of Poblet. This foundation dates from 1151 and is the epitome of a grand, rich monastery where, in Richard Ford's words, "the mitred abbot purple as his vines reigned in Palatinate pomp".

Work started around 1160 on the church, which is built in the standard Cistercian style (a slightly pointed central nave, flanked by two more sharply pointed lateral aisles). In its heyday the monastery would have been served by at least 200 monks, now reduced to 30 or so. But in the evening, when they are singing vespers, the pure and lofty building still echoes with restrained but glorious sound.

Poblet was officially designated as the royal pantheon by Pere III (Peter the Ceremonious, 1336–87). The unusual gabled sepulchres raised on either side of the crossing of the church are royal tombs, containing most of the count-kings of the Catalan-Aragonese federation and their consorts, from Alfons I (the Chaste, 1162–96) to Joan II

Preceding pages: the monastery at Poblet. Below, its nearby rival, Santes Creus.

(1458–79), father of Fernando the Catholic who took Catalonia into union with Castile. During the disentailment of the monasteries in 1835, Poblet was ravaged. The royal remains were rescued by a Tarragona curate and only returned in 1953 when their tombs were ingeniously reconstructed by the sculptor Frederic Marès.

This spacious, airy church is a marvellous last abode. But perhaps the most enchanting feature of Poblet is the cloister with its hybrid combination of Romanesque capitals and Gothic tracery, and its octagonal pavilion complete with basin and fountain in the north corner of the quadrangle.

From L'Espluga de Francolí it is less than an hour's drive northwards, via **Solivella** and **Rocallaura**, to **Vallbona de les Monges**, which has been in continuous occupation by Cistercian nuns since 1157. Vallbona is much smaller than its male counterparts but somehow more haunting, possibly because of the pervasive atmosphere of continuity and prayer. Its variegated cloister, with each

arm of a different period, is charming. The nuns are justly proud of the octagonal lantern which pours light over the crossing of the church and makes a fine external effect.

The cross-country drive from Vallbona to **Santes Creus** leads pleasantly through undulating vine slopes topped by spinneys and copses. All three monasteries of the "triangle" are nicely situated but Santes Creus (the name means "Holy Crosses") enjoys the prettiest surroundings of all, flanked as it is by market gardens and a single village street above a riverside walk. The entrance courtyard, dedicated to St Bernard, is bordered by former monastic buildings, all decorated with *esgrafiats* or stencilled white patterns, some geometric, some floral, in exuberant contrast with the severely military aspect of the west front of the church.

Entry is through the cloister, which immediately invites comparison with Poblet's and testifies to their rivalry. But the arcade, particularly the south arm (1331–41) by the Englishman Reinard Fonoll, is more fully Gothic with neat scrolled or floral capitals, while some of the corner columns are topped off with popular scenes not usually found in more solemn Romanesque decoration. There is also a rear cloister called the "Posterior", off which are cellars, kitchen, refectory and royal apartments.

Two monarchs broke ranks with their fellows and elected to be buried at Santes Creus: Pere II (Peter the Great, 1276–85) and Jaume II (James the Just, 1291–1327), the latter with his wife, Blanche of Anjou. Pere's casket is raised on a porphyry urn carried by a pair of Mesopotamian lions—said to have been brought back from some foray to the East by the famous corsair Roger de Llúria, who is buried a few metres from his master.

The three Cistercian monasteries can be seen (in a rush) in one day from Tarragona but they are best savoured through a more leisurely approach, breaking the journey either at a hotel in L'Espluga or at Santes Creus, where the Hostal Grau is a haven of peace.

Jaume I (d. 1276) is returned to Poblet, 1953.

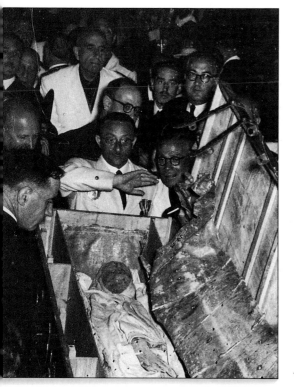

TARRAGONA PROVINCE

It takes time to get a feel for the shape of the 2,425 sq. mile (6,283 sq. km) Tarragona province since, underneath the common bond of *catalanisme*, it is a geographical hotch-potch of small segments with very different personalities. The easiest to characterise are the mountainous inland areas, which merge into a magnificent silhouette when seen from the coast but in close-up break up into distinct landscapes squeezed together cheek by jowl: the rust and emerald hills of **Terra Alta** and slaty black slopes of **Priorat**, the small but craggy **Serres de Prades** and more gently undulating **Conca de Barberà**.

A subtler eye is needed to pick out the divisions of the coastal plain. Away from the watery Ebre delta, tourist developments and towns fringed by modern suburbs blur the geography of the coast, while the main market towns as well as the agricultural zones give the flat, often featureless countryside its character. Oranges, rice and orchard fruits make the south unexpectedly lush; spiky hazelnut and almond groves cover the central plain with blossom in spring; vines, cereals and plane-tree-lined avenues lend the north a more temperate air.

Since the civil war, industry, tourist development and the building boom have accelerated the slow shift of prosperity and population from the mountains to the once impoverished coast and brought in their wake a flood of immigration, largely from the País Valencià and Andalucía. This, the *tarraconenses* say, has generally tempered their *catalanisme* (one-fifth of education is still in Castilian) and taught them a greater tolerance of others' ways. But also it has opened up a new gap between the industrial towns north of Cambrils, which are increasingly integrated with Barcelona's economy, and the more closed, conservative areas of the mountains and southern plain.

Anti-centralism is evident in gentle jibes against Barcelona and there are fierce local loyalties, but it shows most clearly in the liveliness of the towns, many of which have their own theatres and arts festivals as well as traditional *festes*. So it is hardly surprising that **Tarragona** city (pop. 100,000) tends to be looked to as an administrative capital rather than the cultural and commercial hub of the province.

Splendour of Rome: The *tarraconenses* are known for their calm, and though their capital is a great city, it has avoided becoming a hectic metropolis. Its ordered urban planning was inherited from the Romans whose original layout, uniquely preserved, imbues the city with its whole character. Tarraco, the splendid capital of Hispani Citerior, was built on three clearly delineated tiers propped up by a remarkable series of tunnelled vaults. Today the old town, girdled by more than half a mile (1 km) of the massive city walls, is a quite separate entity from the grid of spacious avenues of shops and offices which began to grow outside the walls in the late 19th century, while the massive

industrial zone and port are tucked away on the south side of the River Francolí.

Arriving through the messy sprawl to the south considerably dampens the spirit of place. But if you come in from the north or east, there are several monuments which keep the Classical splendour and scale that so impressed travellers during the six centuries of Roman occupation. A superb domed villa lies 3 miles (5 km) north at **Constanti**, the **Aqueducte de les Farreres** (named after the local rusty-red water and also known as the Ponte del Diable) straddles a small valley just off the old Via Aurelia leading to Lleida, and 5 miles (8 km) to the north on the Via Augusta is the **Cantol de Medol**, a great gladed hollow where the Romans quarried, leaving a stone needle to mark its depth.

The first impact of the city proper, now largely hidden by the spread of the suburbs, can be felt at the end of the Rambla Vella. Below, the **amphitheatre** drops down to the beach; above,

Preceding pages: Tortosa's well buttressed cathedral beside the Ebre.

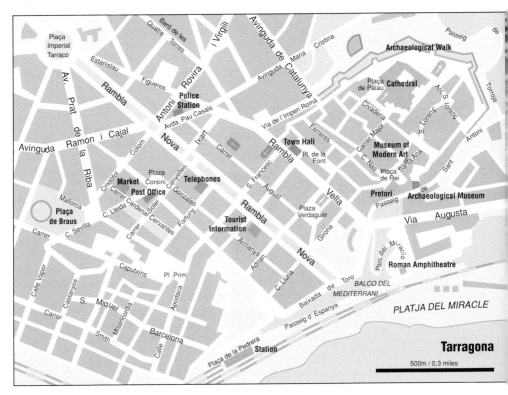

the walls rise up behind the **praetorium** and the newly excavated Roman **circus**.

The main sights, immaculately laid out and clearly explained in a series of illustrated pamphlets, are best broached at the **Passeig Arqueologic**, which leads round to the **history museum** and the stunning **archaeological museum**. They help to evoke life in the worn stones, often eroded by the salty air, and make sense of the striking symmetries and parallels in the city's development over nearly 2,000 years: the gold and tawny 12th/13th-century **cathedral** built over the **temple** (do not miss the glorious small retable, full of human detail, over the altar); the **praetorium**, or Roman tower, which became a royal palace in medieval times; the neo-classical Plaça de la Font, used for public *festes*, built above the circus; the splendid ironmongers of the Modernist **food market** close to the commercial forum; the bronze of Augustus given to the city by Mussolini.

These echoes of the past, found all around the old city, gave the English

writer Rose Macaulay the sense of a haunting ancient undertow, but today, in the wake of post-Modernism, they seem a natural underpinning to the modern city.

Recently, the *casc antic* (old quarter) has again been growing a new skin inside its old shell. Decaying quarters have been renovated (gingerly, so as not to disturb the bed of archaeological riches below), the hilly cobbled streets are being pedestrianised, cafés and restaurants are moving back in. But, apart from *festa* time (the main one is Santa Tecla, at the end of September, when giants from each quarter and *castells* or human towers move slowly around the old alleys), the bars and cafés around the Rambla Nova are the main meeting places.

The Rambla, a breezy 19th-century promenade, is the main *passejada* of the modern town. As straight and purposeful as any Roman road, it abruptly stops high over the sea beneath a statue of the great Catalan naval commander Roger de Llúria. This is the Balcó Mediterrani,

15th-century high altar, Tarragona Cathedral.

the city's much-loved terrace with a view, which embraces the sea that gave birth to the town.

Second city: Reus, 8 miles (13 km) west on the N420, is the province's second town. It is to Tarragona as Barcelona is to Madrid: two-thirds of the size, commercially dynamic and still jostling for recognition. At Carnival time pranksters put up derogatory roadsigns to *"Tarragona, barri marítim"*. Around the kernel of the old *barri jueu* (Jewish quarter), the stylishly window-dressed shops and Modernist facades by Domènech i Montaner (notably the splendid, encrusted **Casa de Navàs**) recall the mercantile heyday of the 19th century, when prices for Spanish wines were quoted around Europe under the tag "Reus, Paris, London", a phrase which has stuck.

Today, the agricultural **Llotja** (commodity exchange) on the Plaça del Prim still fills up on Mondays, when the prices of products are set, but now it is the price of hazelnuts which travels the world. These are grown on the sur-rounding plain and they are best viewed from the Romanesque church at **Vila-nova d' Escornalbou**, 12 miles (20 km) southwest on the T310. Unfortunately, neither of Reus's most famous sons, Antoni Gaudí and the 19th-century painter Marià Fortuny, left his imprint here, although the wonderful small theatre bears Fortuny's name.

Around Valls: Most people drive back through the northern plain only to reach Santes Creus and Poblet, the great Cistercian monasteries (see previous chapter). This is a shame. The **Baix Penedès**, awkwardly cut off from the other *co-marques* of the wine region to which it belongs, is focused on coastal tourism, but the rest of the plain, looking inland to **Valls** (12 miles/20 km north of Tarragona on the N240), keeps a more rural, traditional feel. The most interesting villages hug the foot of the mountains or follow the River Gaià which rises near **Santa Coloma de Queralt** in the most northerly corner of the province and runs east of Valls, coming out into the sea at Altafulla. At **Vilabella**, 5

The Roman amphitheatre Tarragona.

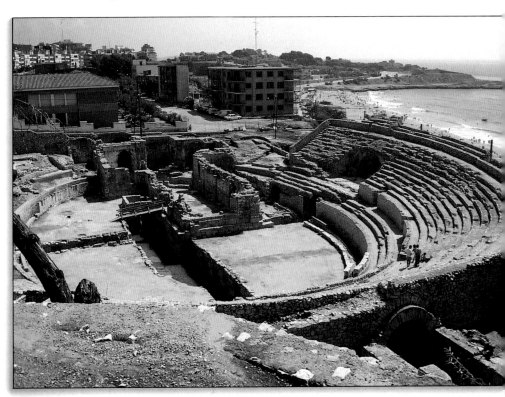

miles (8 km) southeast of Valls, there is a small **rural museum** and in summer a local group performs folk dances in the patio of the 12th-century church. At **El Pla de Santa Maria**, 5 miles (8 km) north of Valls on the T200, known for its outstanding 13th-century church, ambitious plans are being hatched for a Catalan **cultural theme park**.

Despite a large light industrial zone, Valls has a much more down-to-earth character than Reus and a strong attachment to traditions: as in an old saying that contrasts *l' home de Valls i el senyor de Reus*. The oldest tradition is the huge round-the-clock agricultural fair of *firagost* and the fastest growing is the *calçotada*, when quantities of giant local spring-onions grilled over charcoal are washed down with wine from *porrós* (beware of being served frozen onions in summer), but the most famous is the *castells*, or human towers, which grew out of a Valencian dance called the *muchaganga* more than two centuries ago. Catalonia's season for *castells* competitions opens here each year on

the feast of Sant Joan (June 24). The *colles*, or teams—originally peasants and artisans, Carlists and Liberals—perform in the lovely Plaça del Blat, under the 230-ft (70-metre) church steeple which dominates the old town.

The picturesque road following the Gaià valley runs into the rolling wheat fields of Tarragona's most northerly *comarca*, La Conca de Barberà, which has some of the most unexpectedly beautiful countryside of the province. As elsewhere, the Moors' presence shows by default, in the wealth of medieval architecture which marks the resettlement after their expulsion. The smaller villages such as **Conesa**, **Passanat**, **Villaverd** and **Saralla del Comtat** have wonderful churches, arcaded *plaças* and Romanesque arches repeated on a larger scale at Sant Coloma de Queralt, which belonged to the Knights Templar.

Travelling further southwest from Santa Coloma down the T221, vineyards begin and the villages have splendid Modernist wine co-operatives built after the reshuffling of the tenure system in the wake of phylloxera blight (the co-operative movement in Catalonia began in **Barberà de la Conca** itself). Most were designed by Gaudí's disciple César Martinell, who was born in Valls.

Base for Poblet: The T221 arrives back on the N240 between Valls and Lleida at **L'Espluga de Francolí**. This has a fine church and museum of rural life, but its tourist complex, catering for visitors to the monastery of Poblet, comes as a bit of a rude shock.

Neighbouring **Montblanc**, the third town of Catalonia in medieval times, is a more attractive base. It now lives almost entirely off industry and services, but its higgledy-piggledy streets are given a miniature grandeur by the 14th-century walls, considered the most important medieval military construction in Catalonia. Within them are aristocratic mansions and churches such as Sant Miquel, a 13th-century building of lovely, rough simplicity (three *Corts*, or Catalan parliaments, met here) and small shops lining closely

A town bar with a name to confuse.

packed streets crowned by Santa Maria la Major, which has beautiful curved Gothic fan vaulting and a grand organ above the door.

In the **Serres de Prades** immediately to the southwest of Montblanc there are no real towns, only thick-walled stone *masies* and villages, many of which are now half-empty, set in fine walking country. To the east are undulating hills patchily covered with the native forest of holm oaks, pines and chestnuts or scrubby heath; to the west craggy, terraced valleys with brickish soil.

One of its most beautiful villages, **Siurana**, off the C242 near **Cornudella de Montsant**, has been preserved by its remoteness. Several walking paths and a winding, rutted 5-mile (8-km) track lead up to the medieval hamlet perched like an eagle's nest on the end of a ridge dividing two deep gorges. The defeat of the Wali of Siurana in 1153 sealed the success of the Reconquest in Catalonia and legend has it that his wife, in defeat, threw herself off a dizzying ledge close to the castle. Remarkably, a dozen families still live in the stone houses and the only concessions to tourism are a car park for visitors and homely *fonda*.

El Priorat: The next mountainous pocket continuing southwest is now an administrative *comarca*, but it is the much smaller core of eight villages and their steeply terraced vineyards on harsh, slaty black hills that Catalans consider the real **Priorat**. These were founded and protected by the first Carthusian monastery in Spain, **Escala Dei**, which grew to glory between the 12th and 19th centuries. The villages survived the loss of the monastery after the state appropriation of Church lands in the 1830s, the terrible poverty that followed the phylloxera vine disease and, finally, the slow closure of the lead mines. They now form a self-contained world bound together by pride in the quality of their wine and their continued struggle with the land.

All of the villages are beautiful and unspoilt and can be dawdled around in a day while you taste and buy some of the best red wines in Spain at the *bodeges*. **Almond grove in February.**

At **Torroja** there is a small private **wine museum** and an altar made from an olive press; at **Bellmunt** a Modernist **Casa de Minas**; at **Gratallops** the only remaining **traditional cooper** and a good restaurant. Escala Dei itself awaits restoration, but is nonetheless a superbly romantic ruin overgrown by ivy and the wild herbs the monks used in their apothecary.

The mighty Ebre: To the west, El Priorat is bounded by the curving snake of the **Ebre Valley**, best seen from the corniche road that winds through peach, cherry and plum orchards on the left bank. Until road and rail took over, the river was an important economic route along which coal, oil, wine and almonds were carried downstream and rice and salt pulled back upstream in barges.

But now it is the huge volume of water—154,000 gallons (700,000 litres) a second—which ensures the valley's prosperity by powering the nuclear complex at **Asco** and industries around **Flix**, by irrigating the delta and alluvial plain, and by providing decent drinking water for Tarragona city (at a price). Riverboats chug back and forth from **Miravet** just south of the N420 and **Amposta** near the river's delta, but the currents and power of the river make it generally dangerous for swimmers.

The valley and the heights overlooking it have paid dearly for their strategic and economic value: the towns and villages were battered variously by Carthaginians, Romans, Moors, Franks and Catalan reconquerors as they fought for control of the valley. More recently, the bulge in the right bank of the river where it arcs eastward was torn apart by the Battle of the Ebre in 1938, which left massive casualties (estimates vary over 100,000) and many of the villages destroyed by Nationalist bombing.

General Franco directed the battle from the heights near the town of **Gandesa** on the N420, 15 miles (24 km) west of the riverside town of **Móra d'Ebre**. The stone needle on an Iberian tumulus which marks the spot has, not surprisingly, been defaced. There is

Grapes fresh off the vine.

another monument, a bizarre iron and stained-glass sculpture actually in the river further downstream at **Tortosa**. But neither of these have the emotional pull of **Corbrera**. Some 4 miles (6 km) west of Gandesa on the N420, the ruins of this village and its church have been left as a silent witness to the destructive power of war.

Pots and pitchers: On the river itself there are three towns worth visiting. **Miravet**, small and sleepy on the right bank, can be reached by an old-fashioned paddle ferry (daytime only) from which you get a good view of the white-and-ochre houses dropping down the cliff under the bulky fortress of the Knights Templar. The outlying *barri de terrissaires*, or potters' quarter, is justly famous. Although it now draws tourist coaches, the family potteries still work traditionally, mixing their own clay and following shapes which go back to Moorish times.

From here, it is a short sidestep into the **Terra Alta**, where the landscape jumps from cultivated valleys to the blue slate peaks in the **Serra de Pandols**. Today many people have abandoned the land to work in the factories and atomic power stations to the north, but the central villages are still surrounded by vineyards and almond and hazelnut groves. The local musky *amber blanc* is sold at the splendid Modernist co-operatives at Gandesa (which also has a lovely small old town) and **Pinell de Brai**, 5 miles (8 km) east on the C221, which is nicknamed "the cathedral of wine".

Horta de Sant Joan, 25 miles (40 km) southwest of Gandesa, draws visitors because Picasso spent two summers there with his friend Manuel Pallarès, but there is nothing associated with him except for the rich rust-and-green landscape of his canvases and apocryphal tales of his drinking habits and his French girlfriend, Fernande. More memorable is the Romanesque sanctuary nearby at the base of a combed quiff of rock. It is also worth tipping over the border into Aragón to catch **Vall-de-Roures**, frozen in time

Oil mill dated 1606 from Cervera del Maestre.

beneath a Gothic cathedral and spilling down the hillside to a river.

Big river towns: The first bridge downstream from Miravet is at **Tortosa**, the largest town of the south, which has a stolidly conservative reputation, smart cake shops, a very good botanical park and a Modernist covered market. In the old town, medievalism predominates. The large Jewish quarter, the Gothic **Llotja** and, above all, the splendid **cathedral** all survived the heavy bombing and destruction of the civil war.

As elsewhere, relatively little is left intact from the Moorish centuries, although for three centuries, as the seat of a *taifa*, the city controlled much of the valley. All that survives are the ruined defences of *la suda* and a small stone with carved Arabic writing, symbolically embedded in the walls of the cathedral's lovely small cloister.

Just before the river reaches its greatest power before slowing to meander through the flat delta, a suspension bridge—the longest in the world for a short time after it was built in 1905—

crosses from the left bank to **Amposta**. Lively, relaxed and largely agricultural, the town now has little except ruined defences to suggest its historic importance. Its rise from Iberian settlements clustered on the alluvial plain and subsequent downfall, due largely to Barbary pirates, can be traced in the excellent small **Museu de Montsià**, which also explains the natural history of the delta. The town also has plenty of lively bars and an excellent regional craft shop in Carrer Jaume I.

Amposta is also a good base for exploring the flat southern plain protected from the sea by the looming bulk of **Serra del Montsià**. Often called *la quinta provincia* (fifth province), this southernmost part of Catalonia is given a languorous air by Moorish place-names, teapot-lid church cupolas, festivals with oxen and bulls—sometimes with flaming horns—and acres of olive trees covering the plain.

The scattered villages, **Ulldecona** and **Alcanar** in particular, have some fine architecture, and above the **Santuari del Remei**, where there is an extraordinary roomful of *ex-votos,* ranging from plastic limbs to a whalebone and an L-plate, a large Iberian village is being excavated. Its streets, rooms and even bread ovens are already clearly outlined.

Moving inland, the road winding along the River Sénia, which marks the border with Valencia, passes a series of old watermills and a massive dam before reaching **Els Ports**, the end of the mountain system which runs down from the central *serres*. To the south of Montsià, beyond the convent of **Benifassà**, whose monks first planted rice on the plain of the Ebre, the architecture changes suddenly to the overhanging eaves and faded colour washes of the lovely mountain villages of Valencia's Baix Maestrat (the Maestrazgo in Castilian). But beneath the altered facades the language remains the same, a reminder that throughout the south of the region's southernmost province and well over the border into the País Valencià, *catalanisme* is as strong as anywhere further north.

Tortosa's altar. Following page: *castellers* in Barcelona.

TRAVEL TIPS

GETTING THERE
248   By Air

TRAVEL ESSENTIALS
250   Virgin Wisdom
250   Visas & Passports
252   Money Matters
252   Health
252   Customs
254   Tipping

GETTING ACQUAINTED
254   Climate
254   Time
254   Business Hours
254   Public Holidays

COMMUNICATIONS
254   Media
256   Postal Services
256   Telephone & Telex

EMERGENCIES
258   Loss
258   Left Luggage

GETTING AROUND
258   Driving
260   Private Transport
260   Public Transport

WHERE TO STAY
263   Hotels
271   Youth Hostels
273   Permanent Arrangements

FOOD DIGEST
274   What to Eat
274   Restaurant Listings
286   Drinking Notes

THINGS TO DO
289   Tours
291   Other Visits

CULTURE PLUS
293   Museums
297   Art Galleries
298   Historical Houses
300   Concerts
302   Ballet
302   Opera
302   Theatre
303   Cinema
303   Diary of Events
306   Architecture
307   Other Must-Do's

NIGHTLIFE
311   Dinner/Dance
311   Drinking Bars
312   Nightclubs
314   Cabaret
314   Casinos
314   Food Around the Clock

SHOPPING
316   Shopping Areas
329   Vat & Export

SPORTS
329   Spectator

FURTHER READING
330

USEFUL ADDRESSES
332   Tourist Information
        Centres (TICS)
332   Embassies

GETTING THERE

BY AIR

There are three international airports in Catalonia. El Prat de Llobregat in Barcelona is 10 miles (15 km) from the city centre. Trains between the airport and Sants station leave every half hour and take 20 minutes. Girona-Costa Brava and Reus-Costa Daurada are charter-only airports which do not operate in winter. Passengers from these airports are reliant on relatively inexpensive taxi services unless they are part of a package holiday, in which case the coach will be waiting. Both have fly/drive facilities. An airport at La Seu d'Urgell near Andorra handles domestic flights. Iberia, the Spanish airline, is the principal operator in Barcelona and offers regular money-saving deals on flights and fly/drive.

BY ROAD

The border is about 13 hours from the Channel ports by motorway, 10 hours from Paris. Allow for an overnight stop unless you're in a hurry. The winding coast road (the N114 in France, becoming the C252 in Spain) crosses the border at Portbou. The N9 national road from Perpignan crosses at Le Pertus and becomes the N11. Beside it the A9 motorway becomes the A7 as it reaches the La Jonquera border point—both are busy in summer and though the motorway queues can be longer, they tend to move faster. From just north of this border at Le Boulou the D115 goes inland to cross into Spain through the Col d'Ares Pass and become the C151 which winds down towards Ripoll and Olot. The N116 rises up along the northern Pyrenees' slopes from Perpignan to Puigcerdà in the Cerdanya Valley, which can also be approached on the N20 from Foix. The N20 also leads into Andorra, and out again into Spain just above La Seu d'Urgell. There is

nowhere else to cross between there and the N125/N230 at Canejan in the Vall d'Aran.

Motorway tolls are charged in Spain: the price from the border to Barcelona on the A7 is a little over 1,000 pesetas (£5). Charges are displayed on screens at exits. There is also a charge of a few hundred pesetas for using the Cadí and Vielha tunnels.

Regular bus services run from most large European cities. Eurolines' regular services from London's Victoria Coach Station (tel: 071-730 0202) go to Alicante, stopping at Figueres, Girona and Barcelona, a journey of 27 hours.

BY RAIL

The Paris–Barcelona line comes over the border at Portbou, and it takes about 11œ hours from Paris Austerlitz to Barcelona's Sants station. Trains stop at Girona, but you will probably have to change at Sants and take a Valencia-bound train (line N2) to go further down the coast to Tarragona, or a Zaragoza train (line R5) for Lleida. From Toulouse, the railways enter Spain via Bourg Madame and Puigcerdà in the Pyrenees. At both borders it is necessary to change trains as Spanish railways have different gauges from the rest of Europe (they were designed to keep the invading French out). This inconvenience may end when new lines are laid to take the French-style high-speed trains.

BY SEA

No direct route, although Barcelona has facilities for international passenger vessels and there are frequent ferries between Barcelona and the Balearic Islands. It is also possible to go by sea to Santander in northwest Spain and drive across, but this is a hefty five-hour haul.

Travel Essentials

VISAS & PASSPORTS

Visitors from EC countries, Switzerland and Malta need only a national identity card. Lacking this, British citizens must have a passport. People from the United States, Canada, Australia and New Zealand must also have a valid passport. South African citizens need a visa.

Motorists need green card insurance and a bail bond. The latter is issued by your insurer when a green card is obtained. An International Driving Licence is not essential for most European visitors, but it does have an explanatory page in Spanish which could prove useful in the event of an accident. Visitors from EC countries may stay for up to three months in Spain. For an extended stay, apply for a *residència* (temporary residence permit) through a local police station.

CUSTOMS

You are allowed to bring into Catalonia: any amount of money in Spanish or foreign currency; personal effects; two still cameras and one 16mm camera; typewriter; bicycle; binoculars; calculator; cassette player; portable radio and musical instruments. But you may bring in only 300 cigarettes, 1.5 litres of spirits and 3 litres of wine—although it is difficult to imagine wanting to take more to a land of such cheapness and plenty. On leaving the country you should take with you only 100,000 pesetas or the equivalent of 500,000 pesetas in foreign currency.

HEALTH

Take out medical insurance before you go. It is well worth it as even a quick visit to a doctor can be expensive. For British visitors, the E111 system (consult your local DSS) does work after a fashion: the form should be taken to an office of the Institut Nacional de Seguretat Social to obtain a book of coupons. But these are only accepted by doctors practising under the INSS system and both the office and the doctor may be far away or hard to find. The DSS plans to simplify the system but this will take time.

Spanish chemists are usually very helpful with minor complaints. Called *farmàcias*, they display a green or red cross and usually open 9 a.m.–1 p.m. and 4.30–8 p.m. They should display a notice giving details of a local emergency service; if not, the police will direct you. Surgery hours of clinics are usually posted outside town halls. Most large towns have a hospital with a 24-hour emergency department. Local police should give details.

The main complaints suffered by visitors to Spain are over-exposure to sun and over-indulgence in alcohol, together with unspecified "tummy bugs" which are usually due simply to change of diet and different drinking water. Most of the tap water in Catalonia is not only drinkable, it is very good, but in Barcelona and some of the coastal resorts it can taste rather unpleasant although it is not harmful. Bottled water, both carbonated and still, is widely available and inexpensive. Take sensible precautions against the sun and against dehydration which can be very debilitating.

No vaccinations are required except if you are coming from a country where cholera, smallpox or yellow fever have not been eliminated.

WHAT TO WEAR

Take cool, comfortable, crease-resistant clothes, as for any warm climate. In summer, you will need nothing thicker than a sweatshirt or cardigan, and that only for occasional cool evenings. In winter and spring a thick jersey or jacket will be needed and some waterproof shoes and an umbrella would be useful. It doesn't rain very often but when it does it can come down in sheets.

Take sensible shoes if you intend to do much walking. Virtually anything goes in Catalonia these days as far as clothes are concerned but you will be less conspicuously a tourist if you avoid beachwear when in towns and cities. On the beaches, styles range from baggy shorts and one-piece costumes to nothing at all, depending on where you are and what you feel like.

WHAT TO BRING

Anything you might need for the beach—masks and snorkels, sunhats, beach mats—can usually be bought more cheaply in Spain. A vast range of sun lotions is also available at similar prices to the rest of Europe. Take an insect repellent and soother in case your Spanish is not up to buying them. Take all the film you will need—it is more expensive in Spain. Take teabags if you are self-catering—in Catalonia they are sold only in small packets. Take a kettle for self-catering if you don't like boiling water in a saucepan. Take all the books you will want to read—the selection of English and other foreign language books in local shops is limited.

ANIMAL QUARANTINE

Domestic animals can be taken in and out of Spain quite freely—but not, of course, in or out of the UK.

GETTING ACQUAINTED

GOVERNMENT & ECONOMY

Spain has been a constitutional monarchy under King Juan Carlos since the death of General Franco in 1975, and a socialist government headed by the Prime Minister, Felipe González, was elected in 1982 and re-elected in 1986. The parliament consists of a Congress and a Senate and all national government offices are in Madrid.

Catalonia, which has a very strong sense of national identity, is a self-governing community within Spain, governed by the Generalitat in Barcelona, an institution which originated in the Corts Catalanes in the Middle Ages. Since it gained its autonomous status in 1977, the Convergencia i Unió (centre-right) party has been in power. There is a strong socialist opposition. The president of the Generalitat is Jordi Pujol. Catalonia's four provinces—Barcelona, Girona, Lleida and Tarragona—are divided into 41 *comarques*, each with its own local administration.

Catalonia is one of the most prosperous regions of Spain with a relatively high standard of living which is reflected in prices for food, clothing and consumer goods comparable to the rest of Western Europe. Some 25 percent of Spain's industry is located in Catalonia, mainly textiles, chemicals and mechanical equipment. 35 percent of the population is engaged in industry, 60 percent in services and only 5 percent in agriculture, which nevertheless flourishes, with olives, grapes, apples and pears as the basic crops. The Olympic Games in Barcelona in 1992 are also a benefit to the economy. Spain is a member of the EC and EVA, the equivalent of VAT, is levied.

GEOGRAPHY & POPULATION

Catalonia, in the extreme northeast corner of Spain, covers an area of approximately 12,300 sq. miles (19,700 sq. km), in between the sizes of Wales and Scotland. Within it there is a great variety of landscape and scenery. The Catalan Pyrenees boast impressive peaks, snow-covered for many months of the year, some up to 9,700 ft (2,950 metres) high. The Vall d'Aran in Lleida and the Cerdanya in Girona are typified by brown, rolling foothills and broad, fertile valleys; the *comarca* of La Garrotxa is a volcanic region and a swathe of wooded hills follows the coast down to Barcelona.

Just to the north of the capital is the spectacular massif of Montserrat, on which the monastery of the Black Virgin stands.

The coast is more than 350 miles (580 km) long and is divided into four main parts: the Costa Brava, from the border to Blanes, mainly an area of attractive rocky coves; the Costa del Maresme, to the north of Barcelona, its long sandy beaches protected from wind by the hills behind; the shorter expanse of the Costa Garraf, which reaches as far south as Cubelles and is often included in the Costa Daurada (Dorada) which stretches the length of Tarragona province and takes its name from the fine golden sand of its beaches.

In the Empordà, in the province of Girona, and the Ebre delta, in Tarragona, there are extensive marshlands, important reserves for migratory birds and areas of rice cultivation. The Alt Penedès, in Tarragona, is one of the biggest wine-producing regions in Spain and the plain of Alcanar at the southern end of the Costa Daurada is covered with citrus groves.

Catalonia has a population of just over six million, of which 1.7 million live in the city of Barcelona and almost one million more in the industrial towns and suburbs surrounding it. Lleida has 108,000 inhabitants, Tarragona 107,000 and Girona 67,000.

THE COMARQUES

Although Catalonia is sub-divided into four provinces, each province is divided into smaller *comarques* (singular: *comarca*), small counties which are taking on an increasingly important administrative role. They are:

Comarca	Capital
Lleida province	
El Segrià	Lleida
Les Garrigues	Les Borges Blanques
Pla d'Urgell	Mollerussa
L'Urgell	Tàrrega
La Noguera	Balaguer
La Segarra	Cervera
El Solsonès	Solsona
El Pallars Jussà	Tremp
L'Alt Urgell	La Seu d'Urgell
Alta Ribagorça	El Port de Suert
El Pallars Sobirà	Salt
La Vall d'Aran	Vielha

Girona province

La Cerdanya	Puigcerdà
El Ripollès	Ripoll
La Garrotxa	Olot
L'Alt Empordà	Figueres
El Baix Empordà	La Bisbal
Pla de l'Estany	Banyoles
Gironès	Girona
La Selva	Santa Coloma de Farners

Barcelona province

El Berguedà	Berga
Osona	Vic
El Bages	Manresa
Vallès Oriental	Granollers
Vallès Occidental	Sabadell and Terrassa
Maresme	Mataró
El Barcelonès	Barcelona
Baix Llobregat	Sant Feliu de Llobregat
Garraf	Vilanova i la Geltrú
L'Alt Penedès	Vilafranca del Penedès
Anoia	Igualada

Tarragona province

La Conca de Barberà	Montblanc
L'Alt Camp	Valls
El Baix Penedès	El Vendrell
Tarragonès	Tarragona
Baix Camp	Reus
El Priorat	Falset
La Ribera d'Ebre	Móra d'Ebre
Terra Alta	Gandesa
Baix Ebre	Tortosa
El Montsià	Amposta

CLIMATE

For a relatively small area, Catalonia has a climate as varied as its geography. In Andorra and the Pyrenees the temperature can drop to below freezing in winter and in the foothills nights can be quite cool even after days of warm summer sun. In the north of the Costa Brava spectacular cloud formations can appear quite suddenly above the mountains, and winds, of which the Tramuntana is the most fierce, whip up apparently out of nowhere and can last for several days. But a little further south the climate is more reliable: there is very little rain from June to September and what there is is usually concentrated in short, heavy showers. The average temperature in coastal resorts is 25° C (77° F) in summer and 11° C (52° F) in winter. Inland, away from cooling sea breezes, it can be much hotter and the mild, sunny seasons of spring and autumn may be preferred for serious sight-seeing or long-distance walking.

WEIGHTS & MEASURES

Catalonia uses the metric system for all measurements. Solid weights are measured in grams and kilograms, liquids in litres and distances in metres and kilometres. 1 kilometre = approximately ⅝ mile, 1 kilo = 2lb 2oz, 1 litre = 1¾ pints.

ELECTRICITY

Except in a very few rural places the voltage is 220. Plugs are usually small, two-point ones, and a universal adaptor can be handy. Some power points are designed only for low output, such as lights, so it is best not to plug an electric fire into a point being used for a lamp.

TIME ZONES

Spanish time is one hour ahead of British summer time and GMT for most of the year. Clocks in Spain are put forward one hour at the end of March (usually the same time as in Britain) and put back one hour at the end of September (about a month before Britain), so during the interim period there is no time-lag.

When it is 12 noon in Barcelona it is: 12 noon in Amsterdam, Bonn, Dublin, Paris and Rome; 11 a.m. in London; 6 a.m. in New York and Montreal and 9 p.m. in Sydney.

LANGUAGE

Catalonia is bilingual in Castilian (Spanish) and Catalan. Everybody speaks Spanish, although some older people in rural areas do so with difficulty, and Catalans much prefer to speak Catalan.

Catalan is a separate language, not a dialect. Its teaching and publication were banned during the Franco era and it has since undergone a great resurgence. It is used in conversation, in schools, in businesses, on radio and television and in newspapers— although the Barcelona daily newspapers, *La Vanguardia* and *El Periódico*, are in Castilian. Most books, including guide books, are in Catalan. All street and place names have been changed and any remaining notice in Spanish may well have *En Català* scrawled across it, for language is a vital part of Catalan nationalism. Nobody, however, expects foreigners to speak the language, though efforts are appreciated. Most people will be very pleased to talk to you in Spanish and are very tolerant and encouraging of even the most excruciating attempts. Here are a few basic words and phrases, in both Catalan (first) and Spanish:

Good morning *Bon dia*; *Buenos días*
Good evening *Bona tarda*; *Buenos tardes*
Hello *Hola*; *Hola*
Goodbye *Adéu*; *Adiós*
Please *Si us plau*; *Por favor*
Thank you *Gracie/Merci*; *Gracias*
You're welcome *De res*; *De nada*
How much is…?
Quant val…?; *Cuanto es…?*
Where is…? *On es…?*; *Donde está…?*
At what time…?
A quina hora…?; *A que hora…?*
How do you say…?
Com es diu…?; *Como se dice…?*
Where can I change money
On pue canviar moneda?; *Donde se puede cambiar dinero?*
Open *Obert*; *Abierto*
Closed *Tancat*; *Cerado*

Most shops and offices open 9 a.m.–1 p.m. and 4 p.m.–8 p.m., Monday–Friday and shops keep the same hours on Saturdays. Banks sometimes have a summer schedule of 9 a.m.–2 p.m. with no afternoon opening. Bakers usually open on Sunday mornings, selling freshly baked bread. However, in coastal resorts in summer most shops open on Sunday and some do not observe the midday closure during the week.

HOLIDAYS

Shops, banks, offices and museums all close on the following days:

1 January *New Year*
6 January *Epiphany*
Good Friday and *Easter Monday*
1 May *Labour Day*
25 July *St James's Day*
15 August *Feast of the Assumption*
11 September *Catalan National Day*
12 October *Spanish National Day*
1 November *All Saints' Day*
6 December *Day of the Constitution*
8 December *Day of the Immaculate Conception*
25 December *Christmas Day*
26 December *St Stephen's Day*

Additionally, each town and village has its patron saint, on whose day banks, shops and offices are usually closed.

FESTIVALS

There are numerous colourful national and local festivals, especially in spring and early summer (see chapter on *Festivals*). The local tourist office will give details of the smaller events, in particular the *festa major*, the main festival of every town and village. Apart from the days mentioned above, other important festivals are:

Carnival: on Shrove Tuesday, celebrated everywhere, particularly in Roses, Sitges and Vilanova i la Geltrú.

Semana Santa: Holy Week, religious processions in most towns.

Festival of the Virgin of Montserrat: 27 April, at the monastery.

Corpus Christi: flower carpets in several towns, including Sitges.

St John's Eve: 23 June, bonfires and other pyrotechnics.

Vendimia: the wine harvest festivals are in mid-September

24 September: the Verge Mercè festival is Barcelona's biggest.

RELIGIOUS SERVICES

Most churches no longer stand open all day but the times of services are usually posted on the door and often on the notice-board outside the local town hall. With all but the Roman Catholic religion outlawed for so long, it is unsurprising that other religions are not well established in the country. In summer some churches, like that of Castelló d'Empúries, hold mass in German, French and English (again, the times are posted on the door). In Barcelona the Parroquia Alemana, Avenir 14, tel: (93) 209 61 80, holds services in German, while the Paroisse Francaise, Angli 15, tel: (93) 204 49 62, has services in English and French.

There is an Anglican church in Barcelona: St George's, Sant Joan de la Salle 41, tel: (93) 417 88 67. Jewish services are held at the Sinagoga de la Comunidad Judía, Avenir 24, tel: (93) 200 61 48, and Islamic services at Mezquita Al-Widadiyah, Balmes 13, tel: (93) 318 67 09.

COMMUNICATIONS

THE MEDIA

Television: There are seven television channels. TVE1 and TVE2 are national, the first broadcasting almost exclusively in Castilian, the second mostly in Catalan. The two Catalan channels supported by the Generalitat are TV3, a popular channel, and Canal 33, which is slightly more high-brow, covering the arts, sports and minority interests. There are three private channels, all brought into operation in 1990: Antena 3 and Tele 5, both Madrid based, and Canal Plus, a subscription-only channel linked to its French counterpart. French television can be seen in some northern areas and people in Tarragona can pick up Valencian television, which is on the same wavelength as Canal 33. There is also a useful device available which allows viewers the choice of watching some films in their original language.

Radio: Between 9.30 and 4.30 on weekdays during July and August Radio Associò de Catalunya broadcasts an hour each of Catalan, English, German, Italian and French (105 MHz on FM). There are local radios in every town and in summer foreign languages burst through the Catalan to advertise shops, discos and events. The most popular radio station is Cadena SER, a national radio with high local input (828 kHz MW). Radio 2 national radio is a very good classical music station.

Print: Catalonia's two main daily newspapers are *El Periódico* and *La Vanguardia*, both in Castilian. The popular Madrid daily, *El País*, has a large Barcelona staff producing a Catalonia edition which alters about six news and features pages plus the sport. *Avui* (Today) is the only Catalan region-wide daily, but there are a number of local daily papers such as the *Diari de Barcelona*, *El Nou* in Vic, and the *Diari de Girona*.

There are no English language papers, but *Lookout*, a monthly magazine published in the Costa del Sol, is distributed here. In summer some freesheets appear, such as *Panorama* in Empúria-brava which has articles in French, German and English.

POSTAL SERVICES

Post offices keep the same hours as other businesses although in smaller places they may only open in the morning. Tobacconists (*Tabac*), clearly identifiable by the red and yellow stripes of the Spanish flag above their premises, also sell stamps and postcards.

Post to most of Europe can take as little as four days or as much as a fortnight particularly in the busy summer months and if posted in rural areas. It is worthwhile putting postcards in envelopes as letters seem to have priority. There is an Express service, called simply "Express", which costs about 130 pesetas for a 20g letter to the UK.

TELEPHONES

Public telephone boxes have clear instructions in English, French and German as to how to make both domestic and international calls. International dialling codes are as follows: UK: 44, France: 33, Germany: 49, USA: 1. All international calls are preceded by 07.

For international information from the province of Barcelona phone 008 for Europe and 005 for other countries; from the provinces of Girona, Lleida and Tarragona phone 9398 for Europe and 9391 elsewhere.

As a rough guide the charge for the first three minutes of a European call is approximately 400 pesetas (£2). Call boxes accept coins of 5, 25 or 100 pesetas but nothing less than 100 will suffice for international calls. Larger towns and popular resorts have *cabines*, kiosks where your calls are metered and paid for when you finish. This saves you accumulating a pocketful of change to make a call.

Telephone numbers in Catalonia run to six

numbers, except in Barcelona province where there are seven. Each province has a different dialling code: Lleida is 973, Girona is 972, Barcelona is 93, Tarragona is 977. If you are dialling a number within the province, you don't need these prefixes. If you are dialling from outside Spain, you need the national code for Spain (34) followed by the provincial code *without* the 9 prefix. The code for Andorra is 9738 (33 628 from the UK).

Telegrams may be sent from hotels and camp sites and all post offices.

Most 3-star and over hotels have telex machines and there are fax services from main post offices in Barcelona, Girona and Tarragona.

EMERGENCIES

SECURITY & CRIME

The crime rate in Catalonia is generally low, although Barcelona has a bad record for purse-snatching and thefts from cars. Take sensible precautions when in crowds and avoid walking alone at night in cities. Leave valuables in hotel safe-deposit boxes; use travellers' cheques and credit cards where possible instead of cash and keep a separate record of your cheques. Report any thefts or losses to the police immediately to enable you to claim on your insurance.

There are three police forces in Catalonia as in all Spain. They are the Policia Municipal ("town police") who usually wear a blue or grey uniform; the Cuerpo Nacional de Policia, an anti-crime squad, who wear blue and white; and the Guardia Civil, who patrol roads and rural areas. They are a paramilitary force and wear drab green uniforms. All police are armed. Although there is a division of duties, call on any of them if you need help. They rarely speak English but are usually helpful.

Where is the nearest police station?
¿Donde está la comisaría más cercana?
I want to report a theft.
Quiero denunciar un robo.
Where is the nearest doctor/chemist?
¿Donde está el médico/la farmácia más cercana?

ILLNESS/ACCIDENTS see under *Health Tips*.

CONSULATES

Britain: Avinguda Diagonal 477, 08036 Barcelona, tel: (93) 322 21 51.

Canada: Via Augusta 125, 08006 Barcelona, tel: (93) 209 06 34.

France: Passeig de Gràcia 111, 08007 Barcelona, tel: (93) 317 82 08.

Germany: Passeig de Gràcia 111, 08008 Barcelona, tel: (93) 218 47 50.

Ireland: Gran Via Carles III 94, 08028 Barcelona, tel: (93) 330 96 52.

USA: Via Laietana 33, 08003 Barcelona, tel: (93) 319 95 50.

There is also a British consulate in Tarragona: Reial 33, 43004 Tarragona, tel: (977) 28 08 12.

GETTING AROUND

Barcelona is the only Catalan city with an underground railway—and the only city large enough to need one. In all other towns and cities, even Lleida, Girona and Tarragona, you can explore and shop on foot or on frequent and inexpensive buses. If footsore and in need of a taxi, there are prominently marked ranks in central areas and fares are very reasonable (a 10 percent tip is usual). In all three provincial towns the railway stations are about 10 minutes' walk from the heart of the old city and signs to places of historic interest are explicit.

Although public transport is adequate and you won't need a car for visiting any of the major towns, to make the most of the country you really do need private transport.

RAILWAYS

There are five main rail links in and out of Barcelona:

R1: Portbou-Girona-Barcelona. This is the main line down from Paris. An additional line operates north of Barcelona in summer: the Vapor de la Costa goes up the Maresme coast to Blanes then picks up the R1 at Massanet.

R2: Puigcerdà-Ripoll-Vic-Barcelona. This is the link-up to Toulouse in France, and a good way into the Pyrenees.

R3: Barcelona-Manresa/Reus/Valls-Lleida. This line continues to Zaragoza, and Madrid. From Lleida a line goes up to Pobla de Segur, half way to the Aigüestortes national park.

R4: Barcelona-Tarragona. The Costa Daurada train continues down the coast to Valencia.

Trains to the northeast resorts use the Cercanías station behind the Estació de França, near the harbour, refurbished in the late 1980s as a major national and international terminus. Trains to the southeast run from the Passeig de Gràcia and from the central station, Sants, in Plaça Països Catalans, from which connections can be made to any part of Spain or Europe. Stations are prominently marked with the national railways acronym RENFE (Red Nacional de Ferrocarriles Española). Travel agents sell tourist cards, valid for unlimited rail travel for periods of 8, 15 or 22 days. Buying tickets at smaller stations can be a bit frustrating as ticket offices tend to stay closed until just before a train is due, by which time a long queue may have formed. But the system seems to work and people catch the right trains.

There are various categories of trains, which will be marked on the prominently displayed timetables. A Tranvía is a local train, second-class only, which stops at all, or most, stations. An Expreso or Rapido is long-distance, stopping only at main stations. The Talgo, Ter and Tren Estrella are luxury trains, first and second-class, and the EuroCity is an international express. All the fast trains are subject to a supplementary charge. Fares are not expensive, particularly on local trains, and there are cheap days—*días azules*—which are also marked on the timetables. Winter and summer timetables are quite different, so do not rely on one which is not up-to-date.

Further information: RENFE, Estació Central Barcelona de Sants, Plaça Països Catalans s/n, 08014 Barcelona, tel: (93) 322 41 41.

Barcelona also has a suburban line, run by the Ferrrocarils de la Generalitat de Catalunya, tel: (93) 205 15 15. From Estació Plaça d'Espanya trains go to Montserrat, Igualada and Manresa. Get off at Santa Coloma de Cervelló to see Gaudí's Colònia Güell. From Plaça Catalunya they go to Sabadell, Terrassa and Sant Cugat.

Useful phrases:
When is the next train/bus to…?
¿Cuando sale el proximo tren/autobus para…?
What is the fare to…?
¿Cuanto es la tarifa a…?
I would like to reserve a seat.
Quiero reservar un asiento.
Single *Ida*
Return *Ida y vuelta.*
Where can I get a taxi?
¿Donde puedo coger un taxi?

THE METRO

Barcelona's underground stations are marked with "Metro" on a red diamond. There are five lines which criss-cross the city, running from 5 a.m.–11 p.m. (until 1 a.m. on Saturday and Sunday); detailed maps are displayed in station entrances and pocket maps are available inside. Tickets cost 65 pesetas (1990) for any length of trip and special tickets, which can be used for up to ten trips on underground or bus, and on the Montjuïc funicular railway, can be bought for about 400 pesetas (£2). Bus tickets, the same price as Metro tickets, are otherwise issued by the driver. A useful route in Barcelona is number 100, which departs every 45 minutes from the Plaça del Palau and takes in all the major sights of the city on a 90-minute journey.

DRIVING

From north to south, Catalonia is well served by motorways: the A7 runs from the border towards Valencia, becoming the A17 briefly before it reaches Barcelona, and the A2 for a short while to the south of the city. A brief stretch of motorway, the A19, runs north from Barcelona to Mataró, and a new ring road, known as the "Olympic belt", should greatly improve the city's severe traffic problems. The N11 (N roads are main, single-lane, national highways) shadows the motorway from the border down to Exit 9, where they part company. It then follows the coast down to Barcelona, emerging to the south of the city and turning inland towards Lleida. For much of its length the N11 has a fairly light traffic flow, although its coastal stretch becomes horribly congested in the summer months and should be avoided if possible. From Barcelona the Autovia 152 (a two-lane highway) goes to Vic and on to Puigcerdà; the 240 links Tarragona and Lleida; and the 141 goes from Lleida to join the 152 just below Vic.

In between these main routes, Catalonia is criss-crossed by a network of regional and local roads, mainly going northsouth, following the rivers coming down from the Pyrenees and making hard work of eastwest journeys. The roads themselves are of varying quality, some of which more than compensate, by scenery and lack of traffic, for what they may lack in width or smoothness.

Car hire: To hire a car you must be at least 19 (21 for some companies) and have a valid licence (an international licence is not essential). Charges are usually calculated at a daily rate, plus mileage and insurance, and are comparable with charges elsewhere in Europe. For example, a "standard" car such as a VW Golf or Renault 21 would cost approximately £45 a day plus 50p per kilometre. The large rental firms, Hertz and Avis, Europcar, etc., operate in most cities and many resorts and towns have smaller local companies. Travel agents and tourist offices (Oficina de Turismo or Oficina Municipal d'Informació) will direct you to a rental firm or make reservations for you. If you are flying to Catalonia you can arrange car hire before you go and collect and leave your car at the airport.

It is not always easy to get children's seats or child-size straps in rented cars, although front seat belts are now compulsory—as are helmets for motor cyclists.

Driving your own car: See *Travel Essentials* for documentation. All cars should display a nationality sticker and carry a red breakdown triangle. Spare bulbs for head and rear lamps should also be carried. If charged with a traffic offence you may be required to pay an on-the-spot fine. Emergency telephones are situated at roadsides and the police emergency number is 092. Speed limits are: 75 mph (120 kph) on motorways, 60 mph (100 kph) on major (national) roads and 55 mph (90 kph) on local roads.

Petrol prices (in 1990) are slightly lower than in England and considerably lower than in France. Unleaded petrol is becoming more widely available.

Useful phrases:
Fill the tank, please.
Llene el depósito, por favor.
Unleaded. *Sin plomo.*
Check the oil/tyres/battery, please.
Controle el aceite/neumaticos/batería, por favor.
I have had a breakdown.
Mi coche se ha estropeado.
Is this the road for…?
¿Es esta la carretera hasta…?

Note: a car battery is *una batería* but a small, domestic battery is *una pila.*

BUSES

Buses run between most large towns and, in summer, from many of the more popular resorts to nearby towns of particular interest, although there is not always a service which links one resort with another. Buses are a good way of seeing the countryside and fares are inexpensive, but it would not be wise to plan a holiday which depended entirely on this form of transport. Bus stations can appear crowded and disorganised but services are generally efficient although not very frequent in rural areas.

HITCHHIKING

Known as "autostop", hitchhiking is legal and commonplace but carries the same risks as elsewhere. As always, you stand a better chance of a lift if you travel in pairs, carry little luggage and look reasonably clean and tidy. There are two organisations in Barcelona which organise lifts at low prices. These are: Barnastop, Pintor Fortuny 21, 08001 Barcelona, tel: (93) 318 27 31, and Comparco, Ribes 31, 08013 Barcelona, tel: (93) 246 69 08.

BOAT TRIPS

Boat trips up and down the coast operate throughout the summer and are a good way to appreciate the fine coastal scenery.

Cruceros Costa Brava: This line sails up and down the Maresme and Costa Brava. Boats leave about four times a day calling at 13 resorts between Tamariu in the north and Calella on the Maresme in the south, but not all go the whole distance which takes a total of about five hours. Prices range between about 750 pesetas and 2,000 pesetas, depending on destination. Cruceros Costa Brava, 17007 Palamós, tel: (972) 31 43 96.

Panoramic: The glass-bottomed boats of the Lineas Azules S.A. line ply between Roses and Blanes with trips in summer starting every 30 minutes.

Medes Islands: Several boats go regularly from L'Estartit either just around the Medes Islands or round the islands and then north beneath the Montgrí cliffs. The extra couple of hundred pesetas for the longer journey are worthwhile. Most of the boats have glass bottoms.

Barcelona: Trips around the harbour go from the quay beside the Columbus statue, cost little more than a Metro ticket and last half an hour. They give a good perspective of the city and Montjuïc.

Balearics: Cruise ships make weekend round trips to Ibiza and Mallorca, leaving Barcelona at 9 p.m. on Friday night and returning at 8 a.m. on Monday morning. The adult fare is around 30,000 pesetas. Transmediteranea, tel: (93) 319 82 12.

Cruceros Costa Daurada: These sail regularly between Cambrils, Salou and Tarragona, and Salou, Cambrils and L'Ametlla de Mar. On summer weekends there are night-time trips between Salou and Cambrils. Prices between 600 and 1,000 pesetas. Cruceros Costa Daurada, Rambla Jaume I, 8, 43850 Cambrils, tel: (977) 36 02 38.

Ebre delta: Boats can be hired to see the river and its delta from Sant Carles de la Ràpita, tel: (977) 74 08 04, Amposta, tel: (977) 70 20 13, and Deltebre, tel: (977) 48 91 22/48 04 73.

NATURAL PARKS

There are more than 30 conservation areas in Catalonia and visitors are encouraged to enjoy many of them. The parks are not fenced off and access is easy—indeed it is often difficult to tell what is park and what is not. For an idea of the flora and fauna of the areas, see the Pyrenean Wildlife and Ebre Delta chapters.

Aigüestortes and Lake Sant Maurici: the region's only National Park is in the mountainous northwest and covers 38 sq. miles (100 sq. km). It has to be approached in one of two completely different directions: the western part from the Boí Valley, off the N230 from Lleida; the eastern part, which includes the Sant Maurici lake, from Espot via the C147 from Balaguer to La Pobla de Segur. The park entrances are 4 miles (6 km) from Boí and 3 miles (4.5 km) from Espot. There are information centres at both villages as well as in Lleida: Carrer

Camp de Mart 35, 25004 Lleida, tel: (973) 24 66 50.

Buses run from Lleida to Boí on the El Pont de Suert line (Automóviles La Oscense S.A., tel: (947) 22 70 11 or (973) 69 02 72). For the Sant Maurici side, the Autobuses Anónima Alsina Graells S.A. company operates from Lleida, tel: (973) 26 85 00, and Barcelona, tel: (93) 302 65 45. The train from Lleida only goes as far as La Pobla de Segur.

Four-wheel-drive hire can easily be arranged on arrival. Jeeps take up to 8 passengers and cost around 18,000 pesetas for a full day. For Lake Sant Maurici Jeeps can be hired from Espot, tel: (973) 63 50 09, or the Hotel Saurat, tel: (973) 63 50 63. For Jeep hire on the Boí side tel: (973) 69 60 36.

There are eight refuges offering mattresses, blankets and food which accommodate 30–80 people. Spartan but adequate and cheap, they cost are around 700 pesetas a night, 400 pesetas for breakfast and 1,200 pesetas for lunch and evening meals. You can book through C.E.C., Paradís 10, 08002 Barcelona, tel: (93) 315 23 11.

Cadí-Moixeró: There are a number of access points into this 160 sq. mile (415 sq. km) natural park covering the Cadí and Moixeró mountain ranges. It is probably best approached from the Cerdanya plain on the north side of the range where the tourist offices in Puigcerdà and Bellver de Cerdanya, tel: (973) 51 00 16, can provide maps and guides. They recommend eight particular excursions, some of which involve overnight stays at one or more of the nine refuges in the park. Most of these are free, and you take your own food. Fishing is forbidden.

Autobuses Anónima Alsina Graells S.A. run from Barcelona to Puigcerdà via La Seu d'Urgell, tel: (93) 302 65 45 or (973) 27 14 70. The RENFE train goes from Barcelona to Puigcerdà.

Four-wheel-drive vehicles can be hired via the tourist offices as well as at the town hall at Baga, on the Barcelona side of the Túnel del Cadí, where a guide service is also offered, tel: (93) 824 41 11.

Garrotxa Volcanic Zone: The natural park based on the defunct cones of this curious volcanic area occupies 46 sq. miles (120 sq. km) and includes the towns of Castellfollit, Sant Joan les Fonts, Santa Pau and Olot. Within this there are pockets designated "Nature Reserves" which cover only 3.5 sq. miles (9 sq. km) and lie mainly between the Garrotxa capital of Olot and the pretty medieval town of Santa Pau. There is a tourist office at both but the Casal dels Volcans on the Santa Coloma road out of Olot, Avinguda de Santa Coloma s/n, 1700 Olot, tel: (972) 26 62 02, is more likely to be open. It also has two exhibition rooms.

The reserves are all good, undemanding walking country, and three places are of interest, all lying beside the GE524 between Olot and Santa Pau. The first is the Fageda d'en Jordà, a large, silent beech wood, the second is the Santa Margarida volcano, whose grassy slopes can be climbed down, and the third the great excavations of El Croscat volcano, a moonscape behind the Santa Margarida restaurant.

The TEISA bus company runs the Garrotxa Express from Barcelona to Olot via Girona and Banyoles, tel: (972) 26 01 96.

Aiguamolls de l'Empordà: The natural park covers 18.5 sq. miles (48 sq. km) and is in two parts, divided by the resort of Empúria-brava, which has destroyed much of the natural wetlands the birds here once enjoyed. The northern half is between Castelló d'Empúries and the village of Palau Saverdera and includes a couple of hides. But the main reserve is signposted half way along the road between Castelló and Sant Pere Pescador. Here is the information centre, Els Cortalet, which supplies maps to the hides and trails which go down to the sea, tel: (972) 45 12 31.

The birdlife is almost identical to that of the Ebre, and it has the distinction of being the only place in Spain where the garganey duck breeds, which is why it has been adopted as the park's symbol. There is a train station at Vilajuïga, 5 miles (8 km) from Castelló d'Empúries.

Delta de l'Ebre: see the relevant chapter for details about this natural park. For any further information contact El Centro de Recepció del Parque Natural del Delta del Ebre, Plaça del 20 de Maig s/n, Deltebre, tel: (977) 48 95 11.

Wine producers, co-operatives and *bodeges* are hospitable places, and at most of them you will be able to taste the wine before buying. Some of the larger wine makers are closed for all or part of July and August for their holidays, while the smaller co-operatives stay open to pick up all the trade they can. If you want wine from the barrel you should take along your own bottles or containers, as they may cost almost as much as the wine. There are six wine regions:

Empordà-Costa Brava: In the most northeasterly corner of the region, this stretches between Figueres and the French border to the sea. There are co-operatives at Roses, Pau, Vilajuïga, Garriguella, Mollet de Peralada, Capmany, Sant Climent Sescebes, Rabós and Espolla, a village whose wines Josep Pla thought the best. At Pont de Molins there is the large Ricardell co-operative and at Capmany is Oliveda, whose label is to be seen on most restaurant tables in the area. The centre for the local CAVA industry, however, is Peralada, a delightful medieval town worth a visit. The castle's wine museum has some great old oak casks, and though the bottling plant is not visitable, the white and pink *méthode champenoise* are on sale in the cafés.

Alella: The smallest of the regions, Alella is in the hills behind the Maresme coast. There are a couple of good wine shops in the town as well as the co-operative. Closed in August: The Parxet vintners is nearby at Santa Maria de Martorelles.

Penedès: Catalonia's largest and best-known wine region (see *Wine Dynasties* chapter), just west of Barcelona, centres on the towns of Vilafranca del Penedès and Sant Sadurní d'Anoia. The famous high-tech Torres Bodega is in Carrer Comercio, Vilafranca (closed: in August). There is a good selection of local wines in the shops, plus the excellent Museu del Vi (closed: Sunday). For a full list of producers contact the tourist office or the Consejo Regulador de la Denominación de Origen Penedès, Carrer Amalia Soler 27, tel: (93) 890 28 81.

Sant Sadurní is the *cava* town, home of Catalonia's two top producers of *méthode champenoise* wine, Codorníu and Freixenet. Caves Codorníu on the edge of the town is a fine Modernist building restored by Puig i Cadafalch and worth a visit. The two companies account for about 80 percent of Catalonia's *cava*, but there are many more producers in the town. Other wine makers in the Penedès region which can be visited can be found at Monistrol d'Anoia, La Bleda and Santa Margarida i Monjos.

Priorat: Perhaps the most charming of the regions, where small villages make wine in small quantities. The precipitous slopes are attractive to look at but hard to work, and few young people remain at home to help out on the land. There are co-operatives at Bellmunt del Priorat, Lloà, Gratallops, Porrera, Torroja del Priorat, La Viella Alta, La Viella Baixa, Pobleda and La Morera de Montsant. The most modern wine makers are at Scala Dei.

Tarragona: De Müller, suppliers of altar wine to the Vatican, is the surviving grand old wine makers in Tarragona, in the Carrer Reial, open during weekday office hours. There are several cavernous *bodeges* in the town. Outside Tarragona, on the N240 towards Valls, there is the modern Lopez Bertrán wine producer.

Terra Alta: This is centred around Gandesa, and most of the tasting can be done in the town, at Pedro Rovira, for example, and Bodegas Pedrola.

WHERE TO STAY

Tourist offices in most towns will send you a list of local hotels. Reservations may be made by phone but should be confirmed by letter and a deposit may be required.

Large hotels will have receptionists who speak English but in smaller places they may not. The following sample letter may prove helpful:

Distinguidos señores:

Quiero reservar una habitación doble/individual con/sin baño para uno/dos/tres noches/una semana, desde el 24 de abril/mayo/junio/julio/agusto/setiembre. *Espero recibir su confirmación. Les saludo atentamente,*

(Dear Sirs:

I would like to reserve a double/single room, with/without a bath for one/two/three nights/a week from 24 April/May/June/July/August/September. I look forward to receiving your confirmation.

Yours faithfully,)

Catalan hotels have the usual star-rating system, but it is also useful to remember the following points: H means *Hostal*, an establishment which will provide a reasonably priced meal but does not necessarily have accommodation. F stands for *Fonda*, or inn, where you will get a clean but very basic room and a substantial set meal for a very reasonable price. *Fondas*, the backbone of good cheap Spanish hospitality, are due to be phased out. *Habitaciones*, or *Habitacions* (HR), a sign seen only in towns, means rooms only—usually inexpensive ones.

When travelling it is worth remembering that apart from motels on motorways it is unusual to find roadside hotels—they are invariably located in towns or villages. Unlike their French counterparts, Spanish and Catalan hoteliers do not assume that you will take your evening meal in the hotel, although a choice of à la carte or set menu is usually available if you wish to do so.

CAMPING

There are 300 camp sites in Catalonia. Tourist offices will provide guides to local sites and the Departament de Comerç, Consum i Turisme at Passeig de Gràcia 105, 08008 Barcelona, has a list of all sites in the region. Called "Campings", the sites are rated 1st, 2nd and 3rd category, depending on facilities. Some are in beautiful settings, many have swimming pools, some are in prime sites beneath pine trees by the sea, and a lot of the nicest ones are small, family-run affairs. It is not always possible to reserve a space, however, and sites get very crowded during late July and August. Prices are posted on an official list in the reception area and most places offer reductions outside the peak season. It must also be said that hotel prices compare favourably with camp sites, particularly if you are a family, and especially away from the coast in high season.

FARMHOUSE HOLIDAYS

Known as Residències-Casa de Pagès, these are farms which cater for up to 15 guests. You may take full or part-board, or in a few cases cooking facilities are provided. Larger tourist offices will provide lists of farmhouses; the list is not extensive, as they are a fairly recent innovation. Many of them are located in the beautiful Vall d'Aran.

YOUTH HOSTELS

Children in Catalonia often seem to spend a week or two at summer camps, which are dotted all over the countryside. Youth hostels display the international sign and their Catalan name, Albergues de Juventud. Lists of addresses can be obtained from YHA offices anywhere in the world. There are five hostels in Barcelona, at the following addresses:

Passeig Mare de Déu del Coll, 41, 08023 Barcelona.

Passeig de La Pujades 29, 08018 Barcelona.

Carrer de Numancia 149, 08029 Barcelona.

Plaça Reial 17, 08002 Barcelona.

Carrer de La Duquessa d'Orleans 56, 08034 Barcelona.

FOOD DIGEST

Catalan cookery is very varied and specialises in unusual and appetising combinations of meat and seafood, known as *mar i muntanya*, literally, sea and mountain. There is chicken with prawns or lobster, rabbit with snails and ragout of pork and rabbit with sole and mussels. Chicken (*pollastre*) appears frequently on Catalan menus and is very good quality. Rabbit is often served grilled with *allioli*, a kind of thick, garlicky mayonnaise. *Samfaina*, a sauce of tomatoes, peppers, aubergines and courgettes is a favourite accompaniment to either meat. Trout is popular inland, particularly in the Pyrenean region. Be warned: by some linguistic quirk the word "truita" means both trout and omelette (and "pi de porc" is not pork pie, but pig's trotters).

On the coast, seafood of all kinds is abundant: two dishes appear on the menus of most seafood restaurants: *sarsuela*, a vast stew of various fish and seafood and *parillada*, an equally large selection of grilled seafood. Don't miss *faves a la catalana*, a dish which appears in spring when *faves*, broad beans, are fresh. They are stewed with local sausages and garlic, and quite delicious. *Calçots* are another speciality, especially in Tarragona: large spring onions, grilled over an open fire and served with spicy sauces, especially *romesco*, which is based on almonds and red peppers. This is an autumn and winter dish; leeks are prepared in the same way throughout Catalonia when they are in season. *Bacallà*, salt cod, features on many menus at all times of the year, most frequently in *brandada*, a superior kind of fish and potato pie; and *esqueixada*, a salad made of shredded cod, onions, peppers, tomatoes and olives, which can be very good indeed. *Arròs negre* is rice cooked with squid and dyed charcoal-black with its ink.

Tapas bars (*tapes* in Catalan) are not a Catalan institution and visitors familiar with other parts of Spain may miss the cafés where little saucers of food are served with drinks. Barcelona's *barri* Gòtic is an exception and has a plethora of bars, each with its own speciality. Most towns, however, do have bars where an appetizing array of dishes lines the counter, for quick snacks. It is a good way of trying out an unfamiliar taste—much better to have a small portion of garlicky snails or baby squid before risking a full course in a restaurant. It is also a good way to stave off hunger pangs until the late Catalan dinner hour. You can eat from 8 p.m. onwards, but you will do so alone or in the company of other foreigners who cannot survive until 10 p.m. which is when restaurants really come to life.

If you are on a self-catering holiday, make the most of the markets. Huge Spanish tomatoes have a wonderful flavour; don't be afraid to buy the pale ones which look unripe, as they often taste best. Baby artichokes, in spring, are a pleasure not to be missed and apricots and greengages taste the way fruit used to taste. Strawberries are abundant and a good accompaniment to cheap sparkling wine. Olives are sold from huge vats, sometimes more than a dozen varieties on display, and you are welcome to taste before buying. Meat is slightly more expensive than in England, but butchers are very obliging and will cut and trim to order.

Charcuterie and chicken are often sold in different shops from other meats and the selection of salamis and sausages is worth experimenting with. There are many varieties of *botifarra* and *llonganisses*, some to be sliced and eaten raw, others to be used in cooking.

Fish and seafood, which are extremely good, often cost half as much in a city market as they do on the coast where they are caught, as most of it is rushed straight off to markets and restaurants. *Bacallà*, mentioned above, is widely available in markets. Hanging in stiff, grey-white slabs, it looks most unappetising but providing it is soaked for 24 hours, preferably with a change of water halfway through, to remove the salt, it forms the basis of some very appetizing dishes. Hake (*lluç*) is the most common white fish.

READING THE MENU

In coastal resorts most menus have translations in several languages, but inland and in towns they are often written only in Catalan and/or Spanish. In Catalan, to eat is *manger*, lunch is *dinar* and dinner is *sopar*. Below is a sample menu including many of the dishes which are frequently found in Catalonia.

Catalan/Spanish/English
*Entrants/Entradas/***First courses**:
*Anxoves fregides/anchoas fritas/*deep-fried anchovies
*Bledes amb panses i pinyons/espinacas a la catalana/*spinach (or chard) with pine nuts and raisins
*Bolets/champiñones/*mushrooms
*Bunyols de bacallà/buñuelos/*balls of salt cod in batter
*Calamars/calamares/*squid
*Canalons/canalones/*cannelloni
*Cargols/caracoles/*snails
*Escalivada/escalivada/*grilled peppers, onions, aubergines, in oil
*Esqueixada/esquixada/*shredded salt-cod salad with onions and black olives
*Gambes/gambas/*prawns
*Musclos/mejillones/*mussels
*Pa amb tomàquet/pan con tomate/*bread spread with oil, tomato and garlic
Pastis/pâté or *pastel/*terrine or cake
*Pebrots farcits/pimientas rellenas/*stuffed peppers
*Pesols amb pernil/guisantes con jamón/*ham and peas

*Sopas/Sopas/***Soup**:
Escudella i carn d'olla/escudella de carne/ meat and vegetable stew traditionally served as two courses, broth first, then the contents.
*Gaspacho/gazpacho/*cold summer soup, based on tomato, bread and garlic, with cucumber, etc, added.
*Sopa de peix/sopa de pescado/*fish soup
*Suquet/suquet/*a superior, local fish soup made with three kinds of white fish.

*Amanides/Ensaladas/***Salads**:
*Amanida catalana/ensalada catalana/*Catalan salad: slices of salami and ham and olives with salad.
Amanida de bacallà/ensalada de bacalao/ salt-cod salad
Amanida de mongets/ensalada de judías/ white-bean salad
*Xató/xató/*salad with salt cod, tuna and *romesco*

*Peix/Pescado/***Fish**:
*Bacallà amb samfaina/bacalao con sanfaina/*salt cod with sauce of tomatoes, peppers, aubergines.
*Llagosta/langosta/*lobster
*Llagostins/langostinos/*large "Dublin Bay" prawns
*Lluç/merluza/*hake
*Peix espasa/pez espada/*swordfish
Pop (*estofat*)*/pulpo* (*estofado*)*/*octopus (stewed)
*Rap/rape/*monkfish
*Sarsuela/zarzuella/*fish and seafood stew
*Sèpia/sepia/*cuttlefish
Truita (*de riu*)*/trucha/*trout (*de riu*, meaning river trout, is sometimes added, but don't count on it).

*Carn/Carne/***Meat**:
*Ànec amb peres/pato con peras/*duck with pears
*Botifarra amb mongetes/butifarra con judías/*sausage with white beans
*Conill amb allioli/conejo con allioli/*rabbit with garlic mayonnaise
*Estofat de bou/estofada de buey/*beef stew
*Faisà/faisán/*pheasant
*Fetge amb ceba/higado con cebollas/*liver and onions
*Guatlle/cordoniz/*quail
*Llom de porc/chuleta de lomo/*pork loin chop

Tripa a la catalana/tripas a la catalana/
tripe in a thick sauce
*Xai rostit/cordero asado/*roast lamb
*Xai amb pesols/cordero con guisantes/*lamb
with peas
*Vedella/ternera/*veal

*Postres/Postre/***Pudding**:
*Crema catalana/crema catalana/*a local
crême broulée
*Flan/flan/*an instant, packaged version of
crema catalana
*Formatge/queso/*cheese
*Fruites seques/frutas secas/*nuts and dried
fruit
*Gelat/helado/*ice cream
*Mel i mató/miel y mató/*cream cheese with
honey
Peres amb vi negre/peras con vino tinto/
pears in red wine

*Fruite/Fruta/***Fruit**:
*Ananas/piña/*pineapple
*Pome/manzana/*apple
*Pressec/melocaton/*peach
*Tronja/naranja/*orange
*Uves/uvas/*grapes

*Begudes/Bebidas/***Drinks**:
*Cremat/cremado/*rum and coffee punch
*Granissats/granizados/*crushed ice and fruit
juice (often lemonade)
Orxata/horchata (*de chufa*)/almond-fla-
voured milk
*Xocolata/chocolate/*thick drinking choco-
late

RESTAURANTS & HOTELS

The writers of each travel-guide section
chose some hotels and restaurants they can
recommend. Many restaurants and some
hotels take a holiday themselves in the autumn at the end of the "season", and in winter
most resort restaurants are closed, with some
opening only at weekends or lunchtime.
Many established urban restaurants close on
Monday or Tuesday. Restaurants are at their
fullest at Sunday lunchtime.

LLEIDA PROVINCE

Lleida: The 2-star **Residència Principal**,
Plaça de la Paeria 8, 25007 Lleida, tel: (973)
24 09 00, in the heart of the old town is a
comfortable, medium-priced hotel. For
good value, typical Lleidan food and wines
try **La Huerta restaurant**, Avinguda de
Tortosa 9, tel: (973) 24 24 13.

Guimerà: A curiosity of the town is the
Restaurant Medieval, which has built its
reputation on serving dishes made from 500-
year-old recipes.

Tàrrega: The 1-star **Hotel España**, Plaça
Rafel Casanova, 25300 Tarrega, tel: (973)
31 13 57, is comfortable. There is good
traditional Catalan cuisine, reasonably
priced, at the **Fengara restaurant**, Carrer
del Mestre Güell 3, tel: (973) 31 11 59.

Cervera: The 2-star **Canciller**, Passeig
Balmes 2, tel: (973) 53 13 50.

Solsona: The 3-star **Gran Sol**, Carretera
Manresa s/n, 25280 Solsona, tel: (973) 48 09
75. Local cheeses, wines and dishes can be
found at the **Sant Roc restaurant**, Plaça de
Sant Roc 2, tel: (973) 81 10 06.

Cellers (Selles): The 2-star **Hostal del
Lago**, Carretera C147 s/n (the main Bal-
aguer-Tremp road) 25631 Cellers, tel: (973)
65 03 50, is beautifully set by a lake. It also
has a good, inexpensive restaurant serving
local dishes as well as a surprisingly good
paella.

Tremp: The 2-star **Hotel Siglo XX** in
Plaça de la Creu 32, 25620 Tremp, tel: (973)
65 00 00, has reasonably priced rooms and a
good cheap restaurant with local dishes.

Aigüestortes Park: There are two hotels
with modern facilities, at a fair price. On the
Val d'Espot side is the 2-star **Hotel Saurat**,
Sant Martí s/n, 25597 Espot, tel: (973) 63 50
63. On the Val de Boí side, the 4-star **Hotel
Manantial**, 25528 Caldes de Boi, tel: (973)
69 01 91. This spa hotel is worth the extra for
a luxury stay and has a good restaurant.

La Seu d'Urgell: The **Parador
Nacional**, Carrer Sant Domènec s/n, 25700
La Seu d'Urgell, tel: (973) 35 20 00, has 3-
stars but should have more. The menu is
excellent. For half the price there is the
comfortable 1-star **Hotel Andria**, Passeig
Joan Brudieu 24, 25700 La Seu d'Urgell, tel:
(973) 35 03 00. The **Can Ton restaurant** in
Carrer de la Font is ridiculously cheap and
very popular.

VALL D'ARAN

Arties: Parador Nacional Gaspar de Portola, Carrer Afores s/n, 25599 Arties, tel: (973) 64 08 81, is a 16th-century house, once home to an explorer who went to California, now converted into an intimate inn which caters for skiiers. The **Hostal Valarties**, Carrer Major 3, 25599 Arties, tel: (973) 64 09 00, has a dozen rooms and a lounge with open fireplace and is attached to the renowned restaurant run by Irene España Plagues. Exceptional cooking can be found at **Casa Irene**, Carrer Major 3, tel: (973) 64 09 00. Dishes include home-smoked salmon with crab sauce, duck with truffles; green walnut liqueur is the house speciality. For something different, try **Patxiku Kintana**, Carrer Remedios s/n, tel: (973) 64 16 13, where fresh seafood is prepared with Basque wizardry—shellfish in filo pastry, pasta with clams, or other seafood which the chef orders from San Sebastian and is served with perfect sauces.

Betrén: The **Hotel Husa-Tuca**, Carretera de Betrén s/n, 25530 Betrén, tel: (973) 64 07 00, is a modern, comfortable, no-nonsense place with ski equipment rental nearby and a shuttle bus up to Baqueira. It also owns its own lifts to take you to the compact resort of Tuca on the mountain behind. Warming soups and honeyed lamb can be had at **La Borda de Betrén**, Carrer Major s/n, tel: (973) 64 00 32.

Escunhau: The **Hostal Casa Estampa**, Carrer Sortan 7, 25539 Escunhau, tel: (973) 64 00 48, is an inexpensive hotel with extensive views. You can eat hearty Aranese dishes at **Casa Turnay**, Plaça Major, tel: (973) 64 02 92. Dishes include *olla* (stew), wild boar casserole, stuffed cabbage and plums roasted in cream.

ANDORRA

Andorra la Vella: Hotel Andorra Palace, Prat de la Creu, Andorra la Vella, tel: (9738) 21072. Very central, overlooking the Valira river but with its back to the main shopping throng. Sauna and restaurant. **Hotel Eden Roc**, Avinguda Dr Mitjavila 1, Andorra la Vella, tel: (9738) 21000, is smack in the town centre, with a car park and restaurant: at the top end of the price range, around 10,000 pesetas a double room. **Res-**taurant **Versailles**, Cap de Ferrer, tel: (9738) 21331, has inspired French cuisine by owner-chef Claudi Martí from Carcassonne. His pâtés, salads and desserts are a delight. **Chez George**, Edifici Prada Casadet, tel: (9738) 29646, has unexpected city elegance in a semi-circular dining room overlooking the Valira river. Reasonably priced à la carte, specialities include sauced meat dishes. (Closed: August.) **Hostal Calones**, Antic Carrer Major 8, tel: (9738) 21312, has robust fare cooked to traditional recipes gathered by the granny of the house, María Montanya. Her grandson, Miguel, now runs the business. **Can Manel**, Carrer Mestre Xavier Plana s/n, tel: (9738) 22397, is a reliable and unpretentious bistro offering excellent value for money. Civets of game in excellent sauces are recommended. The **Pyrenees** store in Avinguda Meritxell has a top-of-the-store buffet offering excellent value for exhausted shoppers with fresh, interesting salads and hors d'oeuvres as well as hot dishes. (Open: 12.30–4.30 p.m.)

Escaldes: Hotel Roc Blanc, Plaça Coprinceps 5, Escaldes–Engordany, tel: (9738) 21468, is a well-appointed, smart hotel set back from the main thoroughfare on a small square. It has a covered thermal swimming pool, fitness centre, terrace and piano bar. A top suite costs around 16,000 pesetas. **Hotel Delfos**, Avinguda de les Escoles 29, Escaldes–Engordany, tel: (9738) 24642, is a large modern hotel in a shop-lined street parallel to the high street. **Residencia Les Closes**, Avinguda Carlemany 93, Escaldes–Engordany, tel: (9738) 28311, is a pleasant, cleanly decorated bed-and-breakfast establishment in a modern cul-de-sac off the main street. Underground carpark; several restaurants nearby. **Restaurant 1900**, Carrer de la Unió 11, tel: (9738) 26716, has plush and pretty decor and, in a similar theme, nouvelle and international cuisine. There is a gastronomic menu for around 6,000 pesetas.

Ordino: Hotel Coma, Carretera General, Ordino, tel: (9738) 35116, is a small family hotel in beautiful countryside. Convenient for skiing at Arcalís, Arinsal and Pal. Satellite TV and tennis.

Sispony: Residencia La Burna, Sispony, tel: (9738) 35355, is a small, simple bed-and-breakfast place in a hamlet above La Massana Valley. Well placed for skiing at Pal and Arinsal and for summer exploring.

La Massana: Borda de l'Avi, Carretera d'Arinsal, La Massana, tel: (9738) 35068, is now part of the HUSA chain, with its chic sister, the **Xopluc**, in Sispony. This serves well-presented country food in agreeably rustic surroundings, but it is not cheap. **Borda Raubert**, Carretera d'Arinsal, La Massana, tel: (9738) 35420, specialises in old Andorran recipes using fruits of the earth—*escudella* soup, casseroles with wild mushrooms and venison among them.

Canillo: Hostal Sant Pere, El Tartar, Canillo, tel: (9738) 51087, has a grill room for ravenous skiiers and a restaurant proper. There is fresh fish and frequently changing dishes which combine local and international ingredients with flair.

GIRONA PROVINCE

Cerdanya: In Puigcerdà hotels fill up at weekends and it is best to book. The 2-star **Maria Victoria Hotel**, Carrer Florença 9, 17520 Puigcerdà, tel: (972) 88 03 00, has a good restaurant and a fine view over the Cerdanya plain. Cosier, and cheaper, is the **Internacional**, Carrer La Baronia s/n, 17520 Puigcerdà, tel: (972) 88 01 58. On the edge of town on the road to Alp, it has the advantage of easy access and parking. The most famous restaurant of the region is **Can Borell** high in the hills at **Meranges**, for many years in the vanguard of Catalan nouvelle cuisine. The restaurant is pretty, the portions are small, the prices are high, but it's worth the experience, just once.

Ripoll: Not a great choice of hotels in this town. The **Hostal Ripollès**, Plaça Nova 11, 17500 Ripoll, tel: (972) 700215, is a cheerful little family establishment.

Olot: A huge open-air family restaurant can be found on the outskirts of town in the rural setting of Font de Moixins. *Purrós*, huge breads and great portions of grilled meats. **Mulleras**, Can Mulleras s/n, 17176 Sant Privat d'En Bas, tel: (972) 69 32 57, is a pretty country *pensió* only a couple of miles outside Olot in the Val d'En Bas. Its walls are covered with local paintings. Bread and tomato with ham for breakfast and an inexpensive evening set menu includes local trout.

Camprodón: The **Güell**, Plaça Espanya 8, 17867 Camprodón, tel: (972) 74 00 11, is an elegant and inexpensive hotel that deserves more than its one star. You will eat heartily, especially meat dishes such as beef with prunes, at any of the restaurants in the rural village of **Setcases**, 8 miles (11 km) to the north.

Figueres: The capital of the Alt Empordà has a couple of 3-star hotels with restaurants which have attracted attention for many years. The **Duran**, Lasauca 5, 17600 Figueres, tel: (972) 50 12 50, has a traditional interior of tiles and high-backed chairs and a *purró* of Muscatel does the rounds at the end of the meal of Empordà dishes. The **Hotel Ampurdán**, Carretera Nacional N11 Km 763, tel: (972) 50 05 62, was one of Josep Pla's favourites, and is often credited as the birthplace of the "new" Catalan cuisine.

Palol de Revardit: Can Mia, tel: (972) 59 42 46, between Girona and Banyoles on the C150, is a kind of zoo restaurant. Thousands of birds of different varieties are kept in cages, plus wild boar and Vietnamese pigs, all waiting to please your taste buds. You don't have to eat, you can just wander around. Best to book in summer.

Bàscara: El Pessebre (The Crib) is signposted at this town on the N11 12 miles (20 km) north of Girona. It is a delightful little restaurant, serving imaginative dishes at reasonable prices.

Girona: The **Peninsular**, Carrer Nou 3, 17001 Girona, tel: (972) 20 38 00, is a well-established hotel, just over on the new side of town. The **Reyma**, Pujada del Rei Martí 15, 17004 Girona, tel: (972) 20 02 28, is a relatively inexpensive 2-star hotel, as is the **Centro**, Carrer Ciutadans 4, 17004 Girona, tel: (972) 20 14 93, a hotel with large rooms which has seen grander days; in the heart of the old town, it is largely taken over by university students in term time. The **Boira** in Plaça d'Independència has an upstairs room which looks out over the Onyar and the painted tenements. Good helpings, reasonably priced. Over the bridge in the old town cheap set menus are on offer in several restaurants in the Carrer Força, and at the top of the *call* is a restaurant of the same name, which serves excellent *mar i muntanya* mixes of dishes in smart but pleasant surroundings.

Arbúcies: Les Pipes, just outside Arbucies on the road to Vic, is the kind of place one always hopes to find by the road: a quaint restaurant of timbered beams and rickety floors, beside a stream. It has its own trout tanks, too.

COSTA BRAVA

Portlligat: The **Hotel Portlligat**, 17488 Portlligat, tel: (972) 25 81 62, is the only commercial establishment in Dalí's bay and it has a salt-water swimming pool alongside it. Quite swish but never very full, one might go for a treat, either staying overnight or just for a meal in the well-appointed dining room overlooking the bay.

Empúries: The 1-star **Hotel Ampurias**, 17130 L'Escala, tel: (972) 77 02 07, is out of town, right by the ruins and right on the beach.

Aiguablava: The 4-star **Aiguablava Hotel**, 17255 Platja de Fornells, tel: (972) 62 20 58, is the classic Costa Brava hotel, beautifully situated in Fornells Bay and presided over by one of the coast's characters, Xiquet Sabater, who choses his guests so that no one nationality dominates. It is a more human-looking place than the modern Parador opposite, though these national hotels have an excellent reputation for local dishes. **Parador Nacional Costa Brava**, 17255 Platja d'Aiguablava, tel: (972) 62 20 58.

Palafrugell: The **Cypsele**, Carrer Ample 30, Palafrugell, tel: (972) 30 01 92, is a 1-star hotel and also a restaurant with a good reputation. One of the few places where you can try the classic local dish, *el niu*, a huge stew based around cod's tripe, but this must be ordered in advance. An unusual hotel on the coast here is the **Sant Sebastià**, Santuari de Sant Sebastià s/n, 17200 Palafrugell, tel: (972) 30 05 86. It is spectacularly placed

above a lighthouse at the top of cliffs. The hotel, built around a courtyard, has character and there is a bar and restaurant attached.

Palamós: The 3-star **Trias**, Passeig del Mar s/n 17230, tel: (972) 31 41 00, is rather pricey, but another of the coast's well-known hotels which has been going for years. There are a number of good fish restaurants around the port, such as **Maria de Cadaqués**, Notaries 39, which also serves Empordà dishes, and **Xivarri**, Reuda 22, where pork and prawns are mixed together.

La Platja d'Aro: Just inland from this disco resort, on the road to Santa Cristina d'Aro, a road to the right leads to Masnou and the golf club. A few minutes up this road and set well back from it in its own grounds is the **Big Rock** restaurant in a typical farmhouse where Carles Comós has made a name for himself as an innovator in modern Catalan cuisine. Foodies should not miss the experience. Best to book in high season, tel: (972) 81 80 12. Closed: Sunday nights and Monday.

S'Agaró: La Gavina, Plaça de la Roselada s/n, S'Agaró, tel: (972) 32 11 00, is the only 5-star hotel on the coast (see *Tourism* chapter). If you are not super-rich, drop in for a coffee and stay instead at the nearby 1-star **Ancla**, Carretera Sant Feliu-Palamós Km 2, S'Agaró, tel: (972) 32 01 28. Or you could simply splash out on a pot of fish (*olla pescadors*) at the up-market beach café, the **Taverna del Mar**.

Sant Feliu de Guíxols: One of the coast's best known restaurants is the **Eldorado Petit**, Rambla Vidal 23, tel: (972) 32 18 18. It has the look of a brasserie, and the dishes are highly imaginative—fresh ravioli stuffed with seafood, or rabbit in Rioja. For a cheaper, simpler meal, the bar next door serves uncomplicated fillers. The **Casa Rovira** *pensió*, Carrer Sant Amanç 106, 17220 Sant Feliu de Guíxols, tel: (972) 32 12 02, was owned by the English writer John Langdon-Davies and is still run by his family.

Tossa: The **Bahia** is a fine seafront restaurant, where Camilla Cruanas has established herself as the queen of the *tossensa* cooks. Try the *brandade de bacallà* starter or the *cim-i-tomba*, the town's fish stew speciality. The **Diana** is an interesting Modernist house-turned-hotel in the centre of town, Plaça Espanya 10-12, 17320 Tossa de Mar, tel: (972) 34 03 04.

COSTA DEL MARESME

Caldes d'Estrac: This Edwardian-looking former spa resort has the large, 4-star **Hotel Colon** at the end of its *passeig marítim*: Ciutat de la Paz 16, 08393 Caldes d'Estrac, tel: (93) 791 05 00. There is also a very pleasant and slightly cheaper hotel, the **Racó de Peix**, Passeig dels Anglesos 3, 08393 Caldetes, tel: (93) 791 01 44. This small, grand house on the seafront has large rooms and bathrooms and a restaurant with terrace attached.

Arenys de Mar: There are good fish restaurants in the port, such as the **Posit de Pescador**. The **Hispania** in Carretera Reial 54 is celebrated for its Catalan cuisine. Counter the effects of a large restaurant bill by staying at the **Los Angeles** *pensió*, Carrer Margarides 8, 08350 Arenys de Mat, tel: (93) 792 38 49.

BARCELONA CITY

Hotels: The capital does not have an abundance of accommodation and better class hotels should be booked, as conventions and such like can fill them up. Middle-priced hotels are particularly in short supply. The tourist information centre at the airport can book you into a hotel on arrival.

Two good 4-star hotels towards the top of the range are **Comtes de Barcelona**, Passeig de Gràcia 75, 08008 Barcelona, tel: (93) 215 06 16, in a converted Modernist mansion, and the slightly cheaper **Colón**, Avinguda Catedral 7, 08002 Barcelona, tel: (93) 301 14 04, in the Gothic quarter, though the cathedral bells may keep you awake. There are two palatial hotels which are not sky-high in price. The 3-star **Hotel Granvia**, Gran Via de les Corts Catalanes 642, 08007 Barcelona, tel: (93) 318 19 00, is near the Plaça Catalunya and has a brocaded, Regency feel. The 2-star **Hotel España**, Sant Pau 9 i 11, 08001 Barcelona, tel: (93) 318 17 58, is a Modernist extravaganza from Domènech i Montaner and though the bedrooms are plain, its public rooms maintain a sense of the *belle époque*.

There are a clutch of pleasant, middle-priced hotels by the Rambla de Catalunya, such as the 2-star **Windsor**, Rambla de Catalunya 84, 0800 Barcelona, tel: (93) 215 11 98, and the **Neutral**, Rambla de Catalunya 42, 08007 Barcelona, tel: (93) 318 73 70.

But most of the hotels are on or near the main Rambla. There are lots of inexpensive places on the roads and lanes leading off both sides of the street, and they become progressively more seedy towards the port. Near the Plaça Catalunya at the top there are 1 and 2-star hotels on Carrer de Santa Anna: the **Catalunya**, tel: (93) 301 91 50; **Cortes**, tel: (93) 317 91 12; and **Nouvel**, tel: (93) 301 82 74. Further down on Carrer del Carme, there are four *pensiós*: the **Carmen**, tel: (93) 317 10 76; **Aneto**, tel: (93) 318 40 83; **Selecta**, tel: (93) 209 19 30; and **Mare Nostrum**, tel: (93) 318 53 40. The 2-star **Sant Agustí**, Plaça Sant Agustí 3, 08001 Barcelona, tel: (93) 317 28 82, is pleasantly situated in a quiet square behind the market, and on the opposite side of the Rambla the **Hotel Jardí**, Plaça St Josep Oriol 1, 08001 Barcelona, tel: (93) 301 59 00, overlooks two attractive, bustling little squares.

Restaurants: as one might expect, the city's restaurants cater to all tastes. These are just a small flavour.

Eldorado Petit, Carrer Dolors Monserdà 51, tel: (93) 204 51 53, is the younger sister of the famous Sant Feliu de Guíxols restaurant. You get the extra you pay for here, in the best modern Catalan cuisine, and there is a fine garden and terrace, plus parking. Also at the top of the bill is **Botafumeiro**, Carrer Gran de Gràcia 81, tel: (93) 218 42 30, *the* seafood restaurant and oyster bar which also serves Galician dishes.

Passadís de'n Pep, Plaça de Palau 2, tel: (93) 310 10 21, is a small but "in" restaurant, where most diners are happy to eat what they are given. **El Raïm**, Carrer Pescaderia 6, tel: (93) 319 29 98, has been "in" for bygone literati and is still a pleasant, informal place. To get an artistic flavour, visit **Els Quatre Gats**, Carrer Montsió 3, tel: (93) 302 41 40. It is a shadow of its former self, and the paintings on the walls are copies, but one really does have to sit in the same place that Rusiñol, Casas, Picasso and the rest did, even if the idea of such smart food in a once-bohemian atmosphere is hard to digest. There is a reasonable lunchtime set menu.

Other characterful spots include **El Gran Café**, Carrer de Avinyó 9, tel: (93) 318 79 86, a turn-of-the-century sewing machine premises, which nostalgically retains its decor and serves good Catalan dishes in bistro style. A good inexpensive restaurant is the **Estevet**, Carrer Valldonzella 46, tel: (93) 302 41 86. Try also one of the **Eqipto** "chain", the latest opened in the Rambla; the one at the back of the market is fun: Carrer Jerusalem 12, tel: (93) 317 74 80.

Barceloneta, the city's seafront, also has some good restaurants and if it is hot it is worth hopping on a metro or bus to cool off under an umbrella at a table at one of these beach shacks. They are popular, and a little more expensive than their ramshackle appearance suggests they are going to be.

BARCELONA PROVINCE

Vilafranca del Penedès: Celler del Penedès, Km 35 on the C244 to Vilanova i la Geltrú, tel: (93) 890 20 01, has country-style food and, above all, good wine.

Sabadell: Can Marcel, Carrer Advocat Cirela 30-40, tel: (93) 723 23 00, has quality cuisine, but is slightly pricey.

Caldes de Montbui: Balneario Termes Victòria, Carrer Barcelona 12, 08140 Caldes de Montbui, tel: (93) 865 01 50, is a spa hotel which is now becoming trendy.

Granollers: La Granolla, Carrer Girona 52, tel: (93) 870 20 07, is not cheap but it has very good Catalan and French cuisine.

Montseny: Sant Bernat, Finca el Cot, 08460 Montseny, tel: (930) 847 30 11, is a pleasant small hotel situated near the forest and mountains of the natural park.

Vic: Parador Nacional, 08500 Vic, 10 miles (15 km) northeast of Vic off the N153, tel: (93) 888 72 11, is very popular and very beautiful. A relatively new building for a Parador, it is wonderfully set in a pine forest overlooking the Sau reservoir. The restaurant serves good traditional Vic dishes.

Monistrol de Montserrat: Monistrol, Carretera Abrera-Manresa (C1411) Km 13, tel: (93) 835 04 77, is a 2-star hotel overshadowed by mountains and an alternative to a cell in the monastery.

El Bruc: El Bruc, Carretera Nacional 11, Km 574, 08194 El Bruc, tel: (93) 771 00 61, is a well-appointed 3-star hotel set in this legendary valley. It also has a good restaurant: listen out for the mythical drummer boy as you eat traditional Catalan cuisine.

Igualada: América, Carretera Madrid-França (N11) Km 557, 08700 Igualada, tel: (93) 803 10 00, is a popular, comfortable 3-star hotel set next to the main road. **Port-Lligat**, San Ferran 42, tel: (93) 804 69 32, has good, reasonably priced Catalan cuisine.

Manresa: Pedro III, Muralla Sant Francesc 49, 08240 Manresa, tel: (93) 872 40 00, is a large, central 3-star hotel; a good base for visiting Barcelona or Montserrat. **L'Aligué**, Carrer El Guix 8, tel: (93) 873 25 62, on the main road to Vic, has a good selection of international and Catalan cuisine.

Cardona: Parador Nacional Duques de Cardona, 08261 Cardona, tel: (93) 869 12 75, is a hilltop castle overlooking the town and salt mines, authentically complete with squeaking floorboards. The restaurant in the baronial hall is pricey but the food is fine and the portions large.

Berga: Queralt, Plaça de la Creu 4, 08600 Berga, tel: (93) 821 06 11, is a small 2-star hotel and a good base for trips to the Pyrenees and Andorra. **Santa Maria de Queralt**, Santuario, tel: (93) 821 24 58, is a hilltop sanctuary just west of Berga where you can enjoy basic Catalan cooking as you look out over the world.

Castellar de N'Hug: Les Fonts, Afores s/n, 08696 Castellar de N'Hug, tel: (93) 823 60 89. Stay at the source of the Llobregat *and* drink the water.

Castelldefels: Rey Don Jaime, Avinguda de l'Hotel s/n, 08860 Castelldefels, tel: (93) 665 13 00, has 4 stars and is expensive, but it is worth it for the beautiful hilltop view of the *costa* as far as Barcelona. Fine food. **Rancho**, Passeig de la Marina 212, 08860 Castelldefels, tel: (93) 665 19 00, is quieter than the beach-front hotels and has good quality cuisine and service. **Nàutic**, Passeig Marítim 374, tel: (93) 665 01 74, facing the beach, serves superior seafood in quaint surroundings. **Las Botas**, Autovía de Castelldefels, tel: (93) 665 40 96, is a busy restaurant right on the main road serving traditional Catalan dishes; grilled meats a speciality.

Sitges: Calípolis, Passeig Marítim s/n, 08870 Sitges, tel: (93) 894 15 00, is a fairly large 4-star hotel just a few hundred metres from the church and museums on the seafront. **Terramar**, Passeig Marítim s/n, 08870 Sitges, tel: (93) 894 00 54, is an older style 4-star establishment facing the beach with gardens and sports facilities. **Vivero,** Platja de Sant Sebastià, tel: (93) 894 21 49, is a basic place with tables outside overlooking the small beach and serving mainly seafood. **Els 4 Gats**, Carrer Sant Pau 13, tel: (93) 894 19 15, is a reasonably priced, quality restaurant on a narrow street descending to the sea.

Vilanova i la Geltrú: César, Isaac Peral 4, 08825, Vilanova, tel: (93) 893 07 04, is a small, reasonably priced 3-star hotel in the main town. Its restaurant is only open at weekends and it is worth waiting for. **Peixerot**, Passeig Marítim 56, tel: (93) 815 06 25, is a beach-front restaurant which specialises in seafood and is extremely popular with weekenders from Barcelona.

Altafulla: Yola, Via Augusta 50, 43893 Altafulla, tel: (977) 65 02 83, is one of the nicest hotels on this part of the coast, with a good restaurant, too.

Cambrils: Can Gatell, Carrer Miramar 27, tel: (977) 36 01 06, is one of three restaurants in the town owned by the Gatell family. All are famous for their classic Tarragona fish dishes (*romesco, àrros a banda, suquet,* etc) but this one is the most traditional.

Tarragona: España, Rambla Nova 49, 43003 Tarragona, tel: (977) 23 27 12, is a small, old-fashioned hotel right in the middle of town, reasonably priced. **Restaurant Les Coques**, Baixada del Patriarca 2, tel: (977) 22 83 00, serves good regional dishes. **El Tiberí**, Carrer Martí Ardenys 5, tel: (977) 23 54 03, isn't much to look at but its buffet food is Catalan, cheap and cooked by one of the best local chefs. **La Rambla**, Rambla Nova 10, tel: (977) 23 87 29, is rather smart and it serves what some consider to be the best and most authentic *romesco* with two courses of different kinds of fish; Pau Aquilo is an old-fashioned owner, always around and running everything immaculately.

El Vendrell: Restaurant Pi, Rambla 2, tel: (977) 66 00 22, is a café-restaurant done in a rather overblown Modernist style. It serves good local dishes such as *xató* salad and their own version of *calçots*.

Valls: Although Valls makes a good base there are only a couple of places to stay. The 2-star *pensió* **Torreblanca**, Carrer Josep M Fàbregas 1, 43800 Valls, tel: (977) 60 10 22, is attractive. **Restaurant Masía Bou**, Carretera de Lleida s/n tel: (972) 60 04 27, is *the* place to eat *calçots*. There are countless photos of celebrities, from Dalí to Suarez, wearing bibs and wolfing down their onions. It is smart and on the pricey side, but the *calçots* are the real thing, grown at the back of the restaurant, cooked in the backyard and followed by the traditional meal of spicey sausage and lamb.

Montblanc: Ducal, Carrer Disputació 11, 434000 Montblanc, tel: (977) 86 00 25, is one of the few reasonably priced hotels in the area, which is infinitely preferable to L'Espluga de Francolí as a base for Poblet. The **Fonda Colom**, Civaderia 3, tel: (977) 86 01 53, is in the old town and serves good local dishes. **Restaurant les Tines**, Finca Riubadella s/n, tel: (977) 87 80 40, serves grilled meats and is set inside an old castle.

Santes Creus: Grau, Carrer Pere III 3, 43815 Santes Creus, tel: (977) 63 83 11, has lots of character, is very quiet and is universally recommended.

Priorat: Residència-Casa de Pàges, Carrer Carrerada 8, 43739 Porrera, tel: (977) 82 80 21, is one of the first of several *casas de pàges* supported by the Generalitat to supply accommodation on a small scale. It is an old house, beautifully converted in a modern Abstract style, and designed for only a dozen guests. **Restaurant Piro**, Carrer Piro 21, Gratallops, tel: (977) 83 90 04, serves really good *platos típicos* with a menu which changes daily according to local ingredients (they collect their own *rovellon* mushrooms).

Gandesa: Piqué, Via Catalunya s/n, 43780 Gandesa, tel: (977) 42 00 68, is a simple road hotel with an excellent restaurant. Near the wine town of Gandesa, with its lovely old centre, it is also a great place for exploring the south.

Santa Bàrbara: (Montsià) **Venta la Punta** is a large basic country restaurant which is very popular with the locals and attracts big family groups. Great local dishes include huge hunks of lamb *a la brassa*, peppery *longaniza* sausages, fresh cheese with honey, rough country bread and local wine.

SPA HOTELS

The following spa hotels or *balnearis* all have a wide range of curative treatments on tap, but they can also be used simply as pleasant places to stay. Most were built at the turn of the century and have Modernist or Noucentist touches, with large bedrooms, elegant dining rooms, pleasant gardens and swimming pools and are surrounded by woods or wide open spaces for walking in. They tend to be a little more expensive than conventional hotels, and this is reflected in their star ratings. Their restaurants are open to non-residents, and to make the most of what the kitchens have to offer it is usually best to avoid the residents' set menus and go *à la carte*. For more detailed information, there is a spas association: Associació Balnearia, Balmes 191, 5è, 4rta B, 08006 Barcelona, tel: (93) 218 36 99.

Caldes de Malavella: (10 miles/16 km south of Girona, off the N11). **Vichy Català**, Avinguda Doctor Furest 8, 17455 Caldes de Malavella, tel: (972) 47 00 00. 4-star, 150 beds. Open: all year round. This large hotel has all possible health and leisure facilities and there is specialised medical supervision. The spa water is recommended for digestive, respiratory and circulation complaints, and for rheumatism, kidneys and the urinary tract. **Balneari Prats**, Plaça de Sant Esteve 7, 17455 Caldes de Malavella, tel: (972) 47 00 51. 4-star. Open: all year round. Although this also has 150 beds, it feels a lot smaller than Vichy, perhaps because it lacks a bottling plant. Part neoclassical, part rather modern, it is situated in the centre of town. Its full range of facilities include beauty and obesity treatments.

Santa Coloma de Farners: (26 miles/43 km southwest of Girona). **Termes Orion**, Carretera del Balneari, 17430 Santa Coloma de Farners, tel: (972) 84 00 65. 2-star, 100 beds. Open: all year round. This elegant neoclassical hotel is set in the countryside just outside Santa Coloma de Farners. Its cool white interiors are very handsome. It has health services with specialised personnel. Its waters are recommended, among other things, for the nervous system.

La Garriga: (15 miles/24 km north of Barcelona on N152). **Balneari Blancafort**, Carrer dels Banys 55, 08530 La Garriga, tel: (93) 871 46 00. 3-star, 100 beds. Open: all year round. This hotel has attracted many of Barcelona's leading lights, among them Eugeni d'Ors who invented the term "Noucentism" and was inspired by the gardens and guests of the time to write a memorable work, *Oceanografia del tedi* (*Oceanography of boredom*). Full health facilities include treatment for obesity and stress. Its sodium chloride-based waters are said to be good for the circulation.

Caldes de Montbui: (10 miles/16 km north of Barcelona on B143). **Balneari Broquetas**, Plaça de la Font del Lleo 1, 08140 Caldes de Montbui, tel: (93) 865 01 00. 3-star, 150 beds. Open: all year round. This is a nice old hotel in the middle of town with some remains of Roman baths. There is specialised medical supervision but no hydrotherapy. **Balneari Termes Victòria**, Carrer Barcelona 12, 08140 Caldes de Montbui, tel: (93) 865 01 50. 2-star, 150 beds. Open: all year round. A hotel with a 1930s look, it has full leisure and health facilities. Its waters are recommended for rheumatism. **Balneari Termes La Salud**, Carrer Joan Samsó 3, 08140 Caldes de Montbui, tel: (93) 865 00 98. 1-star, 90 beds. Open: all year round. Catalonia's oldest spa hotel, opened in 1674, has a pleasant terrace and health services, but no restaurant, though eating in the town should be no particular hardship. **Balneari Termes Solà**, Plaça de l'Angel 5, 08140 Caldes de Montbui, tel: (93) 865 00 95. 1-star, 50 beds. Open: March to November. Perhaps the cosiest of them all, it has been run by the same family since 1680, and it has a family feel which has attracted a number of painters, including Joaquim Mír. Full spa facilities and good home cooking.

Vallfonga de Riucorb: (equidistant between Barcelona, Lleida and Tarragona, 20 miles/32 km north of the N240). **Balneari Vallfonga de Riucorb**, Carretera del Balneari s/n, 43427 Vallfogona de Riucorb, tel: (977) 88 00 25. 3-star, 160 beds. Open: mid-May to end-October. A mile (2 km) from the town, this hotel was built at the turn of the century amid the pleasant, hilly countryside. There is medical supervision but no hydrotherapy. The water is recommended for infections of the liver.

Caldes de Boí: (88 miles/140 km north of Lleida on N230). **El Manantial**, 25528 Caldes de Boí, tel: (973) 69 01 91. 4-star, 216 beds. **Hotel Caldes**, 25528 Caldes de Boí, tel: (973) 69 04 49. 1-star, 226 beds. Both open 24 June–30 September. These two adjacent hotels are administratively linked and reservations to either must be made to Carrer Balmes 7, atic B, 08007 Barcelona, tel: (93) 302 40 88 (1 October–15 June), or Apartat de Correus, 25520 El Pont de Suert, Prov Lleida (16 June–20 September). The huge complex provides many facilities in a modern hotel (El Manantial) and a rebuilt medieval hospice (Caldes). They have no less than five hot and cold swimming pools among their sports facilities as well as a full range of health and beauty treatments. Water comes from 37 springs. The joys of the

Romanesque churches of the Boí Valley and Aigüestortes Park are within striking distance.

SPORTS

SAILING

There are 36 marinas along the 360 miles (580 km) of Catalonia's coast. Even though facilities have been expanding rapidly since the mid-1980s, berths can still be hard to come by in summer. For most of the summer all club berths are accounted for. There are some anchorage points along the rockier northern coast, and temporary berths on public jetties or in harbours are either very cheap or free. See the port authorities on arrival. A helmsman's certificate is required for any boating activity. General points about sailing in Catalonia are given in the chapter on *Outdoor Activities*.

Costa Brava: The main facilities are at the top end of the Bay of Roses, where large boat showrooms and chandleries serve Santa Margarida and Empúria-brava, Spain's largest marina, built on 15 miles (25 km) of canals: Club Nàutic Empúria-brava, Port, 17486 Castelló d'Empúries, tel: (972) 25 05 04. Palamós, the new Port d'Aro at Platja d'Aro and Sant Feliu de Guíxols all have safe ports and good nautical facilities. Blanes has a small second-hand boat fair in April on the seafront.

A number of coves and bays also provide anchorages, but remember the Tramuntana can blow up quickly, so make sure that your vessel is secure even on the balmiest nights. **Maresme:** Breakwater arms have been growing out of the long sandy stretches of the Maresme to provide "recreational" ports and a lot of money has been sunk into them to make sure their facilities are up to scratch. The most modern are El Balís and El Masnou, which has an active yacht club. (Promóciónes Portuarias S.A., Port, 08320 El Masnou, tel: (93) 555 30 00.)

Barcelona: There are two clubs in the capital's port, both dating back to the last century. The Reial Club Marítim de Barcelona, tel: (93) 315 00 07, and the Reial Club Nàutic de Barcelona, tel: (93) 315 11 61, are both at Port, 08002 Barcelona. The sailing federation, Federació Catalana de Vela, is at Passeig Manuel Girona 2, tel: (93) 204 83 63, and the sailing school, Esola Catalana de Vela, is at Moll Adossat s/n, tel: (93) 315 39 72. The cruising association, Asociació Nacional de Cruceros, is at Moll d'Espanya s/n, tel: (93) 310 41 23. Traditional *patí a vela* catamarans sail from the yacht club at Barcelona.

Costa Daurada: As on the Maresme, many new jetties, breakwaters and recreational facilities have been creeping out from the Costa Daurada's sandy shores. Catalonia's latest port is the 1,011-berth La Ginesta just north of Sitges: Port Ginesta S.A., Port, 08870 La Ginesta, tel: (93) 664 36 61. Aiguadolç, another new port, is just to the south: Port de Aiguadolç S.A., Port, 08870 Sitges, tel: (93) 894 26 00. Tarragona is a busier port than Barcelona, mainly due to its oil refinery, and it also has Catalonia's oldest yacht club, Club Nàutic de Tarragona, Port, 43004 Tarragona, tel: (977) 21 03 60. Other recreational ports exist all down the coast to Sant Carles de la Ràpita on the Ebre delta. Pilots are needed to sail into the Ebre itself.

DIVING

Anyone wishing to dive in Spanish waters must have a diving permit. Permits cannot be obtained by post. It is best to get one of the reputable diving centres or schools to organ-

ise a permit on your behalf from the local marine commandant. They are only issued for the period of your stay and they cost around 1,000 pesetas.

Visiting divers need the following documents which they should hand in at the diving centre where they make their first dives:

1. Photocopies of identification pages in passport (in a British passport these are pages 1, 2, 3 and 4).

2. Photocopy of your current diving qualification page in logbook, or of diving certificate.

3. Photocopy of current diving medical certificate.

4. Two passport photographs with your name in full on the back.

The following are air stations on the Costa Brava where divers can get their bottles filled. Most supply other diving services, such as boats.

El Port de la Selva: Mononàutica Hidalgo, Muelle Balleu 5. Antonio Hidalgo is president of the Cap de Creus diving club and, given notice, can arrange boats.

Cadaqués: Club Poseidon-Nemrod, Platja Cayals. Boat diving available. The Club Meditérranée, just north of Cadaqués, has a diving centre for its guests.

Roses: Diving Company, Platja. Hermanos Roda, Carrer Astilleros.

L'Escala: Montgo-Sub, Platja Montgó, run by Joaquim and Maria Pallas. Boat diving available.

L'Estartit: Unisub, Bar Tortuga, Carretera de Torroella. Owner Tony Murray. Boat diving available. Medas-Sub, Passeig Marítim. Boat diving available.

Tamariu: Stolli's Diving Base. Owner Gunter Stollburg. Boat diving available.

Llafranc: Triton Diving Centre, Plaça dels Pins, run by Emili and Lotti Agusti. Boat diving available.

Calella de Palafrugell: Poseidon-Nemrod, Platja Port Pelegri. Divemaster Rudi Pacena. Boat diving available.

Palamós: Club Nàutic Costa Brava, Cantera, Port de Palamós.

Sant Feliu de Guíxols: Club de Mar, Passeig Marítim. Run by Peter and Jeanette Tatka. Boat diving available.

Tossa de Mar: Centro de Actividades Subacuáticas Mar Menuda, Platja.

Lloret de Mar: Motonàutica La Marina,

Passeig del Caleta.

Blanes: Astilleros Esteveta, Final Muelle Comercial.

Some of the fish that can be seen in the waters along the coast have the following names in Catalan: Anchovy: *anxova* or *seitó*. Barracuda: *espetón*. Bass: *llobarro* or *llop*. Corb: *corba*. Dentex: *déntol*. Gilthead: *daurada*. Goldline bream: *saupa*. Grouper: *nero*. Sardine: *sardina*. Sea flies or chromis: *castanyola*. White bream: *sard* or *verada*. Wrasse: *tord massot*.

GOLF

At the beginning of the 1990s a number of applications for golf courses had been filed. These will take a few years to become reality, but the chances are that the original nine clubs of the region, listed here, could be more than doubled by 1995. Eight of these clubs are by the coast, and so are easily accessible to tourists. The ninth is in the Pyrenean valley of the Cerdanya. All have club and trolley hire. Green fees go up to around 7,000 pesetas.

Club de Golf Pals: Platja de Pals, 17256 Pals, province of Girona, tel: (972) 63 60 06. Open: all year round. Closed: Tuesday between 1 September and 30 June. Finely set among pine woods beside the beach at Pals, the main hazard is the Tramuntana wind. The Spanish Open was held here in 1984 and, though not excessive by European standards, it is the most expensive of Catalonia's clubs.

Club de Golf Costa Brava: La Masia, 17246 Santa Cristina d'Aro, province of Girona, tel: (972) 83 71 50. Open: all year round. Closed: Wednesday October–May. Just inland between Sant Feliu de Guíxols and La Platja d'Aro, this course has some narrow doglegs. The clubhouse is a fine traditional *masia*. There are special weekly and monthly rates.

Club de Golf Llavaneres: 08392 Sant Andreu de Llavaneres, province of Barcelona, tel: (93) 792 60 50. Open: all year round. Closed: Monday in winter. Between Mataró and Arenys de Mar on the Maresme coast, this is Spain's smallest course, but the nine holes cover 2,350 yards (2,149 metres) and require full-blooded strokes. Green fees are obviously less than on a full course, at around 3,000 pesetas.

Club de Golf Vallromanes: Apartat de Correus 43, 08170 Montornès del Vallès, province of Barcelona, tel: (93) 568 03 62. Open: all year round. Closed: Tuesday. Behind Mataró on the Maresme coast, the first half of the course is flat, the second half on a hilly slope. Weekday green fees are half weekend and holiday fees.

Club de Golf Sant Cugat: 08190 Sant Cugat del Vallès, province of Barcelona, tel: (93) 674 39 58. Open: all year except Monday. Just inland from Barcelona city, the prewar course here was built by English expatriates. It has since been re-laid out, and this is where Severiano Ballesteros made his professional debut. Weekday green fees are about 2,000 pesetas cheaper than at weekends.

Reial Club de Golf El Prat: Apartat de Correus 10, 08820 El Prat de Llobregat, province of Barcelona, tel: (93) 379 02 78. Open: all year round. Visitors arriving by air fly over this course just before touchdown at Barcelona's El Prats airport. It is the closest to the city, and has the most members of Catalonia's clubs. Although the course is completely flat, it demands the use of a variety of clubs. The club's facilities include a children's nursery.

Club de Golf Terramar: Apartat de Correus 6, 08870 Sitges, province of Barcelona, tel: (93) 894 05 80. Open: all year round. An interesting course overlooking the sea on the south side of Sitges. It also has swimming pools, tennis courts and a nursery. Weekday fees are much cheaper than weekends or holidays.

Club de Golf Costa Daurada: Apartat de Correus 600, 43080 Tarragona, tel: (977) 65 54 16. Open: all year round. Closed: Monday. Just off the main road north of Tarragona, this is a nine-hole course. It has a pleasant club house, plus squash courts.

Reial Club de Golf de Cerdanya: Apartat de Correus 63, 17520 Puigcerdà, province of Girona, tel: (972) 88 13 38. Open: all year unless snowed off. The Cerdanya Valley is a beautiful setting for a golf course, and this club makes the most of it, among poplars and oaks. The green fees are modest, but the course has many championships, particularly in August and September as well as at Easter. The club house complex includes a hotel.

WALKING

You can walk your boots off in Catalonia. Some 1,875 miles (3,000 km) of footpaths have been mapped out by trail-blazing Catalans who have been tramping the hills and plains for a century. It is, however, crucial not to get lost, so most of these are marked with parallel red-and-white stripes painted on rocks and trees. If they are accompanied by an arrow it shows a change of direction. If the two lines are crossed it shows you where not to go. If there are several paths and they cross each other, as they do in parts of the Volcanic Park in Garrotxa, each one is separately colour coded in yellow or green instead of red.

There are some long-distance "G.R." routes, which have small signposts with the numbers of the routes and the names of the next village. These are ambitious walks. The G.R. 92 stretches the whole length of the coast from Portbou to Ulldecona; the G.R. 1 covers the entire Catalan Pyrenees, from Cap de Creus to Aragón.

Booklets called *Topo-guides* give details of the walks. Tourist offices or specialist shops should also be able to help. Two useful Barcelona addresses are: Centre d' Excursionisme de Catalunya, Paradís 10, tel: (93) 315 39 72, and a good bookshop, Librería Quera, Carrer Peritxol 2, in the *barri* Gòtic just off the Plaça del Pi.

HUNTING & FISHING

Details of how to go about hunting and fishing are given in the *Outdoor Activities* chapter. To find a suitable place to hunt, approach the relevant provincial hunting federation:

Federació Provincial de Caça de Lleida, Avinguda Prat de la Riba 80 4-2, Lleida, tel: (977) 21 27 77.

Federació Provincial de Caça de Girona, Carrer Emilio Grahit 122, Girona, tel: (972) 20 56 08.

Federació Provincial de Caça de Barce-
lona, Via Laietana 9 4-2, Barcelona, tel: (93) 301 23 07. The hunting federation for the whole of Catalonia (Federació Catalana de Caça) is at the same address.

Federació Provincial de Caça de Tarragona, Carrer San Françesc 3, Tarragona, tel: (977) 21 27 66.

For permits for hunting mountain goat, apply to:

Direcció General del Medi Natural, Córcega 329, Barcelona, tel: (93) 237 80 24.

Fishing licences: can usually be bought on the spot from tourist offices. For more detailed information approach the relevant government departments:

Servei Territorial d'Agricultura, Ramedería i Pesca de Lleida, Camp de Mart 35, Lleida, tel: (973) 24 66 50.

Servei Territorial d'Agricultura, Ramedería i Pesca de Girona, Avinguda de Sant Françesc 29, Girona, tel: (972) 21 24 00.

Servei Territorial d'Agricultura, Ramedería i Pesca de Barcelona, Carrer Sabí d'Arana 22-24, Barcelona, tel: (93) 330 64 51.

Servei Territorial d'Agricultura, Ramedería i Pesca de Tarragona, Avinguda de Catalunya 50, Tarragona, tel: (977) 21 79 55.

For general information:

Federació Catalana de Pesca, Avinguda Madrid 118, Barcelona, tel: (93) 330 48 18.

SKIING

There are 12 resorts in the region, all in the Pyrenees, plus five in Andorra. Their season extends from the beginning of December to the end of April. For a general view of the skiing scene, see *Outdoor Activity* chapter.

Baqueira-Beret: 43 pistes from 4,820–8,200 ft (1,500–2,500 metres). The "in" place where the royal family go. The twin towns are situated in the Vall d'Aran, and there are both high peaks and some flatter land for cross-country skiers. Further information: Oficina de Baqueira-Beret, Apartat 60, 25530 Vielha, Lleida, tel: (973) 64 50 25. Snow report: tel: (973) 64 50 52

Tuca-Mall Blanc: 20 pistes from 3,280–7,380 ft (1,000–2,250 metres). Also in the Vall d'Aran, this is a mile (2 km) from the region's main town of Vielha. It has some tricky trails and a slalom stadium. Further information: Tuca-Mall Blanc, Carretera Betrén-Tressens, 25530 Vielha, Lleida, tel: (973) 64 10 50.

Boí-Taüll: 14 pistes from 6,685–8,060 ft (2,040–2,455 metres). The newest resort started operating in the 1988–89 season. Its lack of sophistication is compensated for by the fine Romanesque villages where private homes open their doors to guests. Further information: Boí-Taüll S.A., Carrer la Granada 25 6è 1a, 08006 Barcelona, tel: (93) 238 04 73.

Super Espot: 24 pistes from 4,890–7,610 ft (1,490–2,320 metres). At the entrance to the Aigüestortes Park, Espot is a popular holiday centre in both summer and winter and is surrounded by magnificent scenery. Further information: Super Espot Estació d'Esquí, Carretera Barrabé s/n, 25597 Espot, Lleida, tel: (973) 63 50 13.

Llesui: 22 pistes from 4,740–7,970 ft (1,445–2,430 metres). A modest resort just north of Sort. The bare slopes of the surrounding mountains make it obstacle-free. Further information: Pallars Turístic S.A., Santa Anna s/n, 25560 Sort, Lleida, tel: (973) 62 08 05.

Port Ainé: 18 pistes from 5,410–8,000 ft (1,650–2,440 metres). Begun in 1986, this resort is also near Sort, 4 miles (6 km) north of Rialp. It has slopes suitable for beginners. Further information: Pallars Industrial S.A., Avinguda Flora Cadena 6, 25594 Rialp, Lleida, tel: (973) 62 03 25.

Port del Comte: 31 pistes from 5,545–7,870 ft (1,690–2,400 metres). This most southerly resort is actually in the pre-Pyrenees. There are meadow and woodland trails and a slalom stadium. Further information: Estació d'Esquí, Port del Comte, Apartat 26, 25280 Solsona, Lleida, tel: (973) 48 09 50.

Rasos de Peguera: 9 pistes from 6,215–6,725 ft (1,895–2,050 metres). South of the great Cadí range and 8 miles (13 km) north of Berga, this is Barcelona's closest resort. It is particularly recommended for family skiing. Further information: Estació d'Esquí Rasos de Peguera, Plaça de Sant Pere II, 08600 Berga, Barcelona, tel: (93) 821 17 48.

La Molina: 29 pistes from 5,215–8,085 ft (1,590–2,465 metres). One of the longest established resorts, on the eastern edge of the Cerdanya Valley, La Molina is always popular, and sometimes very full. There are artificial snow cannons and a great variety of pistes between the peaks of Puigllançada and Tossa d'Alp. Further information: Avinguda Supermolina s/n, 17573 La Molina-Alp, Girona, tel: (972) 89 20 31.

Masella: 88 pistes from 5,248–8,300 ft (1,600–2,530 metres). Next to La Molina, on the north face of Tossa d'Alp. Most of its 40 miles (62 km) of trails go through pine woods. Facilities include a heated indoor pool, sauna and gymnasium. Further information: Estació d'Esquí Masella, 17538 Alp, Girona, tel: (972) 89 01 06.

Vall de Núria: 9 pistes from 6,440–7,440 ft (1,965–2,270 metres). Inaccessible by road, skiiers must take the "zip" train up the Freser Valley from Ribes. Uncomplicated slopes, plus ice skating on the lake in front of the large sanctuary. Further information: Estació d'Esquí Vall de Núria, Passeig de Gràcia 26 3r, 08007 Barcelona, tel: (93) 301 97 77.

Vallter 2000: 16 pistes from 6,595–8,201 ft (2,010–2,500 metres). The most easterly resort, from here on a clear day you can see the Bay of Roses. Accommodation is in two refuges, or in the nearby village of Setcases, or the town of Camprodón. Further information: Estació d'Esquí Vallter 2000, Carrer Freixenet 1, 17867 Camprodón, Girona, tel: (972) 74 03 53.

ANDORRA

Pas de la Casa-Grau Roig: 38 miles (58 km) of pistes from 6,890–9,185 ft (2,100–2,800 metres). 134 snow cannons. Car parks at foot of slope. Close to French border and reliable snow. Tel (9738) 31816

Soldeu-El Tarter: 37 miles (60 km) of pistes from 6,364–8,530 ft (1,940–2,600 metres). 126 snow cannons. Lift to station from car park on main road. Tel (9738) 51151.

Pal: 28 miles (35 km) of pistes among pine forests from 5,840–7,735 ft (1,780–2,358 metres). 135 snow cannons. Car park at foot of slopes. Tel (9738) 36236.

Arinsal: 17 miles (28 km) of pistes from 5,085–8,530 ft (1,550–2,600 metres). 59 snow cannons. Two car parks at different altitudes. Tel (9738) 36236.

Arcalís: 12 miles (20 km) of pistes from 6,365–8,530 ft (1,940–2,600 metres). These north-facing slopes are cold in the early season, but snow stays later. Two car parks. Tel (9738) 36400.

Cross-country skiing: As well as these ski resorts, there are several centres for Nordic or cross-country skiing: Salardú in the Vall d'Aran, Bonabé in Pallars Sobirá, Sant Joan de l'Erm and Tuixén-la Vansa in Alt Urgell and Lles and Aránser in the Cerdanya.

Weather reports: These are usually given in the daily press. Snow and road reports can also be obtained from Associó Catalana d'Estacións d'Esquí i Muntanya, Carrer Menéndez Pelayo 191, 4t, 1a, 08012 Barcelona, tel: (93) 238 31 35, or (93) 217 46 80.

MISCELLANEOUS ACTIVITIES

Cycling: Federació Catalana de Ciclisme, Passeig Vall d'Hebron s/n, Barcelona, tel: (93) 427 01 86.

Kayaking: Federació Catalana Piragüisme, Avinguda Madrid 118, Barcelona, tel: (93) 330 44 48.

Speleology: Federació Catalana d'Espeleología, Avinguda Portal L'Angel 38, Barcelona, tel: (93) 318 07 77.

Water skiing: Federació Catalana d'Esquí Nàutic, Avinguda Madrid 118, Barcelona, tel: (93) 330 47 42.

CULTURE PLUS

ARCHITECTURE

Caves, wall paintings and dolmens: Early man left his mark throughout the region. The Cova del Moro at El Cogul in Lleida province has interesting Mesolithic wall paintings. La Cova d'en Daina near Girona has a large and well-preserved passage grave. Dolmens are often marked on maps, and signs indicating their presence seen at roadsides, but in practice they are very hard to find. There is a menhir at Can Ferrer in the province of Tarragona and wall paintings in the Cova de Vallmajor at Albinyana nearby. Paintings also in L'Agulla cave, Benifallet and Cabrafeixet cave, El Perello, and rock paintings near the Ermita de la Pieta at Ulldecona

Iberian sites: Ullastret, in the province of Girona, has a large Greco-Iberian site and museum. In Tarragona province Coll de Moro de Gandesa is worth a visit, as are La Ferradura, La Moleta del Remei and Alcanar. There are Ibero-Romano remains at Montmell, La Costa and at La Bisbal de Penedès, and at Tivissa where there is a picturesque hilltop village.

Greek and Roman: Empúries in Girona province has an extensive and very well preserved site, which has both a Greek and a Roman section and is attractively set by the sea. Isona, in Lleida, has interesting Roman remains, but Tarragona city is the principal site; there is a Passeig Arqueològic along the Roman walls, which are larger than Girona's, an amphitheatre and circus, the remains of the Via Augusta and, outside the city, two monumental tombs and the remains of an aqueduct.

Romanesque: There are some 2,000 Romanesque buildings in Catalonia Tourist offices will give details of local sites and can provide "Romanesque routes" designed to take in as much as possible. Perhaps the greatest of these buildings are: the monastery of Sant Pere de Rodes, overlooking Cap de Creus in the province of Girona; Sant Pere de Galligants in the city of Girona, now used as a museum; the Santa Maria Cathedral in La Seu d'Urgell; the collegiate church of Sant Vicenç in Cardona; the parish church of Sant Jaume de Frontanya near Berga and the cluster of Visigothic-Romanesque churches of Santa Maria, Sant Miquel and Sant Pere in Terrassa.

Among the best Romanesque doorways are those of Santa Maria de Ripoll in the province of Girona, and Santa Maria in Agramunt, in the *comarca* of Urgell, Lleida province. Most of the churches are bare of ornamentation and some of the best of the paintings and sculptures can be found in the Museu d'Art de Catalunya in Barcelona and the Museu Episcopal in Vic. (See the chapter on *Romanesque*.)

Gothic: Catalonia also has a wealth of Gothic buildings, details of which can be obtained from local tourist offices. Barcelona has some prime examples in the *barri* Gòtic, or Gothic quarter. The cathedral and the monastery of Pedralbes in the Sarria suburb are particularly noteworthy. Other important buildings are the collegiate church of Santa Maria in Manresa, which is known as La Seu—the cathedral—although in fact it is not, and the genuine cathedrals of Tarragona and Tortosa, in the province of Tarragona. As with Romanesque, much of the sculpture and paintings from Gothic churches can be found in the Museu d'Art de Catalunya and the Museu Episcopal, Vic. Girona's art museum has some fine, if rather grisly, Gothic retables.

Modernism: Barcelona is the showcase for Modernism, with such places as the Parc Güell and the Puig/Montaner/Gaudí block on Passeig de Gràcia. But there are sudden surprises all around Catalonia, from fanciful tombs in Lloret de Mar to the weird converted farmhouses in Sant Josep Despi, now a Barcelona suburb, where Josep Jujol's Can Negre heralded Surrealism. The tourist offices have information about routes. (See also *Nineteenth-century* and *Modernism* chapters.)

MUSEUMS

Catalonia is rich in museums of all kinds, from the Museu Picasso in Barcelona to the local museums in the capital towns of each *comarca*, called "*comarcal*" museums. The following is but a brief selection of some of the more interesting ones. Tourist offices will provide full details (in several languages) of those in their localities. Museums change their opening times, and sometimes even their locality, with great alacrity, but generally opening hours are 9 a.m.–1 p.m. and 4–7 p.m., although the Picasso museum in Barcelona and the Dalí in Figueres are both open all day. The Dalí museum, the second most popular in Spain after the Prado in Madrid, is also the exception to the rule that museums close on Mondays. Addresses are given only for those in large cities; those in smaller places will be easily located. Entrance fees are usually a few hundred pesetas.

BARCELONA

• CITY

Museu Arqueològic, Passeig Santa Madrona, Parc de Montjuïc. Archaeology.

Museu d'Art de Catalunya, Palau Nacional, Parc de Montjuïc. The place to go to understand what all the fuss over Romanesque art is about.

Museu d'Art Modern, Plaça d'Armes, Parc de la Ciutadella. Catalonia's artists, from the 19th century to today.

Museu de la Ciencia, Teodor Roviralta 55. Science.

Museu Frederic Marès, Carrer Comtes de Barcelona, 10. Idiosyncratic collection of Romanesque, Gothic, Renaissance and baroque sculpture.

Museu d'Historia de la Ciutat, Plaça del Rei. City history with Roman basement.

Museu Marítim, Plaça Portal de la Pau, 1. Maritime museum in the extraordinary Drassanes docks.

Museu Militar, Castell de Montjuïc, Parc de Montjuïc. Military—principally interesting for the 18th-century castle itself.

Fundació Joan Miró, Plaça Neptu, Parc de Montjuïc. Miró's work and that of other contemporary artists.

Museu Picasso, Montcada 14–19. Mostly early work, donated by the artist and his widow, housed in a medieval building.

Museu Tèxtil i d'Indumentària, Montcada 12–14. Textiles and costumes. Opposite the Picasso museum, it's worth seeing both.

• PROVINCE

Arenys de Mar: Museu de la Punta Frederic Marès. Large collection of lace, both local and from other parts of Spain.

Martorell: Museu Santacanca "L'Enrajolada". Catalan and Hispano-Arabic dishes and tiles, plus furniture and 19th-century paintings.

Montserrat: Museu del Monastir de Montserrat. Archaeology and paintings. The monastery, 32 miles (50 km) from Barcelona, is an important spiritual centre, home of the Black Virgin, La Mare de Deu de Montserrat (see *Barcelona Province* chapter). The mountain itself is a popular area for walking and rock climbing. Access from exit 25 on A2/A7 motorway from Barcelona to Tarragona, or by train from Barcelona's Plaça Espanya.

Sabadell: Museu-Institut de Paleontologia. One of the most important palaeontological museums in Spain.

Vic: Museu Episcopal. Second only to Barcelona's Museu d'Art de Catalunya for Romanesque and Gothic.

Vilafranca de Penedès: Museu de Vilafranca. Housed in 12th-century Palau de Comtes-Reis, it comprises six separate museums, among which is the Museu del Vi, Spain's only museum devoted to wine and viniculture. Art, geology, archaeology and ornithology are in the other five.

GINORA

• CITY

Museu Arqueològic de Sant Pere de Galligants, Plaça de Santa Lucia. Archaeology in fine Romanesque monastery.

Museu Capitular i Claustres del Catedral, Plaça de la Catedral. Contains the wonderful 12th-century Tapestry of the Creation.

Museu d'Art, Palau Episcopal, Pujada de la Catedral. From Romanesque to modern art.

Museu de la Ciutat, Carrer de la Força. City history. *Sardana* instruments.

Centre Isaac del Cec, Carrer de Sant Llorenç. Part of newly renovated Jewish quarter; centre for Hebrew studies.

• PROVINCE

Banyoles: Museu Arqueològic Comarcal. Prehistoric finds including the famous Neanderthal jaw. Museu Darder: anthropology and ethnology, including some grotesque mummies.

Figueres: Teatro-Museu Dalí, Figueres. Designed by Dalí as well as containing many of his works. Museu de Joguets: private museum with huge collection of old toys.

Llagostera: Fundació Emili Vila. Vila's former family home; his paintings (some still for sale) plus works by Modigliani and a Lautrec self-portrait.

Llivia: Museu Municipal. Contains the oldest pharmacy in Europe.

Olot: Museu Comarcal. Housed in ancient hospice; paintings by Olot School and exhibition of work from local saint-making industry. Open: Monday. Closed: Tuesday.

Peralada: Museu-Biblioteca del Convent del Carme. Library, wine museum, pottery. Housed in castle; regular guided tours.

Ripoll: Arxiu-Museu Folklòric. Famous Catalan forges, armaments, pottery and shepherds' artefacts.

Sant Joan de les Abadesses: Museu del Monestir. Gold and silverware and sculpture from the monastery.

Sils: Colleció d'Automòbils de Salvador Claret. Large collection of antique cars, situated on the N11.

Tossa: Museu de la Vila Vella. Paintings by local and other European artists, including Chagall.

Ullastret: Museu Monogràfic del Poblat Iberic. Finds from a large Iberian settlement.

TARRAGONA

• CITY

Museu d'Història de Tarragona, Escales de Sant Hermenegild. Roman and medieval artefacts. Housed in the Roman Pilatus Castle.

Museu Nacional Arqueològic, Plaça del Rei. Most important Roman collection in Catalonia.

Museu de la Necròpolis, Passeig de la Independencia. Mosaics and sarcophagi from important early Christian necropolis.

Museu Diocesà, Catedral de Tarragona. Romanesque and Gothic art.

• PROVINCE

Amposta: Museu del Montsià. Local ornithology.

El Vendrell: Casa-Museu Pau Casals, El Vendrell. Birthplace of Pau Casals, who is buried in local cemetery. Personal belongings, art, music scores, etc. A new auditorium is being built nearby. Casa Museu Guimerà, home of 19th-century Catalan poet and playwright; personal belongings.

Poblet: Museu del Monestir de Santa Maria. Archaeology and fine art.

Reus: Museu Comarcal. Paintings by Fortuny, sculpture by Rebull, plus Romanesque and Gothic remains. Museu Arqueologìa Salvador Vilasec, important prehistoric remains.

Santes Creus: Museu del Reial Monestir. Housed in 18th-century rooms of the monastery.

Tortosa: Museu del Catedral. Religious art.

LLEIDA

• CITY

Museu Capitular, Plaça de la Catedral, Lleida. Flemish tapestries, ecclesiastic treasures.

Museu Diocesà de Pintura Medieval, Carrer del Bisbe, Lleida. Gothic art.

Museu Diocesà d'Escultura Medieval, Sant Martí church, Carrer Jaume el Conqueridor. Medieval sculpture.

Museu de la Paeria, Plaça de la Paeria. Archaeology and history.

Museu Arqueològic, Plaça de la Catedral. Archaeology.

• PROVINCE

Balaguer: Museu Comarcal. Ceramics and Arabic artefacts.

Cervera: Museu Duran i Sanpere. Roman and Iberian remains.

La Seu d'Urgell: Museu Diocesà. Paintings, sculpture, 11th-century gold and silverware. Miniatures by El Beat de Lièbana are of special interest. Note: Open on Monday but closed on Sunday afternoon.

Solsona: Museu Diocesà i Comarcal. Housed in Bishop's Palace. Medieval paintings and sculpture, Iberian remains.

ANDORRA

Andorra la Vella: Casa de la Vall (old quarter). 16th-century fortified mansion, now the seat of government.

Ordino: Casa Areny de Plandolit. 17th-century nobleman's house, restored as museum of Pyrenean husbandry.

Escaldes-Engordany: Museu d'Escultura Viladomat, Edifici Salita Parc, Parc de la Mola. Sculpture by local artist, Josep Viladomat.

Sanctuari de Meritxell, near Canillo: Modern shrine by Ricardo Bofill, next to site of ancient chapel. Regarded as spiritual heart of Andorra.

MUSIC

The *sardana* is danced to the traditional tunes in village squares and city avenues all over Catalonia and there is a festival of *habaneros*, songs which sailors brought back from Havana, in Calella de la Palafrugell every summer. But the region is also rich in music festivals and concerts of all kinds. Barcelona, as befits the capital, has a splendid opera house, the Gran Teatro del Liceo, in which both opera and ballet are performed.

Tickets are extremely difficult to get but for those who would like to try, programmes can be obtained from beside the theatre at Carrer Sant Pau 1, bis, 08003 Barcelona, tel:

(93) 318 92 77. Barcelona also has the Palau de la Música Catalana, a beautiful Modernist building in which jazz concerts are held as well as recitals of classical and ancient music.

Excellent and well supported local choirs, such as the Orfeó Catalá and Coros Clavé, tour the region, and a number of music festivals are held each summer. Staged in monasteries, churches and castles, they attract top popular and classical artists. Yehudi Menuhin makes highly acclaimed appearances, as does the Spanish guitarist Narciso Yepes, the National Ballet Company, and the favourite local opera stars, Montserrat Caballé and Josep Carreras. On the popular side, Julio Iglesias can clog up the traffic for miles around, while Liza Minelli has also attracted capacity crowds.

The telephone numbers for information about some of the best-known festival venues are:

Festival Internacional de Música Castell de Peralada, tel: (972) 53 81 25.

Festival Internacional de Música de Cadaqués, tel: (972) 25 83 15.

Festival Internacional de Música de Torroella de Montgrí, tel: (972) 75 80 37.

Festival Internacional de Música de Cantonigrós, tel: (93) 200 39 26.

Festival Internacional de Jazz de Terrassa, tel: (93) 783 51 37.

Ticket prices are between 2,500 and 5,000 pesetas (£12.50–£25) depending on the artist, and may be reserved by phone and picked up before the performance. Travel or tour agents will usually make the booking for you.

NIGHTLIFE

CLUBS & DISCOS

The brightest night spots tend to be in the kind of crowded resorts one wants to avoid: the spectacular razzmatazz of the Grand Palace in Lloret de Mar or the Galas in Salou; or the laser shows of La Platja d'Aro, which boasts the greatest concentration of discos on the coast.

In the summer months discos spring up in all the resorts, charging perhaps 2–3,000 pesetas to get in and adding several hundred pesetas to the price of a drink. With meals eaten late, nightlife doesn't begin to get going until after midnight, continuing until around 5 a.m. when the tradition in some resorts is to have fresh *churros* (doughnuts) dunked in hot chocolate.

In the more established resorts discotheques and night clubs are open on winter weekends, too.

Many of the late drinking places in Barcelona, like the Zsa Zsa, have no entrance fee: they just demand a lot of money for their drinks. Others, such as Otto Zutz, like you to queue up so they can then refuse you entrance because they don't like your face. It is hard to recommend any of these, not least because they come in and out of fashion so fast.

CASINOS

Public gambling is a relatively new experience in Spain, as it was banned under Franco. There are three casinos in Catalonia and they are open from about 7 p.m.–4 a.m.

There is a small entry fee of around 600 pesetas and you will need to take your passport.

Peralada: The casino is part of the castle in this medieval, sparkling-wine village. Though the gaming rooms are tastefully hung with tapestries, the hostesses in glittering top hats and tails look quite out of place. Tel: (972) 50 31 62.

Lloret de Mar: Part of the modern Hotel Casino de Lloret, it has all the usual games, plus a slot machine room, restaurant, disco and swimming pool. Carrer de Tossa s/n, tel: (972) 36 65 12.

Sant Pere de Ribes: Called the Gran Casino de Barcelona, this is actually 26 miles (42 km) from the city on the outskirts of Sitges. There is a dance hall with an orchestra on Fridays and an open-air concert theatre. Tel: (93) 893 36 66.

SHOPPING

WHAT TO BUY

Leather goods are very good value, from belts and purses to jackets, boots and shoes. These can be found everywhere, from smart shops in large towns to weekly markets in villages and resorts, with prices and quality varying accordingly. Shoes of all kinds are a good buy: apart from leather there is a range of inexpensive and attractive canvas styles and, of course, *espadrilles*. For local use, plastic buckled sandals are sold very cheaply in most resorts and are ideal for stony beaches and rocky coves.

Basketwork is no longer as cheap as it was, but some items are still good value and there is a large variety.

Ceramics: There is a wonderful and inexpensive range of kitchen, garden and decorative ceramics available in small shops, at markets and in huge roadside emporiums. La Bisbal is the largest Catalan ceramic centre with nearly 100 shops in the town.

Miravet, in Tarragona is also an important pottery town, as is Verdu in the Urgell (Lleida) where most of the ceramic ware is black. It is often possible to watch ceramics being made and painted in the smaller workshops.

Hand made lace can be bought, especially in L'Arboc in Baix Penedès, Tarragona.

Olive oil and wine vinegar (*aceite de oliva* and *vinaigre de vino*) are good value. Wine and spirits are still ridiculously cheap. Table wine can cost as little as 90 pesetas (about 45p) a litre and a good quality Rioja or Valdepeñas can be had for less than 300 pesetas (£1.50). There are some very good Spanish brandies costing about 850 pesetas (about £4.50) a litre.

WHERE TO BUY

Barcelona has large department stores in the city centre: El Corte Inglés in Plaça de Catalunya and Galerías Preciadas in Avinguda Portal del'Angel, and a number of large shopping arcades. Smaller, more traditional shops abound in the rest of the city as in other towns. Shops in Catalonia still tend to specialise, and you will find haberdashers, drapers, dry-goods stores, knife vendors and ironmongers—which makes shopping more time-consuming but far more interesting. For food shopping, there are supermarkets, but not to the exclusion of many individual shops. Many towns have pedestrianised shopping precincts but, again, the stores in these are mainly small, privately owned ones.

Markets: Markets flourish throughout the region, selling everything from food to caged birds. Barcelona has Els Encants, an outdoor market open on Monday, Wednesday, Friday and Saturday, selling second-hand and antique goods and a stamp and coin market in the Plaça Reial on Sunday morning. The main Barcelona food market is the Mercat de Sant Josep, known as La Boqueria, in the main *rambla*, a colonnaded,

19th-century building which is open daily, selling beautifully displayed food of every kind.

Every town and many villages have a weekly market: some are large, noisy affairs, others have just a dozen stalls. They principally sell food, household linen, kitchenware, flowers and a limited selection of clothes. The fruit and vegetable markets can be a joy to look at even if you do not intend to buy. The *rambla* in Barcelona, between Plaça de Catalunya and the port, has its famous, permanent market of books, flowers and caged birds, which runs almost the whole length of the central avenue, a colourful and fascinating display, especially during the hours of the evening *passejada*.

Most coastal resorts have markets which are swelled in summer by vendors of tourist goods: souvenirs, bikinis, leather goods, cheap T-shirts and gimmicky toys. Quality varies but prices are usually fair. Some stallholders will bargain, some won't—and they will be quite definite about it.

EXPORT PROCEDURES

Members of EC countries can buy consumer goods costing more than 47,000 pesetas for export and obtain tax discounts. You must present your passport or identity card to the vendor and ask for an application form which will be filled in by the store and stamped by customs when you return to your own country. For people from non-EC countries, discounts are also available but the forms must be stamped by Spanish customs on departure and the discount will be paid to you when you return to your own country. If buying works of art, dealers will provide information about export regulations.

COMPLAINTS

Official complaints forms are available in hotels, bars, restaurants, camp sites and travel agents to enable visitors to register complaints. Formal complaints may also be made to tourist information offices or to regional tourist services (Servei Territorial de Comerç, Consum i Turisme).

SPECIAL INFORMATION

CHILDREN

Catalonia, like all of Spain, is a great place to be a child, or to be a parent travelling with one, for they are generally welcomed and often totally indulged. Children are allowed in bars where fridges containing ice lollies are as important as the vast array of bottles behind the counters. Family meals in restaurants are part of the national culture and most menus offer chicken and chips and spaghetti for those who won't be tempted by the thought of trying something new.

Some hotels have babysitting services, otherwise ask for a *canguru* (a kangaroo) to sit. The larger resorts have day centres, *guarderías*. But you may do better befriending other people on the beach and arranging swaps.

Most towns have a play park in a central area and the coastal resorts offer a wealth of amusements from water chutes and go-karts in the larger places to hoop-la stalls and mini rifle ranges in the quieter ones. Many beaches have pedaloes and some hire out child-size windsurfing boards. Spanish children rarely go to bed before midnight on hot summer nights and, as meals are eaten late and most entertainments don't start until after 10, your main problem may be tired and fractious children who can't cope with the changes in their sleeping habits—but are determined to try.

Provision for people with disabilities leaves something to be desired. There are no special facilities on Spanish railways, although wheelchairs are available at the main city and frontier stations. All the airports offer this service if they are informed, through a booking agent, when the ticket is bought. It is not possible to hire a car which has been converted to hand controls, but Hertz does have some automatic models. Details from Hertz UK reservations, tel: (081) 679 1799, or through a travel agent.

Most of the main tour operators, including Intasun, Horizon, Thompson and Wallace Arnold, cater for disabled people and travel agents should be able to find out where you can have the type of holiday best suited to your needs. Most Catalan hotels, however, are not well equipped to deal with wheelchair-bound people and, from the point of view of sightseeing, remember that the Costa Brava is a very rocky place, and the old towns were built with cobbled streets and steep flights of steps; the Costa Daurada is much flatter. The Spanish Private Organisation for the Disabled (ECOM) is at Carrer de Balmes 311, ent 2, 08006 Barcelona, tel: (93) 217 38 82.

FURTHER READING

The following books are in print in English:

General:
Handbook for Spain 1845 by Richard Ford. Just 80 pages of Vol II deal with Catalonia, but this 19th-century writer on Spain was the best. Centaur Press.

Homage to Catalonia. George Orwell's classic account of the civil war. Penguin.

The Catalans by Jan Read. The most comprehensive history of the nation. Faber and Faber. Though actually out of print, most public libraries have it in stock.

The Essence of Catalonia by Alastair Boyd. A personal and very readable guide to the region and its culture. Andre Deutsch.

Fabled Shore by Rose Macaulay. Written in 1949 and now republished, it is full of her delightful wit and observations, and covers the coast all the way round to the Algarve in Portugal. OUP.

Voices from the Old Sea by Norman Lewis. The name of the Costa Brava town of Farol was invented by Lewis in this true story of a fishing village being transformed into a 20th-century tourist resort over three seasons. Penguin. His novel *The Day of the Fox* is also set on the Costa Brava,

Homage to Barcelona by Colm Tóibín, an account of the city's culture, history and politics. Simon and Schuster. Also by Tóibín is a novel set in Catalonia, *The South*. Serpent's Tail.

Forbidden Territory by Juan Goytisolo, an autobiography, offers an invaluable account of Barcelona during the Franco years. Quartet.

Art and Architecture:
Homage to Barcelona edited by Michael Raeburn. A lavish catalogue to the Hayward Gallery's exhibition about the city during the Renaixença and Modernist periods. Arts Council of Great Britain.

Picasso by Patrick O'Brian. An excellent biography, which gives a full account of the influence of Catalonia on the painter. Collins.

Secret Life by Salvador Dalí. There are many books about Dalí, but new readers should start with the autobiography. Vision Press. *Salvador Dalí, The Surrealist Jester* by Meryle Secrest is also recommended. Grafton.

Miró by Roland Penrose. Written in the 1930s, this remains in print and gives a good understanding of the artist and his work. Thames and Hudson.

Language:
Teach Yourself Catalan by Alan Yates.

The only grammar available in English, and a good one. Hodder and Stoughton.

Food and Wine:
Catalan Cuisine by Colman Andrews. A full and enthusiastic appraisal with a cook's tour of the region. Headline Book Publishing.
The Spanish Table by Marimar Torres. Recipes from all over Spain by this top Catalan cookery writer. Ebury Press.
Mediterranean Seafood by Alan Davidson. An encyclopaedic work for fishermen, gastronomes and market shoppers. Penguin.
Wine from Spain by Jan Read. A rundown of all Spain's wine by one of the first foreign writers to be honoured by Spanish vintners. Faber and Faber.
Travellers Wine Guide: Spain by Desmond Begg. A where-to-taste guide produced with the Automobile Association. Waymark Publications.

Wildlife:
Where to Watch Birds in Catalonia by Josep del Hoyo and Hordi Sargatal is the English edition of a Catalan book published by Edicions Lynx in Barcelona.
Flora and Fauna of the Mediterranean. No pocket guide can be comprehensive, but this is a start. Collins.

The Anglo-Catalan Society publishes papers from time to time, as well as holding annual meetings, though it has lost a bit of steam since Catalan has been reinstated in Spain. Anyone interested in the society's activities should contact Dr David George, Honorary Secretary, Dept of Romance Studies, University College, Singleton Park, Swansea, Wales SA2 899.

USEFUL ADDRESSES

TOURIST OFFICES

Most towns and resorts have a tourist information office, usually centrally located and marked with a large "i". They keep similar hours to other offices. Staff are generally helpful; those in main resorts and large towns usually speak some English, French and German. In smaller places they probably will not but they always have plenty of literature on their area, printed in several languages.

The addresses of a few main offices are as follows:

Lleida: Oficina d'Informació Turistica, Arc del Pont, 25007.

Andorra: Sindicat d'Iniciativa, Carrer Dr Vilanova, Andorra La Vella, tel: (9738) 20214. Oficina de Turisme del Principat d'Andorra, Carrer Marià Cubí 159, 08021 Barcelona.

Puigcerdà: Oficina de Turisme del C.I.T., Carrer Querol.

La Jonquera: Oficina de Turisme, Porta Catalana, A7 motorway.

Portbou: Oficina d'Informació Turistica, Estació RENFE, 17497.

Girona: Oficina de Turisme, Rambla Libertat, 1, 17004; Oficina Municipal de Turisme, Estació (Station) RENFE, 17007.

Barcelona: Patronat Municipal de Turisme, Estació (Station) de Rodales, 08003; Oficina de Turisme, Gran Via de les Corts Catalanes 658, 08010; Patronat Municipal de Turisme, Passeig de Gràcia 35, 08007; Patronat Municipal de Turisme, Estació (Station) de Sants, 08014.

Reus: Oficina de Turisme, Aeroport de Reus, 43204.

Tarragona: Oficina de Turisme, Carrer Fortuny 4, 43001. Patronat Municipal de Turisme, Carrer Major, 39, 43003.

Government regional tourist services: (for registering complaints, etc.)

Servei Territorial de Comerç, Consum i Turisme:

Lleida: Avinguda Prat de la Riba 76, 25004.

Girona: Travessia de la Creu 1, 17002.

Barcelona: Avinguda Diagonal 431 bis, 5a, planta, 08071.

Tarragona: Rambla Vella 7, 43003.

In the UK: Spanish National Tourist Office, 57 St James's Street, London SW1A 1 LD, tel: (071) 499 0901.

Andorran Delegation Tourist Office, 63 Westover Road, London SW18, tel: (081) 874 4806.

Consulates: see Emergencies.

AIRLINES

Air France: Passeig de Gràcia 63, Barcelona, tel: (93) 215 28 66.

British Airways: Passeig de Gràcia 59, Barcelona, tel: (93) 215 21 12.

Lufthansa: Passeig de Gràcia 55, Barcelona, tel: (93) 215 03 00.

TWA: Gran Via de les Corts Catalanes 634, Barcelona, tel: (93) 318 00 31.

Iberia: Plaça Espanya, Barcelona, tel: (93) 301 39 93; Plaça Marques de Camps 8, Girona, tel: (972) 20 58 00; Rambla Nova 116, Tarragona, tel: (977) 21 03 09.

Iberia in London are at 130 Regent Street, London W1R 5FE. Reservations, tel: (071) 437 5622.

MOTORING ORGANISATIONS

Offices which provide information and emergency road services to members of foreign motoring and camping associations:

Reial Automobil Club de Catalunya: Carrer Santalò 8, Barcelona, tel: (93) 209 83 85.

Europ Assistance Espanya SA: Avinguda Diagonal 652, Bl.C. 6°, 2a, Barcelona, tel: (93) 204 61 11.

Caravan Club: Alarm Centre ANWB, Gran Via de Carles III, 86, Barcelona, tel: (93) 330 75 51.

Camping Club FICC: Servei Turística S. Heinze Latzke SA, Carrer Ricardo Calvo 6, Barcelona, tel: (93) 247 56 02.

ART/PHOTO CREDITS

INDEX

A

Ager 177
Agramunt 98
Aiguablava 234
Aiguadolç 283
Aiguafreda 234
Aiguamolls nature reserve 230–231
Aigüestortes National Park 178–179, 202–203
Albinyana 286
Alcanar 311
Alella 120, 248
Alp 212
Alt Urgell 27
Altafulla 286–287
Amer 93
L'Ametlla de Mar 288–289
Amposta 289, 293, 309
Andorra 106, 157, 158, 193–196
Arbúcies 223
Arenys de Mar 247
Arenys de Munt 247
Argentona 248
Arties 97, 188
Asco 309

B

Bagà 84
Baix Empordà 27
Balaguer 176
Balsareny 88
Banyoles 27, 217
Baqueira-Beret 157, 187
Barberà de la Conca 307
Barcelona 29, 31, 37, 44, 50, 51, 52, 58, 60, 61, 67, 68, 69, 84, 87, 88, 103, 104, 105, 106, 107, 111, 112, 137, 138, 154, 253–269
    Antic Hospital de la Santa Creu 258
    Archaeological Museum 28, 267
    Avinguada de la Meridiana 106
    Barcelona World Fair 104, 266
    Barri Gòtic 220, 264, 269
    Barri Xines 269
    Betlem church 258
    Bulevards Rosa 140
    Carrer Almirall Cervera 104
    Carrer Bisbe Irurita 265
    Carrer de Boqueria 265
    Carrer de Montcada 263
    Carrer del Consell de Cent 115
    Carrer Ferran 265
    Carrer Nou de la Rambla 259
    Carriage Museum 268
    Casa Caritat 258
    Casa de la Ciutat 265
    Casa del Ardica 265
    Castell 266
    Cathedral of Saint Eulàlia 264
    City of Barcelona Museum 264
    Col.legi de Arquitectes 105, 264
    Diagonal 253
    Eixample 256
    Els Quatre Gats 111
    Frederic Marés Museum 265
    Gaudí Museum 256
    Geological Museum 263
    German Pavilion (El Pavellò Barcelona) 104, 266
    Gran Teatre del Liceu 259
    Gran Via de les Corts Catalanes 253, 260
    La Barceloneta 262
    Llotja 262
    Maritime Museum 261
    Mercat de Sant Josep (La Boqueria) 258
    Military Museum 266
    Miró Foundation 113, 115, 267
    Montjuïc 104, 220, 269
    Monument a Colom 261
    Municipal Institute of History 265
    Museu d'Art de Catalunya 98, 178, 266–267
    Museu d'Art Modern 111, 261, 263
    Museu de Cera 261
    Museu Tèxtil i d'Indumentària 137, 263–264
    Museum of Automata 268
    Museum of Graphic Arts 267
    Museum of Popular Arts and Industries 269
    Natural History Museum 263
    Palau de la Generalitat 265
    Palau de la Música Catalana 69, 83
    Palau de la Virreina 258
    Palau Güell 259
    Palau Moja 258
    Palau Reial 268
    Paral.lel 266
    Parc d'Espanya Industriel 107, 257
    Parc de la Ciutadella 262
    Parc Güell 256
    Parc Joan Miró 107
    Parliament 263
    Passeig de Colom 262
    Passeig de Gràcia 253, 256
    Passeig de Picasso 115, 263
    Passeig Nacional 262
    Pavellons Güell 268
    Pedralbes 268
    Pedralbes Monastery 268
    Picasso Museum 112, 263
    Plaça Catalunya 253, 256, 257
    Plaça del Pi 265–266
    Plaça del Rei 264
    Plaça dels Paisos Catalans 257
    Plaça Espanya 266
    Plaça Ramon Berenguer el Gran
    Plaça Reial 259
    Plaça Sant Jaume 265
    Plaça Sant Josep Oriol 265
    Poble Espanyol 147, 267, 269
    Rambla 253, 257–261, 269
    Reials Drassanes 261
    Sagrada Família 52, 103, 256
    Santa Maria del Mar 262

354

Tibidabo 266, 267
Vallvidrera 266
Zoo 263
Baronia de Sant Oisme, La 177
Barceló, Miquel 115
Barruera 178
Bàscara 84
Beget 216
Begur 234
Bellmunt 309
Bellpuig de les Avellanes 177
Bellver de Cerdanya 155, 211
Benifassà 311
Berga 88, 93, 277, 279
Besalú 216–217
Betlan 189
Betrén 189
Bisbal, La 223
Blanes 227, 238
Boí 97, 178
Borges Blanques, Les 182
Bossost 188
Breda 223
Bruc, El 275
Buda Island 294

C

Cabrils 248
Cadaqués 228
Cadí-Moixeró Natural Park 203–205, 211, 279
Cal Mosques 288
Cal Vidrell 288
Calafell 286
Caldes d'Estrac 248
Caldes de Boí 178, 214
Caldes de Malavella 214
Caldes de Montbui 214, 276
Caldetas 105
Calella de la Costa 247
Calella de Palafrugell 235
Cambrils 288
Campdevànol 213
Camprodón 157, 215
Canal d'Urgell 182
Canet de Mar 247
Cantol de Medol 304
Cap Begur 234
Cap de Creus 227, 232
Cap Roig 234, 235
Capmany 219
Cardona 94, 96, 275–276
Casarilh 189
Casas, Ramon 111
Cases d'Alcanar, Les 289
Cassà 222
Cassals, Pau 86, 114, 286
Castellar de la Ribera 181
Castellar de N'Hug 88, 273, 278, 279
Castelldefels 156, 283
Castellfollit de la Roca 84, 207, 216
Castello d'Empúrias 231–232
Catalan history
    Autonomy 57–58, 59, 60–61
    Carthaginian colonisation 29
    Charlemagne 31–32, 37
    Christianity 30

First Carlist War 48
Franco regime 59–60, 74–75, 104–105, 113–114
Greek colonisation 28
Industrial development 47–50, 60
Jaume I 38–39
Moorish rule 31–32, 37
Peninsula War 47–48
Pere II 39, 41
Pere III 41–42
Prehistory 27
Renaixença 43, 49, 74, 86
Roman colonisation 29–30
Spanish Civil War 58–59
Visigothic invasions 30–31
Catalan language and literature 39, 49, 60–61, 67–68, 73–76
Catalanism 49, 51–52, 57, 60
Cellers 177
Cerdà, Idelfons 256
La Cerdanya region 157, 211–212
Cervello 121
Cervera 87, 182
Codorníu Group 119–123, 176, 275
Colera 227
Collegats gorge 180
Conca de Barbarà 303
Conesa 307
Constanti 304
Corbrera 310
Cornudella de Montsant 308
Corts (parliament) 42
Costa Brava 145–148, 227–238
Costa Daurada 283–289
Cova d'en Daina 222
Cubelles 284
Cuixá 93
Cunit 285

D – E

Dalí, Salvador 111, 113–114, 115, 217, 228, 230, 232
Delta de L'Ebre 155, 289, 293–296
Deltebre 294
Domènech i Montaner, Lluís 52, 103
L'Empordà region 86, 126, 130, 132, 232
Empúriabrava 230
Empúries 28–30, 32, 126, 230, 231
Erill-le-vall 97, 98, 178
L'Escala 132, 233
Escribá, Antoni 260
Escunhau 189
Esparreguera 87
L'Espluga de Francolí 89, 307
Espot 179
L'Estartit 233, 242, 244

F – G

Figueres 86, 113
fishing 155–156
Flix 309
Folhuera, Francesc 147
Font Romeu 158
food 126–132
Formigues Islands 235
Fornells 234

Fortuny, Mariano 138
Gandesa 309
Garraf 283, 284–285
Garrotxa Volcanic Park 201, 207, 216
Gasch, Sebastià 114–115
Gaudí, Antoni 52, 74, 103, 112, 114, 130, 256, 259, 268, 273, 306
Gausac 189
Gavà 283
Generalitat 58
Gerri de la Sal 180
Girona city 44, 47–48, 67, 69, 86, 87, 219–222
Gósol 111
Granollers 70, 276–277
Gratallops 309
Guàrdia de Noguera 177
Guimera 182

H – L

l'Hospitalet 285, 288
Els Hostalets d'En Bas 216
Horta de Sant Joan 112, 310
Hostalric 47–48, 223
Hunting 154–155
Igualada 275
Illes Medes reserve 241–244
Jews in Catalonia 69, 220
Juia 220
Lavaix 177
Llafranc 241, 244
Llanars 215
Llança 227–228
Lleida city 30, 44, 67, 98, 174–176
Llivia 212
Llofriu 222
Lloret de Mar 89, 145, 238
Lorca, Federico García 115

M – N

Macià, Francesc 57–58
Malgrat de Mar 247
Manresa 47–48, 273, 275
Maresme, El 132, 247–249
Masnou, El 156, 248
Masó, Rafael 146, 147, 222, 233
Mataró 248
Medes Islands 233, 241–244
Meranges 211
Miami Platja 288
Miravet 309, 310
Miró, Joan 104, 111, 112–113, 114, 115, 257, 260, 267
modern architecture 103–107
Modernism 52, 74, 103–104, 111
Molina, La 154
Mollet 106
Molló 216
Monells 223
Montblanc 307–308
Montgarri 189
Montgrí massif 233
Montserrat 47–48, 60, 274, 275
Monzón 38
Móra d'Ebre 309
mountaineering 154

Nonell, Isidre 112
Noucentism 57
Núria 154, 212
Núria valley 205–207

O – Q

Ogassa 215
Oliba, Abbot 94, 213
Olot 84, 207, 216
Olympic Games (1992) 61, 107, 262
Organyà 181
Pagés family 119–123
Palafrugell 222–223, 235
Palamós 146, 235–236
Pals 222
Passanat 307
Penedès 119
Penedès region 120, 273, 285
Peralada 83, 120, 219
Peratallada 223
Picasso, Pablo 74, 105, 111–112, 113, 114, 115, 260, 264, 284, 310
Pineda de Mar 247, 248
Pinell de Braia 310
Pla de Santa Maria, El 289
Platja d'Aro, La 146, 227, 236
Platja de Pals 234
Platja dels Eucaliptus 289
Pobla de Montornes, La 84
Pobla de Segur, La 177
Poblet 98, 300–301
Pont de Suert, El 177
Ponts 155, 182
Porqueres 217
Port de la Selva, El 94, 228
Port Ginesta 283
Portbou 227
Portlligat 113, 228
Ports, Els 311
Prat d'Aguiló 154
Prat, El 283
Prats 211
Premiá de Mar 248
Priorat, El 120, 303, 308
Prullans 211
Puig i Cadafalch, Josep 52, 98, 103, 104, 121, 176, 248
Puigcerdà 104, 153, 157, 158, 211–212
Puigmal 154
Punta de la Mora 286
Quart 223
Queralbs 212

R – S

Raïmet 176
Rasos de Peguera 279
Raventós family 119–123
Reus 48–49, 67, 306
Ribes de Freser 212
Ridaura 89
Ripoll 88, 94, 96, 213
Roc Sant Gaietà 286
van der Rohe, Mies 104
Romanesque art and architecture 93–98
Roses 28, 41, 47–48, 85, 156, 230

Rupit 279
Rusiñol, Santiago 111
S'Agaró resort 145–148, 236, 237
Sa Conca 237
Sa Riera 234
Sa Tuna 234
Sabadell 137, 140, 276
Sailing 156–157
Salardú 97, 189
Salou 179, 283, 288
Sant Antonio 227
Sant Carles de la Ràpita 289
Sant Cugat del Vallès 273
Sant Daniel 236
Sant Elm 237
Sant Esteve Sesrovires 121
Sant Feliu de Guíxols 145, 236–237
Sant Feliu de Pallerols 88
Sant Hilari Sacalm 214, 223
Sant Iscle de Vallalta 248
Sant Jaume d'Enveja 289
Sant Jaume de Frontanyà 98
Sant Joan de les Abadesses 96, 215
Sant Julià de Cerdanyola 84
Sant Martí 231
Sant Martí del Brull 98
Sant Miquel de Crüilles 223
Sant Pau 237
Sant Pau de Casserres 98
Sant Pere de Galligants 96, 97
Sant Pere de Ponts 97
Sant Pere de Ribes 285
Sant Pere de Rodes 94, 96, 97, 228
Sant Pere Pescador 231
Sant Pol de Mar 247
Sant Privat d'En Bas 216
Sant Quirze de Pedret 93, 98
Sant Sadurní 223
Sant Sadurní d'Anoia 120, 121, 275
Sant Sadurní d'Osomort 98
Sant Salvador 228
Sant Sebastià 235, 283
Sant Vicenç de Calders 286
Sant Vicenç de Montalt 248
Sant Vicenç dels Horts 87
Santa Coloma de Cervello 273
Santa Coloma de Farners 85
Santa Coloma de Queralt 306
Santa Helena 227
Santa Julià de Boada 223
Santa Margarida 227, 230
Santa Maria monastery, Gerri de la Sal 180
Santa Pau 216
Santes Creus 83, 300–301
Santuari de Queralt 279
Saralla del Comtat 307
Sardana 69, 83, 86
Segre valley 181
Serra de Montseny 130, 154, 276
Serra de Pandols 310
Serra del Cadí 154
Serra del Montsià 311
Serres de Prades 303, 308
Sert, Josep Lluís 113, 267
Sert, Josep Maria 146
Setcases 157, 215–216
Seu d'Urgell, La 96, 180–181
Sitges 85, 88, 105, 283–284

Siurana 308
skiing 157–158
Solsona 98, 181
Sort 180

T – U

Talarn 177
Tamarit 286
Tamariu 234–235
Tàpies, Antoni 111, 115
Tarragona city 29, 47–48, 67, 83, 129, 287–288, 304
Tarrega 182
Taull 97, 98, 178
Terra Alta 303
Terradets gorge 177
Terrassa 83, 137, 276
textile industry 47, 137–141, 276, 284
Torredembarra 286
Torres family 122–123
Torroella de Montgrí 86, 233
Torroja 309
Tort valley 97
Tortosa 310, 311
Tossa de Mar 84, 145, 237–238
Tredòs 189
Tremp 177
Tuc-Betrén 187
Ullastret 223
Ulldecona 27, 311
Unya 189
Urtz 212

V – W

Vall d'Aran 97, 154, 155, 157, 179, 187–189, 202
Vall d'Espot 179
Vall de Boí 178–179, 214
Vall de Ter 157
Vallbona de les Monges 182, 300–301
Valls 89, 306
Vallsanta 182
Vallter 2000 ski resort 157
Vallvidrera 74
Vandellòs 285, 288
Vendrell, El 286
Verdaguer, Jacint 73–74
Verdu 182
Verges 87
Vic 97, 98, 273, 277
Vielha 187, 188–189
Vilabella 306–307
Vilabertran 219
Vilac 189
Vilafranca del Penedès 89, 120, 273–274
Vilajuiga 219, 220
Vilanova i la Geltrú 85, 284
Vilassar de Mar 248
Villaverd 307
wine 119--123